The South As It Is

THE SOUTH

Edited and with an Introduction by Henry M. Christman

NEW YORK

AS IT IS: 1865-1866

BY JOHN RICHARD DENNETT

THE VIKING PRESS

Published in 1965 by The Viking Press, Inc.
625 Madison Avenue, New York, N.Y. 10022

Published simultaneously in Canada by
The Macmillan Company of Canada Limited

Library of Congress catalog card number: 65-19271

Set in Times Roman and Perpetua types and
printed in U.S.A. by The Colonial Press Inc.

MBG

Introduction

By the beginning of 1865, the Civil War was rapidly reaching its conclusive stage. Union troops were sweeping through Confederate territory, and the Federal Government was laying the groundwork for the postwar period. On March 4, Lincoln was inaugurated for his second term, proclaiming in his inaugural address, as a policy toward the South, the words "With malice toward none, with charity for all." And, only the day before, the Freedman's Bureau had been established to provide education and advancement for Negroes.

Within a month, the Confederacy had collapsed. On April 3, Union troops entered Richmond, the Confederate capital, and on April 9, Lee surrendered the Confederate army to Grant at Appomattox Court House. History took an unexpected turn, however, with the tragic assassination of Lincoln on April 14, less than one week after the Confederate capitulation. Andrew Johnson, who had been Vice President for little more than a month, succeeded to the Presidency the following day.

The sudden death of Lincoln greatly confused the shape of events to come. The North was divided on many questions. Some Northerners favored a rapid reconciliation with the South; others were deeply suspicious of the defeated Confederates and genuinely doubted that the South could be integrated into the nation without extensive prior reformation. Some ardently pointed out that the Negro, with freedom, became a full citizen, and, legally and morally, was automatically and immediately entitled to all the rights and privileges of citizenship; others argued that the Negro was not yet ready for full equality. Still others were blinded by passion—

v

some, embittered by the bloody war, would be satisfied with nothing less than sweeping vengeance against the vanquished South; others, also Unionist in loyalty, had always been antiabolitionist and still hated the Negro. To all these divisions were now added the complications and exacerbations of the ideological, political, regional, and personal differences and antagonisms between the new President, Democrat Andrew Johnson of Tennessee, and the Radical Republican forces in Congress, led by Senator Charles Sumner of Massachusetts and Representative Thaddeus Stevens of Pennsylvania.

Since the average Northerner could have only vague, general impressions of what actually was happening in the South, it was timely, indeed imperative, to have facts with which the issues could be sensibly discussed and debated. In July of 1865, a new magazine, *The Nation*—"a weekly journal devoted to Politics, Literature, Science, and Art"—published its first issue in New York. This new publication was founded by a group of forty headed by James Miller McKim, the Philadelphia philanthropist and abolitionist, and E. L. Godkin, the Anglo-Irish journalist, who became the first editor. Among the other major sponsors were Frederick Law Olmsted, the architect and writer; Charles Eliot Norton, Harvard scholar; and journalist Wendell Phillips Garrison, son of the abolitionist spokesman William Lloyd Garrison.

From the very first, *The Nation* was deeply concerned with the South and the problems faced by the American Negro. Godkin and Olmsted had traveled extensively through the Southern states, an experience that greatly affected both of them, while McKim, Garrison, and others associated with the founding of *The Nation* had been dedicated participants in the abolitionist movement.

Of the seven "main objects" which *The Nation* specified in its prospectus announcing the first issue, three pertained directly to this concern, and others were related to it. The first "object" was to discuss the political, social, and economic issues of the day; the second was to promote "true democratic principles" in government and in society as a whole. The third goal was "The earnest and persistent consideration of the condition of the laboring class at the South, as a matter of vital interest to the nation at large, with a view to the removal of all artificial distinctions between them and the rest of the population, and the securing to them, as far as education and justice can do it, of an equal chance in the race of life." This was reinforced by the fourth point, which was "The enforcement and illustration of the doctrine that the whole community has the strongest interest, both moral, political, and material, in their elevation, and that there can be no real stability for the Republic so long as they are left in ignorance and degradation." The fifth goal specified in the prospectus was the promotion of popular education, and the sixth point returned directly to the question of the South, promising "The collection and diffusion of trustworthy information as to the condition and prospects of the Southern States, the openings they offer to capital, the supply and kind of labor which can be obtained in them, and the progress made by the colored population in acquiring the habits and desires of civilized life." The seventh and concluding objective was to provide criticism of books and the arts.

Further on in the prospectus was the following: "A special correspondent, who has been selected for his work with some care, is about to start in a few days for a journey through the South. His letters will appear every week, and he is charged with the duty of simply reporting what he sees and hears, leaving the public as far as possible to draw its own inferences."

This special correspondent was John Richard Dennett, born at Chatham, New Brunswick, on November 5, 1838, and brought to Massachusetts as a child. Young Dennett attended Harvard College, serving as an editor of the *Harvard Magazine*. He was graduated from Harvard in 1862 with the degree of Bachelor of Arts, and was Class Poet.

A significant opportunity awaited Dennett upon graduation, one that was to help prepare him for the writing of his *Nation* articles from the South. The previous November, Union forces had seized the Sea Islands off the coast of South Carolina; the plantation owners fled, while their slaves remained and welcomed the Northerners. Union military personnel held and developed the Sea Islands as a major naval base, and Federal officials joined with abolitionist volunteers to educate the freed slaves in a showcase demonstration of democracy. Dennett participated in this famous "Port Royal Experiment" as a superintendent of plantations.

Returning to Harvard for the 1864–1865 academic year, he studied at the Law School. In the summer of 1865, the twenty-six-year-old Dennett undertook the special assignment described in the prospectus of *The Nation,* that of traveling through the South and dispatching a series of articles, "The South As It Is," objectively reporting conditions as he found them.

By July, Dennett was writing from Richmond. Then, moving into central Virginia, he used Lynchburg as his base, making a special side trip to the little village of Appomattox Court House. Dennett spent July, August, and early September in Virginia, devoting most of his first ten articles to a detailed study of that state.

Traveling southward, Dennett next passed through central North Carolina, visiting various communities, including Greensboro, Charlotte, and Raleigh, the capital. Most of September and October were allotted to North Carolina.

Entering South Carolina from the north, Dennett moved rapidly downstate to the coast, writing from Charleston in early November. By mid-November, he was reporting from the Sea Islands, scene of the Port Royal Experiment. Returning upstate, he again surveyed central South Carolina, pausing at the capital, Columbia. He stayed nearly two months in the state.

Moving westward from Columbia, Dennett spent the Christmas season and the beginning of 1866 in Georgia, visiting Augusta, Atlanta, Macon, and Columbus. By late January, he was in Alabama's capital, Montgomery, and then he turned south again, reaching the sea at Mobile.

February was devoted to Louisiana—New Orleans and the surrounding Parish of Orleans, and up the Mississippi River to Baton Rouge. By early March, Dennett had reached Vicksburg, Mississippi, site of his last dispatch from the South itself. Returning to Boston after his nine-month tour, he wrote the two concluding selections of the thirty-six-article series.

After completing this assignment he joined the staff of *The Nation* as an assistant editor, and also was admitted to the bar in New York. He remained at *The Nation* until November 1869, when he became Assistant Professor of Rhetoric at Harvard. Dissatisfied with the routine of teaching, he returned to *The Nation* in

1872. He died in Westborough, Massachusetts, on November 26, 1874, a few weeks after his thirty-sixth birthday.

This series—which was published unsigned, not unusual at the time—is Dennett's sole literary achievement. It was well received, the London *Spectator* asserting that it was "far the best instructive picture that has yet been furnished us of the condition of the Southern states." And these articles have equal and perhaps even greater interest for us now, exactly one hundred years later. They are remarkable literature, living history vividly and faithfully recorded, providing an unexcelled view and feeling of the period. Moreover, Dennett presents revealing insights into the origins and history of the racial problems and tensions which dramatically challenge the United States today.

The reader is struck by the objective description of Southern views; Dennett conveys with care the outlook of many Southerners from all walks of life, even preserving their distinctive dialects and accents. He does not restrict himself to the obvious, easily secured interviews in accessible urban centers, but also penetrates into little-traveled parts of the countryside, seeking out isolated rural Southerners who had never seen a journalist, much less been interviewed by one.

Dennett seeks to provide the widest possible coverage of differing types, attitudes, and regions; and in doing so, he sometimes illustrates neglected aspects of American history. For instance, he gives an unusual picture of the white Southern Unionists, particularly in North Carolina, whose character and role is largely forgotten.

Dennett's articles are at sharp variance with the Southern view of an oppressive, corrupt Reconstruction which subjugated and exploited the virtuous, chivalrous South. Dennett, after all, was a Massachusetts man who had participated in the Port Royal Experiment. It is probable that his observations in the postwar South reinforced his convictions. And it is significant to note his interview with a fellow Northerner, an Ohioan whom Dennett met in Louisiana. Dennett quotes this gentleman as follows:

> In 1860 I was a strong Douglas man. I didn't like Lincoln, and the abolitionists I hated; but, of course, I was Union. As the war went on I began to believe in Lincoln, and, by the time the Eman-

x *Introduction*

cipation Proclamation was issued, I had been educated up to it and endorsed it. As a war measure, I mean; that was how Mr. Lincoln regarded it, and so did I. Well, since the war ended I've been a conservative; I've considered Stevens and Sumner dangerous men, who didn't understand the South, wanted to humble it and so on, and were standing in the way of peace. I believed what we used to hear, that the North didn't understand the South. I believe it yet, but in a very different sense. . . . I came out with the kindest feelings for these people down here; I wanted to see it made easy; we had whipped them, and I wanted it to rest there. I thought the South wanted it to end there. But I was tremendously mistaken. They hate us and despise us and all belonging to us. . . . The only people I find that a Northern man can make a friend of, the only ones that like the Government and believe in it, are the Negroes. I'm convinced they can vote just as intelligently as the poor whites. . . . I've learned to hate Southerners as I find them, and they can hate me if they want to. I'm a Sumner man after I get back, and I shall write out my experience for some of our papers. . . . I'm going to help our people to see two or three things: That the chivalry hate us and despise us; that a "nigger" they don't consider human; that whatever harm they can do us without getting another whipping, they've got the will to do, and mean to do, too. I wish every county in the North would send out two men, who have the confidence of their fellow-citizens, and make them travel through the South and report the true condition of things.

No doubt Dennett approved these sentiments about the South, but his subsequent reportage shows that he did not share this Ohioan's faith in attempting to arouse the North. As a matter of fact, Dennett already was deeply discouraged. He believed the Federal Government had missed its only real opportunity to effect permanent change, which he felt might have been achieved immediately after the Confederate capitulation. Once the South began to revive, however, the determination grew to preserve the old way of life. It was soon obvious that Reconstruction reforms were maintained only by the force of Union arms. Most Southerners made no attempt to disguise their attitude; they were determined to undo Reconstruction as rapidly and as thoroughly as possible, just as soon as the Union troops left. Confident that time was on their side, they eagerly awaited the opportunity to crush the Negroes and the white Southern Unionists. Dennett's forebodings were verified by history. And because of the tragic failure of Reconstruction, the unsolved problems of the South were bequeathed to subsequent generations of Americans.

This volume brings the Dennett articles together for the first time, in permanent form. They are presented here in their entirety, without cuts; the text has been altered only by the modernization of a small number of nineteenth-century conventions of spelling and punctuation, which it was felt would have distracted the reader for no good reason.

HENRY M. CHRISTMAN

The South As It Is

RICHMOND, VA., July 8, 1865

IT was a very pleasant change from the roar and heat of a June day in New York City to the cool breeze and the plash of the waves that greeted us sailing down the harbor on our way to Richmond. The voyage from wharf to wharf occupied three days, for a day was added to its length by our picking up at sea a disabled steamer, which we towed into Hampton Roads. The three days, however, were agreeably spent. In the little things, as well as in the great, one may perceive that the country has returned from war to peace. In the treatment which he receives in one of these private steamers the traveller finds a pleasing contrast to that indifference or insolence which he was forced to put up with in the days of army transports, when contracting owners were paid the same whether their vessels were full or empty, and when every official on board, from captain to steward, resented as an unnecessary evil the presence of every passenger.

Our cabin passengers on the *Creole* were perhaps fifty in number. There were officers returning to their regiments; officers' wives going down with children and waiting-maids to join their husbands; half a dozen excursionists intending to see Petersburg and to spend the Fourth of July in Richmond; a party of German Jews, ill-mannered and dirty, who fraternized closely with each other, and were profuse of attentions to the German nurses and waiting-maids. "Look at those fellows now!" said a young man from Connecticut to me; "a'n't they a 'penny-ante' lookin' lot? But they'll make more money in the Southern country in this next year than you or I will." I afterwards saw one of them in the street at Portsmouth with two or three hoop-skirts under his arm, and a box of paper-collars in his hand, trudging along, as I suppose, to his shop; and another I saw and heard playing the harp on the boat between Norfolk and Richmond.

Besides these we had also some of the vanguard of that army of immigrants which is to occupy the South. My acquaintance from Connecticut was travelling with a friend of his, and they hoped to find somewhere in North Carolina an opportunity to establish themselves in business. The Southern climate would be better for him, he thought, than that of his native State. He wasn't particular what sort of business he engaged in, but he'd a little prefer to bring down a good lot of goods and sell them. There were eight or ten other men aboard going South with similar plans. None of them, so far as I could learn, had any intention of becoming farmers. They all looked forward to trading. Most of them were young men, and seemed to me imbued with all the love of change as well as all the acuteness that is to said to characterize the Yankee. Of quite a different class was a German family going out to be laborers on the estate of a gentleman who owns a plantation not far from City Point. Neither the man nor the woman could speak a word of English, and I was told that they had been but a few days in this country. The woman wore a thick stuff dress and heavy shoes, and was without shawl or bonnet. She seemed home-sick, and spent a good part of her time in tears or in gazing out upon the water. The man was more cheerful. Both seemed robust and healthy, and their employer expected the substitution of their labor for that of Negroes to prove a great success. Certainly, they looked as if they might be depended upon for steady, stolid industry for some years to come. What wages he proposed to pay them I could not learn.

We had on board, among the other passengers and not easily distinguishable from them, several rebels. Rebels I suppose they may fairly be called, for those with whom I have talked, while ready enough to admit themselves conquered, still declare that it is only because their country has been subjugated that they now pay obedience to the United States. With one of these Confederate soldiers I entered into conversation. He was a youth apparently not more than twenty-two years old, intelligent and of pleasing manners. He said he had been up to New York to look round a little and to get himself some clothes. Everybody South was pretty hard up for clothes, and he reckoned they would be for some time if they had to pay New York prices for them. I noticed that he wore a full suit of black broadcloth, and said to him that if a man bought that of course he had to pay high for it. "Yes," he replied, "but look at those boots. I paid a hundred and seventy-five dollars for them in Richmond a while ago, but I reckon it's just as bad to charge me sixteen dollars for boots in New York and make me pay in greenbacks." I asked him if the Northerners seemed to him friendly and well disposed. "Well, yes," he said; "they did so. Well, anyhow, the war was all a d——d foolish piece of business, he supposed. Still his State went out, and if she was to go again he'd go with her. He liked the Northerners better, now that he'd fought against them. He reckoned that a thousand Southern soldiers would whip a thousand Northern, because half the Northern army was made up of foreigners and bought men, to say nothing of the niggers. If the thousand men on each side were picked, of course that would be a different thing. All he knew about that was that he didn't want to be there. What troops did you call the poorest in your army?" I told him that not having served, I did not know the army opinion. "Well, we always used to say in the army that your meanest troops were from Massachusetts, and ours were from South Carolina. But I reckon they only said so." The grand mistake of the Southerners, he thought, the mistake which cost them their independence, was in not having built a navy in the very first of the war. "Where would you have got seamen?" I inquired. "Seamen? we had Buchanan; you can't find better seamen than he is. The *Merrimac* whipped the *Monitor* pretty badly, and it would have been so right along if the Confederate government had turned their attention to naval matters instead of just keeping afloat a vessel here and a vessel there."

He denied strenuously that there had ever been any ill usage of Union soldiers in the rebel prisons. If there had been any such bad treatment, the President did not know of it, nor did General Lee. Of course President Davis didn't believe what he read in the Northern newspapers. No, sir, I might depend on it, Union soldiers in Libby and Belle Isle, or any other rebel prison, were just as well treated as rebel soldiers were in Federal prisons. His denial, though emphatic, was not at all indignant, as if the question was purely one of fact, and had no concern with morality. He seemed as much beyond the reach of argument as people in general, so we changed the subject, and I listened to some reminiscences of the battle of Manassas, and to a detailed account of the plot and incidents of the *Willow Copse*—"the very best play that ever was written, *he* believed."

This young man was quite frank and bold in his conversation, and his manners and language were gentlemanly. His opinions, I suppose, were the same, and his sentiments and feelings somewhat better, than those of his Confederate companions on board, whose appearance and language certainly were inferior to his.

A little after noon of a very hot day we arrived at the city of Norfolk. On the pier was a motley assemblage of whites and blacks, vociferous in their offers of pies, June apples, lemonade, and carriages to the hotels. The Negroes and whites were seemingly on very good terms with each other, though for a week we had been reading of the murderous riots that had taken place between them. But strolling through the streets of the town, it was not difficult to see marks of past violence as well as indications of future trouble. Now and then I would meet a soldier with a black eye, or a Negro with his head bound up; and the Negroes, though here and there one would touch his hat as he met a well-dressed white man, seemed generally to wear a lowering and sullen aspect. Parties of sailors were frequent in the streets, and as one of these passed a drinking shop a sailor did or said something to a man lounging by the door. What the offense was I do not know; my attention was first attracted by seeing the citizen hurl a brick. The missile struck the sailor in the head and knocked him down. He rose, his head and face streaming with blood, and clamored to be let loose on his assailant. His friends, after a good deal of pulling and hauling, induced him to move on. The disturbance lasted for ten minutes, occurred in the main street of Norfolk, and attracted a large crowd, but no policeman made his appearance.

In the evening I had a long conversation with a gentleman resident in the city. The picture which he gives of its condition is not pleasing.

"Sir," said he, "there is no town in Virginia more violently secessionist than Norfolk. For all practical purposes, I mean. To be sure, we Union men cast over two hundred votes the other day at the election, and the Tabb men did not cast much over eight hundred, and some of our men voted the Tabb ticket because Mr. Tabb is a gentleman, and very well liked. But the secessionists are in the majority; then we've got between one and two hundred returned Confederate soldiers in the city; we've got the Navy Yard right handy, and that gives us a good many disorderly men; the city is full of low drinking saloons, and what these men wouldn't do sober they will do when they're drunk, and our secesh folks know it; and I tell you, sir, Norfolk isn't a very safe place for a Union man unless he's a very mild sort of a Union man. There are two men in Norfolk that are very strong Republicans. One of them is in favor of allowing the niggers to vote immediately. Well, sir, they'd better both of them leave the city at once. I wouldn't be in either of those men's shoes for half Norfolk. They'll be shot some night—someone'll hear a cry, and that'll be all any one'll ever know about it."

"I suppose everybody goes armed."

"Of course. I wouldn't think of walking two blocks at night without my revolver. The Tabb government have increased the police force, and perhaps for the sake of its own reputation it may keep order in the city, or, at any rate, try to do so. But if a vote of the Union men could be taken tomorrow, I'm not afraid to say that there would be a unanimous vote to bring back the military government that has just left us. There never was a worse mistake made than giving back a civil government to a place like Norfolk, where all the power at once gets into the hands of the rebels. The loyal men right through the South ought to be protected by the Government for some time to come."

The Negro, this Norfolk gentleman thought, must necessarily sink lower and lower in the social scale when working under a system of free labor. Slavery he believed to have been a curse to the white man, and to all the industrial interests of the country, but the Negro freed would be a greater curse to it than he ever had been as a slave. Unless the colored people were removed to Texas, or some South American country, they would surely die out by reason of their laziness and shiftlessness.

A day or two after this conversation, looking over the *Old Dominion,* a newspaper published at Norfolk, my curiosity was excited by seeing at the head of a column the name of one of the two men whose lives I had been told were in danger if they remained in the city. "A card (somewhat lengthy) from Calvin Pepper," was the caption of the article. This card, it seemed to me as I read it, might fairly be taken as evidence corroborative of that given by my informant, although in it Mr. Pepper states that he intends to absent himself from the city for six weeks, and leaves the reader to imply that he means to return. He appends to the card two letters, showing that he fought bravely in beating back the New York rioters in the summer of 1863, and that he was ready and eager to fight at Washington in 1861. "The annexed certificates are published," he says, "in order that there may be no mistake in regard, at least, to my courage, and that it may not be said that I left Norfolk, or any other place, from fear."

Mr. Pepper says that both his health and business demand that he should absent himself from the city, and he prints his card to notify his debtors and his creditors of his intention to go away. He then goes on as follows:

And now I would say to my personal friends who are so apprehensive, without just cause, it seems to me, for my personal safety, on account of my radical, so-called, and outspoken views of the right of suffrage to colored citizens, and the *rumored threats* that have been so industriously and from sinister motives spread abroad, that since I have been in Norfolk I have not received, *to my face,* from man, woman, or child, a personal insult or threat, or disrespectful treatment of any kind, and that I verily believe that liberty of speech is freer and safer today in the city of Norfolk than in the city of New York.

Mr. Pepper sets forth his political views at some length. "The simple, just, and effectual remedy 'for preventing another rebellion' is equal rights of suffrage to all, and with loyal men in a majority nothing more is to be hoped or desired." These views he declares that he will always advocate—

> And in the exercise of this right of a freeman I shall not be deterred by any threats of violence, or persecution, or prosecution without law, or the perversion of its form and spirit. Free speech without licentiousness, or its abuse, I will exercise while life last, and if need be in the face of death.

At City Point the steamer from New York transfers its passengers to a small river boat. The trip thence to Richmond is made in about four hours, and the traveller is taken past many points that have become the property of history. The river is very winding, the banks are green and hilly, and as one approaches the city are filled with earthworks. We passed but little land under cultivation. Here and there could be seen a field in which the wheat sheaves were piled in stacks, and there were a few fields of Indian corn, but it was low and must have been planted late. In Norfolk I saw stalks nine and ten feet high, but on the James none that was more than three feet, and the greater part of the crop was somewhat less. The water in the river was rather higher than is usual at this time of year, I was told, but however that may be, our pilot took the vessel through the Dutch Gap Canal, thus shortening the voyage by about seven miles. Our boat was a small one, and she thumped on the bottom at the entrance, but in the Richmond papers I saw it stated that a steamer of forty-three feet beam had made the passage a week before. We passed the famous Fort Darling and several ruined bridges, and every now and then saw, just showing above the russet-colored water, the ribs of some sunken vessel. At last we could discern the three spires of Richmond on a distant hill, and the square bulk of the Capitol. The wharves at Rocket's were not so busy as those of Norfolk, and there were, perhaps, not more than twenty small craft in the port.

A little way from the landing stood a "Broadway and Ninth Avenue" omnibus, which rattled us over the ill paved streets to the hotel. Two rudely painted wooden signs, projecting from the corners of two ugly brick warehouses, told us where stood "Castle Thunder" and "Libby." Of these buildings the former is used as a city prison; the latter is set apart for the use of soldiers waiting for their regiments, and for the families of Negro laborers working for the United States Quartermaster. Cannon balls can be seen lying about in the streets, which are little used by any vehicles but army wagons and public.

Traversing the main street, going up the hill, on which the Capitol is situated, in the centre of what was formerly the business part of the city, is the burnt district. For a quarter of a mile one passes nothing but toppling walls, forlorn-looking chimneys, heaps of bricks, with here and there a ruined safe lying in the midst, warped and red from the effects of intense heat. Some Virginia agent of a Hudson Street firm has painted and pasted in half a dozen places the advertisement of "Hubbell's Golden Bitters," but besides this evidence of enterprise, there is very little sign of business activity.

In the shops that still stand there seem to be plentiful stocks of goods, but no customers for anything except the bare necessaries of life. One readily believes the often-repeated statement, "Our people haven't any money, sir." I went into two stores this morning to make some purchases, and perceived illustrations of this truth. In the first of the two I stood waiting to be served, while the shopman and a respectable-looking man talked about a tobacco transaction. The two men seemed to have been acquaintances. One, addressed as "Captain," urged the other to buy of him fifty pounds of hand tobacco. "I haven't got a cent, and I must get home. Pay what you think is right for it. There's only fifty pounds, and if I can't sell it I'll have to pawn my watch. Must get home, you know." The tobacco was such as would command a dollar a pound at the North, and it was offered at fifty cents. At the second store which I entered, the article I wanted was a tobacco-pouch. I noticed among the new ones a pouch of better workmanship than they, but which had evidently been in use. I asked the price of it. "Sam, what do you want for that bag of yours?" said the man to the attendant. "Well, I don't know; it was given to me; I reckon fifty cents will be about right."

In almost all the Richmond shopkeepers there is an eagerness to sell which, to one accustomed to Northern traders, seems strange, and, when one considers the reasons for it, quite touching. As might be expected, goods are cheap. Just after the evacuation the city was filled full of merchandize of all kinds by the Northern dealers. The people could not purchase; and the result is that many articles can be bought cheaper in Richmond today than in Baltimore or New York. "Flour," says the *Whig*, "that sold in New York on Saturday for $7 and $8, sold here for $5, and meats that were selling here for 15 to 20c., there stood on their dignity at 25 to 35c." A market with so little money was easily overstocked.

The Fourth of July may be said to have been celebrated in Richmond this year. Cannon were fired at morning, noon, and night. A few Chinese crackers were fired off by the vagabond boys, white and black, at the corners of the streets in the early morning and in the evening, their pyrotechnic resources, I take it, being too scanty not to make it advisable to husband them closely. In the morning a flag was hoisted at the Spottiswood Hotel, and a short speech made from the roof of the building by General Osgood. Somewhat later in the day a small crowd, made up mainly of Negroes and Union soldiers, with a sprinkling of citizens and children, congregated in the Capitol Square. A lady was introduced to the assembly and read the Declaration of Independence, but in so low a tone and amid such noise of talking and walking about as made it quite impossible for anyone to hear her. The conclusion of her reading was marked by music from a military band which was in attendance. Speeches were then made by a surgeon and two chaplains, and after a benediction the company dispersed. No applause was elicited by any of the speakers. The soldiers evidently were there in the character of onlookers; the Negroes were doubtful if they were expected to applaud or would be allowed to do so (they were carefully removed by the soldiers detailed as police from the crowded steps near the speakers' stand); and as for the citizens— to ask any men, Union or secessionist, to hear such speeches and applaud them, would be asking too much. All places of business were closed throughout the day, but the city wore no holiday aspect. That part of the rebel population which appeared in the streets were seemingly indifferent spectators of what went on around them. The boys and the Negroes, and the Union soldiers in a graver way, alone seemed to enjoy the occasion.

RICHMOND, VA., July 12, 1865

SITTING in the piazza of the hotel today were two Virginian ladies. The younger, whose home lay on the western side of the Blue Ridge, was making her first visit to Richmond since the war ended. She had many questions to ask and answer, and while she and her friend gossipped, her two little boys ran about, barefooted, and certainly not so well dressed as children who are staying with their parents at good hotels in New York.

"There," said the mother, "just look at Charley! Do see him! Stop that, sir. You're bad looking enough as it is. Anybody might tell that you're no Unionist. I'm sure the child appears like he was a little Confederate."

"I a'n't a Unionist," said the boy.

"No, I'm sure you're not. If you were I'd disinherit you, sure, and so would the captain."

"How is it," she enquired, turning to the hostess, "do you give our officers their rank now, or don't the Yankees let you?"

"Oh, yes, just as we always did."

"My soul! I thought they wouldn't let you speak above your breath here. The other side the mountains they told me I'd be hung sure if I was to come to Richmond, I speak right out so. But I told 'em they wouldn't hang me."

The people on the other side of the mountains are tolerably well represented by this lady, I suppose, for, so far as my observation extends, the feelings of the people in Eastern Virginia are the same with hers. This condition of mind is very easily discernible in the ordinary conversation of the street and other public places, and is also discoverable now and then in the more deliberate and cautious utterances of the pulpit and the press. Last Sunday I formed one of the somewhat scanty audience in a Congregational church. The last few minutes or so the preacher devoted to a eulogium on the character of a young man who, like many other members of that church and society, had died in the service of his country. The few closing sentences of the sermon proper were, as nearly as I can recollect them, as follows:

> And does it seem to you, my brethren, that during the last terrible four years the prayers of God's people in these Southern States, because they have not been answered in just the way you had chosen, have not been heard at all? Be not cast down. Do we not know that the fervent prayers of the saints cannot fail of an answer? But now we see through a glass, darkly. By-and-bye, if we will but wait, in God's good time we shall see, and know, and understand.

Doubtless there was much in the discourse to edify the believer, and the audience seemed to derive consolation and instruction from it, but it is easy to see that such preaching tends to make its hearers neither repent of rebellion nor forget it.

The press of Richmond is of course under strict surveillance, and it is not so much in its set articles as in its tone that one finds evidence of its being printed for a people not yet reconciled to the Government which has overthrown the cause of their choice. But in one of the city papers I find addressed to the voters these words of guidance for their action in future elections—advice, I venture to say, far from being needless:

> There is one admonition, however, which cannot be too often given to the people of the South. The election of candidates to office who are notorious for radical, violent, and extreme political opinions should be carefully avoided, as their success would be pointed to by our most dangerous enemies as evidences of most stubborn and unyielding disloyalty.
>
> Men prominent in the past for their secession doctrines would, if elected and admitted to seats on the floor of the national Congress, prove most useless and inefficient representatives at this time. The prejudices of the North would be so strongly arrayed against them

that they would not be able to accomplish a tithe as much good as men of moderate and conservative views.

Occasionally, however, an editor furnishes outspoken proof of his misconception of the privileges and duties which belong to a writer who addresses a community so recently in arms and making deadly war against the Federal Government. The *Whig* of yesterday contained an article which caused the suppression of the paper, for stigmatizing a certain clause of the Amnesty Proclamation as heathenish, and pronouncing a law of the land, enacted by Congress and approved by the President, "mean, brutal, and cowardly, revoltingly absurd and atrociously unjust." The *Whig,* I am told, has hitherto been the most popular journal in Richmond.

I was the other day thrown into the company of a gentleman residing in Amelia County in this State, and for two or three hours conversed with him upon the topics now uppermost in the minds of all men. He was past the prime of life, evidently was well educated and well read, and apparently a pious man. He was, or before the war had been, wealthy, carrying on business in Richmond, and owning a plantation about forty miles distant from the city. I found him disposed to be communicative, and was much interested in hearing his views and opinions. This year's crop in his section, he said, promises to be a good one. The country had not been much devastated, and there was no lack of farming utensils or laborers. A better yield of oats has not been seen for many years, and the wheat, which is already harvested, is quite up to the average. There will, however, be no tobacco, as in February last, when the ground should have been prepared, the future was too uncertain for farmers to risk putting in seed. Indian corn is backward, but there is hope of a fair crop. Corn-planting should have been done about the time of the evacuation, but people then were thinking more of Richmond and Lee's army than of farming, and just after that the Negroes began going away from home, and labor for a time was scarce.

I asked if many of his Negroes left him. "I had about a hundred and fifteen servants on my land. I own a tract of fifteen hundred

acres, but I have never been anything more than an amateur
farmer. My people were always well treated, and never were
worked hard. A number of them had been with my father, and
there were a good many that I had grown up with from boyhood. I
loved some of them. Of course, if a servant has the charge of one
of my little ones, and I see the child grow fond of her, and that she
loves the child, I cannot but feel kindly towards her. When the city
was evacuated, of course, they heard that they were free. Well, sir,
today, out of more than a hundred servants that were on my place
on the first of April, I haven't six left, and those are mostly infirm
old people. Some of them came up with tears in their eyes to shake
hands with me and say good-bye.

" 'Sorry to lef' you, massa; good-bye, massa.' 'But why do you
go, Toby (Sam, Sue, what not); what makes you leave?' I said.
'Oh, sah, we 'bleege to go, sah.' 'Well, what is it obliges you? Do
you expect to find a better place than this? Haven't you always
been well treated here?' 'Yes, massa, but we 'bleege to go, massa.' "
So they went, and I have been working my crop with Negroes that
I have hired, and I suppose somebody else has hired mine."

I asked what wages farmers were paying the freedmen in his
part of the country, and if there had been any concert among them
in reference to prices. He said he was not aware that there had
been any measures taken by the planters to regulate wages in any
part of Virginia. At any rate, there had been none in his county
nor in the adjoining counties. Some owners paid six dollars per
month, some seven, and some eight. He himself paid eight, and
knew of no one that paid less than six. Each hand that he hired
had, besides his wages, a house, fuel, board, and about two acres
of ground on which to raise corn or what he liked. These things,
together with the privilege of keeping poultry and a pig, he considered equivalent to at least eight dollars per month added to the
laborer's wages. He thought he was doing very well by his Negroes,
and they were working very well, about as they had in old times,
perhaps a little harder, but, on the whole, except in the degree of
power which he possessed over the laborers, he did not find the

practical working of the present system very different from that of
the old one.

Two or three colored men to whom I have since spoken on this
subject, set the proper rate of wages as high as ten dollars a
month, and thought the employer paying no more than that sum
ought also to clothe his laborers, as well as provide them quarters
in which to live and the ordinary rations of corn and bacon. But
these men had no expectation that such wages would be
obtainable. Indeed, they appeared to have as little faith in the
whites as the latter profess to have in the Negro. "What kin we do,
sah?" they say; "dey kin give us jes what dey choose. Man couldn't
starve, nohow; got no place to go; we 'bleege to take what dey give
us."

"The Negro," said Mr. K——, "I sincerely hope may disappoint
my expectations. But if he does not, he is doomed to undergo
extinction. Less than a hundred years of freedom will see the race
practically exterminated. The Negro will not work more than
enough to supply his bare necessities. There isn't a county of Virginia where we haven't had some hundreds of free Negroes, and
they have been always perfectly worthless and lived in wretched-
ness. The Negro stands as much in need of a master to guide him
as a child does. When I look at my servants, I feel weighing upon
me all the responsibilities of a parent. In the course of my life I
have known many men who for that reason alone would never
become the owner of a slave. I have brought up my children to
feel so, and accustomed them to the thought of dispensing with
slave labor. Those of them who are old enough share my views on
the subject. But the Negro will always need the care of someone
superior to him, and unless in one form or another it is extended
to him, the race will first become pauper and then disappear. Nothing but the most careful legislation will prevent it. Now take an
example: of my Negroes, nearly half were not on the working list;
but I had to support them all. What will the Negro do when he is
called upon to support not only himself (he isn't inclined to do
that, and I don't believe he will do it), but also to get food, and

clothes, and physic for the infants and disabled people belonging to him? Why, I doubt if my farm ever returned me one per cent. interest on the capital invested in it. He cannot do it. He couldn't do it if all the Southern States were confiscated and given him to do it with."

This last assertion was called forth by my suggestion that perhaps the self-supporting character of the colored communities of Port Royal was due to their having become possessors of confiscated lands in that district, and that if a like policy were adopted in Virginia like results might be expected. "So far as the owners of land are concerned," he continued, "emancipation will prove advantageous. I shall not be obliged to support sixteen people for every nine that work for me. But in order for me to reap any benefit from emancipation, the relation between master and man must be made the subject of wise legislation. That matter ought to be left to the States separately, for, of course, in many matters of detail there will be great differences of requirement."

Happening to have with me a late copy of *Harper's Weekly*, I called his attention to an editorial article containing an extract from one of the Nashville papers, which states that the Legislature of Tennessee have recently placed the Negroes of that State under almost every conceivable civil disability, and left them in a condition differing little from their former slavery, and asked him if the course taken by Virginia would not be identical with that of Tennessee. The statement we had just read, he replied, was probably entirely partisan. He supposed, however, that if it were true, a remedy for the evil would be found by requiring the States to take such action as should be satisfactory to the general Government. The general Government seemed to be doing what it liked. But, after all, the great hope of Virginia lay in the influx of immigrants that might be expected from Europe and the North. He knew many men in the State who owned five and six thousand acres of land. Of course they could not attend to all of it. Let such immense half-cleared tracts be broken up into small farms, and he had no doubt the soil would yield a product fourfold greater than now. The mineral resources of the State were inexhaustible, and certainly there was nothing to prevent its becoming a great commercial country. They only needed men. But between the day of those things and today there were many years, and perhaps fearful suffering. Immigrants might come fast, but the South would not be peopled in one year, nor in fifty. He should not live to see it.

If the Negro must go before Southern prosperity can come, perhaps Mr. K—— will never see it. But, of course, denying the possibility that the blacks can ever become a respectable, self-supporting peasantry, it is impossible for him to believe that by the side of his German, Yankee, and white Virginian manufacturers and farmers of the future there may exist also an intelligent and industrious yeomanry composed of colored Virginians.

As we sat and talked, we had been watching a boat of the "new line for Baltimore" which was rushing along close beside us. Acquaintances were exchanging morning salutations across the few yards of water that separated the steamers. Our speed was not far from seventeen miles an hour, and as we shot along, the near green banks and the yellow stream seemed to be gliding swiftly past us. Now one and now the other boat would gain a foot or two. At last, after several miles of this neck-and-neck running, we placed between our boat and the *Dictator* some rods of clear water. "Fare you well, chile, we can't always be with you," shouted a deck-hand to the beaten steamer, and we went on our way alone. Turning a sharp bend in the river we came upon a small encampment. A few soldiers sat about drinking their coffee, and near one of the tents a rude effigy clad in female apparel was dangling from a tree.

"Ah, what have they there?" asked my companion. I told him it was probably meant to represent Jefferson Davis in the dress he wore when he was captured. "Do people in the North believe that absurd story? I thought Mr. Davis's character, indeed I thought the state of his health for a long time past, was too well known all over the country for anyone not very ignorant to give credence to such a tale. I never was particularly friendly to Mr. Davis, but of course I set the thing down as a fabrication as soon as I heard it. For many years he has been a great sufferer from neuralgia, and obliged to protect himself from the slightest draught of cold air. When he was taken it happened that he had his wife's shawl thrown over his head and shoulders for that reason. It was this which gave rise to the story, but the story ought not to be believed by men of intelligence."

Mr. K—— was curious to know how the Northern people felt in reference to the Southern ex-President. I replied that I thought they were bitterest against him when they thought of the miseries inflicted upon Union soldiers in rebel military prisons. Mr. K—— could not believe that there was much truth in those reports, nor that Mr. Davis could justly be held responsible if they were in the main true. He knew that during the war such charges were constantly made by the Northern papers, and he felt concerned for the honor of the South. He visited Libby Prison in order to satisfy himself, and found that the Union soldiers confined there were fed in the same way with the Confederate soldiers in the intrenchments. In the Southern local papers it was common to see paragraphs stating that such a one had just arrived home from the North, where he had been so treated while in confinement that it was impossible he should recover. The whole South was full of such stories. He was free to confess, however, that he himself had never met a returned prisoner who seemed to have been ill used. He thought that, cleared of all exaggerations, the stories of barbarity to prisoners would be found to be of very slight importance. He believed the people of the North to be humane, and he knew that there was no humaner people in the world than the Southern people. In reference to the responsibility of the rebel leader for the cruelties of Andersonville and Salisbury, and in reply to a question of mine, he said that he thought charges of equal magnitude might have been brought against the North during Mr. Lincoln's administration of office, and yet have received no investigation nor attention from him. At the same time, he said, Mr. Lincoln differed from Mr. Davis in many respects.

I may say here that I have never heard Mr. Lincoln mentioned by any Southerner except in terms of respect and liking.

Continuing our conversation, I asked Mr. K—— if he did not

believe that the inhabitants of the two sections would come together again with the old friendly feeling and be one people as
before. Our talk had been so pleasant that, though I retained a
vague sense of an antagonism between the North and the South, I
had half forgotten that men had been killing each other in the
quarrel, and it was a little surprising to note the bitterness of his
answer.

"No, sir, never. The people of the South feel that they have
been most unjustly, most tyrannically oppressed by the North. All
our rights have been trampled upon. We knew that we had a perfect right to go and leave you. We were only carrying out the
principles of the Revolution. It was our deliberate opinion that we
ought to go out from the old Union. We could no longer give to
the general Government the consent of the governed, and the general Government could therefore no longer have any just powers
over us. But aside from that, our right to secede was perfect. Mr.
Calhoun demonstrated that. Mr. Webster's speeches in reply are
powerful appeals to sentiment and imagination, but the argument
of Mr. Calhoun is irresistible. And even Mr. Webster allows that
one party to a compact having violated it, the other is released
from all obligation. Now the North has repeatedly violated the
constitutional guaranties of slavery. Yes, sir, we had a most perfect
right to secede, and we have been slaughtered by thousands for
attempting to exercise it. And yet it is the fashion to call us
traitors! Now the people of the South are not going to stand that.
They are subjugated, conquered, and in their collective capacity
they must submit to whatever may be inflicted upon them. But
individually, between man and man, they are not going to endure
the infamous charge of having committed treason.

"If the United States Government bring Mr. Davis to trial, and
he defends himself, or if his counsel do their duty, this matter will
be set forth so plainly and convincingly that I for one am willing
the nations of the earth should judge and pronounce if we were not
right, and did not act within our powers. It was not slavery that
caused this war, for it was not the South that began it. We endured
the encroachments of the North upon our rights, and then quietly

availed ourselves of the reserved right of secession. We fired upon
Sumter. True; but not till Sumter had become a South Carolinian
fort, in which you maintained our enemies. Few men at the South
owned slaves. We wanted to leave you. At first I voted for what
was then called a Union candidate for the State Convention. We
elected him by a large majority. We thought it would not be necessary to secede. The whole State thought so, and an overwhelming
majority of that convention were anti-secessionists. Yet they voted
the State out of the Union, and when our members came back to
their constituents, we justified them and ratified what they had
done. I don't think there was a vote cast in our county against
immediate secession when the ordinance came before the people.
You see Mr. Lincoln had issued his proclamation calling for seventy-five thousand men. We all, whether we owned slaves or not,
believed that coercion was mere tyranny, and that we ought not to
submit to it. No, sir, I believe that if the North were to engage in
foreign war, or in any way to need the help of the South during the
lifetime of the present generation, ninety-nine men in a hundred
throughout the South would take up arms against the Washington
Government. I have no doubt of that, sir. You may have a new
Union with these States kept in it by force, but it cannot be said
that this war has perpetuated the old Union."

He believed all Southerners felt so; from the meanest private in
the army up to the highest men in the land, up to General Lee, all
felt that the South had been most deeply injured. He went on to
say that for a time his high admiration for the character of General
Lee had sensibly declined. He had been told that the General had
made application to the Washington authorities for pardon. He
had supposed that rather than do that the General would undergo
exile or death. Not long afterwards an opportunity had presented
itself for speaking to General Lee on the subject. The report
proved to be correct and not a slander. A voluminous application
had been sent in, to which, however, no answer has yet been made.
Since the time of his visit a reply may have been received. Having
learned the motives which had actuated General Lee in asking for
a pardon, his admiration, his veneration, for the man and the pa-

triot was profounder than ever. Had the General considered his
own feelings alone, he would have died sooner than humble himself and a just cause by a seeming admission that it was wrong. His
application was one more proof of his love for his country. There
were thousands of high-toned young men in the South who medi-
tated expatriating themselves, and who, when asked why they did
not seek for a pardon, replied, that until General Lee had done so
they would not. After a long struggle with his inclinations, believing that these young men ought to be saved to the country whose
future they were so well qualified to adorn, and, by participating in
the rights of citizenship, to guide and shape, the General had done
violence to his own feelings, and made the request. Still he had
made no abject submission, but had accompanied the petition for
pardon with a full statement of those things which made his past
conduct seem to him right and proper, and had avowed his
unchanging devotion to his former principles.

I asked Mr. K—— if he supposed the Government would send
General Lee a favorable answer. "Oh, yes," he replied, "undoubtedly."

"And does he expect to be restored to full enjoyment of all the
rights of citizenship?"

"Yes, sir; he has asked for that. And if it is refused him, he will
at any rate have done all that he intended to do. The class of men
whom he intended to benefit have, many of them, applied to be
pardoned, and probably all will do so. Thus General Lee's sacrifice
will have saved many of our first young men from exile, and
opened to them a public career from which they would otherwise
have shut themselves out."

Among other things which I might quote to show how honest
and how earnest this gentleman was in his devotion to the cause
which has just been so signally defeated, he asked me if, at the
North, there was not among the intelligent classes, at any rate
among the religious people, an expectation that God would visit
upon that section some terrible retribution for the unjust war they
had waged upon their brethren, the calamities they had inflicted on
the South.

He seemed surprised and perplexed when I answered that the Northern people were so far from feeling any apprehensions of that sort, that they believed it was God's blessing which had enabled them to carry on so exhausting a war till it was at last successful, and that they regarded themselves as having done much for the cause of humanity and true democracy; in short, that they considered themselves as crusaders rather than criminals.

"Possible!" he said. "The people here look for some heavy visitation of Divine Providence upon you. But God will judge, and judge more wisely than we." By this time Norfolk and Fort Monroe were at hand, and we separated.

III

RICHMOND, VA., July 17, 1865

SINCE Richmond was evacuated, more than half of its inhabitants have been compelled to seek a part or all of their sustenance at the hands of charity. And this relief is received not only by those classes of the population that always were poor, but, in many instances, by families that a few weeks ago were affluent. On the first of March last the head of the family may have owned a great warehouse filled with goods, containing perhaps many hundred hogsheads of the highest priced tobacco, the gradual accumulation of the last two or three years. Tobacco of the cheaper kinds soon becomes spoiled if kept for a long time in the original packages. But the warehouse with all its stores perished in the great conflagration, business is at a standstill, and the merchant finds himself upon the world absolutely a beggar without bread. He lives, perhaps, in a fine house; but nobody will buy it, nobody will take a mortgage upon it, until it can be known whether or not the owner's treason is to be pardoned, and his property left at his own disposal.

So great and wide-spread is the destitution that the military authorities have divided the city into districts, and soldiers detailed for the purpose go about from house to house, finding out whoever may be in need of aid, and giving them orders on the commissariat for stores. Besides the provisions thus distributed by the Government, the American Union Commission is engaged in ministering to the necessities of the people. One of the very few national flags to be seen in Richmond waves over the tent of its agency in the

Capitol Square. There, since a week after the evacuation, tickets have every day been issued, which secured to their holders a dinner of soup from the Commission's soup-house, or flour—of which several hundred barrels have been distributed—or meal and rice. Sometimes as many as fifteen hundred soup tickets have been given away in a day. The charities of the Government are of course upon a much more extended scale. In addition to its labors in relieving these more immediate wants, the Commission has furnished garden seeds, and farming utensils of various kinds, to such cultivators of land as could bring satisfactory evidence of honesty and poverty. Certificates of loyalty are not required. No public announcement of this latter distribution was made, and the persons benefited since the first of this month, at which time it commenced, are not more than twenty in number, and are, for the most part, residents of Henrico County. From the account books of the Commission I am allowed to copy two or three returns, which are of interest as showing the unfortunate condition in which the ravages of war have placed very many farmers in the tide-water section of Virginia:

"Mrs. N—— N—— owns a hundred and twenty acres of land, of which there are thirty under cultivation; she has one horse and a small cart, but no farming implements, nor money to get them; her house is occupied by Federal troops.

"G—— M—— has a wife and nine children; owns and cultivates six acres of land; has now a borrowed horse and plough, and no farming implements of his own.

"W—— C—— owns a hundred acres, and cultivates forty-five; borrows a horse; all the implements on his place destroyed by General Butler's army; and he has nothing left but his farm.

"Mrs. M—— C—— owns a hundred and fifty acres of land, has twenty-five acres under cultivation; hires a horse and cart from Negroes; has no implements left that can be used; has not a dollar."

No one not quite destitute of means was allowed to procure seeds or tools; but people in the condition set forth by the extracts given above received spades, shovels, rakes, hoes, and ploughs. In one or two instances a bill was taken with the articles, and the recipient hoped soon to pay for them, but most of the parties were content to take them as a gift. Now that the new crop is coming in, the Commission proposes, I believe, to suspend operations for a time, and not recommence its labor until the fall, when the inclement season will make more imperative demands upon its resources, and for clothing and fuel as well as for food.

So much has been said of late about the lofty hopes which the emancipated slave entertains in reference to his future, of the insolence of his demeanor, of the certainty that in his hands freedom will become license, that I have looked with care to find indications of these things. So far as concerns the Negro's manners, it seems to me that he has by no means removed all traces of his former servility of demeanor. My observation has, of course, been confined within narrow limits of time and space, but as far as I have seen, in the hotels, at barber shops, in public conveyances, in the streets, the colored people appear good-natured, well behaved, and certainly far more respectful and deferential than one ever expects to find white Americans. At Norfolk and Portsmouth, towns where, a short time previous to my visit and a short time after, whites and blacks were engaged in savage party fights, I met some Negroes who might be classed as exceptions to this general description; but even in those towns, though there was little visible good humor, there was no insolence. How long the deportment of the blacks will retain the characteristic marks of their servitude, and how long a time will elapse before white people cease to be more angry at a Negro's impudence than at a white man's, are questions only to be decided by future experience.

The colored people, at the instance of Negroes resident in Alexandria, will shortly hold a convention at that city, and take into consideration the prospects of their race in Virginia. The public generally will then be informed as to the nature of their demands, and in my opinion these will not be so extravagant as many people now suppose and declare.

Not long since I availed myself of a favorable opportunity to converse with two Richmond Negroes who had been members of the delegation that recently visited President Johnson, and who expected to be in the Alexandria Convention. Both were mulattoes. One had long been free; the other was a slave up to the evacuation of the city. They were men of respectable appearance and of intelligence, speaking with propriety, and evidently not unaccustomed to reflection.

They thought a good many of their people in the more remote and secluded parts of Virginia were hardly aware as yet that they were free. But the great majority not only had a knowledge of the fact, but also knew pretty well in what respects their present differed from their former situation. They all knew they were their own men, and had got themselves to work for. There was great need for some law to regulate the price of labor, so that the people might be able to stay at their own homes and yet not be forced to take less wages than they ought to receive. They thought the relations between capital and labor could not safely be left to natural laws at present, and that they would not be at any rate. Legislation, if not used in behalf of the colored laborer, would be used against him. While the better class of planters would use the people fairly and well, there were many to whose good-will the Negro could not trust, and these would join with the worst classes of voters to oppress him. It was not the slaveholders that were most to be feared; it was the rabble—the same people that were beating the Negroes at Norfolk. Both took it for granted that the colored population was to form a class of hired laborers. Very few of them would be able to buy land now, and they had no expectation that land would be given them.

I asked them what they thought of the immediate enfranchisement of the Negro. One of the two men was in favor of it, and urged all the ordinary arguments in support of it. Unless his people obtained a share of political power, they would have no protection against rapacity and oppression. They would always be kept in poverty and ignorance. They would become a class most dangerous to the peace of society. Nor should rebels be allowed to make laws for Union men. His friend did not think the Negroes in Virginia were fit to exercise the right of suffrage immediately, nor that they would be for some years. Most of them knew nothing about the country. Virginian politics had done nothing but get worse and worse ever since the State, some fifteen or twenty years ago, adopted a more democratic constitution, and let every man cast a vote who was able to bear arms. The gentlemen couldn't get anywhere near the polls on election day, and the men who knew nothing and were worth nothing had everything their own way. The other replied that, unless such men had the right of voting, they never would know anything or be worth anything, and that, at any rate, they had taxes to pay. It would be the same, he said, with the Negroes. The convention, both thought, would go no further than to ask that, if ignorant white men were allowed to vote, ignorant black men should have the same privilege. On that point the two men were at one, but they differed still as to the question whether all men, without distinction of color, should have the right of suffrage, or only the intelligent men of both races. They agreed, too, that there was very faint hope of the convention's being able to effect anything in reference to that matter, whatever good might flow from its efforts to obtain a system of laws regulating the price of labor.

Unlike the Negro population with which I have been best acquainted, these men, as well as others of their race whom I have met in Virginia, seem to look for an improvement in their condition more to their own exertions and to local action, and less to the general Government and the people of the North. They are decidedly more intelligent than the Negroes of Southern Georgia and South Carolina, and evince their superiority by their language, dress, and alertness of demeanor.

As one sits in the hotel parlor or in the cool piazza after tea, it is probable that the group surrounding him consists of men from all parts of the South. Military titles are frequent, and the majority have on, if not a full suit, at least some article of clothing made of

Confederate gray cloth, or of butternut brown. Few are without a pipe and a tobacco pouch. Among themselves they are very frank in manners and speech, nor do I observe that a Northerner is treated with particular coldness. The old gentleman from Columbia whose property has all been destroyed, and who is on his way North to make a composition with creditors whom he will never be able to pay in full; the man from Louisiana who thinks he has as good a right to live in this country as any other man, who is going to stay and live easy if they leave him his property, and stay and take it rough-and-tumble if they don't; the gentleman who was born and raised in East Tennessee, and who has left his native State because he considers it unsafe for any man that has been a Southern sympathizer to try and live there, and who is now looking for a place to locate; the young man from North Carolina who deserted from Lee's army after Gettysburg and worked as a farm-laborer in Maryland—all furnish a share of the smoke and the talk. The last named person, however, does not, like the rest, confide his past history to the company in general. He tells it to me, knowing that I am from the North, and adds that he reckons "they'll be pretty hard on a man round here if they knew he didn't go plum through to the surrender. Down in Moore County he has two brothers that were just as strong for the war as any two fellows could be. He don't know what they'll say to him. He reckons they stuck it out. He'd like to get a good mule and carry on with him when he goes."

The conversation relates to the crops, the condition of the Negroes, the behavior of the Yankees in each man's neighborhood, the probable action of the Federal Government, Southern prospects in business and politics, the state of public opinion in the North, all mingled with stories of the war—perhaps an anecdote of "Prince" John Magruder, an adventure with bushwhackers, a description of the wholesale destruction caused by Sherman's march, or of midnight robbery of a rebel family in Tennessee.

A remark made by the Tennesseean attracts the attention of his neighbor, who says: "Ah, doctor, have you been North recently?" "Yes, sir, I had to leave my home in Tennessee. My wife is a New

England woman, and I've been staying with her folks. In fact, I hadn't any other place to stay at, and was very thankful to stay there."

"Oh, we're all poor together, sir; and no Southern man need be ashamed to confess it. How did you find the people up there?"

"Well, of course, they think they were right, and they're mighty well pleased to think that we're subjugated, but everybody was kind and pleasant. The business men were all glad to see Southern men coming back. You see they never liked Western men so well as us. Westerners would often buy when they meant to fail and smash up, but we Southerners never had the name of doing that, and they like to see us again."

Here the gentleman from South Carolina interrupts. He is a short, small man, quite sixty years old, slow of speech but emphatic, and with a careworn expression of face.

"Were you owing much, sir, at the North?"

"Well, yes, sir; I owed near forty thousand dollars when the war broke out."

"What did they do with you? I am expecting in a few days to meet creditors of my own, and I would like to know how they feel up there."

"They'll treat you well. Very likely you'll find that your creditors are not the men that you think. Some of my paper had passed into second and third hands. The original holders had failed, been smashed up by the war, and my notes were sold at auction. I got them back cheap. I heard of one Norfolk house whose paper had been sold in that way, and they got it again for ten cents on a dollar. Others of my creditors asked me for a full statement, made on my honor, of what my debts were, and the amount of property that I had saved. I gave it, and they dealt very fairly with me. I couldn't pay fifty cents. Oh, they leave a man a little. Of course it depends a good deal on the kind of a man the creditor is, and a good deal on your own character."

"Will they let a man have more goods?"

"On credit?—no, sir. Won't do that. You may get them to fix it up in the way of consignment."

"Well, sir, is it reasonable for them to expect us to pay our debts? Now here am I. I may say that I haven't a cent in the world. Sherman's army burnt my store and my house."

"Sherman says he didn't."

"He did, sir. There can be no doubt of it. One of the Yankee officers told my wife not two hours before the fire began, 'Columbia is a doomed city.' I cannot but think that the moral obligation resting upon me to fulfil my contracts with my Northern creditor is neutralized. That was not civilized warfare. Maybe it was not my creditors who were responsible for that devastation. But some of us down here were innocent of the sin of secession, yet we had to suffer with the guilty. Why should not the innocent and the guilty at the North suffer together in the same way? I do not believe that I am morally bound to spend my old age in toiling to repay my Northern creditors. I ought to be legally released from my indebtedness, and not feel that there is a burden upon me which I can never shake off."

Thereupon followed an animated discussion. The question, considered as one of pure abstract morality, was decided against the old man; but it seemed to be the general opinion that he would have little practical difficulty in settling his affairs with his creditors. The company seemed to think that whatever might be abstractly right, they, individually, if they could not discharge all their obligations, would prefer paying a Southern creditor in full to making a division amongst Southern and Northern creditors.

"Well, doctor, how do the people up there feel about Negro suffrage?"

"I think they're in favor of it. In New England they are, at any rate. In the first place, there's a class that think if the nigger gets a vote, they'll come down here and ride into office right away. Always been friends of the black man, philanthropic, and that sort of thing, you know. They all go in for it. Then there's a very large class who think that the South will always be raising the devil, seceding or something, if they don't give a vote to the niggers. 'The niggers have all been loyal,' they say. They all go in for it. Then a good many think that we, at the South, if we are left to ourselves, won't treat the niggers well; and that class goes in for it. I wish all our people could see it as I do, and they'd go in for it, too."

"How's that? Do you believe in Negro suffrage?"

"Yes, I do; and I'll tell you why I do. It will work just the same here as it does there. The class of people there that represent our niggers, the laborers, have a right to vote. My father-in-law employs thirty-five Irishmen. They always vote the right ticket, and he tells them which is the right one. Now, major, if you hire thirty-five niggers, work 'em well, pay 'em well, and feed 'em well—they don't know Wm. H. Seward from a foreign war, they care nothing about the country (we all know what their 'loyalty' amounted to— Cuffee struck out for himself)—now how are they going to vote?"

"Why, they're going to vote as you say."

"Vote themselves white wives more likely," said a young man from Charlotte County. "No, no, sir; you are mistaken," said another, and there was a general expression of dissent. Some other way than that must be discovered for the South to obtain political power in the Union.

"The Northern friends of the Negro," said the major, "if they want to benefit their protégé, had better abstain from any interference in that matter, for the Southern people will not be apt to stand it. Everybody admits that the Negro is incapable of intelligently exercising the right of suffrage. Why give it to him, then? No people ever fought more bravely than ours have fought for the last four years. We have been obliged to succumb. With how small forces we carried on the war has never yet been told. General Lee could tell, and some time may. We were outnumbered five to one, and here we are subjugated. History records no example of such a war, followed by such a peace. Our people are quiet. No one talks of insurrection. We go peaceably about our business. Every difficulty that has arisen in our streets is directly traceable to Yankee soldiers and the teachings of Yankee Negroes. Why should the North profess to fear that we are not yet conquered, or are not honest when we say so? We are conquered, and all our actions acknowledge it. We may not love the Yankees; I don't think we pretend to do that, do we, captain? but we have made up our

minds to behave as peaceable citizens. We can keep these States in
the Union, and we mean to do it. We have tried our best to take
them out, and we admit that we can't." This, in substance, the
major delivered in an oratorical style, and seemingly with the ap-
probation of all present. He then continued, "But, of course, doctor, the North is not unanimous on this question? I am given to
understand that Mr. Johnson is opposed to Negro suffrage."

"Yes, he is. He takes the same view of the thing that I do, and
you may be sure that he'll be like a flint. They won't turn him."

"You know Mr. Johnson?"

"Yes, sir, I saw him when I was on there."

The conversation continued, and it seemed the conviction of all
present that nothing could be more preposterous, and nothing was
more improbable, than that Virginia should grant the right of
suffrage to her Negro population. If such a thing should happen,
nothing but calamity could be reasonably expected. The national
debt would be repudiated. What Negro would deny himself a
pound of sugar in order that he might honorably pay his share of
the interest on it? The Negroes could vote us into a war at any
time. Anything would serve as a pretext. Cuba was full of slaves,
make war on Spain and free them.

Every demagogue would do with them precisely as he chose.
The doctor might talk of laborers voting as the capitalist directed,
but if the laborer could vote he'd soon vote himself a living out of
the capitalist's property. And even if he should obey the directions
of his employer, that would be of little good, as the great majority
of them would never have a regular employer.

A young man residing near Fort Monroe thought that a great
many niggers would find employment in the Federal army, as he
had been told by an officer whom he met there that the Government intended to distribute nigger regiments here and there
throughout the South to keep the people quiet.

This statement provoked a good deal of indignant comment.
Nothing would make the people angrier than that. It was said the
people would universally regard it as an insult. They had borne a
good deal, and were ready to bear more; but to have Negro troops

put over them was not a natural consequence of their defeat, and they would not bear that. There was a point at which forbearance ceased to be a virtue.

These remarks were made by the younger men of the little circle. The major enquired if the Federal officer who had made the remarks reported had seen service, for, said he, "he doesn't talk like an old soldier. Did you find out how many fights he'd been in?"

The young man replied that the officer was a surgeon, who had entered the service with a view of improving himself in his business, and who, when asked about his battles, replied that he had never seen so much of the active operations as he would have liked. The young man found him in his mother's house. His mother, much against her will, had taken him as a boarder, because the surgeon very much wished it, and offered to have a guard put on the property if the lady would consent to receive him.

"You are not likely to hear such talk from the old soldiers on either side," said the major, who seemed to fill the position of mentor in the party. "I do not believe the War Department proposes to follow any such plan. If Mr. Stanton does adopt that policy, it will produce great evil, and postpone the day of peace. He need not put the Negro on top of us. We will stay down without that."

LYNCHBURG, VA., July 24, 1865

THE Southside Railroad Company promises in its advertisements to take passengers through from Richmond to Lynchburg, a distance of about one hundred and thirty miles, in twenty-four hours. Packet-boats ply between the two cities, but that mode of travelling, besides being very slow and tedious, is made uncomfortable by the heat, and I decided to make the journey by rail. At half after six in the morning, I was assured, the train would leave the station; so breakfasting at five, I set out for the south bank of the James River. All the railway bridges were destroyed by Lee's retreating forces, and trains going southward start from the town of Manchester. I found no depot nor baggage-master. Half a dozen dilapidated cars were standing about, and a rusty looking engine was cracking and puffing up and down, shifting them from one track to another, and making up a train. Of this two passenger carriages formed a part, both on the outside adorned with a painted representation of two Confederate flags, and splashed half way up with the yellowish-red mud of this region, and, inside, both dirty and exceedingly uncomfortable.

Long ago, I suppose, cushions had disappeared, the only vestiges of them that remained being an occasional wad of horse-hair, or a shred of faded plush still clinging to the frame-work of the seats. In the window-sashes were many broken panes, and where the glass was wholly gone wood had been substituted. The floors were filthy. Such as they were, these two carriages were given up to the occupancy of ladies and the gentlemen accompanying them, together with a number of sick and wounded Confederate soldiers; other passengers found sitting and standing room in the freight cars. Even at that early hour the sun began to shine hotly down upon the baked and cracked soil of the railroad, and moving my trunk into the shadow cast by the leaving train, I sat and watched the crowd assembled at the station.

There were, perhaps, a hundred and fifty people collected together. Negro drivers, liberal of the whip and vociferous in expostulation with their mules, drove loaded wagons to the baggage cars. Dirty-looking whites and dirtier Negroes were selling "fried pies" and other uninviting edibles. A crippled Negro was retailing cider, which he poured from a jug with a cornstalk stopper into a tin can that once had held preserved salmon. Newsboys were crying the New York *Daily News* and *Herald*, and the Richmond morning papers. Here in Virginia it is possible, I observe, to get a copy of the *Herald* for some time after every copy of the *News* has been sold. At last the train was got together, and at about half after seven o'clock we began our southward journey, pitching and jolting slowly along.

Indeed, throughout the day the rate of speed was but seldom so great that an active man might not have got off the train and on again without inconvenience or danger. I was told that even in the times before the war the trains never made much more than fifteen miles an hour. The country through which this railway passes lies south of the James, and at a distance varying from ten to forty miles. Between Lynchburg and Richmond the river makes a great curve to the north, that it may skirt the elevated ridge of land on the crown of which the road is built. The land is comparatively unproductive, and Virginians ask the traveller not to form an opinion of the fertility of their State from the appearance of this particular region. Yet there is some good bottom land. The country has many creeks, for in this ridge, close by the line of the road, are the head-waters both of the streams that flow north-easterly into the Appomattox and James, and also of those which seek the tributaries of the Roanoke on the south. I saw but little land under cultivation; indeed, the greater portion of the surface seemed to be not

cleared at all. An occasional field of wheat-stubble, a cluster of farm
buildings, surrounded by a field of corn, the railroad itself, here
and there a tortuous footpath, winding away into the hot and solitary forest, furnished for the greater part of the way the only indications that the almost unbroken woodland was not an undisturbed wilderness. Every hour or two the train is stopped; the
passengers get out and drink water at the tank that is supplying the
engine; Negroes beside the track are busy chopping the wood short
for the furnace and throwing it on the tender; nobody seems to be
in any hurry. When two screams from the whistle give the signal,
we leisurely get aboard again.

At longer intervals a way station presents itself, where two or
three passengers get on or off. Commonly a country road crosses
the track, and two or three mean buildings are in sight; probably
some Federal soldiers are standing about, and an officer inquires
for newspapers. A dozen or more Negroes, one or two men in
Confederate gray, and some white women offer for sale cigars,
apples, and peaches at ten cents a dozen, or for a quarter of a
dollar will sell "a right good snack." This, in some instances, consisted of corn-bread with the leg of a fowl; in others, I saw tied
together into a compact package a piece of bread, three fried eggs,
and a slice of ham. At some places there were, I should think, as
many as thirty people engaged in this traffic, which, however,
seemed not to be lucrative, except, perhaps, at Burkesville Junction, where was a train loaded with two or three happy regiments
of Kentucky soldiers, who seemed overjoyed at the prospect of
being soon at home again. They were as boisterous in their delight
as boys, and the Burkesville market was speedily cleared of eatables and drinkables.

It was understood that passengers for Lynchburg were to
change cars at the Junction, while the other train proceeded to
Danville. At the depot I could find no one to tell me when the
train would leave, nor whether it would start from that station.
The train itself, meantime, was nowhere to be seen, nor could I
learn where it was to be found, till at last a man who had heard me
several times making fruitless inquiries, told me it was "up thar a

short piece," pointing to a curve in the railroad. Getting a Negro to carry my trunk, I walked along the track for a quarter of a mile till I came to an engine and three freight cars, into one of which I put my luggage. Some Negroes loading freight thought the train went to High Bridge and Far'ville. A white man whom I approached on the subject "reckoned it did," and went on chewing tobacco. A conductor I could not find, but finally a brakeman whom I asked, after carefully scrutinizing me as if to see if I might be trusted to keep a secret, told me that it didn't go to Lynchburg, but was the Lynchburg train; that it would start from the place where it stood, and added that I would have to look out for my own baggage. It was then about one o'clock, and a little after three we started. We went on a little way, then stopped and went back. Someone connected with the train had dropped a five-dollar note, and the conductor returned to let him find it. Then we set out again, the engine in the rear of the train, pushing us along to High Bridge. This structure is a trestle-work viaduct, about twelve hundred feet long, and resting upon twenty lofty brick pillars that span a valley, through which runs a narrow creek. Lee's army destroyed the timbers at the western end of the bridge in its retreat before Sheridan, and it became necessary for us to change cars. Carriages of various descriptions were at hand to remove passengers and freight to the other cars. The fare from Burkesville to High Bridge, a distance of twelve miles, was a dollar and fifty cents. The wagon ride from one end of the bridge to the other was about half a mile in length. The fare charged was one dollar for a passenger with a trunk.

One could not help being impressed with the desolateness of the scene as we rode over the pits and gullies of the road. Up or down the narrow valley I could see no dwelling and no cultivated field. On a little knoll near the bed of the creek was a dark-red fort of earth standing out distinct amid the green. High aloft on our left hand broken fragments of trestle-work projected into the empty air between the last pillars of the bridge. We passed over a little bridge of logs, whose timbers were blackened by fire and burnt nearly through. In the open wagon in which I was riding an old North Carolinian, dressed in homespun, sat silent upon a rough

board coffin containing the corpse of his son, and his seat was
shared by two wounded Confederate soldiers. Everything around
seemed to have felt the fire and sword of the war. We found the
train awaiting us in the middle of an earthwork, built by the Confederates to protect the bridge against Federal raiding parties. Here
we had another hour or two of tedious waiting in the blaze of the
afternoon sun. But at last the conductor addressed the engineer,
"Well, Oscar, reckon we'd better go"—and we took our departure
for Farmville. This little town presents a not unpleasant aspect.
The land in the immediate vicinity seems more fertile and better
cultivated than any other which I had seen during the day. The
principal business of the place is the manufacture of the tobacco
raised in the adjacent districts. Here were more Federal soldiers,
and an office of the United States military telegraph. Soon after
leaving Farmville the cars became more comfortable, for it was
near sunset, and the heat somewhat abated. It was not pleasant,
however, to learn that we should be compelled to pass the night in
the train, which would reach Concord at twelve o'clock, and there
wait till six in the morning. I asked if a bed could not be obtained,
but was told that there was nothing at Concord but the railroad
depot.

With the man who gave me this information I had some further
conversation on a variety of topics. He was going up the road, he
said, to see about the loading of a material train which would go
down to High Bridge the next day with timber for repairing the
trestle-work. I asked him if green timber was used in the repairs.
He said, "Yes, it's safe enough; we allow for shrinking." But on
the very next day the same train broke through a defective trestle-
work, about ten miles from this city, and was precipitated over a
bluff nearly fifty feet high. Thirty or forty people were injured,
seven of them severely, and two men were killed. What I have said
of the inconveniences of railway travelling at the South has been
said merely to give some account of the matter. Probably it would
be very unfair to blame the companies for the worn-out rails, comfortless cars, and long delays of which I have spoken. And,
perhaps, it is not the companies but the military authorities who

should be held responsible and blamed for such accidents as this one. To take passengers over a railroad in the present condition of that between this city and Richmond, is to put them in fear and imminent danger of death. Yet the eagerness of the people for mails and transportation is so great that repairs of the most temporary character are made, and probably will continue to be made for months to come, unless some authoritative inspection is instituted. The scene, as described by eye-witnesses, must have been most impressive and distressing. The accident happened about midnight; nearly everybody on board was more or less injured. There was no assistance rendered by any of the country people till morning, for none lived at all near.

By the light of a fire kindled among the ruins of the cars the wounded were removed to a bank of sand in the dry bed of the creek, and the wounds of some were dressed by a Confederate surgeon who was among the passengers. Watches, money, and jewelry were taken from those who lay insensible by some marauding soldiers who robbed in the dark. Of these some who were seen at their work were forced to give up a part of their plunder, but a much greater part was not restored. One gentleman from the North is reported to have lost many thousands of dollars in Government bonds, and others lost sums amounting to hundreds of dollars. I have heard of no investigations into the accident or the robberies.

My travelling acquaintance said he was then going up the road for a load of timber. The gang of hands of which he had charge were getting out stuff in the woods, and it was to go down the next day. He had both black and white laborers.

I asked him what wages were paid. White men that were good carpenters got fifty dollars a month and their board. Ordinary laborers got eighteen dollars a month and the same board as the others. The company had the food cooked for them. It consisted of bread, bacon, vegetables, sugar, and coffee.

I asked if the company got laborers in sufficient numbers, for I remembered having seen an advertisement of theirs in the Richmond papers.

"Can't get white men enough. They're too damned proud to

work. Rather loaf round Richmond and Petersburg. But they'll
have to come to it. I've had to pull off my coat since peace came. I
lost what money I had in the great fire. I had thirty-seven hogsheads of tobacco burnt thar. It would have been worth more than
twenty thousand dollars in gold today. When this war broke out I
had one hundred and sixty-one hogsheads in store. But I had to
live off it. Had a wife and four children, and I couldn't begin to
keep 'em on my pay. They conscripted me, and I had to serve
eighteen months. Well, I got a little money from the Government,
but Lord! you'd have to give two months' pay in Confederate
money before they'd let you give one look at a barrel of flour.
Well, I had to sell a hogshead every now and then till I got it
reduced down to thirty-seven, and them they burnt. So I had to go
to work, and more than me'll have to do it. No, if we could get
white men enough we wouldn't hire niggers."

"They don't work so well?"

"A nigger's work a'n't much. Rather have one white man than
three niggers. They'll work a day, and then they want to lay off a
day. Now with me they used to lay off after they got their week's
rations, and I wouldn't see anything of 'em for two or three days.
But I broke 'em of that, just set 'em to work till they'd worked out
what the rations come to, and then I told 'em to leave."

"You don't board Negroes like whites, then?"

"No; we give 'em an allowance—fourteen pounds of meal a
week and three pounds of bacon."

I asked if any Negro mechanics were employed, and found there
were none. The Negroes are paid fifteen dollars per month, which
is the amount paid hotel servants in this town and in Richmond.
On the railroad the colored laborers when employed in cutting
cord-wood are expected to cut what a white man usually cuts—
three cords a day. The railway company buys the wood as it stands
growing for thirty-five dollars an acre, or already cut at the rate of
one dollar and sixty cents a cord. It is piled up at the various wood
and watering stations along the line, and the hands are employed
in chopping the four feet sticks in two. It is at this work, as I
suppose, that a man is required to go through three cords in a day.

In the other kinds of work done on the railroad I was told that the Negro did not perform nearly so much labor as the white man, and that he needed so much watching and driving that one white man was worth as much as three colored men.

Having discussed the Negro in his capacity of working-man, I asked what he thought of the extension of the franchise so as to make the Negro a voter. Like almost every other man with whom I have talked in this State, he was utterly opposed to it. The Negro was not fit to vote; it wasn't in his nature ever to become fit to vote; and the Southern people wouldn't stand it if the North should put the Negro and the white man on an equality. That would make the South fight. All the secessionists to whom I have mentioned the subject, plant themselves firmly on those three propositions. Let the Negro vote, and the Southern people will have to be kept down by a standing army. The point will have been reached at which forbearance ceases to be a virtue, and perhaps at that point they will have to make a virtue of necessity, but it will be because the bayonet forces them.

Among Virginian Unionists also opposition is manifested, and is based upon grounds hardly different. There is already far too much ignorance and depravity existing among the voters. The servant will be almost sure to vote for the master's favorite candidate.

Ask a Unionist why, if the Negro vote would be so much at the service of the masters, the masters as a rule are so strongly adverse to Negro suffrage, and the reply is that just at present the master is inclined to hate the newly emancipated slaves; that, moreover, the former owners of slaves expect very soon to get the States back into their own hands, and have no fears that they will not be able, as in old times, to get a majority to carry the measures which they propose. If they needed the Negro vote, they would hardly take it, and till they do need it they would much prefer that the freedmen be kept in a condition as nearly as possible resembling their former slavery.

If you then ask the Unionist, who is, I may say always, a disbeliever in the professions of loyalty made by his neighbors who have been in rebellion; who always predicts repudiation of the national debt, a factious questioning of any acts of Congress that were not passed when all the States were represented, persecution of Unionists, and a practical re-establishment of slavery—if you ask him what remedy he sees for these evils of the future, *he* will tell you that he has no hope except in the maintenance of a standing army throughout the South.

The Unionist and the secessionist both declare that the suffrage should not be made more but less extensive. The former seems to think so because he believes the rebellion could not have begun if a majority of the voters in the Southern States had been sufficiently intelligent to comprehend clearly the state of affairs in the country, and to discern their own interests. This has been said to me by several Union men—by one no longer ago than this morning, and in nearly the words I have used. The secessionist, when he says so, proceeds immediately to deduce the conclusion that it would be most unwise to give the right of voting to several millions of people who now are without it, and who confessedly are very ignorant. Which party is with most justice afraid of the Negro vote, and which party will longest continue to fear it, I do not undertake to say.

"How do the Negroes behave since they became free?" was the next question I put to the man with whom I was talking in the car.

"Sassy and lazy. They go round stealing. Two niggers were shot up here at Appomattox a while ago. They got into the way of going round to the houses, and taking what they wanted. The people complained, and a guard was sent after 'em; they wouldn't stop when they were ordered, but run, so the guard fired and shot 'em both."

I asked the same question of another person, saying that the general report was that they had become impudent and idle.

"Don't you believe it," he replied; "they behave well enough. But some people can't see a nigger go along the street now-a-days that they don't damn him for putting on airs. They are pretty much all at work. Their wages are not what they ought to be yet, but that matter will soon regulate itself. A good many of the masters forget pretty often that their niggers are free, and take a stick to

them, or give them a cuff with the fist, though they don't attempt
to administer a regular flogging."

This view of the case, so far as concerns the deportment of the
Negroes, I find confirmed by the Lynchburg *Virginian* of July 24,
which, combating a report that there had been a Negro riot in the
city, says:

> There has been no riot here, nor anything bearing the slightest
> resemblance to a riot. The Negroes have been orderly and respectful
> in their deportment, and the whites have been kind, just, and con-
> siderate towards them. The *entente cordiale* of old between the
> classes has been well preserved. There have been a few individual
> cases of insolence on the part of the one, and of unkindness on the
> part of the other; but such cases are exceptions to the rule.

The white people of the neighboring county of Franklin do not,
however, appear altogether satisfied with the state of affairs in
their district, and on the 13th of July held a meeting at the court-
house, and passed a series of resolutions. The first acknowledges
the supremacy of the Federal Government, and announces that the
citizens of Franklin "are willing to discharge their duties as
citizens, and are ready to appreciate and properly reciprocate a
forbearing and conciliatory policy towards them on the part of the
authorities and the people of the Northern States." The second
resolution declares that "without expressing any opinion as to the
constitutionality or expediency of the measures which have been
used for the emancipation of the slaves, they are desirous to adopt
such measures as will most alleviate the evils and best develop the
good likely to result from so great a change in our social and
industrial system." The resolution goes on to say that the laborer
must content himself with small wages, or in the present bad condition of the country he will have to go without work. Arrangements
already made this year ought not to be disturbed by the military
authorities. The right is claimed of punishing minors whose parents
will not keep proper discipline over them, and of summarily dis-
missing for idleness and misconduct adults and those properly dependent on them.

The resolutions were published in the Lynchburg papers of

Monday, and on Tuesday morning appeared an order of General Gregg, directing his subordinate in that county to notify the persons holding the meeting that "their proceedings are disapproved, and that their resolutions, or any part of them, will not be carried into effect."

The wages now paid to farm hands in this section of country, under the arrangements with which the citizens of Franklin deprecate interference, are in no case higher than five dollars a month. While some planters allow their servants to cultivate a patch of ground for themselves, others do not. On the very great majority of plantations no tobacco is growing this year. A very well informed resident of the city told me that he knew of but four farms where any attempt was making to raise it, and on those the quantity planted was very small. Of corn and oats the yield will be so large as to be remarkable.

Money, however, is exceedingly scarce, and less business is done in proportion to the size of the place than in Richmond. The shopkeepers are not yet wholly free from the habits of Confederate times, and when one asks the price one is told two prices—so much in gold, so much in greenbacks. But this practice, it is said, becomes less common daily, and less and less gold is seen. "Business will be stagnant," says the general voice, "until we can find out what is going to be done with the thirteenth clause of the Amnesty Proclamation."

To return to my friend on the Southside train:

"I reckon I'll have to wait awhile, till they get things straightened out a little. Reckon my credit's good at the North. Baltimore men tell me to come on thar and get what goods I want; and I could do it in New York. Don't owe a dollar up thar. I sent one pretty large bill through to a house in New York after the war had begun. But I reckon I'd better stick to the road yet awhile. I'll be ready for trade aginst the people are."

"I suppose when trade begins it won't be long before the North and South are friendly again?"

"Well, I reckon not."

"I have been told that your people are hostile yet in their feel-

ings, and that if the Government was engaged in a foreign war—
say in Mexico—the Southerners would be in arms against the
North?"

"Well, now, there's a hundred of 'em working right along with
me, and mo'. I hear how they talk, and I know what their feelings
are. They don't hate the North. Except the radicals; they hate
them. But there's nothing they'd like any better than a war with
France. England either. Those two nations encouraged us to fight,
and then backed out and wouldn't recognize us. North and South
together, reckon they'd make short work down in Mexico. A good
many of our people haven't anything else to do, and they'd like it."

They seem to have nothing else to do. To judge by the numbers
of able-bodied men that one sees lounging in the streets and in the
bar-rooms, listlessly sitting about the railway stations, and by the
difficulty that is experienced in getting white laborers to work on
the railroad repairs, there may be some necessity for the recently
promulgated modifications of one of General Gregg's orders, "so
as to include all white persons found loafing about the streets,
without any ostensible means of making a living." The number of
idle white persons is much too great, and will account for much of
the pilfering complained of by the newspapers.

V

LYNCHBURG, VA., July 31, 1865

SIX miles below Lynchburg, a gray stone barn that crowns a hill near the river is pointed out to the traveller as the place where, in the summer of 1864, Hunter's men first showed themselves. There an advance party of his troops made an unsuccessful attempt to burn a railroad bridge. The little earthwork which beat them off still frowns from a neighboring eminence. Behind the city, upon the mountains two or three miles away, can be seen the spot whence a day or two afterwards the baffled Federal general turned back and began his hasty retreat up the valley.

The escape of the Lynchburgers at that time was a narrow one, but until after Lee's surrender the town had never been molested nor occupied by the Union army, and, except that a Confederate storehouse was then destroyed by Sheridan's soldiers, the actual ravages of war have never visited the citizens. But the more indirect evils which the rebellion brought upon all the South this city has evidently suffered. Trade is dead, the people have no money, nor is there a prospect of their soon getting any, for nothing but breadstuffs has been raised this season, and the stock of tobacco, more or less injured, which is all they have to sell, is in the hands of comparatively few men. The shelves of the shops are scantily supplied with poor goods, and several times after purchasing some small article I have been obliged to leave it untaken, because the merchant was not able to give me change for a five-dollar note. Silver and gold are, however, oftener seen in circulation here than in the ordinary trade of any Northern city, and the people show a somewhat extravagant reference for a specie currency. I was yesterday an eye-witness of the following transaction. Two soldiers bought a quart of buttermilk from a small Negro boy. "What d'ye want for it?" said one. The prompt answer was : "Five cents in silver, or ten cents in greenbacks."

The method of the adult traders in computing the relative values of the two kinds of money is a little better than this. It is not perfect, however, and the aid of the provost-marshal is not unfrequently called in to settle disputes between buyer and seller. If gold is quoted in Richmond at 140, the dealer in small wares at Lynchburg, if I understand the process, deducts from the face value of a paper dollar the excess over one hundred in the price of gold, and considers the dollar greenback to be worth not seventy-one cents but sixty. He finds some who put up with the imposition, while others, familiar with general orders and not wholly ignorant of arithmetic, resist, and summon the military power.

The rough little city is built on several round-topped hills that descend abruptly to the banks of the James, which is here an insignificant stream at the bottom of a rocky valley hardly wider than the river's bed. The streets, which run towards the water, are almost precipitous, and all the streets, whether steep or not, are dirty and ill-paved. At present they are unlighted at night, and, though guarded by soldiers, are considered unsafe after nightfall. The warehouses, manufactories, and private residences are, for the most part, mean in appearance, and the stranger is surprised to learn that, before the war, in proportion to the number of inhabitants, Lynchburg was, with the single exception of New Bedford, Massachusetts, the richest city in the United States. But if there is little which, to the casual eye, is indicative of wealth, there are many signs that the reputation of the place as a famous tobacco mart was well deserved. In the business portion of the town the air is redolent of the favorite weed. The windows of half the shops make a display of earthen pipes, bundles of tobacco in the leaf, packages of smoking tobacco, and boxes of tobacco to be chewed. One is everywhere attracted by such titles as "the Celebrated Killikinnick," or "the Celebrated Garibaldi Smoking Tobacco," the

"Tony Lumpkin," "Bob Lee," "Lone Jack," and "Billy Bowlegs, Last King of the Everglades." On the papers of this last named variety the inscription says that, "as Billy was without an equal in love for his tribe and hunting-grounds, so this tobacco stands unrivalled in point of delicacy." But, apparently, for all the varieties there are customers. Nearly every one uses tobacco in one or two of its forms, and no public place is without an array of spittoons. In the pews of the most fashionable church in Lynchburg I noticed spittoons in use.

The opinion seems to prevail among the people that the renown of their city as the tobacco metropolis has passed away with slavery, and that, for a long time at least, it will not return. They say that free labor cannot be profitably applied to the culture of tobacco on a large scale. This opinion may or not be of weight. The men who hold it express great contempt for free Negro labor in general. "Free nigger labor may do on a trucking farm, or something like that, but it won't raise tobacco. You can't place any dependence on it. We may be able to do something with white labor by-and-bye."

These gentlemen firmly believe that the Negro not only will be, but that in most parts of the South he today is, a pauper. Yet I find no man who does not admit that in his own particular neighborhood the Negroes are doing tolerably well—are performing whatever agricultural labor is done. From the most trustworthy sources I learn that, in the vicinity of Lynchburg, of Danville, of Wytheville—in counties embracing a great part of southern and southwestern Virginia—the colored population may be truly described as orderly, industrious, and self-supporting. And this seems to be plainly shown by the reports, drawn up by Government officials, of the issue to citizens of what are known as "Destitute Rations." The exact figures I have in the case of two counties only. During the month of June, relief was furnished 961 persons in Bedford County: of these, 13 were blacks. In Campbell County 530 persons received sustenance from the Government: of these 530 persons, 12 were blacks. In other counties sometimes less, sometimes greater, numbers of persons than in Bedford and Campbell were supplied with food, and in them all the proportion of the Negroes to the white people was substantially the same with that given above.

This distribution has been going on ever since the end of May, but very recently the general commanding in this district has deemed it proper to stop all issues of rations to citizens, except in well authenticated instances of actual pauperism.

The personal knowledge of the issuing officer that the person who asks for food is, by reason of age or infirmity, unable to earn his living, and that he has no relative whose duty it is to support him, is now made the only ground of bestowing the ration. Heretofore it could be obtained if the person demanding it would first swear allegiance to the United States, and then subscribe to an oath which set forth in the following words the requisite degree of poverty in the petitioner: "I do solemnly swear before Almighty God, the searcher of all hearts, that I am in destitute circumstances; that I have nothing to subsist upon; that I have no money to purchase subsistence; that I have made every effort in my power to obtain employment, and without success; that I am ——, with —— helpless children, and that unless relief is afforded me I must perish: So help me God." But the fact that a man had taken these two oaths was found to be no perfect criterion of his honesty or poverty. Whatever may have been the case immediately after the occupation of this part of Virginia by the Federal troops, for some time past it has been plainly discernible that the very large majority of those claiming to be destitute might easily support life without taxing the charity of the Government.

One man was discovered to have come in from the country, drawn rations for himself and his family, and before leaving the city to have expended several dollars in purchasing apple-brandy. Another drew rations who had four adult sons, any one of whom might have kept their father from the necessity of begging, as all were at work and earning fair wages. An old lady coming to the place of distribution was accosted by the clerk with the enquiry if

she were not the owner of several tenements in the town, the rents
of which she was regularly receiving. After some hesitation she
replied in the affirmative. The officer then asked if it was true that
she had stood upon the bridge one day a little while before and
cursed the Yankees? The old woman, finding denial vain, and per-
ceiving that she was to have no more rations, replied in the affirmative to this question also, and went away declaring that she wanted
no more Yankee rations, and that she still had sons left to fight for
the Confederacy if ever there should be another war.

The continual occurrence of such cases as these; the enormous
number of rations required; the evidence afforded by the face of
the country that the crop now about to be gathered is a plentiful
one; and the seeming certainty that, without regard to actual want,
the demand for rations would continue as long as the Government
would continue to give them away, caused General Curtis to pro-
hibit the issue on and after August 1, 1865. An order made in May
last, by General Gregg, which allows farmers, in order that they
may be the better able to provide for the laborers upon their
plantations, to buy supplies from the military stores, paying for
them in cash, or giving bonds to pay for them in cash or in kind
when the crops shall have been harvested, has not, I think, been
rescinded by General Curtis, but is still in force. In the earlier part
of the season many planters availed themselves of the permission
thus granted, which was doubtless of advantage to them and to the
Negroes.

In reference to the remarkable fact that so very few Negroes
of all the great number inhabiting the region round about
Lynchburg have sought food from the Government, it is fair to say
that the military authorities, when the matter was wholly in their
hands, and in those of the agency of the Freedmen's Bureau recently established, have not permitted the planters to set adrift all
or any of the Negroes from their homes. It is considered that the
crops, which in part were planted before the slaves became free,
and which have all been worked by them throughout the year, are
justly chargeable with the support of the laborers and those dependent upon them. Some planters have shown a disposition to turn

loose all such Negroes as were neither able-bodied themselves nor had near relations able to work, and whose labor could be taken as payment for the board and lodging of all. One gentleman, somewhat advanced in years and averse to the trouble of managing free Negroes, wished to let his farm stand idle, and to send away at once about sixty people, who might, very likely, have become a burden on the community at large. He was very angry when informed that no such discharge could be permitted, and that for the present, at least, the Negroes must stay where they were. But the large majority of farmers have kept with them those of their former slaves who would stay, and the large majority of these latter willingly remain in their old homes and work for wages. The amount of pay given them varies a good deal. When wages are paid in money, five dollars per month seems to be the usual rate. But it is believed that on many plantations nothing more is given than the food and clothes of the laborer and his family. Whether this is true or not, I do not know. The Superintendent of Freedmen in this district informs me that among the poorer farmers, whose operations this year are confined to raising food only, it is very probably true that the laborer gets only his board and lodging. Some plantations are "worked on shares." In one case which has fallen under my observation, the employer agrees to feed and clothe the laborers, to allow each family a patch of ground for a garden, and at the end of the year to divide among them one-seventh of the total produce of the farm. The crops planted are corn, oats, wheat, potatoes, and sorghum. The wheat has been already divided. On that plantation there is no dissatisfaction now existing. Not long since the blacksmith refused to do field-work, but afterwards agreed when not at work in the shop to work with the other hands. His view of the subject was that his labor was skilled labor, that it was necessary to the plantation, and that he was entitled to his share of the crop, even though he worked but one half of the time. There are a thousand questions of this sort which are very embarrassing to the agents of the Freedmen's Bureau. They labor with the disadvantage of having as yet no very definite instructions to guide them in the performance of their perplexing duties.

The planters, the Negroes, and they themselves have no certain knowledge of the precise nature and extent of the power lodged in their hands. The Negroes go in blind faith to the superintendent or his local assistant, as the "head Yankee" of whom everything is to be expected, sometimes on a reasonable errand, as to complain that they have been beaten, sometimes with such a request as that the farm on which they live be divided amongst them. A few words of sensible advice usually settles the affair, though now and then warning and reproof are required. For example: a Negro charges his employer with having knocked him down. The master being called on for his defence asserts that the Negro was insolent. The insolence, however, consisting in nothing worse than his saying "Mister" Smith instead of "master," the employer is instructed that now, before the law, the colored man is the equal of the white, and that corporal punishment of farm servants is not allowed.

The white people are often very far wrong in their notions of the object for which the Bureau of Freedmen was organized, and the power committed to its officers. I was waiting the other day in the office of the superintendent when two gentlemen of respectable appearance entered and announced themselves as planters from the State of Mississippi. The conversation on their part was carried on by one, the other saying nothing. Both seemed to listen with very great interest to all that was said to them. The speaker said their business with the superintendent was to get from him about a hundred Virginia Negroes to be taken down to Mississippi to work on cotton. They were informed that the officer had no power to send away Negroes unless they chose to go. They asked if they couldn't get a hundred paupers or criminals. But the superintendent had not at command so many of either class or of both together. They asked if Negroes could not be apprenticed to them for a term of years. But apprenticeship, except of boys in cities, who in exceptional cases may be put with a tradesman to learn his craft, is not permitted.

"Well, now," said the gentleman, "this is how the thing is. I've got land there, and I'm going to raise cotton. I've spent pretty nearly $20,000 for mules and harnesses and a complete outfit generally. What I want to know is this—you say you can't use compulsion to make these Virginia niggers go down there—what compulsion will the Government let me use to make them work when I've got them there, anyhow?"

"You seem to think all Negro labor must be compulsory."

"Why, of course it must. How long have you lived in a slave State, sir?"

"I have lived within twenty-five miles of one a good part of my life. But you must look to the experience of those who have tried free labor. There is Mr. B. G——, on the James. He has about two hundred and eighty-seven Negroes. They were with him as slaves, and he has employed them all since they were emancipated. Only three went away from the place, and the rest, he says, are doing very well indeed. One example like that is worth a great deal of theory."

"Yes, I know him very well. Didn't know he had so many as that, though. But I know the nigger. The employer must have some sort of punishment. I don't care what it is. If you'll let me tie him up by the thumbs, or keep him on bread and water, that will do. Over here in Rockbridge County, as I came along I saw a nigger tied up by the wrists. His hands were away up above his head. I went along to him, and says I, 'Boy, which would you like best now, to stay there where you are, or to have me take you down, give you forty good cuts, and let you go?' 'Rather have the forty lash,' says he. So he would, too. You folks used to make a good deal of talk because we gave our niggers a flogging when they deserved it. I won't ask leave to flog, if you'll let me use some of your Northern punishments. All I want is just to have it so that when I get the niggers on to my place, and the work is begun, they can't sit down and look me square in the face and do nothing."

The superintendent could not encourage him to hope that the Bureau would deport Negroes to Mississippi, nor that it would allow him to use on his plantation the punishments which he seemed to think necessary. If the Negro wouldn't work, he could be complained of. When a Northern laborer violated a contract he was sued.

"Ah! sue the nigger! Can he give his testimony in court? Will his testimony be taken?"

"It is taken here, sir; and it will be in Mississippi—at any rate, while that State is occupied by Federal troops."

"Why, no nigger can be believed whether he is under oath or not. No one that knows a nigger will ever think of believing him if it's for his interest to lie."

The gentlemen took their leave, very much dissatisfied with the state of affairs in Virginia, and with the prospects of planters throughout the Southern country. They were particularly severe upon the policy of obliging a master who wished to discharge his servants to keep them and feed them on his plantation till the Government might be ready to remove them. It was nothing more or less than a confiscation of white men's property to the use and benefit of the black man. It was a most unjust measure. They were reminded that the Negro had done work on the crop, and had a lien upon it for his labor, and that it could be no great hardship to the land-owner if the Government compelled him to relieve it of a heavy burden at no greater cost to himself than giving up to the use of the Negroes some cabins and some land which would otherwise remain empty and uncultivated. But they were not disposed to look upon the matter as anything but an act of mere power on the part of the Government. Of course, it would have to be submitted to. The man did not free his own slaves. The Government freed them. Let the Government take care of them.

The gentleman in charge of the interests of freedmen who resides in this city is superintendent of nine counties. He has one assistant superintendent here in Lynchburg, another at Danville. Both of these are of the rank of lieutenant. At each county seat he has an infantry sergeant and four men, belonging to the company which is in garrison at the village. In these large Virginian counties people sometimes come from a distance of seventeen or twenty miles to make an enquiry or to answer to a complaint. The mere length of way to be traversed before a case can be examined must often prove an almost insurmountable obstacle to the proper or the speedy transaction of business. A Negro, perhaps, comes in from a plantation ten or fifteen miles from the court-house, and makes a complaint of having been ill-treated. To the stories of Negroes, as to those of most other men, there are two sides, but to hear the statement of the man's employer it will be necessary for the sergeant to make a journey of twenty or thirty miles. Probably the case is dismissed without investigation, or an investigation, if made, imposes on someone an undue amount of labor.

In quantity the business of a day is sometimes very great, for both the white men and the Negroes make constant application to the officers of the Bureau, very many of the cases, of course, being trivial, but others being of importance and requiring for their settlement a good deal of tact and judgment. At present there seems to be need of more and somewhat better labor in this field. The higher officers of the Bureau, as it exists in this part of Virginia, are apparently men well qualified for their position. Generally they have served in the army as bonded officers (commissaries, quartermasters, etc.), and, by the terms of their commissions, being held in the service during the good pleasure of the President, are not mustered out of service with other officers of their rank, but remain and are available for the position and duties of superintendents. The lower offices are by no means so well filled. Probably, when it shall be no longer doubtful whether the civil or the military power is to have control of the affairs of freedmen, the local agencies will be made more efficient or replaced by something of a different nature. The agents of the Bureau may perhaps find all their energies taxed in the proper performance of their duties during the coming winter. They certainly will, if the prophecy to which I listened yesterday afternoon should be fulfilled. It was from the lips of a poor white with whom I talked for half an hour or so. He enlisted my services to read to him a hand-bill advertising a sale of Government horses and mules. Here and there, where the letters were capitals, he could spell out a word, but was unable to master the smaller type. I read it to him, and he asked me if the horses would probably be branded as condemned animals. I said I supposed they would be, in order that they might be distinguished from those marked "U. S.," as there would very

likely be a good many Government horses in the South as long as
the country was occupied by the Federal soldiers.

"That will be for more than one twelvemonth. Why, down in
Georgia they is killin' each other yet. I'm told that them secessionists make threats that they'll kill every Union man and every nigger
as soon as the soldiers go away from thar. Why will they keep on
contendin'? We Southerners will have it all to pay for. The niggers
didn't make theirselves free. 'Twas another man done that. But
some do hate the niggers. You mark me, thar'll be a heap o' trouble when Christmas comes, when the end o' the year comes, and
the niggers' time's out that they's hired for. They'll be awfully
defrauded. I can see it goin' on right under my own observation. I
know houses yer whar they keep a nigger till his month's most out,
and then they make a muss with him, and kick him out without
any wages. Poor men like me has got to pay for it. Of course, if
they don't pay, the niggers can't keep themselves, and it'll come on
us. They'll be cheated all kinds o' ways. Don't I know it? You
mark me, a heap o' them niggers'll die like rotten sheep."

Walking along the main street the other morning, I met several
parties of Negro boys and girls with primers in their hands, evidently on their way to school. Turning about in my walk, I followed two grotesque-looking little creatures till I came to the door
of a large brick tobacco warehouse or manufactory. Looking in, I
saw that it was empty of merchandise, and fitted up with benches
as if for a school. The scholars were there also, and two soldiers,
to whom I introduced myself, and by whom I was invited to stay
and see the school when in session. Both teachers were enlisted
men, privates in a Pennsylvania regiment. They were detailed at
their own request for this duty. No pay is given them, but while
engaged in teaching they are relieved from all camp duties. One
was without experience as a teacher, the other told me he had been
a schoolmaster before entering the army.

By nine o'clock about one hundred and thirty children, of all
ages between three and twenty, were assembled, and the school
exercises began. "I want to be an Angel" was sung in clear and
pleasant tones, and with great correctness of emphasis and pro-

nunciation. The first stanza and the chorus all the children knew, and the rest of the hymn they sang two lines at a time as the teacher dealt it out to them.

While the singing went on, I amused myself by counting the faces which gave unmistakable evidence of their owners being of mixed blood. There were all tints and shades of yellow among the forty-nine boys present, and I could find but twenty-seven who seemed to me to be purely African. Among the girls the proportion was much the same.

After the singing a chapter of the New Testament was read, and then the alphabet class recited. They knew their letters backwards and forwards, they could pick out the letters by name, and they could tell which were vowels and which were consonants. I thought they had made rapid progress in the four weeks during which they had been under instruction.

A more advanced class then read a column of a child's paper. One or two of the little girls read exceedingly well. They had been taught, they said, when they were slaves.

In Lynchburg, besides this school, which contains about one hundred and fifty pupils, there is another, taught in the same way, which contains three hundred and fifty more children. It is a pleasant and encouraging sight to see the willingness with which the scholars apply themselves to their lessons, and the very respectable measure of success which rewards their efforts.

It is a sight, too, which has attracted some attention in Lynchburg. The *Republican,* urging upon its readers the importance of providing for the education of their children, speaks of the freedmen's schools, and says, "How utterly important is it that benefits should not accrue through governmental or other philanthropy to these children of a degraded race of which our own are deprived through our culpable neglect and thoughtlessness."

VI

DURING the past week I have been making short journeys into the country round about Lynchburg, travelling by the canal or on horseback, and visiting parts of the counties of Appomattox, Campbell, Amherst, Bedford, and Rockbridge.

Everywhere the country presents the same general aspect, except that as the traveller goes westward and enters the limestone region, the streams no longer look as if they ran with puddlewater, and the eye is not wearied by the hot, bricklike consistency and color of the red clay soil as it glares and cracks in the sun. But everywhere are steep hills bright green with grass, or darker with a heavy growth of walnut and chestnut trees laden with their fruit, pines, gum trees, and black, red, and white oaks; little brooks fall in successive cascades down ledges of rock, or trickle over the face of cliffs that overhang the road and shade it; and almost always blue mountains are to be seen upon the verge of the horizon. Almost always, too, the roads are rough and lonely, so that, travelling slowly along, one has time and opportunity to enjoy the great beauty of the scenery. Occasionally a Negro man or woman is met, perhaps leading a child and carrying a bundle of clothes, perhaps driving home a long string of cows from pasture, who makes a low bow or curtsey and trudges on, turning often to stare at the stranger; or a white man, mounted on a mule or horse, rides slowly along, invariably giving a salutation as he passes, wishing a "Good morning" if the time is earlier than one o'clock in the day, and, if it is later, always saying "Good evening, sir." At every house there is

58

a field of corn, which seems to grow with an almost rank luxu-
riance of leaf and stalk, though I noticed that seldom any single
plant bore more than one ear. Fields of wheat and oat stubble
were of rare occurrence, and I saw none at all of any great extent.
Of these two crops the former, I am informed, is very light in all
this section. I was told of one farmer whose ill fortune had been
remarkable. He had sown forty bushels of seed, and from it all got
but eleven bushels of wheat, and these in the aggregate weighed
only one hundred and twenty-six pounds. As to the character of
his husbandry I made no enquiries.

Where I have been, houses of the better sort are few, or, at
least, few are visible from the road as one rides along. Some, however, I saw, standing among trees, and well built of wood or of
brick—roomy and pleasant mansions, that looked as if they
might be the residences of people at once farmers and educated
gentlemen, and the abodes of a hospitality of which we may read
in Virginian histories. Not far from such houses were usually the
cabins of the Negro laborers, huts, framed and boarded in some
instances, in some instances built of unhewn logs. Similar to these
are the greater number of the detached houses occupied by the
white population of the country through which I have been travelling.
Very simple architectural rules govern the construction of these
dwellings, and a description of one is a description of all. They are
about fourteen feet in length and from ten to twelve feet in width.
The height from the ridge-pole to the ground does not exceed
fourteen feet. The chimney, which is always at one of the gable
ends of the building, and on the outside of it, sometimes just peers
above the roof and sometimes stops short a yard or so below it,
and vents its smoke against the wall. The dwelling has two
windows, unglazed, but furnished with a shutter, which is closed
when the rain comes in or when the wind is in such a quarter that
there is difficulty in persuading the smoke to go up the chimney if
there is any interference with the draft from the door. The floor
may be of earth trodden hard, or, as is more common, of boards;
and there are also boards laid upon the cross beams which, termi-
nating just beneath the eaves, separate the lower room from the

space immediately under the rafters. These boards form the floor
of a loft, which contains the beds of the children, and which also
serves as the granary and general store-room of the family. Most
likely the apartment on the ground floor is unequally divided by a
rough partition wall of home-made clapboards, and thus another
private sleeping place is obtained; opposite the bedroom-door is
the fire-place, six feet high and four feet wide, an oblong hole of
these dimensions having been cut in the logs that form the end
wall. Outside the house two upright posts, one opposite each side
of the above-mentioned aperture, and about four feet distant from
it, are planted in the ground. Then "puncheons," pieces of wood
roughly resembling laths, and used for the same purpose, are so
arranged as to form the three sides of the fire-place, shorter puncheons, laid as children lay sticks in making cob-houses, are piled
one on another till the frame-work of the chimney, growing narrower as it ascends, is properly made. Over all is spread a thick
coat of mud, which commonly is well enough prepared, or often
enough renewed, to protect the sides and back of the fire-place
from the action of the fire, but higher up the bare puncheons are
charred and in places burnt into holes where the sparks have at
some time kindled the dry wood. Within and without, the house,
unwhitened by paint or whitewash, bears traces of continual smoke
and the blackening power of time and weather. The furniture is of
course scanty and of the poorest kind. The objects that most strike
the attention on entering are the large fire-place with its cooking
utensils, and the range of pipkins and tubs, with the drinking
gourds, containing water; for few of these houses are provided
with a well, and the water is brought from the nearest spring at set
times of the day, the vessels being usually carried on the heads of
the children. A fence of palings, or of pickets interwoven with
brushwood, encloses a small patch of garden ground, planted with
cabbages, string-beans, and tomatoes. Just at the door-step, where
the soil is likely to be richest, a dozen of tobacco plants, raised for
home consumption, grow strong and tall, and near by is a bush or
two of red peppers, much used by these people in medicine and in
cookery. Probably a small fowl-hutch stands at the corner of the

garden, two or three pigs lie at length by the road-side, and there is never wanting a noisy cur to bark at the passer-by. Sometimes it is a group of white children, sometimes of little Negroes, that gaze at me from the doorway. Always there is corn growing beside such cabins, and beside one I saw the only cotton that I have yet observed in Virginia. There was, perhaps, half or three-eighths of an acre of it, and the plants were in full blossom. The field seemed clear of grass and weeds, but the cotton was not two feet high, and must, I should think, have been unmanured. The people who inhabit these houses must be the poorest of those who draw rations from the Government stores, and so far as my observation has extended, the military order which remands them to their own resources for a livelihood is perfectly justifiable, as relieving the Government of an unnecessary burden, and discouraging indolence.

Nearly as often seen as houses of this kind are the dwellings of the ordinary class of farmers, who cultivate from one to three hundred acres of land. They are usually of wood, painted white, and surrounded by a post and rail fence, inside of which are plum and peach trees, and, very likely, one or two forest trees for shade. A little in the rear, in a condition more or less dilapidated, stands a row of three or four Negro cabins. The farm-houses seem to contain three rooms or four, uncarpeted and otherwise poorly furnished; but in external appearance the house itself, the farm outbuildings, and the fences are a good deal superior to those which have just been described, and offer many indications of the greater means, if not of the greater thrift, of the owner. The inmates differ less than their habitations, being alike in manners and speech, and generally giving one the impression that, without having much knowledge or having been greatly indebted to education, they are intelligent and tolerably civil and good-natured. There is an occasional exception. Fatigued with riding the other day, and the weather being very hot, I came to one of these houses, which stood invitingly in a cool and shady yard. Dismounting, I walked in. A lean and dirty-looking woman of some forty years of age sat, without occupation, beside the door, and of her I begged a drink of water.

"Thar's the well."

I drew some water, and drank from the little tin pail which served for a bucket. The not very gracious reception I had met with made me think it not best to try to get a dinner from the woman, and I asked if there was any house near, where travellers were taken in.

"Go on down to the station. Heap o' people lives thar."

"Is there any place there where I can get a dinner and have my horse fed?"

"Reckon ye kin. Kin try it. Heap o' people lives thar, anyhow."

"Is there a hotel or anything of that kind?"

"They used to keep a kind o' tavern thar. Don't know what they do now. Country yerabouts is mighty bar."

"I suppose you couldn't get me a dinner, ma'am?"

"Hed our dinner at half-past eleven."

"How far is it to the station?"

"Mile, maybe; maybe mo'."

So I rode on, and soon crossing a railroad track came to a "kind o' tavern." It was a farm-house, not dissimilar to the one I had just left. The landlady, with a sun-bonnet perched on the back of her head, met me in the yard with a look of close scrutiny, and informed me that my horse could have some chopped oats, and that for me there was some lamb, she reckoned. I followed her into the house. There was a hall with a door at each end. Sitting in the draft, and in the full blaze of the afternoon sun, was a man in his shirt-sleeves and with an empty pipe in his mouth. Beside his feet lay an old hat, which he seemed to have been using as a spittoon. Without looking up, he said something as I entered, and I stopped to hear his remark.

"Never heed," said the woman; "old man's been drinkin' apple brandy. Walk into the parlor." Dinner was made ready, and I ate it to the accompaniment of a song which was unintelligibly droned out by the old gentleman in the hall. The flies bothered him a good deal, and the song was interrupted by growling at them. By the time dinner was over, he was thoroughly awake and quite attentive to his guests.

A Negro man-servant waited at the table, over which presided the landlady, with a palmetto fan in her hand. From a silver-plated pitcher, bearing an inscription to the effect that at an agricultural fair it had been awarded to the landlord as a prize, she offered me cider, made the day before. It had been pressed from apples laid in a trough and beaten with a pestle. A good part of their cider, she said, was made by that process. Sitting in the parlor after dinner, a pale young man, limping as he walked, came into the room and accosted me. He wore the gray uniform jacket and trousers which, especially in the country, are so very common as to seem almost the universal male dress. He apologized for addressing a stranger, but wished to know, he said, if I were not a relation of General Wise of Norfolk, as I bore a marked resemblance to that gentleman. I informed him that I had never been in Virginia until the middle of this year; that I was from the North. Having thus begun to talk, we conversed for some time about the war, the soldiers of the two sections, the state of the country at present, and its future prospects.

Yes, that was a quiet place, he said, a mighty quiet little place, but it was none too quiet for him. He never wanted to hear another gun fired in war as long as he lived. There was no more fight left in him. Ever since the 6th day of April, 1861, he had been in the army, knocking round in camps, or marching or fighting, and he had no desire to shoot at anybody or to be shot at by anybody any more. He was eager to go in when he first went, but if they had another war they'd have to burn the woods and sift the ashes before they'd find him in it. His sympathies were with the Southern cause, and always would be, but there wouldn't be another war in behalf of it. The South was sick of fighting, and the North was too strong. How was it down there at Appomattox Court-House? When Lee started from Petersburg he had only a handful of men; nearly all he had he lost on the way up by desertion and death in battle; and on the Sunday when he surrendered, Grant's army was one hundred and fifty thousand strong. Yes, he was willing to acknowledge himself beaten for good and all.

Did he think a foreign war would unite the North and South?

No, nor anything else. Three-fourths of the Confederate soldiers would be more inclined to join Maximilian, if Andy Johnson should make war on him, than to fight for the United States. But he hoped and thought there would be no more war. He wanted to go to Brazil himself, if he could. That was the place for Southerners, and the emperor wanted them there, too. But a man needed capital, and what was he to do who hadn't had more than six dollars since he got out of a Federal prison, over two months ago? That was his case. He had been captured before Petersburg, badly wounded, and had been in hospital or in jail ever since last January. He had a little money when he went in, but since he came out six dollars was all he'd seen, and that he got by borrowing it. He had been for a good while in prison when the news came of Lee's surrender. He did not give up then. When the news of Johnston's surrender came, he concluded the Confederacy was done. His father, who owned some property in Norfolk, came down to get it back again if he could, and he succeeded in getting released at about that time. But his father had failed to get his estate restored to him and had left the city, so that when he reached it he found himself without money. He lived a while with some relations, all as poor as himself, and at last went up to see an uncle, who was a wealthy man and owned a fine place near the Potomac. After a short stay at his house, he asked for the loan of enough money to carry him home. His uncle told him he had none, but he would endeavor to get him a little. So he made his niggers kill some sheep and carry the mutton down to the crews of a couple of Yankee schooners lying in the river. When the meat was sold, his uncle gave him six dollars. Since then, being sick, he had been staying round among his relations, and if he were well, he didn't know what he should be able to do. Could get corn-bread enough, he supposed, to keep the life in him for some years to come, but that didn't seem much of a show for a man, and the worst of it was that all the people were in about that same state, and there didn't seem to be much chance that their condition would improve for the next ten or twenty years.

I said that I supposed things were bad enough in the Southern country, but that it seemed to me not impossible that farmers and planters in Virginia and in most parts of the South might get a better living, if they hired their laborers as Northern farmers did, than they formerly got by working slaves.

"Yes, sir," he replied, "of course you think so. Every man from your section says the same thing. You don't know the niggers. No nigger, free or slave, in these Southern States, nor in any part of the known world, ever would work or ever will work unless he's made to. Have you ever been in Norfolk?"

"Yes, I was there for a day or two; in the city merely."

"Well, when you are there again, just go out ten miles on any road leading from the city. All along by the roadside you'll see that the niggers have built little shanties of old boards and so on, and they've got a little corn growing beside them, and you won't find one in ten of the patches that hasn't got more grass in it than corn. They wouldn't hoe it. There's the grass higher than the corn, and there are the niggers sitting in the shade. Now, do you think those Norfolk niggers won't starve by the thousand this winter? Wait and see. They're sure to starve if they are left to their own means of support."

"But aren't they like other people? Won't the experience of starvation be enough to make them work?"

"They may scratch a living one way and another—those of them that are left after these two winters are over; but starvation isn't going to make them good steady laborers. Our free niggers used to starve enough. Steady labor is what we want; and it's what we're not going to get from them."

"Do you have a good deal of trouble with them here?"

"I don't really know much about this vicinity. I believe they are doing very well. They haven't been free long enough here, and haven't had time to get saucy. Down in Norfolk, where they've been free this two years, it's a different thing. Besides, the niggers in this State haven't had enough to do this year. There hasn't been work enough done to test them. It is next year and the next after that will tell the story. There's no work in a nigger, and so you would say if you knew them as well as I do."

"Do you think that giving them a vote would tend to make them better laborers and better members of society? There's some talk of that at the North."

"Give them a vote! I would rather die, sir, than see a nigger voting in old Virginia. I would rather die," repeated the young man with emphasis, "and so every citizen of this State will say."

"Why," said I, "free Negroes once had a vote in nearly, if not quite, every Southern State, so it would not be without precedent if the right of suffrage were now given to free Negroes. And for the rest, would it be safe to trust white men at the South with the power to repudiate the national debt? I believe many Northern men fear that might happen."

"Repudiate? I should hope they would. I'm whipped, and I'll own it; but I'm not so fond of a whipping that I'm going to pay a man's expenses, while he gives it to me. Of course, there are not ten men in the whole South that wouldn't repudiate."

The young man had evidently become somewhat heated during the latter part of our talk, and said things which, I dare say, he did not wholly believe, and would not have said at the beginning of it.

Leaving the tavern, after paying "a dollar and a quarter in greenbacks" for the entertainment, I rode on over a hilly road, and just at evening came to the famous little hamlet of Appomattox Court-House, where I rested during the night, neither the one sheet, which was all that the bed boasted, nor the vermin, nor the heat, preventing my sleeping soundly.

VII

LIBERTY, VA., August 17, 1865

THE little village of Appomattox Court-House, distant from Lynchburg about twenty-five miles, is situated on low ground at the source of the Appomattox River, and in a district devoted exclusively to farming. It is, therefore, small even among Virginian towns, containing, besides the court-house and a jail in ruins, only some twenty or thirty buildings, mostly the dwellings of farmers; but small as it is, no other collection of houses in all the county so well merits the name of town. It boasts one hotel and one country store, the stock of goods in the latter sadly needing to be replenished. During the time of my visit, both of these buildings were pretty constantly occupied by men who seemed to have no other business on their hands than to lounge in some easy attitude chewing tobacco and talking to each other, or watching across the muddy road and pools of rain water the movements of the soldiers quartered opposite in the court-house yard. In the country parts of Virginia I have seen at one time and another hundreds of white men, and I doubt if I have seen in all more than ten men engaged in labor of any sort. At the store or tavern of every village just such a group of idlers is sure to be found. In accounting for these assemblages, the fact that apple brandy is always for sale by the glass at such places can hardly be considered a sufficient cause, apple brandy being exceedingly abundant in all this region, as nearly every farmer has a still in operation on his own premises. It is to the custom of the country, which throws all work upon the Negroes, that the general idleness must in great part be attributed,

67

and in part also, I suppose, to the unsettled condition of public and private affairs, which furnishes to every man a wide and fertile field for conjecture and conversation.

Within musket-shot of the court-house and the store is the range of low hills where Lee's army was drawn up on the morning of its surrender; on a parallel ridge was the centre of Grant's line of battle; and in the valley between, the town's people point out the spot where the commanders met for conference. It is marked by a deep hole, made by the relic-hunters, who have dug up even the roots of the tree beneath which the generals met. At the invitation of Mr. McLean I visited his house, and sat for a while in the parlor where the articles of capitulation were signed.

Nearly all the furniture which it then contained has been taken away by people anxious to possess some memento of the famous transaction. Tables, chairs, vases, fans, pens, books, everything small and great that could be removed from the room, were eagerly bought, or appropriated without purchase, by enthusiastic visitors. All the movables were exhausted, while yet the demands of the curiosity-seekers were unsatisfied. The standish which the generals used happened to be overturned, and a splash of ink was left upon the window-seat and wall. Urgent requests were repeatedly made for permission to cut out the stained wood and plaster, but this one remembrancer of the event, it having thus become part and parcel of the real estate, Mr. McLean has been able to keep for himself. His other souvenirs of the war are less pleasing, for they consist chiefly of Negroes set free, lands abandoned, and houses and barns destroyed in the early campaigns. "Yes, sir," he said to me, "I was the alpha and omega of this contest—the beginning and the end. The first battle of Bull Run, as you call it, was fought on my plantation, and it was in my house that General Lee surrendered his army. But my first state was far worse than my last. At the time of the surrender I escaped all molestation. I could overhear your soldiers saying, 'Well, boys, we can afford to let this old fellow alone; he's seen about enough of it.' It was true; I had seen plenty to satisfy me, and I may say that I was truly thankful that the thing was all over." So far as I could learn none of the villagers suffered at all in person or property at the hands of the Union army, but, on the contrary, its occupation of their district was an advantage to them; for no fighting of any consequence took place in the neighborhood, and when the soldiers of the two armies marched away, they left behind many cows and horses, which of course came into the possession of the people. The requisitions of rebel collecting agents had left the country almost bare of animals fit for the plough or for carting, and the supply of horses thus obtained was very seasonable. The Government has made known its intention of not calling in these animals, at least for the present; and, furthermore, in pursuance of the same benevolent policy, has recently been selling a large number of mules and cavalry horses at Lynchburg. Some of the animals are nearly worthless, but many of them are valuable, and all are cheap; and these sales will doubtless enable the farmers much more easily to get this year's produce to a market, and to prepare a much greater breadth of land for the new wheat crop than they otherwise could.

The town of Liberty, the county seat of Bedford, lies nearly west of Lynchburg on the line of the Virginia and Tennessee Railroad. I made the journey by rail, and though the iron of the track was much worn, the rolling stock seemed to be in very good order, and we passed over the twenty-four miles between the two towns very comfortably at the rate of ten miles an hour. The fare charged was eight cents a mile. The town, which contains no more than six or seven hundred inhabitants, is very prettily situated on high rolling hills that command fine views in every direction, and particularly where in the north-west, ten miles away, are the blue Peaks of Otter, with the cultivated green slopes at their feet. Half the male population was at the depot to witness the arrival of our train—the one event that breaks the monotony of the day.

In company with an agent of the Freedmen's Bureau I climbed the hill to the main street of the town, and made my way to the court-house. Here are the offices of the provost-marshal of the county and his subordinates, and of the sergeant who acts as local superintendent of freedmen's affairs. The basement of the large court-house is occupied by attorneys' offices, and the first floor is reached by means of a high flight of stone steps. Four stone pillars ornament the front of the building, and are themselves adorned by circulars and printed orders of various Union generals. In one corner of the empty court-room the sergeant had set up his desk, and near it I sat down and watched for an hour the transaction of business. A good many people came in—now it was an old farmer who entered, dressed in an oddly cut, shrunken suit of homespun, wearing a spur on one heel or carrying in his hand a short whip made of leather thongs plaited together; now it was a Negro, hat in hand, with a question or a grievance or a request for transportation; now it was a citizen who came in to hear what decision had been made in reference to the case of a friend, or to vouch for the friend's good character, or, more likely, to spend an idle half-hour in a busy place; or a soldier walked listlessly in and out again.

One rough-looking old farmer ties his horse at the foot of the steps and, coming up, enquires for the "provo." His business relates to Negroes, and the sergeant tells him that he has charge of all Negroes in Bedford County, and will hear what he has to say.

"Two o' my niggers, sir, out thar on my place, are roamin' about and refusin' to work in any shape or manner, and I've come in this mornin' to see if anything kin be done."

"You want to get them back to your farm?"

"Yes, sir; they'd ought to be thar. Both of 'em's got a fahmly thar—women and children—and I have to feed 'em reg'lar, and I want the men to come back and work."

"Have they been at work for you?"

"Yes, they begun this spring, but about a fortnight ago they quit; say 'they'll be dogged if they'll work for me any mo',' and walked off and left their fahmly with me."

"Are they at work anywhere else?"

"I can't say; reckon not. Oh, no, they a'n't goin' to work; not while their women folks take my corn to feed 'em. The women feed 'em."

"Have you been paying any wages?"

"Well, they get what the other niggers get. I a'n't payin' great wages this year, an' I a'n't doin' any great work—makin' a little corn's about all. But they'd ought to be whar their fahmly is. One o' the women's no good to me, and they've both got children to feed, an' they can't take care of 'em without the men. The men agreed to stay on the place."

"Well, what do you want us to do?"

"Well, I thought like enough you'd give me a guard to bring 'em back."

"I haven't any horses, and I can't send men out afoot to hunt up your darkies. They ought to be at home supporting their wives and children, of course; but I guess if the truth was known they've got plenty of wives and children in other places as well as there."

"Like enough they may, but I know these women belong to 'em. They're hanging round the quarters pretty often, for I've seen 'em, and talked to 'em. 'T a'n't fur out."

"Say, sergeant," said a soldier, "I'll go out with the old man."

"Will you go? All right, you know what to say to them. It's just a chance if you get hold of them, though."

"Oh, they'll be thar. They'll know I'm away from home today."

The old man and the soldier walked off together, and probably the Negroes are now at work on the plantation, for whenever they are not brought too closely in contact with the soldiers, so as to receive ill treatment from the badly disposed men who are to be found in every company, they pay unhesitating obedience and respect to a soldier's advice and command. Such, at least, is the testimony given by military men quartered in the country places.

Soon a planter of a better class came in to find out if he could not discharge his Negroes. Of course they didn't work to his satisfaction, he said; there was nothing to make them work; employers couldn't punish their servants, he believed; punish a Negro, and he immediately dropped his hoe and set off for the Yankees. He could manage his Negroes if he could have leave to punish them, otherwise they managed themselves, and no work was done.

The sergeant informed him that punishment was not permitted, and probably would not be.

"So I supposed. Well, will the Government take them off our

hands? I'm sure I don't want mine any longer. I can't feed them, and I don't want to be bothered with them. They are free, and the Government ought to take them, or it ought to give the employers such power as would enable them to control the Negroes and make them work. At any rate, a good part of mine are unable to work, and the Government ought to take them."

"Were the Negroes on your place at work for you this spring?"

"Yes, they are what I owned."

"Did you make any contract with them?"

"No, I told them to stay and keep on with their work. They were there, and there appeared to be nothing else to do with them. I should have been very glad to have had them go; their work hasn't paid for their food."

"You'll have to keep them on the plantation, sir, for the present. We can't take them until we get different orders in reference to this whole matter. The Government has no place for them, and if they've worked on your crops all the year so far, I guess they've got a claim on you to keep them a while longer. At any rate, I can't do anything about it. We'll do what we can to make them work for you while they stay, but they can't be moved."

The planter went out with every appearance of dissatisfaction, and as he passed out of hearing, the sergeant remarked:

"We have lots of those cases now. That man, now, has worked his niggers till he's made all his crops, and when his year's work's done he wants to get shut of 'em."

A very good-looking mulatto man had been standing near the desk while this colloquy was going on, and listened to it with a great deal of interest. In dress he was quite a dandy; his waistcoat and trowsers were snow-white, and he wore a long-skirted uniform coat, that had formerly belonged to some Confederate officer, for it was still garnished with the interdicted buttons. When his turn came to speak, he said that he was a deputy from a number of Negroes living out in the country, and that he came in to ask two or three questions.

"All right, go ahead, and ask them."

"Is it true, sir, I hear, sir, that all we colored folks is a goin' to be hired out for five years? I said no, I didn't believe it, but I am informed we is; that's to be the law."

"No, it a'n't true. You can hire yourselves out for as long as you want to—one year or two years. You can hire out for five years if you like, but nobody's going to make you. If you can get a good place, I recommend you to hire for as long a time as you can."

"Yes, sir. Well, I got the rights of that, anyhow. Now, sir, some of we would wish to hire land to work for ourself, or, perhaps, buy a piece of ground, and we would wish to know, sir, from you, sir, if we can do it."

"Yes, rent or buy. I don't know why you can't do it if you can find anyone that'll let you have the ground. There's no objection to it so far as I know."

"Yes, sir. Well, sir, perhaps we can do so, sir. Perhaps we can do so. But we hasn't any horses, or mules, or ploughs, and what we would wish to know is, if the Government would help us out after we get the land. We could rent a place up here if we had some horses to plough, and so on."

"No; the Government hasn't any ploughs or mules to give you. You must get those things for yourselves. Well, do you want anything else?"

"Yes." He wanted "a paper, a writing," before he went home, that should authorize him to buy or rent land. It was given him, and he went away contented.

A field-hand was the next applicant: a stalwart young fellow, as straight as an arrow, and perfectly black. He complained that his master had been beating him with a stout stick.

"What did you do to him? You've been sassy?"

"No, boss; never was sassy; never *was* sassy nigger sence I'se born."

"Well, I suppose you were lazy."

"Boss, I been working all de time; ask any nigger on de plantashn ef I'se ever lazy nigger. Me! me and dem oder boys do all de work on de plantashn same as 'foretime."

"Well, then, what did he strike you for?"

"Dat jest it, sah. Wot'd he strike me for? Dat ar jest it. I done nothin'."

"How many of you are there on the plantation?"

"Right smart family on de plantashn, sah. Dunno how many."

"Did he strike any other boy but you?"

"No, sah, me one."

"You must have been doing something?"

"No, boss; boss, I tell you; I'se in at de quarters, me and two o' dem boys, and he came in de do', jump on me wid a stick, say 'he teach me.' "

"What did you do then?"

"Run, come yer."

"Well, now you go back home and go to your work again; don't be sassy, don't be lazy when you've got work to do; and I guess he won't trouble you."

Very reluctantly the man took his departure.

"That's a sassy looking darkey," said the sergeant. I could not deny it; he certainly had a face that would add much to the force of any insolent speech he might make.

In a minute he came back and asked for a letter to carry to his master, enjoining him to keep the peace, as he feared the man would shoot him, he having on two or three occasions threatened to do so.

"Oh, you go on. He won't shoot you. If he does we'll have him up here. You go back and go to work, and if he don't use you well come in again and we'll see about it. There's any quantity of those cases," continued he, "and we couldn't begin to hear half nor quarter of 'em. When there's one that looks bad, we investigate it; but most of 'em are trifling."

This jurisdiction of the military authorities over the relations existing between whites and blacks is very distasteful to the former masters. "Last Sunday," said my landlord at dinner, "the captain here sent out more than ten miles and made a gentleman and his wife come into town and appear before him to answer to some charge one of their own niggers had made against them. I tell you, sir, it's mighty humiliating. The lady did nothing but cry all the way in and out."

"Did the Negro prove his charge?"

"I don't know. Don't know whether he did or not. But I know if that captain over there is going to do that, if he's going to listen to nigger evidence, he'll have his hands full. Why, we'd never let a nigger give evidence against anybody but people of his own color. They never gave evidence against a white man in no court in Virginia. But this captain lets 'em, and it would make you laugh to see the way they flock in to him with complaints. Always a crowd."

"Nothing would make me cut a nigger's throat from ear to ear so quick," said a shoemaker at whose shop I stopped for a minute the other day, "as having him set up his impudent face to tell that a thing wasn't so when I said it was so. The idea of letting one o' them be sworn to give his evidence! But I'm d——d if they didn't convict the man," he said, continuing a conversation that I had interrupted, "and not a word of evidence against him but them blamed niggers."

Just before dinner I took a stroll through the quiet streets of the town, in company with an officer of the little Federal garrison.

"That house," said he, pointing to one at a little distance, "had a window or two broken the other evening. I don't blame the boys much; whenever any of us went past, if any of the women were outside they would go in, banging the door as they went, or perhaps hurry to the piano and strike up some rebel tune. On this particular evening they were singing:

> 'Farewell forever to the star-spangled banner,
> No more shall it wave o'er the land of the free.'

They stopped when the stones were sent against the shutters, and sent down a complaint to me the next morning. I told them they shouldn't be molested, and asked if they would please to give up insulting the men by singing disloyal songs. I don't suppose the men would have cared about the singing so much, but it's not that alone. They're very bitter in these little country places where they haven't seen much of the Yankees yet. The women cross the street

if they see us on the same side with themselves, they make faces—
indeed, I've been called after—and the men would be just as bad if
they were not afraid to make so open a display. I was in one of the
churches on the first Sunday that our company spent here, and, as
there wasn't any sexton, I thought I'd find a seat for myself. There
was one pew a little way down nearly empty—there was one
woman sitting in the end of it—so I opened the door and was
going to take a seat there. But the lady rose hastily, looking very
angry, and showed that she intended to leave the pew if I took a
seat in it. I begged her to be seated again, as I wouldn't enter
against her wishes, and kept on my way down the aisle. There was
a chair at the end of it, standing back against the wall, and I took
that. Nobody offered me a seat. The minister had seen it all, and
when he saw me sitting in the aisle alone he came down from the
pulpit and insisted on my going into his pew. I had to go at last,
and, returning to the pulpit, he laid away his sermon, and lectured
the congregation on the folly of cherishing a rebellious spirit, now
that the rebellion is dead, and on the duty of showing themselves
good citizens of the United States by living in peace and amity with
their fellow-citizens of the North."

One of the citizens of Liberty announces himself as a candidate
for a seat in Congress, and expresses opinions that, I dare say, will
ensure him a strong vote in his native district:

> "I shall favor and encourage the emigration and colonization of
> the Negro population as a measure calculated, under present circum-
> stances, to promote the interest of both races, as well as the repeal
> of all laws for the confiscation of the property of those who co-
> operated with the South in the late terrible struggle between the two
> sections of this country. . . . I shall oppose any law or amendment
> of the Constitution of the United States having a tendency to give
> to the Negro the right of suffrage, or to so change his status as to
> place him upon terms of equality with the white man." He can see
> "no necessity for continuing in the limits of the State armed forces
> of the United States, and will do all he can to effect their removal."

VIII

LYNCHBURG, VA., August 24, 1865

IN compliance with an invitation given me yesterday, I paid a visit to a large farm, situated within twenty miles of this city, and, so far as I could, examined the working of the new system of labor, as it exists under an employer utterly opposed to it, who denies its justice and expediency, disbelieves in its long continuance, and accepts it only on compulsion, and only so much of it as he is forced to accept. On his plantation it is a failure, he says, and he thinks it destined to fail everywhere.

The farm contains nearly twelve hundred acres, of which the greater part is covered with timber, and but four hundred and fifty acres are of arable land. Formerly, a good deal of tobacco was got from it, but during and since the war it has been used for the production of Indian corn and wheat. "I did not consider it patriotic to raise anything else," said the owner; "I could not plant tobacco while the country was starving for food. This year I have a few hills—an acre and a half—just to give the people what they want for chewing and smoking."

There are now on the place about sixty Negroes, of whom twenty-one are able-bodied men and women, who have been employed upon the crops of this year; the rest are reported as being infirm people and children. I learned, however, that the care of infants, the cooking of the laborers' meals, and all house service at the owner's residence, is done by persons classed among the children and infirm. This latter class I was told, is exceptionally large on this plantation, because the old gentleman who owns it, and

77

whose long life has been mainly passed in the practice of his profession and in congressional service, has never carried on farming with a view to making it profitable, and has always been an indulgent master. He claims this character for himself. "I never bought a nigger in all my life, sir; and I never sold or whipped but one. Have I ever ordered you to punish any one of them, Mr. W——?" said he to his overseer. "I believe you never did, colonel." "That single one was a thief in grain, sir. As good a laborer as we had, but he would steal a sheep every week of his life. He baffled us repeatedly, but, finally, sir, we caught the rascal; took him red-handed—the mutton in his cabin and the skin in his yard. I ordered him a sound whipping, which he richly deserved, though I knew he was entirely incorrigible. Then I told my overseer to take him down, tie the skin on his back, with the ram's horns over his head, lead him into the city with a rope around his neck, and sell him for whatever he'd bring. The overseer begged to be excused from cutting such a figure in the streets, so I sold him in his own skin only, and satisfied my conscience by a verbal announcement that he was the most accomplished sheep-stealer in the Old Dominion. I have owned slaves now for five-and-forty years, and he is the only one ever whipped by my order; so you can judge if I am a hard master.

"I wish still," he continued, "to treat my people in the same way, but they are fast making it impossible for me to do so. There are always some bad men in every hundred, and now the bad niggers spoil the rest. Since mine were freed, they have become lazy, stubborn, and impudent. They know that they have escaped from all government; that we cannot chastise them. And they are not like white people. I begin to believe that they are without gratitude. Mine appear to have forgotten all the kindness and lenity with which they have been treated by me and my family."

"You've had considerable trouble, colonel, I understand," said my companion, who was armed with authority to investigate and settle disturbances and disputes on the plantations.

"Yes, sir. I am sorry to put you gentlemen in Lynchburg to so much inconvenience, but what can we do? The Government has taken away all coercive power from us; a Negro does what he likes, and I cannot inflict adequate punishment, nor have him punished without riding up to the city. The troubles we have all grow out of the complete anarchy in which our Negro population now is. It was only day before yesterday that my daughter-in-law told one of the servants to do some simple thing—hang out clothes, I believe. Three times she told her without being able to secure her obedience, and I had to be called in. Really, gentlemen, I did not know how to proceed. I decided to banish her. We have on the place a house that stands alone at some distance from any other, occupied by an old blind man, Uncle Tom by name. 'Go, Elsie,' said I, 'go down to Uncle Tom's cabin; I banish you the house till you can behave yourself. Take your rations along, and stay till we send for you to come back. You shall live in exile, with nothing to do but to eat and sleep.' I could think of nothing else to do with her. We have no means of making them obey, unless they choose to do it of their own free will."

"What's today's case, colonel?"

"Another one of the house girls, on the day after this occurred, was rebuked by my son for negligence, and made a very improper reply. My son boxed her ears—gave her two slaps on the side of the face with his hand, that was the whole of it. She immediately left her work, all unfinished, and betook herself to her father's house. My son sent for her, but she did not return, and we have seen nothing of her since."

"Is she at home now?"

"In the woods, I reckon," said the overseer; "she a'n't on the place. It's her father's fault. I told him, 'London, take the gal and give her a whalin' for her impudence, and make her beg Mr. John's pardon.' He wouldn't though. He's the one's in fault, he's so grouty."

"I went to him, myself," said the colonel, "and told him he must chastise the girl, and that she must express contrition for the offence. What answer do you think he made, gentlemen? 'That up at Lynchburg they knew the law better than he did, and I'd better go there if I had a complaint against Rose: that Rose said she hadn't done anything.'

"Now, sir, I want that man removed from my plantation. Nothing would induce me to let him stay here, and he shall not, unless the authorities in Lynchburg compel me to permit him. Such insubordination I cannot tolerate."

"Where is the man?" said my companion; "I'd like to see him if he can be found."

"He a'n't in the field," the overseer answered. "I'm just in from that, and he a'n't out today. He's at his house, I believe."

"Well, sir, the overseer will take you down to the quarters. I will not go. I do not wish my presence to be a restraint upon their answers."

We went to the Negro cabins, the overseer, as we walked along, talking about the condition of the plantation.

"I swar, I thought we'd go through without any more durn trouble; didn't think you'd have to come up again. I've been gettin' on right well with 'em, myself: ha'n't had to strike a lick. We had a considerable muss about two month ago, but the man quieted down again, and now I wouldn't ask no better hand than he is. His brother had been havin' some hard talk with the colonel one day, and, as I come on up from the tobacco lot, I seen 'em all round the corn-house, and I went along toward 'em. On the way, this boy met me, and he opened on me right away. 'It's you,' he says, 'made this muss 'twixt the master and Jim: it's all through what you told on him.' I was perfectly clar, you see; didn't know what the to-do was, anyhow, and it made me mad to hear him. Oh, he spoke almighty careless, I kin tell you, gentlemen—sassy. Says I, 'You shet up, quick.' I had my pistol with me, and I drawed it. 'Say another word,' says I, 'and durn me but I'll blow your brains out. I'll put a hole through you whar you stand.' He shet right up. If he hadn't I'd ha' killed him, sure, I would. He was dreadful nigh it for a minute. Since then, everything's gone on quiet and peaceable; but the colonel's pretty mad, now: it's the old man he's mad with. Well, it's his fault. I told one o' these gals, the other day, to

go get the cows out o' the corn. They'd broke in. She started, after
two or three biddins, and she went so deliberate it fretted me so
that I went after her. 'I told you to jump,' says I, and I give her a
whalin'. Her father he thought that warn't right. 'You make her
step, then, old man,' says I; 'she's got to move when I talk; but if
you'll take the whalin' part on yourself, I'll give it up.' Well, now,
when I find fault he does whale her. That's what London ought to
do."

While this discourse was going on we reached the Negro cabins.
Two or three women were there, and some nursing children. As
we approached they eyed us with no very pleasant expression of
countenance. The overseer enquired whether London was at home.
The woman who answered was his sister-in-law, and the cause of
her sulky manner appeared in her reply:

"How! Bro' Lunnon no gone since mornin'? Bro' Lunnon hear
say master gone to Lynchburg yesterday, come back, say Lunnon,
for leave dis place today. I dunno whar Bro' Lunnon now."

The wife, however, was at home, and was requested to give her
version of the trouble between her employer and Rose. "Her
daughter had been sick," she said, "and went late to her work on
the morning in question. When asked why she had not come earlier, she answered that she came as soon as she could—that she was
sick. Rose was not very late."

" 'Twas an hour by sun when I see her," said the overseer,
"and I heerd she said she couldn't come, she was a-makin' her
bed."

"Well, Juliana, did her master strike her?"

"Not master," the woman said, "mass' John he hit her over the
head; 'cordin' to what Rose say."

"Did he hit her hard?"

"No more'n her nose was bleedin' when she came back."

"Well now, aunty, she's a little girl; you box her ears when she
offends you; why didn't London promise the colonel to make her
behave herself?"

The woman knew nothing about what talk the colonel had with
London, she said; the servants at the house would get along well

enough, except that one of the ladies was too hard to please. Rose had done nothing. Yes, she knew she was bound to work, and keep a good character; so she did.

After the women had received some exhortations to industry and respectful deportment, we went up to the overseer's house, a mud-plastered cabin with two rooms, where the colonel was awaiting our return. He persisted in his request that the man London, and his family, should be at once sent away from the place.

"Why, gentlemen, such insubordination sets an awful example. We have no armed patrols here, no police, no discipline on the plantations, and there are five hundred Negroes around me, and not thirty white men. We live in an isolated place, and my house contains three or four women; and it is essential that they be protected. My corn-house was broken into not long ago, and, I think, my wheat is going out of the barn. Something must be done. It is a very cumbrous mode of enforcing good order to summon you from the city to come down here and discharge my laborers, but it is the only method you have left me. And now I want an example made; I shall not feel safe unless you do what I ask, and, if it cannot be done, I would like to send them all off the plantation. I should feel better to work my garden with my own hands than to endure such insolence."

The colonel was asked if he paid his people anything for their services. "No sir," he answered, "no money wages. If you give money to a nigger he goes and spends it for whiskey, and I have no intention of making the country any more unsafe to live in than it is at present. Besides, sir, and Mr. W—— will tell you the same, they are not worth it; a white man will do the work of three niggers, and one slave did more than three of these freedmen."

"So, sure," said the overseer, "anyhow they ha'n't done a third part what they might this year."

"I called my people together when your army first came here, after General Lee's defeat, and told them I should not pay wages. 'You are free,' I said, 'to go where you please, but if you choose to stay here you may; you shall work for me as you have heretofore, and I will give you the same treatment you have always had, the same quantity and quality of food, and the same amount of cloth-ing.' Most of them have stayed, and I have no specific complaints to make against any family but London's, though all, as I have said, are unprofitable servants. Two men chose to go away.''

Of these two who refused the colonel's terms, one, it was inci-dentally told in the course of the conversation, now acts as cook on a canal packet-boat, and earns fifteen dollars per month besides his board. He visits the plantation once in a while to see his former fellow-servants, and is well contented with his new condition. The colonel would not be harassed and overworked again, he said him-self, by an attempt at farming under the free labor system. He had leased the place to his overseer, and washed his hands of the whole business.

Mr. W——, the lessee, expected success. He showed me the rough draft of a written contract which the Negroes have signified their willingness to sign, and under which he and they are to work together during the coming year. While my friend conversed with the colonel and brought the affair of London to a conclusion, I studied the agreement. It reads nearly as follows: "The under-signed bind themselves to stay on the —— —— plantation from Nov. 15th, year of 1865, to Nov. 15th, year of 1866. We agree to work on said plantation for Mr. W——. He is to pay the rent of the plantation, and he is to pay all the expense of the crops. Mr. W—— agrees to give us payment for labor by sharing equally with the Negroes—one half the crop to be his, one half to be ours, one half the wheat, one half the oats, one half the corn, one half of every crop on the place, excepting that all the fodder and straw is to belong to Mr. W——. Mr. W—— is to give us rations and clothing, and the expense is to be paid back out of our half of the crop. We are to act polite to him, and to be obedient and indus-trious, and make no disturbance in the place."

The crops this year have been small. Next year the new em-ployer intends they shall be very much larger, and I venture to predict that his hopes will be fulfilled. For the causes of the trouble on this plantation are sufficiently obvious, and they may all be removed. The owner of it is, I should say, a humane man, and I

could readily believe that he himself, whatever his overseers may
be able to boast, had ordered but one of his Negroes to be
whipped. His people probably found him kind and indulgent in all
his intercourse with them, and he is now conscious of none but the
friendliest and best intentions towards them. But as a wealthy slaveholder and a veritable descendant of Pocahontas, he is proud, and
will have nothing less than complete deference; he believes that the
blacks were born for slavery, and is intolerant of anything resembling independence and self-reliance in them; moreover, he is an
original secessionist, and thinks emancipation unjust. In short, he
wishes still to be master, is willing to be a kind master, but will not
be a just employer. Perhaps he is now too old to learn; but they,
on the other hand, are not, and his endeavor to keep them tracta-
ble slaves has had no better success than to make them unpaid and
discontented freedmen. Having tried the new labor system, with
the essential feature of it left out, he, of course, finds it a failure.

As we talked, he seemed to please himself by painting a gloomy
picture of Southern society as it is to be when the military occupation ends—smoke-houses broken open by the laborers, and bacon
stolen; corn-houses robbed, and the corn sold for whiskey; then
the worst of crimes committed by drunken niggers, murders like
that on the canal-boat the other night, houses pillaged and burnt
because their owners would not yield to every demand that ignorance and insolence could make; the woods full of outlaws; idleness followed by want, and the country impoverished for lack of
laborers—all because fanatics were determined, by main force, to
lift up the nigger to a level which of himself he could never attain,
and which, if let alone, he never would have sought. Negro
suffrage, if it became a fact, would strip the white man—it would
in his county, where niggers were in a majority—of all his property; perhaps reduce him to servitude. Why not? "You in Massachusetts, sir," he said, "are all abolitionists, and think a nigger is
the equal of the white man, and, of course, you have a right to
hold that opinion there. We, in Virginia, know that he is not; that
God made him our inferior. Perhaps we know nothing about it.
You may know best. The fortune of war has enabled you to try

and prove your theory correct; but I feel so well assured of the result, that I wish from the bottom of my heart you had chosen some other place for your experiment. I wish you had confined it to Massachusetts."

I said but little in answer: that so far as Massachusetts was concerned, the matter was now out of the region of experiment; free Negroes in that State were an estimable class of citizens, whose condition vindicated the good policy of paying wages for labor; that I supposed most men to be industrious, as most religious men are religious—either from hope of reward or fear of punishment; and that, as Negroes in Virginia could not now be whipped, the payment of wages was the only course left open; that it was important, if Negroes were to constitute so dangerous an element in Southern society, to use all fair means to keep them contented.

The experience gained in this first year of freedom has, I think, taught most farmers who intend to live on their land the necessity, for the sake of their own comfort and profit, of paying something like fair wages. The existence of the Freedmen's Bureau probably does not diminish the pressure of this necessity. Applications for a supply of laborers frequently come in to the superintendents, and the wages offered are considerably higher than those now paid; one man offers one hundred dollars a year, board, clothing, and a week's holidays at Christmas; others offer one-fourth, or one-half, the crop. As a rule, the farmers say very little about colonization.

I see that one of the Lynchburg newspapers urges all persons needing the services of mechanics to hire white men in preference to black. Their labor, the paper says, though more costly than that of Negroes, is better, and, moreover, to give them employment is a charitable work, for many of them are needy. An acquaintance of mine in the city, having some rough work to be done not long since, offered it to a white man, who was willing to undertake it, but would not do it for less than sixty-five dollars in specie, and was much displeased when the gentleman gave it into the hands of a Negro. There were twenty days' work, and it was done for fifteen dollars. "I'm told," said the aggrieved mechanic, "that a man's

house won't be very safe if he puts niggers to work on it and shuts
out white men."

While there undoubtedly is a good deal of this feeling in some
portions of the community, I do not perceive that its existence
prevents employers from hiring whom they please, whether he is
black or white, their choice being governed not so much by con-
siderations of color as of cost.

IX

August 29, 1865

LATE this forenoon I left Lynchburg, and set out on a horseback journey into North Carolina. The weather has been bright and hot all day, and the road hilly and dusty, so that I have ridden slowly, and travelled no more than twenty-one miles. In that distance I found but one person going the same way with myself, although the country, especially in the vicinity of the city, is pretty thickly settled, and a good half the land lying along the road is cleared and laid out in farms. The man was a German from Hesse-Darmstadt, going out to look at some land which he hoped to purchase.

He was in the United States five years, he said, and had been forced to spend two of it in the Confederate army. Except for that, he liked America better than Germany; more money could be made here than there, and the climate pleased him much better. He came to Virginia because he had a good heap of friends here, and had found it a good State; but the Virginian people did not like foreigners. They said if it had not been for the foreigners in the Yankee army, the South never would have been whipped. He reckoned that was so. Nearly half the Northern soldiers were German, Irish, and Dutch. But the people round here did not want to part with their land to anybody; they thought it made them great to own much land. He wished the Government would confiscate, so that land would become cheap.

I said that in the Lynchburg papers I had seen quite a large number of farms advertised as for sale. Yes, he said, but they wanted more than the right price; it was one of those farms that he was then going to look at, but he would not give twenty-five or thirty dollars an acre. He would buy or lease two hundred acres and raise grain; his brother would help him, and they would hire as few Negroes as they could. Some would be necessary, but all of them were bad—great liars and unfaithful workers.

As I rode along, Negroes were everywhere busy stripping off the corn-blades and tying them into small bundles, which are hung upon the stalks to be cured by the sun. Later in the day they could be seen coming up out of the fields, carrying on their heads great stacks of the dried fodder, which is at once stowed away in blade-houses. These are small buildings with walls of logs, between which are left wide apertures for the admission of air, as the fodder is apt to grow musty. Besides blade stripping no field work seemed to be going on, except here and there a little mowing, and on one farm a white man and a boy were laying a stone wall, the first I have seen in the State. Out of the towns, the zigzag fence of rails is almost universal.

The surface of the country over which I have travelled today is rolling and much diversified. The landscape is a good deal shut in by woods, but often today I have been able to see the distant Peaks of Otter, dark blue against the pale blue of the horizon, and almost to be mistaken for clouds, except that every other cloud was fleecy white. The soil seemed fertile; there was abundance of timber, the apple trees and the late peach trees were laden with fruit, and all the crops appeared to be thriving well. Indian corn was everywhere, and I saw occasional patches of cotton, tobacco, and broom-corn growing near the houses. More frequent were fields of sorghum. But a small portion of the land is under cultivation.

The people living in this section of the country have no railway or water communication with their markets, and all produce designed for Lynchburg and Danville has to be transported by wagon. I have met seven or eight of these heavy vehicles today, toiling slowly along the road. They are canvas-covered, drawn by four or six mules or oxen, and loaded with tobacco in hogsheads or packed loose. Some were driven by Negroes, but more usually they were in charge of white men, who walked beside the team, while on top of the load, among the hay and corn-blades, were the women and children going up to the city to make purchases. Baskets of eggs and chickens are hung at the end of the cart, and a bag of meal or of cooked provisions. Besides these parties and the man from Hesse-Darmstadt I believe I have met no one today.

At sunset I arrived at the Old Stand, which, as a small shield above the door announces, is a house of "entertainment by S. Simmons." It may serve as a sample of the Virginia country taverns. The house stands in a large yard of short clean grass shaded by tall red oaks; it is two stories high, unpainted, and without window-shutters. Beside the door is a little shelf with a water-pail on it, and a drinking gourd hangs just above. The corn-house, blade-house, stable, and cow-yard are across the road. The dwelling contains four rooms; on the ground-floor one has a bed in it, a chair, and a clock; the other has half a dozen chairs, a table, and a chest of drawers, on which are a three-weeks-old copy of the New York *Daily News* and four or six books—a life of Whitefield, Wesley's *Journal*, and some more modern Methodist publications.

No one about the house seemed to be stirring, so I tied my horse at the gate and walked in. An old man with a handkerchief thrown over his face to protect it from the flies lay asleep on the bed, and not wishing to awake him I read the *News* for more than half an hour. Then he came out, had my horse fed, and told me I might stay all night. His wife had gone away for an hour or two— when she came back I could have some supper, such as it was.

He was poorly himself, had a misery in his head, and had to get sleep when he could. Was I used to travelling that road? No, I said, I had never been over it till today. He thought he'd never seen me before; didn't hardly reckon I was a Virginian; wasn't raised in these parts, anyhow? From Massachusetts, hey? That's one o' the Northern States. The people up there want the niggers freed, don't they?

"Yes," I said, "they want them free, and, indeed, they think they are freed now."

"Allow they're free, do they? The war freed 'em, hey?"

"Yes, the Emancipation Proclamation and the war. Don't you think they're free?"

"No, I don't. They seem to think they be: go here and there and everywhere, as if they was free; but we can tell better when the next Congress meets and after the Supreme Court has decided. Niggers can't do nothin' with themselves. Of course not. How are they behaving in Lynchburg?"

"Very well, I believe."

"No, they a'n't. Up at Acquia Creek they're rioting, and so they'll do everywhere."

He never owned any of 'em, he said, and never wanted to. Didn't they let 'em vote in Massachusetts? Did I belong to any church? No, I answered, I did not; did he? Yes, he was a Methodist. What made him ask me the question was because he had heard that the President was going to do something or other to make the South Church unite with the North. I had heard nothing of it, I said; did he think they would come together of their own accord? No, he didn't; they couldn't unite, and they oughtn't to. He thought the people of the North and South had better just have nothing to say to each other; better keep apart for a time, anyhow. Did I want to buy a farm? He'd sell that one for twenty-five dollars an acre; there were three hundred acres of good land, all in good order. He'd never been raised to farming, and wanted to give it up.

He asked me many questions about Massachusetts—how large it was; what was the capital; if the people mostly followed farming or sheep-raising; if they lived as well as the people of Virginia; if the Methodists were a numerous and powerful sect there; if the Northern people didn't hate the Southerners; if Jeff. Davis would be hung; all of which I answered as well as I could, but without securing credence for my assertion that the North could not be said to hate the South. Massachusetts was ahead of Virginia, he reckoned, because more emigrants came there and there were more small farms. Perhaps Massachusetts people might live better than folks in Virginia, but he'd heerd that they lived mostly on fried peas with bacon in 'em. Virginia people used to live pretty well once, before the war.

While we talked his wife returned, and we were soon summoned to supper. The landlady apologized for the scantiness of the meal, and said the war had accustomed her to poor living; in fact, she hardly knew now when it was necessary to make an apology. Coffee without sugar, corn-bread and butter, and a dish of boiled eggs were set before us, together with a pitcher of buttermilk. Supper was served in a little kitchen behind the main dwelling house, and connected with it by a covered plank-walk. In a corner of the room stood a very large wooden loom, in which the landlady said she had woven all the cloth used in the family for all purposes. Now that peace had come, she reckoned she'd depend on my country for things of that kind and let the spinning-wheel and loom rest awhile.

The old man's opinion that slavery is in some way to be restored, or that, at any rate, uncompensated emancipation will not be permitted by the judiciary, nor by Congress, when the whole country is represented in that body, is an opinion that I have more than once heard expressed, and sometimes by men of more intelligence than the tavern-keeper. One day last week, I walked into a hotel parlor in Lynchburg, where quite a crowd of men were listening to the very amusing talk of "a true-blue, dyed-in-the-wool, Daniel Webster, old-line Whig, sir." By anecdotes and original comicalities he kept his audience in continual laughter. While I heard it, his conversation was, for the most, a humorous but caustic tirade against the Democratic party, which, he said, was chargeable with all the calamities of the past four years. Democracy had killed those nephews of his who fell fighting for the Confederacy; Democracy had dragged him through thirty-two battles and got him ridiculously whipped at the end of 'em; Democracy had reduced the Southern people to corn-feed for the last three years; Democracy had piled up a national debt on the South that had all been—well, call it *paid,* gentlemen. But the Yankee debt, the United States debt, *our* debt, if you will have it so—that's going to be repudiated in less than twelve months. Democracy had emancipated all the niggers—took away his, whom he thought a d——d sight more of than of all the Democrats since General

Jackson. However, they were all staying with him now, and in less than a year every nigger in the South would be a slave again. There are two words about their freedom.

"Come, come, Uncle Billy," said a bystander, "you one of Governor Pierpont's Commissioners of Elections and talking like that! What becomes of your oath?"

"Oath? I've taken every oath that's come into —— County since General Lee's surrender, and I'll take all the rest that come; and I'll keep 'em all. But the Supreme Court has got to talk about this thing yet, you know, and so has Congress—the Congress of the *United* States, you know; when they've talked we'll keep our mouths shut, but till then we'll talk. I've got Andy's pardon right here in my pocket, and I can say what I like. Besides, my son, if I hadn't, I'm not afraid to die; I never cast a Democratic vote in my life—yes, just one: I did cast one vote for that d——d infernal scoundrel of a Jeff. Davis. But I've bitterly repented of that."

"You needn't," said one of his hearers, "that's the best vote you ever cast in your life."

"See here, my friend," said the commissioner, "when I began life I had one most important rule to guide me, and it brought me luck and a good conscience: whenever they brought along anything Democratic, 'No, I thank you,' says I, 'I wouldn't choose any, thank you.' I departed from my rule once, voted for Jeff. Davis and secession, and after being whipped for four years under one Democratic President I had to go and beg a pardon from another. Henceforth, I'm subjugated, and I'm a Whig."

August 30, 1865

This morning at six o'clock I had breakfast, which consisted of the same materials that composed our supper last night, and started for Pittsylvania Court-House, which is fifty-five miles from Lynchburg.

The sky for half the day was cloudy, and the day pleasanter for travelling than yesterday. Four miles of riding brought me to the Roanoke River, which is here not more than a hundred and twenty-five yards wide, flowing between green banks with a strong and rapid stream. In this part of its course the people call it the Staunton River, while fifty miles above and the same distance below it gets its name of Roanoke. The bridge which formerly spanned it was destroyed in May last by General Rosser, acting under the orders of General Johnston, and travellers are ferried across.

The journey of today has been more lonesome than that of yesterday, the country being less thickly settled, and the road for a much greater part of the distance being entirely in the forest. In many places the hills were very steep, and the road was often rugged where the rains had cut deep channels and gulleys in the earth, or had washed bare the rough ledges of rock. Some of these places were so dangerous that turn-outs had been made by the wagoners, and for a few rods the traveller, forsaking the road, rides along among the trees, and emerges into the beaten track after he has passed the obstruction, which is sometimes a gulley or a ledge, sometimes the fallen trunk of a great tree which has lain so long unrotted that the old road marks are half obliterated, sometimes when the road crosses a low or spongy spot. Obstructions of the latter sort were however oftener overcome by corduroying the wet place with branches of trees and rails. I had ridden several hours without meeting anyone, and began to be doubtful if I had not made a wrong turn at some one of the many forks in the road; so I waited for an hour at noon to rest my horse and to see if some traveller would not overtake me. The sun was shining bright, for the clouds of the morning had wholly disappeared, but there was not the faintest breeze nor the least sound in the forest. It was so hot and so still, with nothing to be seen but the trees and the sand, and it had been so monotonously still and dull all day, that I could not help thinking that people living in such a country were excusable, amid their dearth of amusements and mental excitants of any kind, if they busied themselves with sectarian differences in theology and speculative questions in politics.

As no traveller passed, I mounted and rode along, giving careful study to the guide-posts as I passed them. Some of them were completely covered with pencillings. One, besides its inscription, "Lynchburg, 40 miles," was filled with messages and directions. I copied two or three: "B. C., Captain Wofford's Georgians will go by way of the Court-House"; "Captain Williams—Charlotte Battery—we will go through Pittsylvania C. H."; "Jack, go the road with the pine branch"; "W. H. B., Raleigh, N. C., gone along April 5, 1865."

I found that I had not lost my way, and pushing on found clearings becoming more frequent, and the land as I got lower improving in appearance, but still seeming less fertile than what I saw yesterday. By the roadside, just before going into the village, I came upon a team of mules feeding beside one of the tobacco wagons mentioned before. An old Negro and a lad of seventeen or eighteen years old were sitting beside a fire they had kindled near a spring, the boy watching a corn-cake baking in an iron pan, and the man kneading together water and white corn meal in a wooden tray. Slices of bacon were already fried.

They had been to Danville, they said, with leaf tobacco, and were now almost home again. The tobacco was two or three years old; no one had raised any tobacco this year. They would have been five days away from home when they got back to the plantation, but it was good fun.

Pittsylvania County Court-House, or Competition, or Chatham as it is called on the map, is a small village containing three or four pretty churches, a fine court-house, and many handsome dwelling houses. It is a pretty little place, and once was busily engaged in the manufacture of tobacco, but since the war nothing whatever has been done,

My fare at the one tavern which supplies the place of four that once existed here seemed to furnish proof of the exhausted condition of the country. Nothing was set on the table but buttermilk and corn-bread. There is meat in the country, the landlord said, and flour is worth fifteen dollars a barrel, haul it yourself at that. He was working his farm without Negroes—himself and his boys did everything. The boys—three or four grown-up young men—

were very sulky at the supper-table because of a freshet which had destroyed a good deal of their corn.

"Oh," said one of them, stretching himself after supper, "I'd rather be in the war ten years than pull fodder two days. D——n farming; it's enough to kill a horse; it's just fit for a nigger."

August 31, 1865

My road today has led me through a country much like what I saw on Tuesday. There are more clearings and more cultivated land than I saw yesterday, and the soil seemed more productive. During all these days the dwellings which I have passed have been such as were described in a previous letter; at rare intervals one sees the mansion-house with pretensions to elegance and comfort, the log-cabin plastered with mud occurs very frequently, and somewhat less often is seen the ordinary farm-house.

At noon today I stopped for a while at one of these log-cabins, rather larger than most of them, but still having but one room and a loft. There was a glazed window, however, and the board floor was beautifully white and clean. As I dismounted at the gate, the man of the house walked down the path to meet me and offered his hand with much cordiality of manner, inviting me to come in and take a seat. His farm was a small one, containing only a hundred and twenty-five acres of land, and he worked it himself without the help of Negroes.

"Never owned a nigger, sir, and never would hire one except a gal to do house work. Too much drivin' and overseein'. They're wanderin' round now since the crops are laid by, so that the roads are full of 'em. I hear they're dying, heaps of 'em, in Danville."

"Have they been working for wages?"

"Board, I reckon. Nobody knew what to do with 'em. The country's full of orders and reports about 'em—some say they're all to be sent up North and kept thar, and some say that the Government's sending 'em all to Cuba, and sellin' 'em for slaves. I don't know what they are doin' with 'em, but I wish they'd clar 'em out

o' this. They're in the way here; the abolitionists like 'em and
they'd better take 'em. I hear that the abolitionists talk of taking
away our right to vote, and giving it to the nigger. Pretty ridic'lous
idee."

While her husband was talking, the wife, a lean, pale woman,
sat nursing an infant, which after a little while went asleep and was
laid away in its crib. Then the woman, going over to the mantel,
took down a small circular tin box and began to dip snuff, a process I had never before witnessed. She held in one hand the box,
and in the other a bit of stick chewed at the end, so that the
displaced fibres formed a rude sort of brush. This she moistened by
putting it into her mouth. Then it was dipped into the snuff and
rubbed upon the teeth and gums both on the back and front teeth
and on the upper and lower jaws. Every little while, being a neat
woman, as the appearance of her house indicated, she walked
across the room and spit carefully into the fire-place, after which
she replenished the supply of snuff in the dip and again applied it
to her teeth. By-and-bye the box was returned to its place upon the
mantel, and the woman, holding the dip-stick in her mouth, began
to talk with me about the social position of the Negro in the North,
for by this time they had learned I was from Massachusetts.

"Thar was a Yankee man," said she, "was travellin' by here,
and he had a nigger gal with him that he was goin' to take up into
your country. He wanted to rest and drink water, and I made him
welcome to come in; so in he came, and in came the nigger gal and
sot down in this yer same cheer. Thar warn't nobody home but
me, but I went across to her and took her by the shoulder. 'You
walk out o' this,' says I. The Yankee he spoke up, and wanted to
know why I did that; in his country, he said, she'd be as good as
anybody. 'Well,' says I, 'she a'n't goin' to walk in here and make
herself even to me. In my country white folks is white folks, and
niggers is brought up to know their place, and she can't set down
in my room when I'm in presence.' "

Leaving the farm-house, it was not long before I overtook an
old Negro driving a cart to Danville loaded with peaches, sweet
potatoes, and chickens. The horse was very old, very thin, and

galled in many places, as the horses of Negroes in the South are
apt to be, for they usually are harnessed with tackle made up of
rope-ends, bits of hide, and old rags. The man himself was about
sixty years old.

He was not going up to Danville for marketing purposes only,
he said; he was going to see the provost-marshal up there. His
master had turned him and his wife off the plantation, and he did
not know where to go. The master had turned off several families
besides his, and he supposed they'd have to get some of their kin
to take them into their houses, or else the Government would have
to feed and shelter them. I asked if his employer had given him
nothing as wages for his work this year, or if he had done any
work. Yes, he said, he had tended the house-garden all the year;
his wife was the cook for the master's family; one of the sons had
been a ploughman, another had been almost a full hand, and still
another had been a table-boy for two or three years. His master
had fed the family and given them summer clothes, but had not
given winter clothing nor shoes. I asked him if he had been working under an agreement this year. He took a paper from his
pocket-book and showed it to me as his contract with his master. I
copied it into my note-book:

> Under an agreement between me and James, a man formerly my
> property, I am to deliver him ten barrels of corn, at my residence,
> when shucked from the present crop, in full of all claims against me
> for wages this year. The same is to be delivered to any one he may
> sell said corn to, provided the terms of said agreement are complied
> with. Said payment is in full of his wages, his wife's and children's,
> who live with me at this time. Said agreement was made 19th of
> August, 1865.   (Signed)   J. M. W.

New corn is now selling in Danville at two dollars per barrel,
and it is expected that it will be cheaper than that before
Christmas. Mr. W——, just after the surrender of Lee, made a
verbal promise to his Negroes that they should have a part of
whatever crops they would raise. The reason why his written acknowledgment of debt bears so late a date, is because it was not
till the middle of August that he definitely decided what quantity of

corn should be given to each hand, and because he did not care to send away any of his laborers before that time. The paper was given them at the same time with a notice to quit the plantation.

The old Negro declared that the people on that plantation had never worked so hard as they have this year. So it would always be, he thought, if the masters would send away the overseers, and work the farms on shares. Under such a system more provisions would be made than have ever yet been raised in Virginia. The people would like it better than wages. He would himself, and all the people would, be believed.

But the masters wouldn't do that. They would rather send away the old niggers and all with too many children, and hire the strong and young.

There is some truth in the assertion which I have everywhere heard made as I came through Campbell and Pittsylvania, that the Negroes are flocking into the towns. In July last, in the city of Danville, 1,329 persons received rations from the Government, 1,079 of these being whites, and 250 Negroes. On the 1st of August General Curtis' prohibitory order went into effect, and during that month the number of white people rationed was only 413, while the number of Negroes increases and becomes 603; the destitute colored population of the town, it thus appears, having been more than doubled by additions from some source or other.

The officers of the Freedmen's Bureau here stationed say that it is true that some Negroes are leaving their homes, but that in their opinion, in the great majority of cases, it is the Negro who abandons his employer, and not the master who sets his servants adrift.

X

DANVILLE, VA., September 5, 1865

DANVILLE is built upon the crown and northern slope of some steep hills which lie along the south bank of the Dan River. It contains rather less than four thousand inhabitants, of all colors, but, on account of its conspicuous site, produces the impression of a larger and finer place than it is. As one approaches it from the north, and, looking across the river at his feet, sees its many handsome residences standing among trees and gardens, and recalls what he has observed of other towns, or of the absence of them, in his travels through Virginia, the general aspect of the place is quite pleasing.

The river contributes as much to this effect as any other feature of the landscape, for it holds less of earth in solution than most of the other streams which I have seen, and is able to reflect the sky and change with it. The Dan is here about sixty rods wide, shallow and full of rocks, that everywhere show above the surface of the water. It is spanned by two ugly covered bridges, over one of which passes the railroad to Richmond, and the other is a tollbridge for ordinary travel. The stream is rapid, and the waterpower furnished by its current once set in motion the machinery of several tobacco factories, but they are now all idle. Business of every kind is said to be dull; most of the tobacco has already come in from the neighboring counties, and the people have almost nothing to sell. No national bank has yet been established, and there is an embarrassing scarcity of money, so that a large part of the local trade is transacted by way of barter—wood, corn, and other country produce being exchanged for salt, dry goods, and groceries.

The interior appearance of the place is not different from that of other small Southern towns. Queer-looking equestrians, on good, bad, or indifferent horses, riding over the ill-paved streets; three or four men sitting or standing at the doorway of every shop; Negro men, with short cotton aprons, rolling casks, or carrying sacks; sunburnt boys, with long bleached hair, guarding country wagons, while the father exchanges a bag of wheat for a bag of salt, or the mother trades eggs for dry-goods; venders of vegetables—these scantily fill the business street; and over everything, street, houses, shops, and men, is diffused an air of languor, and neglect, and half-decay, for which, perhaps, the relaxing influence of heat and glare is a good deal responsible. The liveliest figures to be seen are the quartermaster's wagon teams, and the corporal's guard, with bright bayonets, at the corner by the pump, who lie in wait to pick up every Negro that has no pass, and march him away to do an hour's work at policing camps or sweeping quarters.

As I stood and watched the amusing incidents of the arrests, I was addressed in sonorous tones by an elderly and ill-dressed gentleman with a very brown face and a red nose:

"My good sir, will you be so kind as to direct me to the Tunstall House? It must be that there is mint somewhere in this town, and they tell me I shall find it there if anywhere." I was going to the hotel he wished to find, and on the way, as well as after we reached the place, the gentleman talked freely. He was from Columbia, and on his way to New York.

"I am going on, sir, to offer a great speculation to some of their rich men there. Friends of mine who have been North since the war ended tell me they found the business men very well intentioned and liberal, and rolling in wealth, sir. They have been coining money up there while we have been gradually coming down, down, down to our last mill. I'm from Bolivar County myself, State of Mississippi. I hail from Columbia, but that's not my native place, nor where I mean to live. I was in Bolivar up to '63, and I own just as good a tract of cotton-land out there now as any man wants. Why, I'll tell you, sir; in the year eighteen hundred and sixty-one, with ninety-nine workers—not hands, mind! workers—I made six hundred and ninety-one bales of cotton! Well, I've heard of better doings than that, but I never saw them. But I can brag of that much. And I can do the same thing again, sir. But I have nothing left, you know, but my land and my experience; not a thing. The Confederate Government, in 1862, issued one of the most blundering, foolish orders that was ever issued by any government on God's earth—to burn all cotton within five miles of the river. My place, you see, is more than ten miles from the river; but the dirty rascal charged with the execution of the order owed me a grudge; hated me as—well, almost as much as I hated him; and he burnt every ounce of cotton I had. Nearly thirteen hundred bales he burned; a fortune, sir, if I had it today. But it's gone. It wasn't a great while after that before the Yankees came and carried off all my mules but five, and destroyed about everything else on the plantation; so I concluded I'd pull up stakes and get away from there. I settled with all my niggers near Columbia. But by-and-bye Mr. Sherman came along, and what was left me before I lost then; all my meat went, all my corn, all my mules, and some of my niggers. Most of them stayed, though, and it became a question what to do with them. I must tell you about that. You see I had brought them out of a good country into a devilish poor one, and though I might have turned them all loose when they became freedmen, that's not my way, so I got a place out in Edgefield, and then I called them up and made a little speech. 'Boys,' said I, 'I got you into this place, where you're like enough to starve, and though we are all going back to Bolivar some day, we can't go just at present; so I've prepared a place for you out in Edgefield district; that's a better region than this, and we'll start for there next week.' But no, sir, they said they didn't wish to go; they'd stay there where they were. 'Stay here? Very good. But how are you going to live? You'll starve; for I won't undertake to feed you.' 'No, master, we won't starve; we've got something.' 'Yes,' said I, 'but you haven't enough to keep you till harvest.' Well, sir, to my astonishment, I found that they had provision for a twelvemonth. The d——d rascals had gone in and helped to sack Columbia. They had everything, sir, from a pound of tobacco to a porcelain egg; bacon, flour, any quantity of clothes. And I found out that Sherman's men, when they broke open my smoke-house and corn-house, had left a share of the plunder with the niggers. I had no more to say. The niggers didn't go to Edgefield, and are there yet, waiting for me to take them home to Mississippi. They're mightily afraid I'll be slipping off and leaving them there, but I'll do the fair thing, and they shall go back. Now this is what I'm going to do in New York. I shall say to some of those capitalists, 'Gentlemen, I've got a good plantation, and not a cent of money. The war has stripped me. I've got no mules, no carts, no blacksmith's shop, no farming implements. I want some of you to loan me ten thousand dollars to get these things with, and within a twelvemonth I engage to give you forty thousand dollars for your ten. Let me have cash enough to stock my plantation so as to set one hundred good niggers to work, and next year I'll pack six hundred bags of cotton, five hundred pounds to the bag.' I might go further, and guarantee more than that, but six hundred bags will do, with cotton where it is now. There's no investment like it. Why, sir, there's untold money in this thing for men with five, ten, and fifteen thousand dollars to lend. The man who loans me the money ought to come right down on the plantation with me or send down an agent. Then he can keep accounts of everything, and see that he is not cheated; he can keep accounts with the hands, and look after things generally. The niggers do work better—there's no use denying it, and I don't blame them—they do work better for a Yankee than for one of us. No doubt, you think, I can get the money? My friends in Columbia say I can, but I'll have to get a pardon first. That I'm not going to do. I don't believe it's necessary, and I'm not going near Washington. The d—d thing is all over, and I'm glad it is; but I sha'n't bother about a pardon."

This gentleman thought that the Negro, poor devil, was fated to disappear; that slavery, if it had oppressed him, had at the same time protected him; give the Negro political and social equality, that would make no difference; being left to stand or fall alone in a competitive struggle for life with a superior race, he would be sure to perish; a system bad for the individual Negro had been the preservation of the Negro race in America; philanthropists, with their schemes for elevating the man, would find they had exterminated the species. A troublesome question would, at any rate, be removed from American politics.

REIDVILLE, N. C., September 6, 1865

"A right smart o' fixins at the railroad thar," was the encouraging description of this place given me by a man who declined to give me a night's lodging, and, moreover, it is laid down on my map of the Southern States, so I was expecting to see twenty or thirty houses and a tavern; but I rode some hundreds of yards beyond the village, and only on enquiry discovered that I had gone through it. Two cars on the railroad, a small way-station, and a store where liquor is sold, is all I could find of Reidville. But going further on my way was a house at which travellers are entertained, and at which I stay for the night.

I have travelled today no more than twenty-five miles, having ridden slowly and stopped often by the way to talk with the people. The country is the poorest I have yet seen, with crops that seem less abundant and healthy than those further north, and with less timber. But the road lies along a high and unproductive ridge, so dry that, during the whole day, I have found no brook or spring, and the good land, I am told, is by the side of the creeks and the Dan River. Large plantations were very few, and the greater number of houses had around them no Negro quarters at all, while others had two or three cabins, which, in many cases, were but little inferior to that occupied by the white family. A large part of the population of the counties of Caswell and Rockingham, I was assured, were "them triflin' people," of whom many were Unionists. The avowal of their sentiments, however, they never attempted, though I am told that such persons were well known to each other, and, during the war, formed secret societies for mutual protection of members, by sharing information and aiding each other's families when it became necessary for the men to flee from the rebel conscripting-officers, or to go away into military service. All the people with whom I have talked profess to have been secessionists. I should think that the majority of the people in these counties belong to the class of small farmers. From the high ground I could often get a view of the country for several miles around, and everywhere was repeated the unvarying scene with which the roadside had made me familiar—rolling ground covered with forest, and here and there, at long intervals, a clearing of one or two hundred acres. Corn, ill-tended, and apparently richer in leaf than in ear, was the chief crop. The blades, in great quantities, were burning up on the stalk. I tried at two plantations to get a feed for my horse at noon, but could not, and I was told this evening that the people most generally were too busy with tobacco to pay much attention to saving fodder. But this year it must be from the force of habit that fodder is spoiling, for I saw only one field of tobacco, and that contained less than two acres.

A third attempt to procure a feed was more successful. The niggers could let me have some, and I could leave fifty cents to pay for it, the farmer said. He was just going down the road a piece, to the church; they were having a "protracted" meeting, and he had been aiming to go for two or three days. So he drove off; and, while the horse ate his chopped oats, I sat in the house-porch talking with his wife, a very fat woman, who laughed continually.

Her husband was a carpenter by trade, she said, but he owned a hundred and thirty acres and farmed as well. He used to raise tobacco right smart; but for three or four years he'd only made corn. She was proper glad to get back to flour again; she told her husband her teeth were done gone chawin' corn-bread, and she reckoned 'twas the corn-meal made the children's throats sore, scratchin' as it went down. She was thankful peace had come. Their land wouldn't bring tobacco without guano. Her husband intended to put in a good crop next year, and she reckoned he'd peddle it out in South Carolina. He'd go thar now if he hadn't sold his tobacco, for it was reported that there was a right smart o' specie in South Carolina, though Sherman did go through.

No, she reckoned he wouldn't do much with his own niggers.

He'd always be able to hire some in the neighborhood when work pressed, and he intended to keep only two of his men with him. And some of the young white men had been talking about hiring themselves out to him; but he didn't know, he was thinking about it. He'd sent off two families, and there was another woman, with five children, that had got to go next week, for her keep cost more than her labor would ever pay for. The woman wanted to stay; so did all their niggers; but 'twas no use; her children were all small but one, and that one had a dreadful har lip, so she couldn't talk plain, and Mr. L—— told her she and her train must start at once, for he couldn't keep her. She reckoned if all the niggers had been sent right away from home immediately after the surrender, they'd ha' found out by this what freedom was like, and they'd ha' been all glad enough to get back with their masters and stay. But they listened to what the Yankees told 'em. This same woman she was speakin' of said to her husband, when he told her to leave, that it seemed like it was mighty hard; she'd been made free, and it did appear as if thar must be something more comin'; the Yankees wouldn't never leave her so. That was the way with 'em all; but they'd find their mistake. There was a man up there a piece that had gone to Washington city with some of the Yankee soldiers, and he come back a while ago. He told how the niggers was treated thar. He said there was a law so that if a nigger stole five dollars' worth he was put in the penitentiary for five years, and if he stole ten dollars' worth he was put in for life, and if he stole anything over ten dollars he must be hung. There was another law that no nigger should have water to drink without paying for it. That, she thought, was too hard; niggers never was treated so cruel down here; water was free to everybody.

It was dusk when I reached this house, which appears to be the residence of a farmer of the better class, and supper was already on the table. The meal consisted of buttermilk, corn-bread, and cold boiled bacon, with peas, and was eaten in complete silence, by the light of a brownish tallow candle. In the evening, sitting in front of the house, the farmer's brother became more talkative, and related to me his experience of life in a Federal military prison. Being asked for news, I said that I believed they were busy in Washington trying Captain Wirtz, the Andersonville jailer.

"I wish they'd let us try the fellows that were jailers at Elmira," said the young man; "they'd get a cussed short trial, and a grape-vine would be the end on't. 'Twouldn't last no ten days."

"Were you confined there? How did they treat you?"

"Treated me mighty bad. I was a prisoner for thirteen months. The Yankees took me at Spottsylvania, and first they sent me to Point Lookout. I was used pretty well thar, but by-and-bye they moved us up to Elmira. That was in August, and I never got home till last June; so you see I know what a Yankee prison was. We never treated them any worse than we was treated. There was forty-two men taken when I was, all out of our company, and there never was but fourteen came back home; so you may know. They killed twenty-eight out o' forty-two, and they tried to kill us all."

"Were any of them wounded?"

"Wounded? No. 'Twas bad food, and usin' 'em hard. The durned weather was enough to kill anybody; the awfulest cold I ever felt. They kept us in tents till a'most Christmas time, and we was about froze to death. Lots of the men had their feet and hands frost-bit, and had to have them cut off. When they did put up quarters for us, they didn't put up half enough. They built great long houses, each one to hold two hundred men, and they only put in one stove at the end of one. Of course we could not keep warm, nor begin to. They didn't mean we should; for they gave us a little bit of wood that wouldn't make ten men comfortable."

"How were the rations? What did they give you?"

"They'd knock down some old cows at the kitchen, and cut 'em up there and then, and fling the meat right so, without washing or anything, into the kettles, and never put in a grain o' salt. That was just their cussed meanness, because they had a plenty. When the meat was boiled, it didn't taste like beef, you know; it tasted of the cow, and heaps of our men couldn't get it down easy anyhow. But they used to cut up the whole of it—the allowance for all the prisoners—and throw the lumps into heaps—great high piles they was—and by the time they'd stand over night the meat would be sour. 'Twasn't good not once in ten times. They gave each man a little small rasher; no account anyhow. We was just half starved."

"Were the men ill-used in other ways?"

"Why, they'd punish us for nothing at all. Every time a commissioned officer came into any room, every prisoner had to jump up and take off his hat and keep standin' till the blasted Yankee was gone. If he didn't, they'd put a barrel-shirt on him. They needn't talk; I know what a Yankee prison is. But I tell you what was the meanest of the mean, worse than the Yankees—them fellows that made application to take the oath. They wanted to take it as soon as they was captured, but they wouldn't go into the Yankee army, and they wouldn't let 'em. But they used to sneak 'round, and lie, and inform on our boys—about tunnelling, you know, and them things. I'd like to come across some o' them fellows now; one in particular."

"You had to take the oath of allegiance, hadn't you, before you came away?"

"Took something. Ha'n't done nothin' but take oaths lately. Have to take an oath for everything I do. What'll you do with me if I don't take it? says I; keep me yer for ever? They'd find something to do with me, they said. I wanted to get home; General Lee had surrendered, yer know; and I concluded I wouldn't let their durned oath stop me, but I'd cuss along with the rest. So I took it and came on home. Don't reckon that's much."

GREENSBORO, N. C., September 7, 1865

Today's ride has been pleasanter than yesterday's, though, on account of my having lost my way, it was a little longer. It has lain through a better country, watered by several streams, and containing more bottom-land. The general features of the landscape have reminded me as much of South Carolina as of Virginia. The surface begins to be more level; among the timber there are more

gums and pines; the road often runs among stumps and close past
the stems of the forest; tall, dead trunks, girdled when the land was
cleared, stand thick together, bleaching in the cultivated fields; the
dark-colored loam has not wholly disappeared, but often the soil is
light and sandy; in the low grounds the trees may be seen rising
out of black pools of stagnant water, and in such places the cardi-
nal-flower forces itself upon the eye, and I noticed the livid
passion-flower; lizards are frequent in the hot sand; I saw, too,
flying among the leaves, a small bird, red as blood, which is common further south.

Today I had an interesting conversation with a man who
belongs to what, as I suppose, must be a new class in the South—
the class of Negro lessees of land. He had been a slave all his life,
he said, and was now "a settled man" (he appeared to be forty-
three or -four), but he was going to strike out for himself and see
what he could do in a state of freedom. He had already rented
some land, and that he thought was what every colored man ought
to do, if he could. Perhaps only a few would be able to do it at
present, because the masters were opposed to it; wanted to keep
the people in such a condition that they could be hired as laborers
at low wages, and preferred to let a "no-account white man" have
a plantation rather than rent it to Negroes. His former master and
the gentlemen living in the neighborhood refused to lease out land
to him. But a few miles away from home he had been more successful. The owner had selected certain parts of his plantation, and
told him to take up as many acres as he could properly care for
and cultivate. The land was not good, most of it being "old field";
but if he could make enough this first year to feed his family, he
would be content. He had bought a condemned horse from the
Government corral for fifteen dollars; he was low in order, but
would be fit to plough next month. His wife had been knocking
about the house most of her life; but he could depend upon her
assistance if the work got too hard for him, and he had two children big enough to do full work in the field. Both were good
ploughmen, and when his own crop did not call for their labor he
could hire them out to the farmers, and he also could do hauling

for his neighbors, and thus pick up a little ready money. If God spared his life, he expected to have twenty acres of corn, eight acres of wheat, five acres of oats, and some potatoes on his land. His landlord was to receive one-third of all the corn raised.

This year he had been working for his old master, who had promised to give his hands such a portion of the crops they made as should be pronounced equitable by two white men whom he designated. The apportionment had not yet been made. On most of the plantations of which he had any knowledge the workmen received some part of the crop in payment for their labor, and, as a rule, the masters were endeavoring to hire them for the coming year at the same price—their board, namely, and so many bushels of corn.

This man said that he knew it to be still usual on some of the plantations to beat the Negroes for any offence; and that especially is this the case in the country districts. Negroes living in the vicinity of Greensboro' could complain to the soldiers, but twenty or thirty miles out they were without redress.

He was very anxious that schools should be established. A while ago some of the colored people had spoken to a white man who lived near, a poor man, but "with good learning," asking him to open a school, which he had promised to do. But he did not like to begin without having first obtained the consent of the gentlemen in the neighborhood; so he called on five or six of them and made known his intention, but he was told that if he tried that game he would be shot in his school-room; he therefore desisted. The gentlemen who told the man so were just the kind of men that would have done it, too; but the Yankees would set up schools, he hoped.

At Greensboro' I made some enquiries with the object of finding out if the statements of this Negro about ill-usage of laborers on the plantations were true.

There is in the town an agent of the Freedmen's Bureau. Like the rest of its agents whom I have seen, he is an overworked officer. He has supervision of seven counties, and has subordinates in but one of them, for police duty in the country is left to the home guard of each county, and consequently there are no Federal

garrisons from which the superintendent might draw assistance. A
Negro who seeks redress for a real or imaginary injury must travel
perhaps ten, perhaps fifty, miles and lay his complaint before the
superintendent in Greensboro', or he must lay it before the home
guard, with what likelihood of getting justice may be guessed from
the fact that the captain of the guard in one of the counties was
much surprised and little pleased to learn, the other day, that he
had no right to whip Negroes whose masters found fault with
them. It is needless to say that the Negro chooses the former alter-
native, and, when he decides to complain at all, he complains at
Greensboro'. Having heard the fifty or sixty complaints of every
day, the superintendent may consider the possibilities of summon-
ing witnesses and all the other circumstances of the case, and may
investigate it if he thinks best and can find time. His office, it will
be seen, is not a sinecure. It would be speaking more accurately to
say that no one man can perform its duties, and that most men,
finding themselves able to do so little where so much calls loudly
to be done, could but become disheartened by the difficulties of the
position.

The officer at Greensboro' has been in the service of the Bureau
only ten days. Within that time two cases of Negro shooting had
been brought to his notice; in one of which the man had been
crippled, in the other only slightly wounded. He would not say that
the sufferer in either case had been absolutely blameless, for he did
not wish to prejudge the matter; but whatever the offence, he
thought some less deadly instrument of punishment might have
been employed. "The fact is," he continued, "it's the first notion
with a great many of these people, if a Negro says anything or
does anything that they don't like, to take a gun and put a bullet
into him, or a charge of shot. But this gentleman knows more
about it than I do; he was provost-marshal of Salisbury down
here." The officer had held that office, he said, from the 19th of
July until the 6th of August, and in that space of time had arrested
and held under guard four persons charged with shooting down
Negroes. Of the four Negroes but one survived. Cases of assault,
both gentlemen said, are very numerous, and almost always with-

out sufficient cause. No day passed without several complaints being made. "Here's a case now," said the superintendent; "I gave this woman an order on her former master for some clothes belonging to her which he withheld. She took it out to him, he read it and it didn't please him, so he knocked the woman down. He only lives eight or ten miles out, and I'm going to try and get a guard so as to have him arrested tomorrow and brought in. I suppose he'll be raging when he finds that Negro testimony is to be used against him, like a man I had here yesterday. We convicted him on what the Negroes swore to, and he *was* mad. He said a good deal; among other things says he, 'If this war ain't done, let us know it, and we can begin over.' 'Exactly,' says I; 'it was done too soon here by three months, *I* always thought, and a good many thought so as well as I after the assassination.' "

He found a good many men who appeared honestly anxious to treat their Negroes kindly, and there were a very few who even interested themselves in schemes for educating the blacks; but it was his opinion, based upon what he had seen while in the army, and confirmed by his experience as superintendent, that the withdrawal of the Federal troops would be the signal for a reign of violence and oppression. From all he could learn, many of the people did not believe the Negroes were legally free, and would not accept the new order of things. The State convention would probably declare slavery dead; but a good many county conventions, if they could speak, would declare that it was not, and in some parts of the State the Negro would see a good deal of trouble.

DAVIDSON CO., N. C., September 11, 1865

I LEFT Greensboro' this morning early, and without regret, for my stay there had been far from comfortable. It is a small, hilly town with only twenty-seven hundred inhabitants; but boasts a hotel styled "The Metropolitan," in which I took up my quarters. To me they gave a room with a bed in it, and a wash-basin, and a chair in which one could sit if the back of it was first set against the wall. My horse had the freedom of a small yard, where, without so much shelter as the shade of a tree, he was constantly exposed to sun or rain. My room, also, was open to the elements, for on one night I was driven from my bed by a deluge of rain-water pouring from the boarded ceiling, which flooded and soaked the floor, and rendered the room nearly uninhabitable for two days afterwards. The hotel table was entirely in keeping with the chambers. Such things in themselves are not unendurable; but the traveller's equanimity is sure to be disturbed when he finds that landlords can push impudence and extortion so far as to demand five dollars a day for such board and lodging. In Danville we fared somewhat better, but not without having somewhat more to pay, the charge for horse and man per day being six dollars and a quarter. Yet nearly every article of food here used is cheaper in these country towns than in the Northern Atlantic States.

As I rode away, the day was gray and soft, promising rain, but soon all the clouds were dissipated and the sun shone oppressively. At the hotel they told me that Salisbury was forty miles distant; at a blacksmith's shop a mile and a half from the village, the distance

was said to be only thirty-five miles; after an hour's riding I enquired again, and was told that the men folks called it forty-six
miles to Salisbury and six miles back to Greensboro'; tonight my
host tells me that really the distance between the two places is
fifty-two miles by the country roads, and that I have travelled
thirty-one miles since morning. Some of these people, I find, have
never passed beyond the bounds of the county in which they were
born, and have learned nothing of places which they have not
visited.

My road has led me over sandy hills, sterile in appearance, and
evidently occupied by people belonging to the class of poor whites;
but the country seemed more thickly settled than the richer districts further north. I saw white women as well as white men busy
in the fields, and there were as many white people at work as
Negroes. Whenever a good opportunity presented itself, I engaged
them in conversation, and usually found them not averse to leave
their labor and talk for a while. Six or seven miles out of Greensboro', seeing a farmer in his sorghum fields stripping the leaves
from the cane, I stopped and enquired about the road. He gave me
the desired information, and, in answer to his questions, I said I
was riding to Salisbury from Lynchburg. He was a lean, hard-fea-
tured man, past the middle age, who owned about a hundred acres
of land, he said, and was "an original secessioner." I asked if he
farmed his land without help.

"I ha'n't no help jest now," he answered. "Most o' our hirelin'
men went off to the war, and pretty much all on 'em got killed, or
died off one way and another. I don't know but all on 'em out o'
this neighborhood is gone; I a'n't sure as one come back. My
wife's brother holp me in plantin'. But we a'n't doin' much anyhow
this season, and I am by myself now."

"I should think you'd hire Negroes; you have employed them, I
suppose."

"Oh yes; before the war, you know, I hed black ones then every
year. But we could make 'em work then. I wouldn't expect to
make a crop with 'em now; they're no account. A'n't it so in your
country?"

"The farmers in Virginia are almost all saying the same thing."

"Exactly; it's jest so everywhar. I tried one this year. He come along about a month, and wanted to come on and work for me; I had a house stannin' empty. 'Yer all so d———n lazy,' says I, 'since ye call yerselves free, running yere and thar from pillar to post, that I don't want none o' ye.' But he 'lowed he could work well, never was a sassy nigger, wouldn't ha' left but his master told him to go; only try him, and so on. 'Wal,' says I, 'I'll try yer, and yer to understand that I won't hev no back-talk, and yer to do jest what I say or ye'll find me out. I sprawl a nigger d———n quick.' That's jest the kind o' man I am; I never could stan' any back-talk from one on 'em. They know me, too; a free nigger'd jest as soon see the devil as see me. This boy promised faithful, and that evenin' I lent him the cart to go and bring up his things and his wife; hedn't much, you know, but sich as 'twas I let him hev the cart to move it, and I put him into the house. Next mornin' I was out in the field with my brother-in-law gittin' out manure, and arter we'd been at it a half hour, along come Mister Nigger. I been knockin' up some shelves,' says he, 'and I come to ax ye for a handful o' nails; that house needs fixin' bad, and I can't live thar unless I do somethin' to it.' 'D'ye see that ar shovel?' says I to him, 'and that ar cart? Pick up and go to work, or I'll run ye off this place faster'n ye come on to it. I didn't hire ye to make houses,' says I; 'I hired ye to work on the farm.' "

"What did he say to that?"

"Nothin'. He knew better. He took the shovel and worked right well for five or six days. Ye know how it is with 'em—for about three days it's work as if they'd break everything to pieces; but arter that it's go out late and come in soon. He didn't say nothin' for a week, but kept at it pretty close, and then one night he packed up, him and his wife, and left. I knew tolerably well whar to find him—down the road a piece, 'long with some free niggers; so I gathered up some o' our boys, and we went down to this place whar I thought he was at, and told him he'd make tracks before night, and if he was found in this neighborhood arter next day we'd shoot him wherever we found him."

"Do you know where he went?"

"He settled down in a place about seven miles over here; but we sent word to some o' the boys thar, and they gathered up agin and run him out o' that. We a'n't agoin' to let niggers walk over us; we can take care o' our black ones as soon as the Yankees is gone. In Virginny, I reckon, yer better off; ye have the civil law thar."

I gave him some information as to the condition of things in Virginia: telling him that there was a Federal garrison at most of the county seats, to whom was entrusted the duty of protecting the colored population, while in North Carolina that matter was left in the hands of the home guards. He agreed with me that the Negro could be more effectually repressed in his own State than in Virginia, but bewailed his proximity to Greensboro' with its Yankees and Superintendent of Freedmen, who appeared to think a Negro was better than a white man.

I asked him if the people of Guilford County were not taking the oath of allegiance. Addressing me as a presumed Southerner and secessionist, he replied, in a slightly apologetic manner: "Yes, we be. I ha'n't tuck it yet myself; but the magistrates hev set a day, and I reckon everybody'll take it. We hev to do it, ye know; we can't vote nor nothin' else till we've tuck it. We've got to git back into the Union, and we mout as well git back as soon as we can, and git the civil law. Don't you look at it that way? Ye've tak'n it in your country, a'n't ye?"

"Yes, every man has to take it before he can vote. I suppose the convention will take the State into the Union again, but it will have to admit that all the slaves are free."

"Yes, I reckon. But it's jest a robbery, stealin' our property like that. That's what I call it; jest what I say about ——. He's up for the convention, and I'm told, I ha'n't heard him myself, but they say he's come out in favor o' repudiatin' all debts that hev been made durin' the war. 'It's a d——n robbery and nothin' else,' says I, 'and we don't need no sich men.' I don't vote for him, and if I hed my way he should be led out with a rope round his neck, then bend down a saplin' and run him up. And I say the same about 'mancipation; it's stealin'.'"

"You have six or seven candidates up, I see. Most of them talk alike, I suppose?"

"Wal, I don't know. No, we know our men, I reckon. There's Mr. H——, up here—you passed his house a mile back—he wants to go. But we don't need him. He was too busy keepin' men out o' the army all through the war, and then he's in with all them triflin' people, and he's a great friend to the black ones. We don't need him, and he won't go, I don't believe. We want men that'll keep the niggers in their place. If we let a nigger git equal with us, the next thing we know he'll be ahead of us. He's so impudent and presumin'."

"Have you many of these Union people in this county? I've been told that they are a majority of your population."

"They a'n't; they're scatterin', sir, scatterin', and the most is no account. I say, friend, would ye take a drink o' brandy? ye'd be welcome if ye would; come up to the house and 'light."

The commander of the post at Greensboro' informed me that more than a hundred persons living in Guilford County had taken out licenses as distillers, and given a bond with two sureties to sell no spirits to enlisted men. There were more than another hundred, he thought, small manufacturers, who had not reported themselves at all, and a great many farmers who distilled no more than supplied the wants of their own families. It is chiefly peach and apple brandy that they manufacture, and most of it is said to be very fiery and unwholesome, on account of their imperfect method of rectifying it. Declining the farmer's courteous invitation, I bade him good morning and rode on my way. At the end of two hours it became time to give my horse something to eat, or rather to begin looking for a house at which a feed could be procured, for I have learned that it is not the first attempt which usually obtains it. Today I stopped at four farms without meeting with success; they hardly had fodder enough for their own horses, they said.

In the course of my inquiries for lodging and horse-feed, I find that in the common speech of people in North Carolina, the phrase, "a poor chance," is not intended to convey any sense of doubt or contingency, but means that certainly the thing desired cannot be had. And, among other variations from ordinary usage in language, *farewell* is often substituted for *good-bye,* and other words of leave-taking; and the past tense of the verb *to help* is formed in the ancient way, *holp* being used instead of *helped.* The *l* is silent in pronouncing the word.

At the fifth house, a long log cabin, my application was successful. "Yes," said the woman to whom I made it, "ye can hev a feed, I reckon, if yer hoss'll eat hay or cane. We ha'n't any corn yit, and we ha'n't raised any oats." I signified my willingness to take hay, and followed the woman to a crazy barn at a little distance from the house. I have seen a great many women on the roads and in the houses of this region whose appearance resembled hers. She was barefooted, and wore a man's hat, from beneath which escaped some locks of tangled hair; her sallow face was thin and dirty, and stained at the corners of the mouth with the juice of tobacco, which she chewed. The original colors of her cotton dress had run together and faded, till it had become of a uniform dingy white or clay color, that matched her complexion, and it clung about her as she walked with long strides. On one shoulder she carried a pitchfork, and a chain halter was thrown over the other. Unsaddling the horse and tying him in a business-like manner, she set hay before him, and then invited me to come into the house and rest; so I entered one of the two rooms and sat down in a rush-bottomed chair. Overhead skeins of brown and blue yarn were hanging from the cross-beams, and at a spinning-wheel near the fire-place a woman, younger than the other, was spinning cotton thread. She looked up as I entered, and nodded, but neither removed the pipe from her mouth nor spoke till I had sat for some minutes looking about me; then she said: "Be you a preacher, sir?" "No, ma'am," I said. "You're a doctor then, I reckon?" I answered in the negative again. "I tuck notice o' your saddle-pockets, and I thought you mout be one or t'other," she said; after which remark she went on spinning and smoking in silence, and I made no attempt to continue the conversation, for half-a-dozen children were crying and fighting on the floor, so that nothing but their noise could be heard. After a while they became a little stiller, one of the older ones amusing the rest by placing my saddle-bags across her back, and creeping up and down in the character of the "preacher's hoss." I took advantage of the lull to ask the woman if they had regular preaching in that neighborhood.

"Over to High P'int they hev, and we hev it yer now and agin."

"What sort? Methodist?"

"Most all kinds—Presbyterian, and Missionary Baptist, and Hardshell, but there's more o' the Methodists."

"What do you mean by Hardshell Baptists?"

"Them as believes in predestination. Everything's foreseen from the foundation o' the world, they say, and nothin' comes out any different from it's ordained. The Missionaries, they holds to free grace."

"What's free grace?"

"Expect you know better'n me. Salvation free, I reckon; but I never tuck to Baptists much. I'm a Methodist myself. My husband's mother was a Hardshell."

"No, I don't know much about it; I come from the North myself, and they haven't any Hardshells where I live."

"They hev the Methodists, don't they?" "Yes," I told her, "a good many," and the thought seemed to please her. By-and-bye she said: "Be they makin' the laws in your country, mister?" "Laws about what?" I enquired. "Why, they do say you're a-goin to take away all our land down yer, because we made the rebellion. But this State never did go out; we's all Union through yer, and they shouldn't harrish us, for we couldn't help it. My man used to lay out many a night for fear them volunteers would git him to go to the war. I hope they'll make good laws."

Her husband had been drowned some months before, and not long afterward her son had died, so she was left alone to manage the farm. She never had been obliged to attend to such things before, she said; she didn't know how much land she owned, nor how heavy a tax she would have to pay; the land was almighty poor; it wouldn't fetch more'n a bushel o' wheat to the acre, so much of it was washed out, and all guttered. She didn't know whar to hunt a man that would crap it for her. It was a mighty hard case for a widow woman with seven gal children and nary boy.

I told her I had seen that some of the landholders were renting out small farms to Negro families. She replied, with less of apathy in her manner:

"Don't want nothin' to do with black ones. They a'n't good for anything on a farm. My man tried some 'fore he died, and they'd eat and steal more'n they'd make. One o' the gals was in the house and she car'd off more soda and sugar than we eat. People ha'n't much use for black ones yer; now they's got their freedom, they say, I expect they'll be worse."

So far as I have seen, all native Southerners, the poorest and most degraded equally with the rich, and people of the most undoubted Unionism as well as secessionists, unaffectedly and heartily despise the Negroes. Truly they are a despised race. Everybody feels contempt, as often, perhaps, mingled with pity as with hatred, for their morals, their mental capacity, and their character as laborers. An old lady who gave me a drink of water this afternoon, a woman of the same class as those whom I have above described, gave me her opinion of colored servants. She was Union, she said, and so was most all the folks along that road till I got down to Lexington. They did say A. L. was a secessioner, but she reckoned they made lies on him. When she learned I was a Northern man, she wanted to know if the black ones wouldn't be sent out of the country, or up North. I said I thought not, and enquired if they were not doing well where they were.

"No, mister, they a'n't goin' to do well. They run about a good deal, I'm told, and they a'n't workin' like they did. There's Captain B——, he's got five young men, and they's allus been treated well; too well, I say. You never could go by the place arter three o'clock but you'd see 'em on the broad o' their backs. They's goin' off, he tells me. They'd better look whose kitchen they's goin' out of, I say; they'll never be so well off agin. He says he wishes they would go, for they don't do what'll keep 'em. They's too sassy, mister. One of 'em come to me last week for work. 'How many rails can you split in a day?' I axed him. I knowed a day's work was a hundred rails if the wood wasn't cut, and two hundred if it was. 'Oh, he could split a right smart o' rails,' he said. 'And how much do you ax?' says I. Wal, he said, he reckoned about a dollar and a half a day would be right. I jest told him to go on, for I hadn't no use for him. He was travellin' to Caswell, he said."

I asked what she could hire Negroes and white men for before the war.

"White men we give nine and ten dollars a month, and we paid a hundred dollars for a nigger. But the owners got to askin' so much shoes and blankets, that it cost as much for the black ones a'most as for the hirelin's. The hirelin's would work jest twice as much, and the black ones would give away your corn, and if they wanted half soles, they like enough cut up your gears."

At three houses, this evening, I found it impossible to procure a supper and lodging, and was obliged to ride for more than an hour after nightfall. There was no moon, and the road was dark among the trees, so that I let my horse pick his way at his own pace along the road, which for some miles had been gradually descending. At last, the rush of water and the sound of machinery warned me that I was approaching a mill, and soon, on the bank of a little stream, I found a shed where three men were sawing boards by the light of pine torches, which sent red reflections across the road and showed me the miller's house. His little girl was sick with the typhoid fever, he said, as he scrutinized me with the light-wood in his hand, and for some moments I dreaded that here, too, was "a poor chance" for entertainment. He took me in, however, and his wife prepared a supper of coffee, wheat bread, and fried fish from the mill stream.

The miller said he ran the saw at night because in the day all the power was needed for the grist-mill. Lumber was scarce, he said, but the people needed bread in this country. My bed-chamber is a very small room, and bids fair to be suffocatingly close before morning, for I can raise neither of the windows. There are feather beds on two lofty bedsteads, which almost fill the room; there are two great piles of folded counterpanes and quilts at the feet of the beds; and I count twenty-nine dresses hanging from pegs and completely covering the walls. The dresses and counterpanes are all of simple cross-barred patterns, and evidently were woven at home in the hand-loom.

SALISBURY, ROWAN CO., N. C., September 12, 1865

Lexington is a small village, wide-streeted, and standing in a little, bare green plain. I passed through it without stopping, and observed nothing noteworthy in its appearance. As I passed the last houses in the village, a well-dressed young woman came to the door-step of a very respectable looking house, with a snuff-dip in her hand, and spat once or twice as she glanced at the stranger. I see that black women as well as white give themselves up to this indulgence, some having even acquired the power of swallowing the snuff.

Apparently a heavy shower had fallen during the night, and for several miles the road from Lexington to the Yadkin River was deep in mud. When I reached the river bank, a ferry-boat was on its way to the other shore, and I bathed in the stream while awaiting its return. The ferryman was an old Negro of seventy, with a gray beard and a face wrinkled but of mild expression. He spoke with deliberation and slowly, and nothing in his language indicated his African descent. Indeed, the language of most of these Negroes is quite as correct and elegant as that employed by the white people, and it is the tone of the voice alone which betrays their origin. Daniel was his name, the old man said, and he had been ferryman there, winter and summer, for forty-three years. Seven masters had owned him since he first put the boat across, but they were all done buried now.

"Well, old man, you're free now," I said.

"I dunno, master. They say all the colored people's free; they do say it certain; but I'm a-goin on same as I allus has been."

"Why, you get wages now, don't you?"

"No, sir; my mistress never said anything to me that I was to have wages, nor yet that I was free; nor I never said anything to her. Ye see I left it to her own honor to talk to me about it, because I was afraid she'd say I was insultin' to her and presumin', so I wouldn't speak first. She ha'n't spoke yet."

"What will you do? work on just the same till you die?"

"Ye see, master, I am ashamed to say anything to her. But I don't 'low to work any longer than to Christmas, and then I'll ask for wages. But I want to leave the ferry. I'm a mighty good farmer, and I'll get a piece of ground and a chunk of a hoss, if I can, and work for myself."

I wished him all success, and bade him good-bye, to which he replied with a "farewell, master," that sounded paternally benevolent.

Salisbury, an old town of three thousand inhabitants, is situated in a wide stretch of comparatively flat ground, and is certainly a pretty place. It is laid out with much regularity, and the wide streets, adorned with fine shade trees and supplied with frequent public wells, are, in general, quiet and clean. Many of the houses have a respectable, old-fashioned look, and are surrounded by spacious yards and gardens, in which the roses are still in bloom and the figs are half ripe. On one of the side streets is the town whipping-post and pillory, and on another a little, dilapidated, crumbling edifice, much like a New England shoemaker's shop, is pointed out as the law-office in which Andrew Jackson was once a student.

But there are two objects connected with the recent history of Salisbury that are also a part of the country's history, and are of universal interest—the prison pen, and its necessary adjunct, the prisoners' burying-ground. The site of the former is upon a gentle eminence at the south-eastern edge of the town. As the visitor approaches it, his eye is first caught by the tall walls of a brick building that stands among oak trees near the road. This was once a cotton factory, and afterwards a hospital. A few rods distant are three smaller houses designed for the operatives, and these, together with the hospital, were ruined by Stoneman in his last great raid. A space of ten acres around these buildings was enclosed by a ditch; outside of that, a high fence was made, and thus the prison-yard was formed. The ditch is still in existence, but of the fence nothing now remains except the posts. The grove near the factory shades but a small part of the enclosure; the open field I found covered with a rank, ill-smelling weed, which conceals the traces of the excavations made by the prisoners. Soon after the town was first occupied by the Federal troops these caves were all filled up by order of General Cooper, for it was feared that the sight of them, recalling the miseries of their fellow-soldiers, might lead the men to acts of violence. Just outside the fence may still be seen the outer orifice of a tunnel that was carried along many feet under the yard, beneath the ditch and the rebel sentry's beat, and by means of which more than a hundred of the men made their escape. It is impossible to estimate the length of the passage, its opening within the prison being now closed, but, whatever the distance, so accurately was it calculated by the diggers, that its outer mouth is not six inches from the fence line. It is hardly bigger than a man's body.

I have looked into a book, found in the town soon after it was first occupied, which contains a report made by the surgeon in charge of the prison during the months of January and February last. A certain part of the report, setting forth the whole number of the prisoners, and various facts in relation to them, I could not clearly understand, and from that part of it I do not venture to quote; but the figures given below are correct, I think, and suggestive. They are from a statement of the number of patients under medical treatment in January, 1865, of the diseases with which they were suffering, and of the number of deaths that occurred:

Disease	Cases	Deaths
Acute Diarrhœa	580	345
Scurvy	28	13
Intermittent Fever	89	62
Frost-bites	21	15

These diseases are only a few of those which are mentioned, and the footing up of the cases and the deaths, as given in the original report, shows that there were 1,342 men sick, and that of these

1,012 died. The book I speak of is in the hands of Colonel Pack-
ard, of the 120th Indiana Volunteers.

The grave-yard lies within eye-shot of the prison pen. Crossing a
field, in which cows were feeding, and a muddy little brook, and
climbing a rough fence, I was in the cemetery. The fence was
erected by Federal soldiers, and encloses about an acre of ground
on the hill-side, nearly bare, for there is only one oak tree among
the graves and perhaps a dozen of the stunted pines that spring up
in worn-out fields. There are a few separate graves with stakes at
the head and foot, and four or five are marked by rude
headboards, on which are inscribed the masonic compass and
square and the names of those interred beneath. But not more than
twenty bodies were so decently buried. The vast majority of those
who died were put into trenches, of which there are fourteen close
beside each other, seventy yards long and wide as the ordinary
length of a human body. In these it is computed that more than
five thousand corpses lie buried. The space seems narrow, but it is
said that, though often the burial was done so carelessly that the
limbs were not covered, yet no room was taken up by coffins,
which were never used, and in some places the bodies are laid one
above another to the number of four and five. The people of the
town dislike to speak of the prison or the cemetery, but I have
heard some dreadful stories of the manner of the interments. Disre-
garding these, however, surely there must be few acres of ground
more dismal than this, or fitter to arouse emotions of painful melancholy tinged with harsher feelings. The effect is aided by the desolate appearance of the spot—a weedy field, a rotting stake here
and there, long red mounds of clay, and a pine fence warping in
the sun.

There is an Assistant Superintendent of Freedmen in Salisbury,
whose office is, of course, thronged by complainants. The great
majority are people who have recently been turned away from
home by their former owners, who are, in most cases, compelled to
pay such persons a certain amount of money, or to give them
sufficient corn to feed them until February 1, 1866. During the

month of August applications for redress were, on an average, twenty-one each day. For the present month the average will be higher.

Having been permitted to look over the superintendent's books, I made this digest of all cases of alleged abuse of Negroes that have been reported during the first fortnight of September: Complaint is made

By colored man, John: that G. S. whipped his wife's sister because she left him, and forced her to go back and work for him. G. S. fined.

By colored man, Norris: that E. J. struck him with a brick, and threatened him with an axe.

By colored man, Anderson: that his master whipped him because he went off the plantation to see his cousin, and threatens to whip him again when he comes back from making his complaint.

By colored man, Dick: that J. W. whipped him severely, striking him seventy-two blows.

By colored woman, Martha: That J. F. Parker overtook her while on her way to the office of the Superintendent of Freedmen, put one end of a rope round her neck, tied the other round the neck of his mule, and so dragged her more than two miles. Showed marks of rope.

By colored man, Julius: That he had been sick of a fever two months, and had not yet recovered, when his master came to his cabin and beat him severely because he was not at work.

By colored woman, Louisa: That J. T. is whipping her children continually, and when she asked him not to do it, ordered her off his place and told her not to come back.

By colored man, Robert: That his sister works for a man named A. S., who ordered her to go out and make fence; that afterwards A. S. went out, and, getting angry, cut her head with a rail.

By colored man, Elias: That some citizens took his gun away from him and told him no nigger had a right to carry a gun.

By colored man, Levi: That W. F. L. has whipped him severely
with a buggy-trace. Shows his back all raw.

By colored man, Sandy: That Ch. and J. L. said he must leave the
plantation, or take a hundred lashes.

XII

CHARLOTTE, N. C., September 20, 1865

JUST before leaving Salisbury I attended a political meeting, at which two of the aspirants to a seat in the State Convention addressed their fellow-citizens. One had been a lieutenant-colonel in the Confederate army; the other during the war was known as a Unionist, and the Salisbury *Union Banner,* which supports his antagonist, even styles him "the radical candidate." His radicalism, however, goes no further, I believe, than to declare it right and expedient to admit the evidence of Negroes as witnesses in the courts of law. The meeting was held in the court-house, during the adjournment of a military commission, which on that day was trying a planter from one of the adjacent counties for the killing of a Negro. While a small audience of two hundred or more persons was assembling, I talked with an officer of the court, who gave me the particulars of the case so far as the testimony had then disclosed them. The planter, it seems, being away from home, the Negro, who was one of his laborers, packed up his clothes and other property, and, going to his mistress, made known his intention of leaving the plantation. Being asked to give his reasons, he said he was not so well treated as the rest of the hands, particularly that the food given his family was inferior to that received by his fellow-servants, and that he thought he could better his condition by seeking work elsewhere. These assertions the planter's wife denied; but the man persisted in them, and it is alleged that in contradicting the lady his language and manner became insolent, so that the planter, returning soon afterwards, found the women of his family indignant and in tears. He shot the man, wounding him fatally.

This is one of the four instances of Negro shooting which, in a previous letter, I mentioned as having occurred in the vicinity of Salisbury. Another is that of a young lady of Davie County, who, having shot and killed a colored woman for forcibly rescuing her child from her mistress, the young lady's mother, who was beating it, has recently been tried for murder. She was found guilty of manslaughter, and, in accordance with a provision of North Carolina statute law, was fined in the sum of one thousand dollars. While I was learning these facts one of the candidates began to speak, and, having delivered an address of half an hour in length, he was followed by his opponent. Each gentleman seemed to spend most of his strength in fiercely attacking the "record" of the other; and obviously the sympathies of the assembly were with the soldier, whose supporters are in a majority in the town, though it is admitted that his opponent will carry the election in the country precincts, and return the Unionist. Both of the candidates, however, professed to be sincere Unionists; both were opposed to armed intervention in Mexican affairs, and they united in pronouncing slavery dead. They were at variance only upon the question of repudiation. All the State debt incurred during the war the colonel would have paid as soon as possible, and in good money, while the doctor advocated the repudiation of all that portion of it incurred for the purpose of prosecuting a rebellious war.

I should say that the interest felt in the result of this election is not universally pervading, nor very intense, and that the vote will not be a heavy one. Today, at noon, stopping at a house about fourteen miles from Salisbury, I found that the farmer supposed the second day of October, at which time the convention assembles in Raleigh, to be the day appointed for choosing the delegates. He had voted to take North Carolina out of the Union, he said, merely because it was plainly impossible that she should remain neutral while South Carolina on the one side of her and Virginia on the other were carrying on hostilities. Still, aside from that, his preference had been for a Southern Confederacy; he was sorry that the

Union was to be restored, and as things stood now he should never again, he thought, take any part in politics. What this man said was confirmation of the statements of a gentleman in the town, an eager canvasser for the colonel above mentioned, who expressed his belief that his favorite candidate would be defeated because a large class of voters who ought to support him, displeased at the ruin of the Confederacy, and reluctant to take the oath of allegiance to the Union, would cast no ballots in this election. The same farmer thought that a nigger was constituted pretty much like a mule, and was most serviceable and best contented when he had plenty of feed, plenty of work, and a little licking. They were getting part of the crop for their labor, he said, in his neighborhood, but some of the farmers hired transient laborers for ten cents a day and a dram. He laughed as he told me that he had heard that, a little to the eastward, it was a common thing when the seines were dropped into the ponds for dead niggers to be fished out. I have seen no one else who had heard anything of such a story, and my informant said he did not believe it was true. It is true, however, that he laughed as he told it.

The nights have now grown cool, though, as yet, there have been no frosts, and the sun is still very hot for many hours of the day; but the leaves are beginning to change, and autumn is evidently here. The gathering of the sorghum has commenced, and I have seen few more pleasing phases of out-of-doors labor than that just now presented on these farms. In almost every house-yard the mill, often a rude one, with cylinders shaped by the axe and with cogs irregularly cut, is in slow motion, and its creaking can be heard a long way off. The horse as he jogs round brushes against huge piles of cane in the whole of his circuit. Women are boiling the syrup under a little shed near by. The crushed canes are mighty good, the Negroes say, to lay in the field furrows and prevent the wash. Much of the hilly land has lost almost all its soil by the action of the rain-water torrents, and the hard clay beneath is scantily covered by thin grass, or stands out bare and barren, refusing to support vegetable life. Still the farmers find it profitable to keep these abandoned fields enclosed. I see small flocks of sheep everywhere, and sometimes fifty or a hundred acres seem to be given up to a herd of half a dozen cattle. Since leaving Lynchburg, I have never got so far from houses as not to find pigs in the woods and by the roadside picking up persimmons, digging for roots, and eating the white oak mast which now begins to fall. The good land of this region is used mainly for the production of cotton, and I saw some small fields white with the opening bolls as I rode along; but the crop was in bad order, the plants often being less than two feet high, and the quantity raised this year will be quite insignificant. These counties were never overrun by either army, and there seems to be a good deal of old cotton still in the hands of the producers. It may be seen, sometimes as many as fifty bales, piled in barns or in open sheds, and I met wagons on the road loaded with it. In Concord, a little village, the capital of Cabarrus County, a factory was in operation where white goods are made and cotton yarn is spun to be sold unmanufactured.

Just before reaching Concord, where I passed the night, I met a middle-aged Negro plodding along, staff in hand, and apparently very footsore and tired. He had walked more than six hundred miles, he said, having set out from a plantation in Georgia, near the Alabama line, and had consumed almost two months in making the journey. He had been sold and sent South four years before, and, as soon as he learned he was free, determined to return to North Carolina and try to find his wife and children. "His own color," he said, "was friendly to him all the way." In Georgia Negroes were doing very well; but in South Carolina "a many doesn't dar to own they is got their liberty." He had no fears but that he would find work to do in Salisbury.

Riding out of Concord this morning I overtook a gentleman who was going out a few miles into the country to visit his plantation, and as long as our roads lay together we travelled in company. The conversation turned upon Negroes as laborers, and he declared that since their emancipation they were nearly useless, and the only hope of the Southern agriculturist was in getting white farm-hands. Most of his acquaintances, in making their plans for next season, had decided to do as much as possible themselves, and to employ only as many colored people as were absolutely indispensable. The worst class of all were the young people of both sexes, who made twice as much noise about their freedom as their fathers and mothers did; but none were good. In his opinion, the first duty to be performed by the Legislature, when North Carolina should be fortunate enough to get a legislature, would be to pass an apprenticeship act, to be applied to all persons of color under twenty-one years of age, who, so far as was practicable, ought to be bound out to their former masters. Enactments with reference to the older Negroes would also be necessary; they were unfit to make contracts or transact any business for themselves; some of them had got money within the last two or three months, and nine times in ten they laid it out in the most inconsiderate manner, spent it for some little notion or other. They had no ideas of economy, and were as destitute of foresight as a child. "Here's a case in point," he said. "A friend of mine owned twenty-five or thirty, who have all been working on for him in the same way in which they have always worked. But last week one old nigger came to him and said he wished to be hired. 'Very well, I'll hire you. How much do you want? Will ten dollars a month do?' The nigger thought it would. 'Then there's your wife; what's she worth?' They agreed that eight dollars a month would be enough for her. 'Well, there's Tom'—that was the oldest child—'I'm willing to give him his victuals and clothes.' Yes, that was fair. 'But you've got four too small to do anything; I can't keep them unless you'll give me something for doing it; I can't undertake to keep them for less than five dollars a month.' The nigger thought that was no more than right, and appeared to be in high glee over his bargain. 'But look here,' said my friend; 'you and your wife I'm to pay eighteen dollars a month, and you are to pay me twenty dollars a month for your four children. Now, where will you be at the end of the year?' The darkey began to consider the subject, and finally concluded that his best way was to go on as he had before."

"But," said I, "isn't five dollars a month a good deal to pay for the board and clothing of four children too small to do any work?"

I had seen boys of not more than thirteen or fourteen years old at the plough, and am told that it is not unusual for boys and even girls of that age to plough quite well.

"No," he answered; "their clothes don't cost much, to be sure; but a child will eat as much as a man—eat and waste."

The usual allowance of food to an adult on these plantations is a bushel of corn a month, and three pounds of bacon a week, though sometimes the ration of meat is omitted. Estimating the cost of these articles at a rate somewhat higher than what I believe to be the average price, the monthly expense of feeding an adult is not far from three dollars and a half. The average monthly cost of feeding children under twelve years of age may probably be two dollars and a half. Clothes, as this gentleman said, doubtless cost little: very many of the Negro boys whom I have seen in Virginia and in this State had on but a single garment, a coarse shirt, flowing nearly to the heels, and the girl's frock, though different in shape, was of similar material. It seems to me, therefore, that the expense of boarding and clothing children whose ages range from infancy to twelve years must be very much less than sixty dollars apiece per annum.

After answering some questions which the gentleman put to me in reference to the political sentiments of the North, I asked in turn if the State Convention would probably declare the evidence of Negroes admissible in courts of justice.

"The right to testify for and against each other in cases where no white man is concerned," he replied, "they have always had, and of course it will be continued to them; but I don't think the Southern people are prepared to admit nigger testimony against a white man. What would be the good of putting niggers in the witness-box? You must have niggers in the jury-box, too, or nigger evidence will not be believed. I don't think you could find twelve men in the whole State who would attach any weight to the testimony of ninety-nine niggers in a hundred."

He was willing that the colored population should be educated, but not without making a proviso which, he thought, would be displeasing to Northern radicals—that white and black children should be taught in separate schools. Nothing should be done that

looked towards the social equality of Negroes and whites. The only
result of that would be a horrible one—miscegenation and the
worst forms of immorality, and, eventually, the driving out of the
white race by a wretched population made up of half-castes and
mixed breeds. His opinions on these subjects are such as seem to
be generally prevalent in this part of the State. The publishers of
the *Carolina Times,* in their prospectus of a daily edition of that
journal, say:

> We trust to see fully inaugurated a generous and humane policy
> towards the freedmen, and all proper means used to educate them
> up to the point that will make them intelligent and useful free
> laborers—beyond *that* the law of nature forbids us to go. . . . To
> ameliorate their condition, and to make them useful and self-sup-
> porting, should be the care of the approaching Legislature. That
> much may be done by that body by the enactment of a compulsory
> code of enforced labor we do not doubt. Experience in the emanci-
> pated colonies proves that that is the only course to keep the
> Negro from dying out or relapsing into barbarism.

One is led to reflect on the propriety of allowing Negroes to
testify in courts by the not infrequent occurrence, even in a community generally well disposed towards the colored people, of scenes
like this. A Negro called Amaziah, formerly owned by a man residing near Charlotte, left the plantation some months ago, because
he found it impossible to live peaceably with his employer, a man
of a violent temper and addicted to drinking. There was no open
outbreak, however. It being desirable to despatch some mowing
speedily, and Amaziah being a very good hand, the gentleman sent
his overseer, and the Negro was induced to return and work for a
few days. One day last week Mr. W—— and his son came into
Charlotte, and both went home intoxicated. As they drove into the
yard the Negro was sharpening a scythe, for the day was wet and
field-work impossible. He was ordered to leave the place, and
come back when the sun shone. Not a damned free nigger should
stay there when he wasn't wanted. The man was on his way out of
the yard when he was attacked by Mr. W—— for moving too
slowly—for not running, the other Negroes say. He resisted, and

his antagonist, being hardly in a fit condition for making a good fight, was being overpowered, when the son, getting a gun from the house, came out to his father's assistance. The gun was snapped twice, but without effect, and then the Negro was beaten with it over the head till it was broken into three pieces. The elder W——— has since crossed the State line, and is for the present in South Carolina. The evidence of which I have given a digest was offered at the son's trial, or rather at a preliminary investigation of the case by the Superintendent of Freedmen.

I see that two schools for colored children are in operation at this point, which are attended by about one hundred and twenty-five pupils. In both of them the teachers are Negroes, but I am informed that larger schools will be opened as soon as buildings can be had, and white teachers are to be sent from Philadelphia by the Society of Friends.

XIII

CONCORD, N. C., September 22, 1865

HAVING determined to ride across from Charlotte to Raleigh by the country roads, it became necessary to retrace my steps for twenty miles, and pass again through Concord. An hour before I reached the village it was dark, and most of the houses were closed; but the stillness of the night, as I turned into the main street, was broken by sounds of loud singing that proceeded from the county jail. The words were those of a hymn, and the singers were evidently Negroes. Going on to the hotel, I found two or three Federal soldiers in the office, who were regarded with no very friendly eyes by some citizen loungers, and I at once surmised that election day in Cabarrus County had not passed in perfect quiet. "Any disturbance here on Thursday, sir?" I asked the landlord. "No," he replied; "seen as much fifty times before. Always some whiskey out election times." In the dining room, eating a late supper, was a citizen of the town whose acquaintance I had made when here before, and of him I made the same enquiry. He said there hadn't been no great trouble; not as he knew; some o' the black ones made a difficulty, but nobody was hurt. There warn't nothin' like what they'd hed in Charlotte, and up here in Salisbury. Forenoon, election day, they run all the black ones out o' Salisbury. He'd heerd the Yankees jined in, and they made a reg'lar cleanin'. I told him he must be mistaken so far as concerned Charlotte, that the election had been conducted very peaceably; and a soldier who had entered the room remarked that he had come from Salisbury on the evening of Thursday, and that no riot had occurred up to the time of his departure. This contradiction was not very well received, and I afterwards heard him repeating his story of riots in other counties to listeners who appeared not ill pleased at the information.

"How did the trouble begin, sir?"

"The commencement of it? I don't know much about it anyhow; I didn't see it all myself, but I've been told that the black ones was crowdin' down round the well, and a young man here in town told 'em to leave that and they wouldn't go, so he threw some water on one fellow, and that was what commenced it. The niggers was stubborn and sassy; come up, some of 'em, with sticks; looked like they was ready prepared."

"Was there any shooting?"

"There was one man by the name o' Smith, he's a Yankee too, I see him shoot once; yes, I believe he shot off two barrels, in the squar', but his pistol warn't loaded with ball, nothin' in it but blank cartridge. I see the sheriff start for him, and I run along too, so's if the sheriff wanted any assistance, but before I got out thar whar he war at, I see as many as eight or ten or a dozen o' the niggers comin' over with rocks and sticks. I turned round to them, and told 'em to drap the rocks. They didn't do it, though they stood, so I drawed my pistol and told 'em agin, 'Boys, drap them rocks,' I said, 'or I'll blow out your damn brains, some o' you'; and then they put 'em down. Well, a crowd came up by that time, and the niggers was run out o' town, and made a scatterment. That's all the shootin' I see."

"I suppose the Negroes carried the news to Charlotte?" "No, up to Salisbury. They went up that same evenin', and I heerd they told the Yankees that we'd killed two niggers and wounded seven, and the fight was still going on when they left. But both of 'em's known, and if they told any such story as I heerd say they told, they'd better look out. That's the great trouble with the niggers, they tell too many lies to the Yankees, and the Yankees believe 'em. Let a nigger tell a lie on me; tell lies, and get me up before the Yankees. First nigger does it, I allow to shoot him. Yes, I do; I'd hate to git into trouble on account of a nigger, nor I don't want to make no trouble with 'em nuther, no more'n with a white man, but they mustn't lie on me. Their freedom's made 'em so sassy there's no livin' with 'em. I heerd that some of 'em's been sayin' the niggers'll rule the day here within two months' time. I just want one to say that to me. The niggers that talk like that'll git killed certain; the people won't stan' that kind o' talk."

A little Negro boy, a servant in the house, gives quite another account of the riot. He says that Mr. Worden, an agent of the Freedmen's Bureau, was expected to address the colored people at Concord on Thursday, and that a great many had come in to hear him, but that always on election day it has been customary for the Negroes to have a holiday, and to watch the voting. He seems to have been too much frightened to observe the events of the riot with accuracy, and was inclined to "allow that all the black ones the sheriff put into the jail would ha' been done hung if the Yankees hadn't come down." He is quite positive that the white men began the fray, and that the knocking down of an old Negro was the signal for a general assault by about thirty men on all the Negroes present. He speaks of one Negro whose arm was broken by a pistol bullet, and of several who were badly beaten.

GOLD HILL, N.C., September 23, 1865

This morning I found the provost-marshal of the district in Concord collecting evidence relating to the riots, and preparing to make arrests. Captain Littler was aided in his investigations by Captain Freeman, of the 128th Indiana Volunteers, who had been for some years a detective officer in his native State—and I was amused to observe the zest with which he resumed the pursuits of his old profession; his keen enjoyment of the chase being tempered only by some natural regrets that he could not work up the thing in a citizen's dress, but was obliged to show himself in uniform. From these gentlemen I learned that the news of the fight, if it can be so called, was first taken to Salisbury by one of the county officers, who, several days previously, had been charged with the duty of laying before the military commander a petition of the magistrates

of Cabarrus that a Federal garrison should be permanently maintained in the county. The provost-marshal had already obtained
sufficient evidence to justify the arrest of some seven or eight citizens, and while I was with him he listened to the complaints of
several men who desired the arrest of two or three other parties.
Of one of these latter cases I took notes.

A young man, with one hand bandaged, came into the office,
and said that if the captain was examining into the difficulty on
election day, he had a charge to prefer against some niggers. He
was requested to tell who they were, and gave the names of two,
but that of another he did not know. "We got him into the jail,
though," said he; "and he's in thar now, I expect; and that's the
one I'm most anxious about, for he's the very man that hurt my
thumb; and he's the same man that demanded me to give up my
pistol."

"Demanded your pistol, did he? What, to fight with? Let us hear
the whole story."

"Yes, sir; I reckon he thought he'd get it, and then he'd make
use of it. You see, I wasn't out much that day. There was niggers
everywhere, blockin' up all the stores, so a man couldn't go in to
buy anything, and fillin' the street up and down till the difficulty
began. I reckon it was about four o'clock in the evenin', I was
standin' in the squar', front o' the court-house, you know, and a
man came up to me and says, 'Yonder goes a nigger, down by the
depot, with rocks in his pocket; le's go down and lick him.' "

"What was that man's name?"

"Well, he's a man I don't know. I know him by sight, but I
don't know as I ever spoke to the man till that day; but since then
I've heerd 'em say his name is Fur. Fur says, 'Yonder's a nigger,
and he's got a pocket full of rocks; le's go and take 'em away from
him, and lick him.' 'All right,' I said; 'I'm going down that way;
come on.' We walked on to the depot. Sometimes we could see
him, and then agin, when he went over a hill, we'd lose sight; and
it so happened we never did git to see him after he went over the
next hill beyond the depot. But right thar, side o' the road, was
these three niggers—Adam, and his son, and this nigger that's in

jail. 'Boys,' says I, 'what you doin' here?'—spoke just in that manner. This nigger he made answer that they wouldn't let 'em stay in town, and they'd run 'em out to that place. 'But never mind,' says he, 'the niggers'll rule the day here yet, and you'll see it in less'n two months.' P'raps he mout ha' said twelve months, but I think it was two months he said. 'You d——n black son, etc.,' says I, 'what d'ye mean by that?' I expect he thought I was goin' to draw my pistol. I hed my hand in my pocket, but I didn't have my pistol in that pocket at all. The niggers began to pick rocks, and I believe Fur said, 'Shoot the black son, etc.' Fur was ahead o' me, and he didn't have any pistol. Then this nigger he says, 'Don't you draw a pistol on me; don't you draw a pistol. Give up that pistol,' demanding me to give up the pistol to him. The other niggers had begun to pitch for Fur, and he came back to me, and then the rocks flew pretty thick."

"Had Fur been throwing any rocks?"

"Well, Fur mout ha' throwed; expect Fur did throw some, but I couldn't see all was done, for this nigger kept demandin' me to give up the pistol, and I was lookin' towards him. I snapped at him twice, but the pistol missed fire, and about that time they'd run in on us with sticks, and this nigger hit me and knocked my thumb out o' place. Well, we had to retreat, and I reckon we fell back all o' thirty paces, and the niggers stood. I got my thumb back agin, and Fur and me went on towards 'em agin, and then the niggers fell back p'raps twenty steps. I don't think it *was* twenty steps. We was goin' to arrest 'em, you see. But they commenced to throw rocks agin, and then I fired. I think I fired twice, but I missed him. I fired at this same nigger. By this time, some o' them up in the squar' see we was in a contention, and five or six went round a-horseback, and come in the rear o' the niggers, and then we arrested 'em."

"You arrested them, and handed them over to the sheriff?"

"Yes, sir. That is, we put 'em into the jail. I was in favor o' putting 'em thar. Some wanted to hang 'em. I might ha' killed that nigger very easy, but I'm a peaceable man. Some of 'em wanted to know why I didn't shoot 'em, but I said, 'No, put 'em in jail'; and when I heerd you'd come to look into it, I thought I'd come and make a complaint."

Captain Littler appeared to think this man's course had not been so peaceable as it might have been, and, after hearing his complaint, ordered him to be taken into custody. Incidentally, his examination showed that the riot began at about eleven o'clock in the morning, and continued, with intermissions, till three o'clock in the afternoon. Several Negroes were beaten severely, and for no better reason, so far as I could learn, than that they were "too sassy and stubborn," and, when the attack was made upon them, waited to be run out of the town, and in some cases even offered resistance, instead of running out of their own accord. Captain Freeman afterwards informed me that the man who came so unsuspectingly to make the accusation had, before leaving the square, pre-arranged the rear attack of the mounted men whom he described as having so opportunely come to his assistance. This, I dare say, he himself would have admitted; he seemed to have no notion that any of his efforts to repress Negro impudence had been marked by irregularity, and repeatedly expressed very great astonishment that "this nigger demanded me to give up my pistol."

I came to this village today, after seventeen miles' riding over the worst of rocky winding roads. "You see when they laid it out," said the landlord, "they didn't want to offend anybody by driving it right through his land, so they carried it round every farm between here and Concord." The village is the most poverty-stricken place in appearance that I have yet seen, with small, poor, unpainted houses, immense piles of slates, disused machinery under weather-beaten sheds, and shafts and mines filled with water, but the inhabitants, destitute of mails and news, give a ready welcome to the traveller, and he fares better than in better towns. They are now awaiting, I had almost said impatiently, but the ideas of Gold Hill and eagerness seem incongruous, the arrival of the president of the mining company from the North, whither he escaped after war had broken out, and who is expected on his return to recover the property from the possession of the Southern stockholders and recommence operations. The people profess to be Unionists, and I was told that many of them were perfectly satisfied with the results of the war, or would be so "when the Government hung Jeff., and made all the niggers settle in South Carolina. The name of South Carolina ought to be taken away, and it ought not to be called a State any more."

RANDOLPH CO., N. C., September 24, 1865

Today I have again been travelling through a country always poor and dry, and now drier than usual in consequence of the long drought, which has seriously affected all the crops, and lowered the streams so much that many of the mills have ceased running. I have seen but a few houses, and only those of small farmers, and it was with difficulty that I found a lodging for the night. The farmer with whom I am staying says the people have so little to eat that they are ashamed to take in a stranger. He is a man of about fifty years of age, of average intelligence, and, like a majority of his neighbors, of his own free will would never have been a rebel, having no cause of complaint against the national Government or the Northern people, and, latterly, having learned to dislike the Confederate authorities for their exactions. He had owned five Negroes, a woman with her four children, and expressed his acquiescence in their emancipation. The mother was anxious to stay with him, but he could afford to give her no wages, as the children were all small, and he wished to know if he was violating any law by taking her work for the family's board and clothing. I re-assured him upon this point, and he stated another perplexity under which he was laboring: a Negro man, with a wife and several children, had left his employer because he could get no wages, no clothes, and not enough to eat, and had come to him begging with tears that he might be permitted to work on the farm. At first he had refused, for he had no money and only a little meat; but the man pleaded so hard, and it seemed so likely that the family would suffer, that he finally gave the desired permission. Since then he had been told several times that he was liable to be prosecuted for harboring another person's runaway servants, and would get into trouble if he persisted in keeping the family. His wife was frightened somewhat; he himself reckoned the black ones were free to go and come where they chose, but he would like me to give my opinion. I was able to quote some decisions of the neighboring Superintendents of Freedmen which covered this case also. He went on to say that many people of his acquaintance thought that the black ones would be re-enslaved, that they were not at present, and probably might never be, legally free. He had been compelled to serve in the home guard last winter, he said, and had been on duty at Salisbury; so, after supper, he lit a pipe and his wife another, and we sat before a light-wood fire talking of the prison. The woman said her brother had been captured by the Yankees, and they treated him fine. She would have been glad to have fed her family on bread and water if them rebels would have let her carry what provisions she could spare to the poor prisoners. Certain sure they were dreadfully worsted, and a heap of people round Salisbury were grieved to see it, but they could do nothing to help them. If one of the guards threw in a piece of tobacco, and they caught him, he was tied up. The farmer's duty had compelled his attendance at the grave-yard on one or two occasions, and the recollection of what he saw there seemed to affect him much. His voice lowered as he told of the earth's being thrown in upon the naked bodies, and of one man thus buried whose face was still wet with the tears he had shed when dying. "I don't say it to flatter you, mister, because you're a Yankee, for I've often said it to my wife before the surrender, and she'll say so; but you wouldn't handle a mutton so careless as them poor men was handled in the carts and them ar trenches."

Not long after crossing the Yadkin, I fell in with an old man who almost insisted on my stopping to talk with him when he learned that I was from the North. He warn't a high larnt fellow, he said, none of 'em *was* round thar, but he was good Union, and it made him mighty glad to come across a man from the Northern States. "And you can't git hurt, stranger," he said, "not in this country, nor no other man that's of a good Union principle. No you can't, stranger. I can tell you what we's done with them ar secessioners that brought this thing on, and they a'n't a-goin to git the upper hands agin. One on 'em couldn't git to oversee that ar dirt road you's stan'in' on, not by vote, not in this county. Expect the road was mighty bad like, warn't it? We ha'n't worked 'em for a good while, but we's goin' to turn to arter the corn's got in, and I'm thinkin' I'll oversee it myself. We ha'n't no use for secessioners, not for nothin', and they begin to know it. Thar was one on 'em found that out this last week up yer at Jackson's Hill, for he was nigh about killed, and they would ha' killed him or beat him to death if he hadn't got on to his mule and they was a-foot. Ye see in the war he was allus a mighty hunter for outlayers and sich, gittin' em into the army, and when he come to the 'lection one o' the boys, a namesake o' mine, see him, and says to him, 'R——, be ye done huntin' deserters?' I don't know what answer he made, but L—— knocked him flat on his face. Then he got up and run, and the boys tuck arter him; but he ran past his mule, and as he run he got a holt o' the bridle and broke it, and made off as fast as ever he could. Oh, them ar hunters has got to keep quiet; they can't bear the sway like they did. I told that same R—— how it would be. He was one of a parcel that was goin' to hang me one day about two years ago. Ye see, mister, I'm a man I allus let my principle be known, and one day I come by the mill, and thar was R—— and his crowd, five or six on 'em, and they'd been drinkin'. R—— he run into the mill and got a rope, and they tied it round my neck: they was for hangin' me right away. Says I, 'R——, ye mout as well make sure work o' this, for 'less ye do ye'll pay fur it. Ye know me, William L——, and I tell ye ye'll pay fur this some day if I git out o' your hands alive.' "

He asked many questions about the national debt, about Northern schools and railroads, about the wages of "hirelin's," the size of farms, the methods of cultivating corn and wheat, and especially about the feelings of the Northern people towards the rebellious States.

"I've heerd ye all reverence General Lee to be a great man. Ye do, don't ye?"

I gave him the popular estimate of Lee's abilities.

"Yes, I've heerd so; the Yankee soldiers with the wagon-train told me so. I tell our boys jest to look at that. 'Thar's the Yankees,' I tell 'em, 'has give us a most etarnal lickin' as ever a parcel o' people did git, I reckon, and see how they hev compassion. Why, if our nasty secession heads had licked your people like they bragged, they'd ha' been crowin',' I tell 'em, 'wuss'n ever roosters. Yes,' I tell 'em, 'the Yankees is a marciful people, and willin' to make friendship with us.' "

PITTSBORO, N. C., September 26, 1865

Yesterday and today I have ridden sixty miles over roads as bad and a country as lean and poor as those I found on Saturday and Sunday. The people in this county of Chatham are richer than their neighbors in Randolph, and there are more secessionists among them; but every man with whom I have talked in the course of the two days until I met my host of this evening, has avowed himself a Unionist; and both counties have sent up anti-secession delegates to the State Convention. My landlord says, however, that the result of this election is not a good criterion of the sentiment of the people; that the solid men of the State have not voted, and the convention will be the weakest body that ever assembled in North Carolina. The two classes seem to entertain and cherish feelings of bitter hostility towards each other, and I everywhere hear stories of assaults made upon persons who were formerly in the service of the Confederate government, and especially upon such as were engaged in picking up deserters. Quite generally these men discreetly absent themselves from election gatherings and other assemblages, and in many instances where they have appeared as voters or as candidates have been forced to fly for their lives. Since leaving Salisbury, I believe I have been in no county where such disturbances were not spoken of as having recently occurred, and offences against property are perhaps more numerous. My landlord tells me that his mother has been obliged to leave her home in Randolph County by a mob who threatened to destroy the house if she stayed in it; and he mentioned several houses, which he said I must have seen as I passed along the road, which are standing empty for similar reasons. I readily believed him, for a man in Ashboro, who was a county magistrate and also an officer of the police, told me that he could count more than a hundred houses owned by secessionists which had been broken into and robbed within the past few months. "Them outlayin' boys had learned a little bushwhackin'," he said, "when the secessioners learn'd 'em to live in the woods." The anti-secession men seem to be having everything their own way at present, in this part of the State at any rate. "Wait two years," my landlord says, "and then you'll see." He openly says, "We've got to get back into the Union, and we'll have to do many things repugnant to our feelings, but we must first of all get back and get our own State into our own hands."

This afternoon I had an amusing interview with a woman whom I found gathering sticks and rotten wood by the roadside. A little girl was with her, and both seemed the poorest of whites, dirty and wretched to the last degree, but yet not so sunk in sulkiness and apathy as most of their class, for the woman talked almost incessantly and laughed a great deal. I asked my way to Pittsboro, and, looking hard at me all the time, she gave me some bewildering directions about the roads to be crossed and the forks to be left on the right hand and the left, and at the end she said:

"Mister, whar be ye frum?"

"I'm from the North."

"The North!" she said, dropping the armful of sticks and coming nearer to me. "Be you a—one o' them—what they call Yankees? Don't be offended, gentleman, that's what they calls 'em; be you a Yankee?"

"I suppose I must be."

"Excuse me, gentleman, but I must look at you, fur I heerd so much about the Yankees and I niver seed one yit. Lord! Lord! A ra'al Yankee! Maria, he looks most like our folks, don't he? He sartin do. Lord, and him to be one on 'em! Well, I must praise the Yankees if they looks like you. Maria, don't they look right nice?"

This compliment she soon afterwards completely spoiled. She went on:

"I see you come ridin' along, and I says to my gal Maria, yer's your cousin comin', I do believe. Don't he look like John, Maria? Indeed you do, gentleman, you're built like him and you're like him in the face. John, he's my sister Bet's son. I wish Bet could see you, and daddy, he'd be proud to see you."

She urged me to ride down a mile from the road and visit her daddy, who was eighty-two years old, and would be very much pleased to see a Yankee, but I was obliged to refuse, for I had still more than twelve miles to ride before reaching Pittsboro, and the afternoon was wearing away. She didn't know what would become of her and her children, now the black ones was free. She said: "We poor folks was about ekil to the niggers, about bein' hard put to it to live, I mean, and now they's free they don't do nothin' but steal, and how we'll live I don't know. They say it's the Yankees rules everything now, and I wish you'd tell me how poor folks is to live among these niggers. I never was married, and daddy's eighty-two years old, and me and my children's afraid to go out when we hear 'em in the corn-field." It would have been useless, I suppose, to counsel her to cleanliness or industry or decency of manners and morals, and I had to decline the difficult post of her adviser.

RALEIGH, N. C., October 5, 1865

I REACHED this city on the evening of the 27th of September, at an hour somewhat later than I had expected, having been detained in the morning at Pittsboro by an incident that I have learned to look upon as a common occurrence. My landlord was obliged to despatch servants through all the neighborhood to get a note changed, but their endeavors, whether honest or otherwise, were not successful, and after being kept from the road for more than an hour it became necessary to depart and leave with him five dollars in payment for one night's stay. The ordinary charge was two dollars in silver, he said; in greenbacks he'd have to charge four dollars. Throughout the country districts there is yet a decided distrust of paper money—a distrust quite natural, founded as it is upon all that the people know of Confederate notes and bonds, and upon their ignorance in respect to the national currency. In Davidson, Randolph, and Chatham counties I found among the farmers some who had heard of greenbacks before I tendered them, but had never seen any and hardly liked to receive them; they'd been told the Government would call in all that kind of money in a year or two and repudiate; understood the traders didn't 'low 'twas worth dollar for dollar: they'd need some money, though, to pay taxes with, and Government money'd ought to be good for that, they reckoned, for the present anyhow.

Not knowing how far confiscation measures may be pushed, they are not a little anxious to have on hand money with which to pay whatever tax-bills may be presented. Some one of the many pamphlets setting forth the country's ability to bear the burden of the national debt would be profitable reading for these North Carolinians, and I think would be willingly read. If not more necessary, the circulation of such a work would be much more easy than that of any tract purely political.

Raleigh is a less considerable city than I had supposed, and the business part of it is neither large nor handsome; but its broad avenues, abundant trees, gentle declivities, and rather elegant private residences, make it the prettiest Southern town, and with the most external evidences of taste and refinement, that I have yet seen. Its name of the City of Oaks must have been given it, I should say, by someone approaching it from the pine lands to the southward, for the number of those trees is not remarkable. The first days of October here are very enjoyable, being hazy and cool without frosts, and the moonlit nights are even finer than the days. But the air is heavy and motionless and cannot expand the chest; it brings with it a faint suggestion of decaying vegetation, and one begins to think of Carolinian slow fevers and agues.

I have been attending some sittings of the colored men's convention recently held in this city. The first steps in the matter were taken by Negroes resident in Newbern, and it seems to have been generally thought by the people of the central and western counties, by such of them as took any thought at all about it, that the call was issued prematurely. They would have had it deferred until after the adjournment of the State Convention, thinking it more proper to address the Legislature in the event of the convention's leaving the colored population unnoticed. An appeal to the convention would wear the appearance of addressing itself not alone to the kindly feelings and the sense of justice of their white fellow-citizens, but partly to their fears also, and thus would provoke resentment. Moreover, the petitioners would put themselves in an attitude of complaint, when as yet they had suffered no injustice by any State action. But, on the other side, it was argued that in this State the Negroes were surely suffering enough at the hands of individuals to justify them in petitioning; that in other States their brethren were suffering under unjust enactments, both ancient and recent; that in the North Carolina statutes there were evils to be cured, and there were other evils to be prevented from getting there; and, finally, with regard to the body before which the Negroes' petition should be laid, that North Carolina would be more likely to slight the claims of her colored citizens after she had obtained full power to legislate for them as she pleased than now, while it is still doubtful if justice towards them may not be the lowest price at which she can purchase the enjoyment of all privileges belonging to a State in the Union. So it was decided to adhere to the original call, which was sent as far as possible throughout the country districts, and on the day of assembling nearly forty counties were represented. Some of the delegates were duly elected by meetings regularly organized for that purpose; others were sent up from churches, from prayer-meetings, from neighborhood conferences where a few men met together in secret. Of course, many were unprovided with credentials, their constituents, very probably, like themselves, being unable to read or write, and but little versed in the business of politics. "They'd hed no time fur credentials," one said; "they'd hed to run off in the night season fur fear"; so it was voted that the convention should be a mass convention, and all should be entitled to seats who had come up to attend. This motion, for which everybody voted, did much to take everything out of the hands of those who originated the convention, but, perhaps, made its action more truly represent the opinions and feelings of the colored people, not of the coast counties and the eastern cities, but of the whole State. For at this present time the Negroes in central and western North Carolina have given but little thought to political subjects, and take no great interest in them. In Wilmington, Newbern, and Beaufort, judging by their representations at the convention, the case is different.

The session was held in the African Methodist church, a small edifice in a back street of the city. The delegates were about a hundred and twenty in number, but crowds of colored citizens were interested spectators throughout the four days, and the house was always filled full. It was neatly but cheaply furnished, the only ornament being a large plaster bust of Lincoln, fixed to the wall above the pulpit, against a background of mourning drapery. Just over his head were inscribed some of the closing words of the last inaugural address—that passage which begins thus: "With malice towards none, with charity for all, with firmness in the right."

Among the delegates were some that wore the Federal uniform, and these were treated with much respect by their fellow-members. In pursuance of a fashion that seems to obtain everywhere, one of them, a sergeant, was chosen to office, and served among the vice-presidents. He, like the others, was a fine-looking young fellow, perfectly neat and clean, with every button polished, and even his face shining. "I's black," he said; "jist as black as ary black man goin', I is."

There were several men dressed in black broadcloth, ministers and chaplains, who did a large share of the talking, and bore a main part in the management of the business, and here and there was a younger man, nattily dressed, and evidently a hotel waiter by profession or a barber; but the great majority were mechanics and plantation hands, men who had grown up in ignorance, whose forms were bent with long labor, whose faces expressed patient endurance rather than thought or any passion, and who for the most part sat mute on the benches. On two or three occasions some one of these men would rise to deprecate long discussion of things merely formal, or debate that was only personal, beginning his speech perhaps in this way: "My dear brothers, I don't place myself in this honorable convention as a Henry Clay or a Webster, fur I know I kin not do it, nor to speak afore you. I know I's a poor, destituted, onlarnt don't-know-A-from-B. I's been rocked in a hard cradle, from my youth up to the present age." And then he would go on to urge the propriety of at once transacting all necessary business, so that delegates could go home, and, warming as he proceeded, he would very likely fall into the sing-song of the class-meeting, and become nearly unintelligible to those whose excitement had not kept pace with his. At the end of his remarks, however, there was always renewed diligence. But these men though ignorant were intelligent, and often spoke exceedingly well. "Yes," said one of the cleverest among them—"yes, we are ignorant. We know it. I am ignorant for one, and they say all niggers is. They say we don't know what the word constitution means. But if we don't know enough to know what the Constitution is, we know enough to know what justice is. I can see for myself down at my own court-house. If they makes a white man pay five dollars for doing something today, and makes a nigger pay ten dollars for doing that thing tomorrow, don't I know that ain't justice? They've got a figure of a woman with a sword hung up thar, sir; Mr. President, I don't know what you call it—('Justice,' 'Justice') —well, she's got a handkercher over her eyes, and the sword is in one hand and a pair o' scales in the other. When a white man and a nigger gets into the scales, don't I know the nigger is always mighty light? Don't we all see it? Ain't it so at your court-house, Mr. President?"

There were three delegates who took very prominent positions in the convention, and who may be called leaders. One was a mulatto, born within the State, but who had received a collegiate education in the North. He was a person of some ability, but it was to his education that he owed his influence. He made many fluent speeches, and was chairman of the business committee, which reported a great many resolutions. A much abler man, one who would be considered a man of more than common ability in any community, was chairman of the committee which reported an address to the State Convention. He, I believe, is of unmixed African blood and a North Carolinian by birth. He, too, spoke often, and always with ease and force. Never attempting the passionate style of oratory which was the kind by far most frequently employed by his fellow-members, but confining himself to straightforward, sensible speaking, he pushed business forward, instructed the ignorant, attained the ends at which he aimed, and, I dare say, won the respect of every man, white or black, in the convention. But perhaps the most remarkable person among the delegates was the last of the three, a light-yellow man whose features seemed to indicate that there was a cross of Indian blood in his veins. His hair was long and black but very curly, and he appeared to be vain of its beauty as he tossed it carelessly off his forehead, or suffered

it to fall heavily and half conceal his eyes. These were twinkling
and slippery, and nearly always half shut, for he laughed much,
and then they partly closed of themselves, and at other times he
had a way of watching from under his dropped lids. He was a well-
shaped man, but it was hardly to be discovered as he lolled in his
seat, or from the insufferably lazy manner of his walking. When he
spoke, however, he stood erect, using forcible and graceful ges-
tures. His voice was powerful, and, though an illiterate man, his
speaking was effective. But sometimes his most impassioned ha-
rangues, made for the purpose of fomenting sectional jealousies between the east and west, or to embarrass the chair, or to defeat
some resolution offered by an opponent, or for the mere pleasure
of contradiction, were brought to an untimely end by his inability
to refrain from laughing. He was really in earnest about nothing,
but his power of sarcasm and brutal invective, and the personal
influence given him by his fearlessness and audacity, always secured him a hearing. It seemed to be his keen sense of the ridicu-
lous only which prevented him from playing the part of demagogue with success. He had artfully spread dissension among the
delegates by declaring it disgraceful to North Carolinians that a
man from the North should have been made president of the convention. That officer, hearing of the murmurs, had tendered his
resignation, accompanying the offer with a speech so judicious that
the convention compelled him to retake his office. A delegate had
declared that such whisperings were born in hell and should return
to their place of birth; they embodied prejudices which, at the
present time, in a restored and liberated country, had no place;
they belonged among the bloody relics of the past. "I come forward, Mr. President," said the man I have been describing, "I
come forward as not bein' one o' the whisperin' class that the
gentleman has referred to. Our young Demosthenes, sir, is very
polite, and shows his good breedin' to this honorable body with his
invitations to his father's house. But who does he suppose is goin'
to accept of 'em when he is not at home? He can talk about the
bloody relics of the past, sir; but as for me, I didn't come here, and

no other man of this convention didn't come here, sir, to have the whip of slavery cracked over us by no slaveholder's son." His opponent was a rather light mulatto. But the brutality of this attack is hardly so great as it seems, the standards for measuring the degree of such insults being different at the South and at the North. The speaker on another occasion announced himself as one well fitted to be a mediator between the black and white races, partaking as he did of the blood of each in equal parts, and being free from the illiberal prejudices of both. It is told of him that, once making a speech in his native town, he said this, among other things: "It'll never do to give these niggers the ballot, they say; if they was to get it that d——d ——— would be mayor. As if I wanted that office, gentleman! I'm goin' to Congress."

But the moderate men among the Negroes, those who thought it best to petition and not to demand, and to petition only for equality before the law and not for admission to all the political rights of citizenship, easily obtained control of the convention. Everything that they thought could justly offend any class of their fellow-citizens at the South or North was carefully rejected. A resolution was offered which declared that if a Negro knew as much when sober as an Irishman knew when drunk, he knew enough to vote on good American principles. This was thrown aside without a dissenting voice. Another one, framed with the praiseworthy intention of encouraging colored youth to educate themselves, and pronouncing it the duty of colored people to employ, whenever practicable, properly prepared pastors and instructors of their own race, became the subject of an animated debate. "I come here to stick fast to my friends," said a delegate; "the white people that done teach my little gals to read, and I'd ha' voted to bite off a snake's head before I'd ha' voted for that ar." The resolution was laid on the table, and a substitute was passed which thanks the Northern aid societies and Northern teachers who have done so much to encourage and elevate the Negro race. The address which has been laid before the State Convention is conceived in a similar spirit and breathes nothing but moderation and conciliation. The Raleigh newspapers praise its ability, and consider it a wonderfully conservative document, undisfigured by the marks of levelling radicalism. Yet it contains these sentences:

> We desire education for our children, that they may be made useful in all the relations of life. We most earnestly desire to have the disabilities under which we formerly labored removed, and to have all the oppressive laws which make unjust discriminations on account of race or color wiped from the statutes of the State.

RALEIGH, N. C., October 16, 1865

THE North Carolina State Convention met at Raleigh, in the hall of the House of Commons, on the morning of Monday, the second of October, and, with praiseworthy despatch, in the course of six days performed all the work which they considered of paramount importance—annulled the secession ordinance of May 20, 1861, and, by a unanimous vote, passed an ordinance forever prohibiting slavery within the State.

During the first two days nothing of interest took place, and there was little for the visitor to do but look about him. Like every other public structure—road, railroad, court-house, bridge, church —that I have seen in the South, the appearance of the capitol showed that for some years only necessary things have been done. Its paint is stained and dingy, the gilding is tarnished, and there is need of new furniture. The Commons Hall is a large square room with a semi-circular gallery on three sides, and a lofty dome-shaped ceiling, from which a chandelier depends. The seats of the members are disposed in the shape of a fan before the Speaker's chair, and the space behind them, beneath the gallery, at the sides and corners of the room, is called the lobby.

Against the wall on the right of the Speaker's chair hangs a full-length portrait of Washington, the only ornament of the hall. There is also a bronze statue of Washington in the capitol yard, the pedestal of which bears the initial letters G. W., A. L., and the inscription, "The saviours of their country." The festoons of mourning drapery are slipping from their fastenings, and some of the black cloth lies upon the ground.

The convention was a more imposing body than I had been expecting to see; for I had been assured by many gentlemen in the western counties that the members elect were all, as a matter of course, Union men; that most of them were, therefore, persons of little property and of no social standing; that the better class of people throughout the State had refrained from voting, and that, in point of ability, the convention would be the weakest ever assembled in North Carolina. A majority of the members wore the appearance of elderly farmers neither very wealthy nor very well educated. One delegate, for instance, said in private conversation: "What do you mean by pro-slavery and anti-slavery? I've always heard those two words, but I was always afraid to make use of 'em, for I didn't feel sure I should get 'em right." Many of them, I dare say, are unintelligent as well as uneducated; narrow-minded men, without the habit of thinking and dominated by illiberal prejudices. One of them said to me the other evening:

"The niggers are having a convention, a'n't they? What do they want? Equal rights, I suppose. How do they talk, anyhow? Going to vote, be they?"

"They don't say much about voting. Their address is very moderate in its tone, but they ask for the right to testify in the courts. What do you think the convention will do in reference to that; grant it?"

"No, sir; they won't get that. It wouldn't do at all. No, sir."

"They say they must work for you, and make contracts with you, in order to live, and that nothing will be more frequent than disputes about work and wages."

"If I make a contract with a nigger, I want it to bind me just as much as him and him just as much as me. I don't want anything but justice, and the contract ought to be fair for the nigger and fair for me, and I'd live up to my agreement."

"But I suppose you know some men in your own neighborhood that won't live up to their contracts unless you go to law and make them—men that will only be just when justice is extorted from them."

Yes, he said, he knew men like that, and he proceeded to give me some instances, to which I listened, and then asked him what a Negro could do in such a case as that he had detailed.

"I don't know," he replied; "don't know. That was a bad case."

"Why, you'll have to let the Negro give testimony, and so, as far as that will enable him, protect himself against such rascality and violence as you describe."

"Oh no," he repeated; "oh no; that won't do. The people won't have niggers giving evidence. They'll never get that. The people won't have it"; and these remarks served him as an answer to all my arguments. But a good majority of the delegates seemed superior to the men of this stamp, and at least would have been able to find some reasons of some sort with which to fortify themselves in their prejudices. The spectator of its deliberations could not but conceive a favorable opinion of the ability of the convention as well as of its dignity and decorum. And though there were some little instances of indecorum, which, in a Northern assemblage of similar character, would have provoked animadversion or laughter, the dignified gravity of the convention remained quite undisturbed. For example, Mr. Giles Mebane, of Alamance, an elderly farmer in snuff-colored clothes, rises to address the house, and, during the delivery of his sensible remarks, holds gingerly between his finger and thumb a quid of tobacco taken from his mouth, a proceeding which leaves his speech unimpeded, though it perhaps takes away something from the freedom and energy of his gesticulation. On another day, Mr. Pool, the member from Bertie, leaving his seat, draws a chair into a convenient position in the lobby, and smokes a long-stemmed pipe within a few feet of the President, and in full view of the convention. Attracted by the scent of tobacco, Mr. Caldwell, of Guilford, also retires to the lobby, and, filling up a pipe with a still longer stem, takes a seat beside Mr. Pool, and, by expressive signs, not to disturb the orator of the moment, begs of him a little fire or a match. In their behavior to each other and to their officers, the delegates were, as a rule, exceedingly respectful; there was no personal crimination and recrimination, and, I believe, it was not found necessary to call any member to order for words spoken in debate.

No one man was the acknowledged master and leader of the convention, as might very likely have been the case had William A. Graham received his pardon, or had Mr. Badger been a delegate. The absence of Mr. Badger, who is now an inmate of the State lunatic asylum, was frequently mentioned with regret, and reference was repeatedly made to him as "that great light." But there were about fifteen men who seemed to think themselves entitled to prominence in debate and the management of business, and of these perhaps four or five were evidently persons not ill-fitted to act as leaders.

The head of the secessionists was Mr. Manly, of Craven County. The doctrines of Calhoun, he said, were not yet devoid of value and utility; they were antagonistic to the principles of centralization, so dangerous and now so much in vogue, and he was still a believer in them as he had been in 1861. Mr. Manly is tall and spare, and speaks in a low voice, as if he were feeble and easily fatigued. Almost always when he spoke his face was turned towards the floor, and his chin rested upon his chest. His eyes, too, were half closed, but now and then as he listlessly let fall a sentence he would cast a quick glance around him as if to watch the effect of his words. The chairman of the committee to report on the ordinance of secession was Mr. Nathaniel Boyden, of Rowan. He is a Massachusetts man by birth, a very well-known lawyer, and once a representative in Congress. His Unionism is something more than a mere intellectual dissent from the doctrine of State sovereignty, which is a common, and perhaps the purest, form that Unionism assumes among native North Carolinians, and it is a great deal more than a mere hatred of secessionists, which is the type of Unionism that I have found most prevalent even in such counties as Randolph. In him it is a warm sentiment of loyalty and affection for his country. How it could happen that he became a member of the Legislature during the rebellion I am unable to explain. From all that I have heard of him, both here and in Salisbury, his place of residence, he must be pronounced to have been an honest and outspoken Unionist. He is a small, gray-haired gentleman, apparently not far from seventy years old, fastidiously neat in his dress. He is a tolerably good speaker. Mr. Bedford Brown, of Caswell, is also an old man, with very suave, agreeable voice and manner. He was a senator from North Carolina about twenty-five years ago, and was a prominent member of the convention of 1861. In this convention, so far as sides were taken, he occupied a middle position between the perfectly uncompromising Unionism of Mr. Boyden and the secessionism of Mr. Manly. Besides these three men, there were Mr. Pool, whom many speak of as the ablest man in the State; Mr. Warren, of Beaufort, one of Governor Holden's provisional judges, who made the best speech that the convention has yet heard; and Mr. Moore, of Wake, whose abilities are, perhaps, fitter to shine in a committee room or a court of law than in a legislative and political assembly, but whose keenness, pugnacity, and talent for detail made him powerful in debate.

The first day of the session was spent in perfecting the organization of the convention, with reference to which there was no contest whatever, but even thus early it became evident that there were present two parties which cherished different recollections of the past, if not different purposes in the future. The delegates had come forward to the secretary's desk, and, kissing the Bible, had sworn to support the Constitution of the United States, Mr. E. G. Reade had been made permanent president of the convention without opposition, and had read a brief speech expressive of the desire of North Carolina to return to the Union: "Fellow-citizens," he said, "we are going home. Let painful reflections upon our late separation and pleasant memories of our early Union quicken our footsteps toward the old mansion, that we may grasp hard again the hand of Friendship, who stands at the door, and, sheltered by the old homestead, which was built upon a rock and has weathered the storm, enjoy together the long, bright future which awaits us." Various subordinate officers had been chosen, and then Mr. Mebane moved that a committee of seven be appointed to frame rules for the government of the convention. Mr. Manly offered an amendment to the effect that, until Mr. Mebane's committee should report, the rules prepared for the convention of

1861 be adopted as rules of order for the present convention. Mr. King at once moved as an amendment to Mr. Manly's amendment that, instead of the rules of 1861, the rules of the Constitutional Convention of 1835 be adopted. Mr. Mebane thought it quite immaterial which set of rules were selected for temporary use, but a delegate immediately informed him that, though there might be no great difference in the rules, there was a very great difference between the two years and between the action of the State at those two periods. It would be just as well to forget 1861. After this little ripple on the surface everything was quiet again, and the convention at once decided that the committee should be appointed, and that, until they reported, rules should be dispensed with.

On the second day a message was received from Governor Holden, who laid before the convention several documents relative to the public institutions and interests of the state.

Several committees were then appointed, among others a committee on the secession ordinance of May 20, 1861, with Mr. Boyden as chairman, and a committee on the abolition of slavery.

On the third day, rather sooner than was expected, Mr. Boyden's committee reported an ordinance drawn up in these terms:

> Be it declared and ordained by the delegates of the good people of the State of North Carolina in convention assembled, and it is hereby declared and ordained, that the ordinance of the Convention of the State of North Carolina, ratified on the 21st day of November, 1789, which adopted and ratified the Constitution of the United States, is now, and at all times since the adoption and ratification thereof, hath been in full force and effect, notwithstanding the supposed ordinance of the 20th day of May, 1861, declaring that the same be repealed, rescinded, and abrogated, and the said supposed ordinance is now, and at all times hath been, null and void.

The clerk read it amid the attentive silence of the house, and immediately Mr. Smith, of Johnson County—"High Smith, of Low Johnson," as he has been called, in reference to the ignorance of his constituents and his own stature—moved that the ordinance be at once put upon its several readings. It was a rule of the convention that all resolutions and ordinances should lie over one day before coming up for consideration. Mr. Manly hoped that the rules would not be suspended nor the ordinance passed hastily. In matters of so great consequence the maturest deliberation was requisite. He objected to the phraseology of the ordinance as reported, and intended on the following day to introduce a substitute. He would, therefore, move that the motion to suspend the rules be laid on the table. As this motion, if successful, would have also carried the ordinance itself to the table, Mr. Smith withdrew his motion, and the convention soon afterwards adjourned.

On Thursday morning Governor Holden transmitted to the convention the address of the colored people of the State, with a recommendation that it be referred to a committee. The clerk read the address, which was received respectfully though not with particular attention, for it had already been published in the newspapers. Two or three members of the colored convention were in the gallery watching the fate of their address, and many significant glances were sent in that direction from the body of the house, one delegate calling the attention of another to the presence of the Negroes. Mr. Caldwell, of Guilford, rose and spoke substantially as follows:

"Mr. President, I endorse the proposition of Governor Holden. I hope the time has come when the situation of these people will receive honest and careful consideration. The time has been, sir, when I have been denounced as an abolitionist—an abolitionist from the Massachusetts of North Carolina. Well, sir, I have always had my own opinions on the subject of slavery; I had them in times past and I have them now. I earnestly desire to see the condition of the Negroes improved all it can be. We all know that it needs improvement, and all our best efforts will be taxed to prevent the misery and trouble that may come upon them. We can see that they've got an idea of running into the towns and trying to pick up a living by a little boot-blacking and a little white-washing. That course of life will not support them, and I am strongly in favor of wise action to prevent these evils of idleness and flocking out of the country into the towns. For my part, I want to see them sifted and scattered all over the country, not only over the South but over the

North, up to the Canada line, till every Northern State, as well as we down in the South, shall be helping to bear this great black burden of humanity. Then I should go in for North Carolina's treating them as well as they can be treated everywhere, and allowing them as many privileges as Connecticut or any other Northern State."

The allusion to the Connecticut election, news of which had just reached Raleigh, was made and received with a smile. The President appointed a committee of five, with Mr. Pool at its head, to take the address into consideration, and they some days afterwards reported it inexpedient for this convention to engage itself with a question so complicated and difficult as that of the relations to be established between the blacks and the whites, and recommending that a board of three commissioners be appointed by the Governor to collect information relative to the matter and lay it before the Legislature at its next session. The report was fair and liberal in its tone, but commits the convention to nothing.

I refrain from any further attempt at a diary of the proceedings, especially since the results have doubtless already been published at the North. I may allude, however, to the warm debate which sprang up upon the question of submitting these two ordinances to the people for ratification. The Unionists were determined that slavery and secession, by name, should come before the people for final and definitive judgment. They carried their point, and the people are to vote on each ordinance separately, ratifying it or rejecting it.

In the long debate on secession, much was said in condemnation of that theory; the loss which it had inflicted on the South was bewailed, and the tyranny of the secessionists and the rebel government was denounced with bitterness. But it was roundly said that this renunciation of secessionism and its works, of itself, entitled North Carolina to her old place and power in the Union. One had to remind himself that the convention itself was an acknowledgment that the State had lost some of her rights and privileges.

The discussion of the basis of representation, the reading of the address presented by the colored convention, the report of the committee to which it had been referred, and the passage of the abolition ordinance, had all alike failed to bring up the freedmen as a topic of discussion. But an ordinance introduced by Mr. Moore, of Wake, contained, among some miscellaneous matters, a section which declared married all Negroes who for six months previously to the ratification of the ordinance, and at the time of its ratification, should be living together as man and wife. Mr. Moore fought hard for his proposition, and Colonel Whittlesey, assistant commissioner of the Freedmen's Bureau in North Carolina, was in the lobby, and was understood to favor it and to desire its passage, but a large majority of the convention were opposed to taking any action whatever in relation to the condition of the Negro population. It would be better to leave the whole matter to the Legislature. Mr. Dockery, of Richmond County, took occasion to state what he knew about the freed people in his part of the State, and to set forth his views of the proper policy to be pursued towards them by the national Government.

He was a friend to the Negro. He could remember how he loved his old nurse, and his children now loved their Negro nurse so that often they would leave the arms of their mother to go to her. But he had little confidence in the elevation of the Negro race. It was true that they were in a condition of demoralization—poor, degraded, and unfortunate—and it would be well to lift them up if possible; but it could not be done by such action as Mr. Moore proposed. He felt a real attachment to the Negroes—many of them —and had often told them that he did not blame them for being free. If he had been enslaved and freed by war in the same way, he himself would have cheerfully accepted his freedom. But he did blame them for their bad conduct since they were emancipated. He wanted a carefully prepared code regulating the conduct of the blacks, or they would become a disgrace and a danger to the community. But he believed that the only effective and satisfactory policy which could be adopted was that which General Jackson had pursued towards the Indians—they must be colonized. The

Government owned plenty of land in the South-west, and the Negroes ought to be separated from the whites and sent into that region by themselves.

When General Jackson decided to move the Indians, there was a great outcry about the inhumanity of his policy. It was cruel, they said, to tear the poor Indian from his hunting-grounds, and his springs, and the grave-yards of his fathers. But General Jackson removed them, and where was the man who would today deny the soundness of that measure? Where was the man to say it was inhuman? Who supposed a single Indian would now be alive in Georgia or South Carolina or North Carolina if they had been left among the whites? It was just so with the Negroes, and he believed it would soon be found so, and the people would decide upon colonization. Mr. Moore's ordinance had two objects in contemplation, the moral elevation of the Negro by compelling him to marry the woman with whom he chose to live; and a material object—to make each Negro support his own children. But the ordinance would not bring about the desired end. The Negroes are determined to have as many wives as they can get. He himself had a nigger with two wives, one of whom he called his Sunday wife and the other his Monday wife; and he was rejoicing in his freedom because he could now get a third wife as soon as he could get a little more money. He had it from a gentleman of undoubted veracity that within a very short time previously there had been seventy marriages of Negroes, and of these seventy, sixty-five had within a week left other wives or husbands to take new ones. As to their working habits, the story was equally bad. He was paying his own niggers $6 a month, but they were getting dissatisfied. There was a constant stream of niggers coming along past his house, some from Raleigh, some from Greensboro' or Salisbury. Perhaps he would become aware that work had stopped in the blacksmith's shop; he would inquire the cause: "Oh, Mr. Smith's Jack or Tom has come back from Raleigh." He tells them that niggers are getting $20 a month up here, and the result is that the niggers all become discontented, and the able-bodied men wander off, leaving their wives and children on the farms. The Pedee country was a poor country anyhow, and all had to work, both white and black, or the farmers could not make buckle and tongue meet. Gentlemen might imagine what the condition of things would be with half the population wandering in idleness. It would be like an army without a leader, resolved into a mob; famine would overtake it. Colonization was the only remedy for such evils.

Mr. Little also favored a reference to a committee who should report to the next Legislature. He was a friend of the Negro, but he wanted to be put on record as a believer in the doctrine that this is a white man's country and a white man's government. He was opposed to Negro suffrage, Negro testimony, miscegenation, and other articles of the radical faith. He was glad to see that such doctrines had been repudiated at the North, he said, and praised General J. D. Cox, formerly of Sherman's army, as a man of sound opinions. He thought there were some people who entertained unjust prejudices against the Negro. He was not one, but would like to see them elevated and would not be averse to their being educated. North Carolina, unfortunately, was not able to educate her white children at present, but in time he hoped to see her educate the black.

The convention having passed an ordinance setting an early day in November for the election of members of the State Legislature, many of the delegates are anxious to return home and meet their constituents, so that it is probable that the convention will soon adjourn. But for some reason it seems to be thought best that another session should be held in the spring. Most likely no definite action will be taken upon the war debt or the condition of the freedmen until it can be known whether or not North Carolina will be admitted by Congress when she makes application, this winter, holding in her hand the ordinance abolishing slavery and that which declares that the State has never been out of the Union at all.

FAYETTEVILLE, N. C., October 20, 1865

ABOUT fifty miles north of this city I came upon the upper edge of the sandy pine country, and left oak timber and red clay roads behind me. As I rode out of Raleigh the weather was bright and beautiful, and a soft wind blowing from the south suggested spring to the feelings, though autumn was visible in the many colored tints. But ten miles of the road were hardly passed before the few morning clouds began to spread over the whole sky, the first drops soon came down, and it was evidently setting in for a day's rain. The effect proper to the scenery of the pine barrens is produced best during an autumnal storm. Melancholy and sad always, it is dismal when the sky hangs low and gray over the landscape, when the tree-tops in the distance are obscured by vapor, and the rain, falling steadily on the sand and brown pine needles and rotten logs, forms wide sheets of water in the white road, and black pools where there is a little vegetable mould and the dead leaves are thickest. It is only necessary to come to a human habitation to make the scene appear still more lonesome and gloomy. The house itself is seldom more than a log-hut; in the brown expanse of cleared land many of the pines have been girdled, and hundreds of the lofty stems, bleached white, are standing and leaning at every angle, while the dark green forest, withdrawn a little from the road, is still more sombre than when one rides among the trees.

Splashing slowly along, I got so thoroughly soaked with rain before reaching any house where it would be pleasant to stay for the night, that it seemed as well to go on to Barclaysville as to stop short and leave my intended day's journey unfinished. Having ridden, according to my reckoning, twenty-four miles, I came to a large white house with several outbuildings. Taught by experience, I dismounted and asked if that was not Barclaysville. The woman said it was, and, therefore, knowing it to be professedly a house of entertainment, I preferred a request for lodging. She listened, and turning away, walked through the hall without making any reply. It was not a warm reception, but one soon gives up expecting that in Southern taverns. I proceeded to bring my saddle-bags under cover and to wring the water out of my clothes. In ten minutes a Negro man came round to the gate and led my horse to the stable. I ventured to take off my spurs and knock again at the door. I asked for a room and a fire. Nearly a quarter of an hour's waiting ensued before I was taken from the piazza to a chamber. By dint of many more knocks I was able to get wood enough in small instalments to keep my fire going till supper time. Meantime a Federal officer had arrived, and the presence of a Yankee in uniform seemed to intensify the landlady's disagreeable feelings: "Sherman's bummers had come to her house on several occasions," she said with asperity. "She never could forget it to the Yankees. They were worse when they had officers with them than at any other time. Wheeler's cavalry always behaved like gentlemen, but the conduct of Sherman's men would have disgraced savages."

After supper the farmer came home, and him we found much more companionable. He was a ponderous man, six feet high, with a good-humored, honest face, and apparently of rather more than ordinary education and intelligence. He put a live coal in a large earthen pipe and asked for news. I spoke of the convention and the two important ordinances to be submitted to the people. "That's what I call nonsense," he said. "Every voter's taken an oath to support Mr. Lincoln's proclamation, and they know we can't vote against the abolition of slavery. What's the good of pretending you can say no when you can't?"

The declaration of the convention that the secession ordinance had always been null and void he also stigmatized as nonsensical. "But we sent them up there to do the work," he added, "and we'll have to be content with their way of doing it. I'm just as loyal as anybody, and I'm going to be a good citizen, but I believe we've had a government here this last four years. There's a good many trying to make out that they've always been sound Union men, when the fact is we were all rebels together. I'm in favor of acknowledging we're whipped and asking forgiveness, and then if the United States won't take us back, why it's not our fault. We've got to eat dirt anyhow, as Vance says, but blamed if I think much of a man that pretends he likes it. I never could keep up with the politicians though."

I remarked that the convention had done nothing in reference to the Negro testimony question, and asked him what he thought of it.

"Well, sir, I'll tell you what I think: a white man can't live in this country if a nigger can get to testify. I want to wait till they have more of an idea of the nature of an oath before I let one of them give evidence against me. Why, our lives wouldn't be safe. They must be educated and elevated first. It won't hurt 'em to wait a little. Let every man, white and black, when he makes a contract, have it in writing, with two witnesses, and there'll be no trouble."

I asked him what he would do in cases where contracts were not in question.

"That might be bad, sure enough, in some ways, but it would produce more evil to let a nigger swear to anything and everything. I haven't any prejudices against 'em because they're free, but you see I can't consider that they're on an equality with a white man. I may like him, but I can't let him come to my table and sit down like either of you gentlemen. I feel better than he is. The nigger has a kind of a scent about him that's enough for me. You Northern men needn't think that we hate 'em; I rather like 'em myself, and I believe we treat 'em better than you would. I know I never got so much work out of a nigger as some Yankees I've seen. In North Carolina it was the hardest kind of work to get a slave convicted for any serious offence. We were so tender of them that we wouldn't let a slave be tried except by a jury of slaveholders.

That don't look much as if we were inclined to be too hard on 'em, does it?"

We discussed the subject at some length. His first answers were dictated by prejudice, and he seemed to have never before made the question a matter of thought; but at the last he admitted that the country would be harder to live in if Negroes could not testify than if they could. In this respect he was like almost every other respectable man with whom I have conversed in North Carolina.

Colonization was the best policy, he thought. A nigger hated work, and had no ambition; he would do just enough to keep him from actual starvation. His wife believed that pretty much all the niggers she knew would a little rather starve to death than work for themselves or others.

The farmer listened with much interest to an account of Minnesota given by the Federal officer. He wanted to know if that State was in the latitude of Ohio, and appeared astonished beyond measure at the idea of an acre of land producing sixty bushels of wheat. He wouldn't mind spending a winter in the snow for the sake of the game and fish, but reckoned he never should get there; all his life he'd wanted to go down in one of those Massachusetts vessels and catch these here mackerel fish, but hadn't been able to do it. The Minnesota Indians must be bad neighbors, sure. 'Twas the British Government taught 'em that fashion of scalping prisoners; paid 'em so much a scalp in the Revolutionary war.

So we spent the rainy evening in conversation and in watching our wet clothes drying before the fire. Candles were not lighted till bed-time, but the hearth was kept supplied with light-wood, and there was no need of lamps or candles. In the morning, which was clear and cool, I set out in company with the officer, who was going as far as the ferry over the Cape Fear River. He was an agent of the Freedmen's Bureau, and was on his way to Harnett County to organize a species of court or mixed commission for the trial of causes in which Negroes and white men are the parties. His orders, based on recent instructions from General Howard, were to associate with himself certain designated gentlemen, and the board thus formed was to have final jurisdiction in cases of comparatively small importance, while serious criminal charges were to be transmitted to the authorities at Raleigh. The citizens acting in these newly instituted courts receive no compensation for their services.

A nine miles' ride in the bracing air, and through a country seemingly almost uninhabited, brought us to the Cape Fear, with its sluggish stream and banks of mud, on which willows were growing. The Negro ferryman had appropriated to his own use about a hundred and fifty yards of telegraph wire, which everywhere lies along the roadside between Raleigh and Fayetteville, and, stretching it from bank to bank, is able to dispense with a pole in setting his scow across. His people in Harnett had no abuse to complain of now, he said. "They'd feel more better if one of the Yankees was on the spot to see about the dividin' of the crop—that was all." He refused to take any money for ferrying over the Superintendent of Freedmen, and walked some distance up the road to show him the way.

From the river I rode on alone through a thin forest, which showed all the signs of a turpentine region. Almost the only large tree to be seen was the long-leaved pine, and of these nearly every one was disfigured by the axe; the bark having been removed from the trunk in strips of various lengths, the naked place in some being eight or nine feet long, in others no more than fourteen inches; their width was from ten to fifteen inches. These broad scars at the top were shaped like a fish's tail, and at the bottom of each, near the root of the tree, was the "box" in which the turpentine is caught. These are holes cut in the trunk of the tree. Their length is precisely the same with the width of the "hacking" which is to supply them; in width, from front to back, they may be five or six inches, and in depth four or five inches, measured from the outer lip downwards and back in a slanting direction towards the heart of the tree. A virgin tree loses only a foot of bark from the box upward, and at the beginning of each successive year a foot more is taken. In trees a foot in diameter, but one box is cut, and in larger trees the hacker leaves a strip of living bark between each hacking, that they may not be girdled and die. It is the rule that the tree large enough for three boxes shall have but two, and that large enough for two, but one.

A little after noon I stopped at a farm-house, to have my horse fed, and listened for a while to the grumbling of the farmer. He was not without excuse, for the house and all its surroundings spoke of poverty. The chimney was blown down, so that a fire could not be made; his farm looked as if seed sown there would be wasted; his son lay on a bed wrapped up in his overcoat, and shaking with the ague, and, it being just after dinner, his wife was dipping snuff. "He didn't know how much land he had," he said; "he knew it was monstrous hard to git a livin' off it; he farmed about thirty acres. Had been away that morning trying to git a nigger to come and help in the harvestin', fur his boy was too sick to do anything. More ager round this year than he ever knew before; but the boy'd been well, if he'd not gone off to a Baptist meeting, and got tuck down agin. He couldn't hire the nigger he wanted; he'd started off somewhar, like all the rest. All wanted to travel, and go from pillar to post. One he had—never did own but one, a kind o' family nigger—was goin' off come New Year's. He didn't know what the old critter wanted, nor how she could live; had relations t'other side of the river, she said. He didn't want to keep her, for that matter; she was so old she couldn't hardly see to thread her needle. The niggers used to be the happiest people on earth, with plenty to eat and plenty to wear, and no hard work, but they'd find the difference now. On most farms they'd been nothin' but a moth, and emancipation wouldn't hurt the farmers much, except some that had their wealth in 'em; but there was only a few large slaveholders in that country. Colonel M. owned about a hundred black ones, and he was about the richest. The Yankees ought to colonize 'em in the territories, and he had heerd they was goin' to do it. He hoped it mout be, for a man that wouldn't work would have to steal, sartin. An industrious one yer and thar's nothin', and the best of 'em a man can't put dependence in."

Within the past month I have heard a good deal said in favor of colonization, and said by owners of large plantations, who might be expected to desire a crowded labor-market. Speak to them about the vast expense, and other practical difficulties in the way of removing a whole nation from the country in which it has lived for generations, and which it loves, and one will say that the Government may have all his share in the public lands to pay it for taking away his niggers; another that he will gladly bear a heavier tax than has ever yet been imposed on him as his part of the expense, and that his acquaintances all say the same thing; and all cite Andrew Jackson's removal of the Indians as a case in point.

Thirteen miles from Fayetteville, I enquired my way of an old gentleman, who very civilly gave me copious directions, and with a crutch cane drew a diagram in the sand to make them the plainer. I spared him a quarter of an hour to give him the Raleigh news, and with the rest spoke of the new court then organizing in Harnett.

"That's a very good thing; we needed something of that kind. Now, just to illustrate how the other system worked, I'll tell you about my own experience. I've been up before one of the Yankee officers myself. Sherman's wagons went along this road, you know, and of course some of the animals were pretty much used up, and they had to take 'em out of the harness. There were four or five that fell down between the bridge and the watering place—just couldn't put one foot before the other; it was too bad to see 'em. One was an amazing lofty creature, too. I never worked so hard over a beast before. Well, I was out in the lot, and the captain came over and told me I was to pick up all these exhausted mules that could be found within a certain distance, and if I could bring 'em round again, the quartermaster at Raleigh would compensate me for my trouble. I wasn't hardly able to do it. I'd been confined to the house ever since '62, and couldn't work much then, but I undertook it, not to see the beasts suffering, and I found five. I had feed carried out, and we raised 'em up on their feet again, and did all we could. Two out of the five I found right here by the pontoon, with a couple of niggers standing over 'em. 'Boys,' said I, 'you've no business with these mules, they're in my charge.' The mules were no good, they said; they'd been working two hours to get 'em half a mile. 'No matter for that,' I told 'em; 'I was responsible for 'em, and they must leave 'em alone.' But they wouldn't; 'they were Sherman's men,' they said, 'and were going to take the mules to Raleigh.' 'Well,' said I, 'take 'em if you can get 'em there, though it's plain they'll die on the way; but remember that I'll report you, and I'd do the same for any man if he were white as the drifted snow from heaven. I don't threaten this because you're black; it's my duty.' Luckily, for me, a soldier had come up and heard the dispute. Well, he began to swear at such a rate that the niggers started off. He was surprised at me to hear me talk so calm and mild with them. 'That's the way a man ought to talk on business,' I told him. I reckon it was about a month afterwards that the same two men came to me with an order directing me at once to deliver to the bearers two mules, their property, or to appear on such a day in Fayetteville, and show cause why not. It was signed by one of these Freedmen's officers. Of course, there was nothing for it but to go to Fayetteville; so my son fixed up a side-saddle, and I went, though it was hard work, for I'm sixty-nine years old, sir, and I hadn't got well of my sickness, and never shall. The officer read me a written statement, that the niggers had made and qualified to, that I had forcibly taken from them, on such and such a day, two mules which they had purchased at the Government sales. Of course it was all a falsehood, and by means of what the soldier knew I convinced the officer that it was. I told him I didn't blame him for what he had done, for he could do no less if he believed their statement, but I thought it was rather hard to put me to the inconvenience of the journey, just on the assertion of the niggers. I told him I was sixty-nine years of age, and his court was the first I had ever been summoned before for any misdemeanor. I'm very glad they've established this court you speak of; it's a vast improvement on the old one."

Leaving the old gentleman, I rode on over a solitary road through the forest, hardly seeing a house till I reached the outskirts of Fayetteville. "Yer seven miles and a half from Fayetteville," said an old woman, whom I found at her doorstep smoking, "and ye'll hev to ride it tonight, stranger. But if ye ride a little peart ye'll be thar early yit. Thar's houses between, but ye won't git tuck in, for everybody's too much worsted, and ye wouldn't git nothin' to eat."

It soon became very dark, and I rode along, wishing for the lights of the town, when suddenly I was startled by a loud whoop from the roadside. It was nothing but a Negro trying to attract the attention of his companions at some distance ahead. Till we overtook them I walked my horse beside him, and listened to his talk. He knew I was a Yankee by my speech, he said. There was a heap of difference always between a Southern man and a Yankee, and he could tell one from the other very easy. He couldn't help laughin' to remember what he used to think about Yankees—how they had horns, some on 'em, and on'y one eye. That's what the rebels told him. He hadn't felt sure which side would whip while the fightin' was goin' on; kept hearin' that the rebels was whippin' studdy, drivin' the Yankees back every battle he didn't know how many miles, so that he didn't know what to think. He pretty much give up. But he used to pray, and he knowed if the good time didn't come in his day it was sure to come sometime; that he knew, for the Scriptures said, "In the latter days all mankind, the small and the great, shall eat his bread in the sweat of his brow"; so the white folks would have to work as well as the black ones. But by-and-bye Sherman came, and his army covered the face of the earth. "Great God, what a company!"

He was employed on a farm now, he said, and got six dollars a month; he should try to get work in a turpentine orchard. Wages were better in that business, and besides it was more agreeable to work in the shade, and the smell of the rosin was healthy.

Fayetteville is a pleasant town of six or seven thousand inhabitants, on the west bank of the Cape Fear River. Its numerous stores and warehouses are large and solidly built of brick, so that the city seems designed, not so much for the residence and workshop of its own people as for the business uses of a wide extent of country. This peculiarity belongs to the appearance of many small Southern towns as distinguished from those of the same size at the North. The chief business of Fayetteville is the shipment of tar, rosin, and spirits of turpentine down the river to Wilmington, and the sale of manufactured goods to the farmers round about. The river has been lower this season than for twenty-seven years previous, and trade is inactive at present, but it appears to be a busy and thriving town.

The following conversation, which I had this morning with a colored citizen of Fayetteville, may serve to show what are the hopes and expectations that have been formed by the most intelligent men of this class—those who deserve to have and who have the most influence with their fellows—the men who framed the recent address of the colored people to the State Convention. He is a barber by trade, a light-colored man, good-looking, and with a face expressive of good sense and good feeling. He had been a slave all his life till set free by the war, but had taught himself reading and writing, and his talk showed that he had made good use of those acquisitions. What he has read, his reflection upon it, and a careful study of events on which so much for him and his race was depending, has furnished him with a set of opinions in which there is nothing of violence, though they are very decided, and has fitted him to be a leader and counsellor among his own people. This prominence seems to affect his interests injuriously, for his white customers have withdrawn their patronage from the shop of a man who allowed himself to be sent as a delegate to the Negro convention.

As to the question whether or not the South shall be re-admitted to the Union before granting the right of suffrage to the Negroes, he says that he and his people are quite indifferent. Many care little or nothing about it at all, and many are perfectly willing to wait a few years, thinking that they will not have long to wait. He himself believed Negro suffrage a necessary consequence of Negro emancipation, if emancipation was made complete. If a black man could testify in court, and in all respects enjoy equality before the law, he would soon begin to educate himself and acquire property, and otherwise make himself respectable, and so prepare the way for his admission to the polls. Both of the great parties would be waiting for them by that time, for the colored population would be an element of such power that the Democrats would try to seize it if the Republicans were not beforehand with them. The South would need them, too, so that all things considered, he expected to be a legal voter in his native State before he was five years older.

But the right of Negroes to testify was something absolutely necessary, and he hoped that Congress would admit no State which had not granted it. If the North Carolina Legislature were to meet today, it would probably exclude the evidence of colored men; hardly a man could be found at present to say a word in favor of it. A year or two would probably change the popular opinion; but he hoped that Congress, to prevent the troubles of this year or two, would declare that no State had a republican form of government if every free man in it was not equal before the law, equal so far as the witness-box was concerned; he wouldn't insist on admission to the jury-box, for it required more sense to be a juror than to be a voter. But who could think it strange if a Negro, ignorant and without friends, when he felt that he had no place to go for justice, should take the law into his own hands? Then white men would do the same, they wouldn't wait either, and there would be nothing but bloodshed and burning.

Very few of the former slave-owners would give a Negro a fair chance, and for this reason, as well as to allow time for the minds of the people to cool and to make it possible for the Legislature to be just, he wanted the Freedmen's Bureau kept in existence another year.

He laughed at the idea of a Negro insurrection, and said he wished those who talked of it could know his people as well as he knew them. The worst to be feared was the occurrence of individual cases of violence or theft, when some Negro saw no other mode of redress; but there never would be a black rebellion. The Negroes wanted nothing so much as to live in peace with the white people of the States. What they had done in this very town, in respect to calling in a garrison of Negro troops, was sufficient proof of that. When Sherman's soldiers were first taken away from Fayetteville, and the town was put into the hands of the citizens, they showed a disposition to revive the slave code, and to enforce certain city ordinances that were full of the old spirit; Negroes were not to be allowed to meet together for worship, unless a white man was present in the assembly; no Negro was to carry a walking-cane; one man, after being convicted of some offence, was publicly whipped, and two men who lay in jail, awaiting trial, were taken out and whipped by persons who had no shadow of authority. The colored people didn't think such doings looked like freedom, and some of them began to talk about petitioning for a garrison of Negro troops. The citizens were very much afraid they'd do it, but after consultation among themselves, my informant said, "it was decided not to ask for a garrison, but for an agent of the Freedmen's Bureau to come up and adjust the difficulties. We knew that if we wanted to bring about a state of bad feeling between the white folks and the darkies, the surest way to do it would be to bring Negro soldiers into town. Besides, we knew from what we had seen in Wilmington, that a Negro regiment always has a bad influence on the other Negroes, who learn to hang around the camp and be idle. The soldiers stir up strife of all kinds."

The action of the Negroes in that matter might have been misconstrued if they had tried to keep white soldiers away. Certainly they prayed about as hard for Sherman to go as they had prayed for him to come. He didn't believe there was a darkey house in the town that the "bummers" hadn't ransacked. A Negro with a good suit of clothes, or a new pair of shoes, was halted at once and made to exchange. He laughed heartily as he described a party of them stealing his razors and other implements of his trade. But at any rate the conduct of Sherman's army had produced this good effect on the minds of the Fayetteville Negroes—they no longer believed that every man of Northern birth must necessarily be their friend, and they more clearly saw the need of looking to themselves for their own elevation. That was the true policy to be adopted, and the policy which eventually was sure of adoption and of success.

LUMBERTON, N. C., October 23, 1865

LUMBERTON stands on the left bank of the Lumber River, at a distance of thirty-three miles from Fayetteville. The village is small, with only four or five hundred inhabitants and without pretensions to beauty, for it lies scattered over a sandy level and on all sides is closely encircled by the pine barren, which here and there pushes itself into the streets and among the straggling houses. It is the capital of Robeson County, and carries on a small trade with Wilmington in the products of the forest, the two towns being connected by a railway on which trains run up and down every other day. The country to the north I found in most respects like that between Fayetteville and Raleigh; the clearings, however, are considerably more numerous, and the road oftener leads across small morasses where sand and pines are replaced by a dense growth of gums and creeping vines, and cypresses, each tree, amid the surrounding water or black mud, standing on a little hummock of earth which its roots hold together. By the roadside in such places a string of hewn logs, raised on props two or three feet high, gives a narrow foot-way to pedestrians, while the horseman finds the swamp water, sometimes for several rods of the road, washing against his stirrups.

The houses of this district are commonly low black buildings of one story, with roofs projecting so as to form a gallery or piazza, and apparently contain two or three rooms. Plaster is often dispensed with in the interior finishing, and sometimes the walls are faced with pine, smooth and unpainted, which becomes quite handsome as it darkens with age. At various distances from the dwelling are half a dozen small out-buildings, which can be distinguished from the Negro huts by the absence of mud chimneys and the looser structure of their walls. Corn is the principal crop, but the wealthier farmers raise some cotton, and a good deal of rosin and turpentine is made. Although the soil and the people seem so poor, more than half the inhabitants of Robeson were formerly held as slaves.

I stopped at one of the poorest houses on the road today and tried to buy a dozen ears of corn, but could only get a sheaf of fodder. Four rickety cabins in the middle of a corn-field, which the wind was whirling into clouds of dust, formed the homestead, and the family consisted of an old woman and five or six white-headed children of all sizes. She civilly set a chair for me beside the hearth, and as I sat down all the household gathered round, a stranger, I suppose, being an unusual sight. One little boy stretched himself out on the floor, with his feet in the ashes, and made many remarks on my dress and equipments: "Mister, be you a Yankee? you wear a Yankee coat." "Them's a bully spurs; gi' me one, mister?"

"Hit a'n't," said his mother; "a Yankee wears a blouse coat. Git up an' go 'long. Ye laugh so large! why can't ye behave smart?"

"I suppose he don't see a man from the North very often."

"Ye be from thar, then. I reckoned ye was. No, he's seed Yankeens, but he behaves just so ugly. Sherman's companies come along here, an' they was dreadful. I allus liked your nation afore, but I can't niver git it over to them soldiers."

"What did they do—rob?"

"No, sir, that warn't hit; 'peard like they thout I warn't worth comin' to see; but they tuck off my man. 'Twas a Sunday mornin' when we heerd the Yankees was comin', and I was scart bad, for my son thar was up to P'int Lookout; they tuck him for a prisoner at Fisher, and the old man had gone off to the dam. The children come running to tell 'Here's the Yankees, here's the Yankees,' and I began to wish the old man was to home, or I warn't. But the first company of 'em went right along that same road, and they looked, but they didn't come into the lot. My man hed been in the army, but he come home; I think 'twas two days before the Yankees come; nor he didn't git leave nuther. Well, mister, he allus was sickly, an' he niver thout the war was right; an', I tell you, he got right sick of it, an' so did a meny, and he jist tuck home, an' I don't blame him; I dunno as I do—not a bit. When he heerd the Yankees was comin', he knowed I'd be scart, and thout he'd come back to the house. He was crossin' the lot, an' hed his uniform on, an' they seed it. I don't reckon they'd ha' come except for that, but a parcel of 'em rode their critters right up to the door, an' filled the house full in a minute. They begun to talk to the old man, an' he talked too. They said he was a Johnny Reb; he said he warn't, and told how he was a deserter; but they swore they wouldn't believe a word he'd say. One of 'em told him to pull off his shoes, an' he hed to. Some of 'em was smart men, you know, mister, an' some was low down. They said he must go with them, and then I began to be scart bad, for I didn't know whether they wanted him for a good thing or what, and I begged 'em hard. But they told me 'twas no use, they was agwine to take every rebel soldier along an' keep 'em prisoner, for they was the very ones shot your men. That was March, an' I niver seed him agin till July, an' then he was a mighty sick man; you couldn't hiv him to take that journey agin, he said, for he was amost starved to death; his feet was so sore he couldn't walk for a week, an' he didn't live long, nohow."

"Well, mister," said the son, "is the fightin' all done now, do ye reckon, or how is it?" I assured him that the war was entirely over. His next question was in relation to the Negroes: "D'ye think the niggers is r'aly free?" I thought there could be no doubt of it.

"Well, what's gwine to be done with 'em? Some say they's to be sent off into another country, into some island somewhar; but no island wouldn't take 'em, would it?"

"Oh no, they'll be kept here where they are."

"Well, then," said the woman, "the Government is agwine to give 'em land, I reckon; we heerd that too."

"No, what land they get they must buy, I believe, as other people do."

"Well, how'll they live then? The rich people won't sell 'em land, nor yit they won't hire 'em."

"No, they hate 'em because they's free," said the son; "an' a many of em's got to die this winter, for they turn 'em off all they can. But I say, mister, if a nigger's free, is he to hev his vote like any man?"

"Is he gwine to hev his oath?" asked the woman.

"I think it's pretty likely that he will be allowed to testify; I don't know about the voting."

"Well, don't it seem kind o' hard to hev a nigger come an' make oath agin ye—a right coal-black nigger? How is that? Is it right or a'n't it?"

I showed how easily it would be possible to inflict great injustice upon the Negroes if they were declared incapable of testifying.

"Well, sartin it does look like it, an' I reckon they will hev to hev it."

"They do hev it now," her son said, "whenever the Superintenders of Freedom arrests yer. Thar was McM——, ye know. He's a man lives about six miles from here. He licked an old nigger woman o' his so 't she couldn't lift up her hand, an' they let her give in her evidence. I heerd it made McM—— mad; he's a proud feller. But the colonel, or the superintender, told him if he was gwine to talk, talk, an' mind himself, or he'd git into trouble. He hed to pay seventy-five cents a day to her till she got well, an' the doctor's bill, an' two or three more bills."

After a little talk about the national currency, which they said some of their neighbors refused to receive, and which they had been told would soon be good for nothing, I bade them good-bye, and rode on to this place, which I reached just before sunset. The landlord, smoking with a friend in the tavern parlor, seems to be angry beyond measure because the State Convention has repudiated the rebel war-debt.

"It's Bill Holden did it," he says, with many expletives, "and it's just like him; it's exactly Bill Holden. I'll tell you the whole story. I had it from our representative. When he went up to Raleigh to attend the convention, he went down to the Yarborough Hotel,

and there he found Judge Reed, and Judge Gilliam, and eighteen
or twenty more prominent gentlemen, who asked him to go up
with them into a private room, for they had a document from
Washington they wanted to show him. He went up, and they read
him a letter written by our State agent in Washington, Doctor—
what is his name? You know who I mean. He said that he had
been admitted to interviews with every member of the cabinet, and
it was the opinion of every one of them, and it was supposed by
them to be the opinion of Andy Johnson, that the question of the
war-debt had better be left alone; it would only make trouble and
divide the people to discuss it now. So the convention did let it
alone, and when any ordinances or resolutions touching on it were
brought forward, they were staved off in some way or other, and
the whole thing was left to the Legislature; that was the general
understanding. And now Bill Holden's part comes in. On Wednes-
day morning Jonathan North was first announced as a candidate
for governor. As soon as Holden knew it he telegraphed to Washington—what he telegraphed you know as well as I do—and
down comes this telegram of Johnson's, commanding the convention to repudiate, and it obeyed. Now, I don't care if it keeps the
State out of the Union for forty years, I'll never vote for Bill
Holden to be the governor of it; no sir, never while my head is
hot."

MARION COURT-HOUSE, S. C., October 25, 1865

Just at dusk yesterday, after wading through Ashpole swamp, a
dreary morass several miles long and a quarter of a mile broad, I
crossed the State line and entered South Carolina. The last North
Carolinian with whom I talked was an old lady living not far from
the swamp, who owns a large farm and cultivates a few acres of it.

"But it's more," she said, "than I'll crap next year; I'll do well, I
expect, if I can make a livin' off it, for the niggers a'n't gwine to do
any more steady work. Eight and ten dollars a month they want,
and twenty days idle time. One o' my gals, Jane, told me they was
to have land given to 'em for themselves. 'Don't think you'll git

mine,' I told her, 'for I'll cut your throat first.' Confound her impudence! But every one of 'em goes off by the first o' January, and what corn and taters we need my son'll have to make, and if he can't I can. The niggers is jest gone to ruin, and I wish old Sherman had taken 'em every one when he freed 'em. I never did have no use for a free nigger anyhow. Some o' my neighbors thinks these poor white men round here is gwine to hire out and make cotton, but I know better. The white men here that didn't own land never was raised to work, and they won't work. Not gwine to do it. I can tell the Yankee nation it's jest cut off its own nose to spite its face, for it's not gwine to git cotton any more, nor corn to eat, and their manufactures is ruined. They've ruined the niggers too, and there never was a happier people than they was. Why don't the Yankees move 'em off? If they don't, they'll be killed up jest as sure's your born. One was killed last Monday was a week, and lots and cords of 'em's goin' the same road."

I asked for the particulars.

"Stealin'. It happened about seven miles from here. Mr. —— had been havin' a corn-shuckin', and he give the niggers a supper afterwards; that's the rule in these parts. Well, he thought it mout be some of the corn would go that night, so after supper he took his gun, and went down to the corn-house. Sure enough, in a little while a man came down with a basket and filled it up full. Mr. —— let him walk off about twenty steps, and then he fired and the man fell. Come to find out, it was one of his own niggers, that he'd raised. He lived the night out and died the next mornin' at ten o'clock."

"What was done about it?"

"Well, I don't jest know. I heerd that Mr. —— went and delivered himself up to the lieutenant o' the home guard; he said he hadn't nothin' to do with it, but to go over with him to the captain, and I believe the captain car'd him up to Lumberton."

These same facts were recounted to me again by the farmer with whom I lodged last night, and, in addition, he told me that the defendant was tried on Saturday last by the agent of the Freedmen's Bureau, and having proved, by Negroes living on the farm, that the deceased was shot while in the act of stealing, was thereupon discharged from custody and exonerated from blame. The farmer approved of this decision, for it seemed to indicate what he had been hoping for, that the agents and superintendents had recently had orders to be much stricter in their government of the Negroes. They needed sharp watching, and one or two such examples as this case furnished would have a good effect. All the stealing, however, was not done by Negroes, he said. He had been down to the village that day to tell a man that he couldn't undertake to buy cotton for him, nor engage any, until the country became a little quieter. Sometimes the bales are quietly taken away in the night; sometimes a party disguise themselves and seize the cotton by violence; sometimes they go with a pretended order from the district commander. Last week three bales had been taken out of that neighborhood by men dressed in the Federal uniform, who demanded the cotton as property formerly belonging to the Confederate government. But the owner knew some of the gang, and next day, with a few of his friends, tracked the thieves and took their plunder away. He had never known such times.

"Well, how do you punish the robbers?"

"We haven't had any law all this time, and we couldn't do much. I expect it'll be better now that we've got back into the Union, and the soldiers are going to be removed."

This last remark somewhat surprised me, but I found on further conversation that he really held the opinion that South Carolina had been fully restored to her place in the Union and to all her powers by the action of the State convention. It was a new idea to him, he said, that Congress had any authority to keep a State out. The war was done, and the convention had freed the niggers; what more could be wanted? The State must be back, for he had seen the representatives going up to Columbia that day.

The dearth of newspapers in Marion District was equally shown by another of his opinions. It was very likely, he thought, that the Congress would pay former slaveholders for the loss of their property. Perhaps a man had been laboring all his life for his money, and had it invested in niggers at the time of the emancipation; it seemed too hard that he should lose it, and he heard a good deal of talk about Government paying a part of the value anyhow. That would be no more than fair.

I thought it would be generally considered unfair.

"Why, I don't mean for the North to pay it all," he explained; "I mean for the United States to pay it in bonds, and then the whole country, South as well as North, could be taxed to meet the interest on 'em. That wouldn't be any harder on the North than on the South, would it?"

He seemed quite nettled because I failed to see the justice of the scheme even in this aspect of it, so much so that I thought he might perhaps be the original author of it; but he said it was a good deal talked about among the neighbors, and that he'd heard it first at the court-house. He didn't care much for himself; hadn't but three or four niggers.

Upon the questions of Negro suffrage, Negro testimony, and colonization of Negroes, he had brought himself to the same conclusions which I have so often heard expressed in this region, and so often presented at length: A nigger's oath wasn't worth a chew of tobacco; any one of 'em would cut a white man's throat for that any time; as to nigger voting, it wasn't worth while talking about it —it meant nigger equality, and white men couldn't and wouldn't stand that; niggers would have to be moved off, they were so lazy that they wouldn't work more than two days at a time, and so worthless that the other five days of the week would be spent in stealing; they couldn't live among white folks.

This man owned a farm of more than two hundred acres, he lived in a very neat log-house, with a trim yard around it, his outhouses and fences were regularly disposed and in good order, nine or ten books were on the mantelpiece, and his surroundings generally, as well as his manners and conversation, showed him to be a good deal above that class commonly called "low-down, triflin' people," or poor white trash.

A ride of twenty miles from his house brought me to this place, a very quiet, pretty little village, full of trees and gardens, and light, elegant houses, among which a huge bare court-house, made of bricks and stucco and iron, seems strangely out of place. In Marion I find, for the first time, the magnolia growing, and not many miles from the village I first noticed branches of the mistletoe, and saw the Spanish moss hanging from the pine and the water-oak.

XVIII

KINGSTREE, S. C., October 30, 1865

THE traveller from North Carolina passes but a little distance into this State before he finds the outward indications of a widely different social organization. The scenery in its general aspect is the same. There, as well as here, for a hundred miles from the coast, the surface is very flat and traversed by many sluggish streams; pine barrens alternate with swamps, and by far the larger portion of the country is covered with forests. But the clearing of the small farmer is rarely seen; the fields of the great plantations spread wide on either hand till their bounding lines of woods appear as irregular black walls; the Negro cabins, often neatly built, are gathered into little villages of twenty or thirty houses, and often it is possible to ride three or four miles in a straight line within the limits of one man's land. The valleys of the creeks and rivers are possessed by the rich planters, the poor whites, whose local designation is "backwoods people," occupy the ridges between. Their dwellings are seldom to be seen from the public thoroughfares, and one is surprised to hear that this class constitutes a great majority of the white population.

Yesterday morning, just after leaving Marion village, I turned from the main road, and, with the intention of making my ride a couple of miles shorter, followed a cart-path leading through the estate of a large cotton planter. Very soon I lost my way among the intricacies of the field-paths, and rode aside to the Negro quarters to ask for information, and, after the road had been pointed out, I said to two of the Negroes: "Well, boys, have you raised much cotton and corn this year?"

"Raise corn, sir? Didn' plan' cotton; dis yer san' hill fiel' don' bring cotton nohow. We jus' done broke corn."

"You'll make cotton this next year, I suppose?"

"Dunno, boss, dunno. We's waiting till Jenewerry come. Den we kin know."

"Are you going to stay here another year?"

" 'Spect so, sir. Major G—— was own dis place. He was master for all we. He says we kin stay ef we work, and we kin have half the cotton we make."

"But you won't make a contract till January, you say?"

"No, sir," said an old man, "we heares dis an' dat, dis an' dat, an' we told him we'd hol' on tell Jenewerry."

While this conversation was going on several men and women had come out of the neighboring cabins, or were standing in the door-ways, and though they pretended to be engaged with something else, and did not approach me very closely, I could see that they all gave careful attention to overhear what was said.

"Well, I should say that Major G—— had made you a very fair offer. Why not sign the agreement now? You don't want to put it off till it's too late to begin work on next year's crop?"

"I ain't agwine to bin' myself," said one young fellow, "not till I kin see better."

"Hush you," said the old man, "you dunno what you talk about. Let de gen'l'man talk."

I waited, however, to see whether or not they would broach the subject of a division of lands among the Negroes, for I am told that such an opinion is universally prevalent in the lower districts of this State. But they also waited, and seemed disinclined to speak plainly, so I asked if that was what they were expecting to take place in January. "Yes," they said with some hesitation, "they'd been told so."

"Yes," said another whom I had not before seen, "we's agwine to wait anyhow. We dunno whar we'll be next year, nor what they'll do with us. They tell what they'll do at Columby, and they tell another thing over to headquarters, and I goes for waitin' any-how."

When I told them it was very unlikely that any land would be given away by the Government, they listened to what I said, but appeared to receive it with dissatisfaction and incredulity. In Virginia and North Carolina I found but one Negro, an old man living near Charlotte, who entertained any expectation of this kind. In this State I have talked with the people of five plantations in Marion and Williamsburg districts, and all seemed to be fully persuaded that some such provision was to be made for them. The terms which they refused these Negroes pronounced fair and reasonable, but they declined to accede to them, and it seemed that their refusal was as much dictated by a profound distrust of the promises made them as by the hope that they themselves might, perhaps, become landholders.

The house at which I stayed last night was that of a planter who lives midway between the Great Pedee River and this village, and it furnished me with exceptionally pleasant and comfortable quarters. Its owner was a Northerner by birth, who, having come out from Connecticut as a trader many years ago, had married a Southern woman and become a wealthy rice and cotton planter. Everything in and about his house was ordered with a methodical neatness not at all common in this region, for he seemed to have retained many of his New England habits. His political opinions, however, were entirely South Carolinian. The Southern States he still called the Confederacy, and he spoke of the battle of Chattanooga as a great calamity.

"Your Government," he said, "ought as a matter of policy to deal gently with President Davis."

"Why," said I, "does anybody in the South care particularly about him?"

"I am sure," said his wife, "if the Yankee Government wants the good-will of the females of the South, it will set him free at once, for we all admire him."

"Yes," said he, "and everybody knows that he had less to do with bringing on the war than many others. He seemed to be more unpopular towards the close of the war, and there was a certain party in this State, with the Rhetts at the head of it, which made a great outcry against his administration and charged every disaster on him; but the mass of our people always thought him a pure-minded statesman and patriot."

He saw it stated in the papers, he went on to say, that Mr. Davis was to be tried for treason. A Northern jury would probably find him guilty, but he had no idea that any punishment would be inflicted. To put him to death would shock the South beyond expression and disgust the whole civilized world, so he had no fears that any such extreme measure would be adopted. And, as he had said before, to conciliate the Southern people, who never would believe that Davis had done wrong, it would be well to release him without trial.

I told him that I had heard a good deal said about a probable Negro insurrection, and asked him for his opinion.

"I look for it, sir, in January. I regard it as almost certain to occur."

"Why, who was that nigger," said his wife, "who said right out that there hadn't been any war to what there would be? One nigger man said that to Mr. B——'s nephew, sir."

"It is a general fear," said Mr. B——. "The Negroes have made up their minds that land is to be given them at New Year's, and of course it will be a great disappointment to them when they find that that time has gone by and nothing has been done for them. Our Negroes here are more intelligent than those thirty miles below us, and we have more white men among them, but I think there will be a rising on the coast. Of course it couldn't extend far, but some families will be murdered and some property destroyed, and a deplorable example will be set to both white and black. It will begin the work of extermination."

In reply to my questions, he said that more than half of his neighbors, he thought, shared his fears. He had no intention of moving his family away, because he expected the fighting to be confined to the tier of counties on the coast. The United States officers would not believe in the possibility of an insurrection. They seemed to despise the Negroes too much to think them capable of becoming dangerous.

As for work, the freedmen were doing absolutely nothing. He had overheard one of his girls saying that she hadn't seen any freedom yet, she had to work just as hard now as ever. And that was the feeling of a great many of them. Then, as he had said, they were waiting for January, and nothing could be done with them till they became convinced that they must work for wages. They were stealing everything that they could lay their hands on. In old times, when a slave was caught stealing he was not prosecuted, for the owners had too much respect for each other; but his master was informed and made restitution to the loser, and the thief escaped with a whipping. He never was whipped severely on such occasions, he had no character to lose, and in a month the whole thing was forgotten. In this way the Negroes were made a race of thieves.

"Oh, Mr. B———," said his wife, "I'm sure they were all thieves in Africa. Wherever you read about them they're always the same."

"And there is a class of white folks," he continued, "meaner than the Negroes, who have been made more lawless by the war, who never would work, and they now encourage the Negroes to come about them. One man, just over the creek, who never earned a dime in his life, has got more than forty Negroes on his farm; if you can call it a farm—he never made corn enough to feed himself three months. They steal whatever they can, and he sells it for them, and the whole parcel expect to live off their neighbors. It is these people who demoralize the Negroes. What with the one and the other, I don't know how we are to live in the country at all. The two classes together are so numerous that I'm afraid we couldn't enforce a good, strict vagrant law if we had it. I candidly confess that I look forward to the extermination of the freedmen."

This gentleman was very desirous of leasing out either his rice or cotton plantation to some Northern man. Then, he said, if he could find someone with five thousand dollars' capital, he would engage in the lumber business, or in distilling spirits of turpentine, for he owned about five thousand acres of woodland, and had a turpentine orchard containing a hundred thousand boxes.

This village of Kingstree is garrisoned by a company of soldiers, and the people of the tavern seem to be in a state of considerable excitement on account of a conflict that has just occurred between the military and civil authorities. The landlord was arrested some three weeks since by the special agent of the Treasury Department on a charge of having secreted, and afterwards sold as his own private property, several bales of cotton which, at the time of Johnston's surrender, were owned by the Confederate Government. Today the sheriff of the district arrested the Treasury agent on a charge of false imprisonment, but his prisoner was immediately taken away from him by the commander of the garrison. This occurrence gives rise to much denunciation of the tyranny of martial law. The landlord, a Bavarian, who can hardly speak English, has been declaring his determination to appeal to General Gillmore, at Charleston, and is exhorted by his friends and his wife to do so.

"That'll do no good," said one young man; "knock the scoundrel down the first time you meet him."

"And if he does," said a lady sitting near, "the Yankees'll put him into jail, and he'll have to buy out. We'll all just have to leave the country, and let the Yankees have it. Don't I love them from the bottom of my heart! Once I had my trunks all packed, ready to start as soon as I could sell my furniture and find a vessel, for it seemed as if I could not stay. Oh, if ever there was a rebel I was one. The agony I suffered when we first got the news of General Lee's surrender was perfectly indescribable. I didn't close my eyes, you know; I walked up and down; it seemed I couldn't believe it, yet I knew it was true, and I just cried and cried. I did say that the Yankees should never make me shed a tear, but that broke me down. That was the time I was going to emigrate. I remember it was the next day Mrs. S—— run over to the house. 'Oh,' says she, 'good news! I've got good news for you.' 'I don't know what good news there can be any more,' says I. 'Old Lincoln's dead,' says she; 'assassinated in Washington city.' Well, I didn't see how that was going to do us any good then; but I couldn't sell my furniture, and I just unpacked my trunks about as fast as I'd packed them, and here I am yet. But I only wish I had plenty of money, and I'd go to some place where I wouldn't have to see a Yankee again as long as I live."

CHARLESTON, S. C., November 3, 1865

On Tuesday morning I set out from Kingstree in a thick mist, and rode all day through the dripping trees and over a very thinly peopled country. Just after sunset I succeeded in getting a lodging at the house of a planter, who hospitably took me in, although the arrival of two relatives to pay him a visit had filled his only spare chamber. But it was his rule, he said, never to turn away a stranger, and I should have a bed before the fire in the parlor.

His property, as he informed me in the morning, consisted of something more than sixty-five hundred acres of land, divided into two plantations, one devoted to rice and one to cotton, and a grazing farm stocked with sheep and cattle. His house was a large, weather-beaten building, with piazzas at the front and back, but appeared to contain only four rooms, the windows of which were unglazed and the walls unplastered. In the parlor, which also served as the dining-room, there was but little furniture, and nothing for purposes of ornament.

At supper the conversation, in which I took no part, turned upon the Negro.

"I met Dr. M——," said one of the ladies, "as I come on down, and he said they'd begun to form a company to protect us against the niggers. He was goin' to be the commissary, he said, and they'd chosen the commander, too. I told him that's what ruined us before; there was too many wanting to be officers, and not enough of soldiers."

"I hadn't heard anything of that," said her uncle, "but it's going to be necessary. I'm told that the nigger soldiers in Georgetown have been getting very independent latterly; but the Yankee officers, they say, make short work of it with 'em. I hear that one or two of 'em were shot down last week, and tumbled into the river, man and gun."

"Who did it?"

"Their own officers, the Yankees. That's a case of nigger shooting that won't be trumpeted all over Lincolndom, I expect."

"I wish they'd shoot 'em all," said his wife; "I'm glad when I
hear o' one of 'em got out o' the way. If I could get up tomorrow
morning and hear that every nigger in the country was dead, I'd
just jump up and down."

"I don't want 'em to go quite so soon as that. They'll go fast
enough for me if they last a few years longer."

"You want to get a little more out of 'em first, don't you, uncle?
So do I; but I don't know how it's to be done. Mine raised me just
a hundred bushels of corn this year; not enough to feed the
horses."

"A hundred bushels? That's pretty well. I've got thirteen able to
work, and I didn't get quite sixty bushels for myself, and I'm sure
they hav'n't got enough to last them into May."

After supper he showed me the prospectus of an emigrant aid
society which it is proposed to establish in Charleston. Landowners are invited to take shares in the stock of the company,
paying for them in money or in land, and European emigrants are
to be induced to settle in South Carolina, and purchase or lease
farms from the society, which will pay out dividends to its stockholders from the funds thus accruing. If the scheme should obtain
the sanction of the Legislature, and some aid from the State, he
proposed to subscribe for as many shares as he could pay for with
five thousand acres of rice land. His cotton plantation he intended
to divide into small farms, and to make his former slaves tenants
upon it, they to pay him as rent one-third of their cotton crop and
two bushels of corn to the acre. He had no intention of attempting
to carry on planting with free Negro labor. By the time affairs were
a little settled, so that he could get rid of his Negroes, he hoped to
be able to get German tenants or laborers. As to the stock farm, he
would attend to that himself. In the spring of 1863 he had over
five hundred head of cattle; he believed that today he hadn't more
than a hundred and fifty. At the same time he sheared three
hundred and seventy sheep, and it was doubtful if he had a

hundred and twenty-five left. The backwoods people all had a gun and a dog, and they had been living at the expense of the cattle and sheep in the woods, and they were expecting to do the same for the next two years. Perhaps by close attention he might be able to prevent such wholesale destruction. At any rate, watching cattle would be less vexatious and unprofitable than trying to drive free niggers.

In the morning, while we were waiting for breakfast, we sat in the piazza, and seeing two human skulls in a corner, I asked if there was any story connected with them.

"Yes, sir," he said, "they belonged to two d——d robbers who got their deserts at my hands one morning in May last. General Gillmore, you know, sent out a raiding expedition under Brown and Potter just before the time of Johnston's surrender. They stripped the country of mules and horses and every description of property, and, of course, they encountered little or no resistance, so that some of our colored friends in Georgetown began to think stealing from what they called a 'reb' was a safe and profitable business. I think it was about the 15th of May—hostilities had ceased, at any rate—when a party of something like twenty came out of Georgetown, and, going further up into this district, began plundering the plantations. When they had got all the horses and carts they could drive, and loaded them down with plunder, they started back. But they didn't all get back. I thought we'd stood enough of that kind of thing; so I got some of my neighbors together; we armed ourselves, and pursued. There were about twenty of them, and only six of us, but I knew we could rout them. I didn't follow too close. I knew the country perfectly, and I wanted to get them where there was no bog or swamp for them to take to. When I had them in the right spot, we closed in at a canter. They showed fight, sir, but 'twas no use. We scattered them easily. Seven of them fell, five of the seven killed on the spot. That fellow, you see, never knew what hurt him."

He handed me one of the skulls as he spoke, and pointed to a hole made by a pistol bullet. I asked how he had prepared the trophies; if he had removed the flesh by boiling.

"No, sir," he replied; "we let them lie where they fell, and the weather prepared them. I didn't bring them in till August."

Leaving the house of this gentleman, a ride of seven miles brought me to the Santee River. The water was so low that the ferry-boat, or scow, could not ply at the regular place of crossing, and for nearly a mile I was obliged to flounder through the tenacious mud of a cypress swamp, my horse often sinking above his knees in the slimy mire and ooze.

At noon I stopped and gave my horse a feed, more for the sake of talking with the people who sold it to me than for any other reason, for they were such as might serve very well as samples of the poor white population of South Carolina. Their house was a poor log cabin, standing alone in the solitude of the pine woods, and around was a little clearing of an acre or two of sand, in which had been made an ill-rewarded attempt to raise a few rows of corn. There was no furniture in the one room which served for all the uses of the family, except a bench and two dirty beds. The children were puny, unwholesome-looking creatures, with tangled whitish hair and complexions of a dingy straw color. All gathered round me and stared while the horse was eating, but to all my remarks and questions the reply was silence or answers as nearly monosyllabic as possible, and I gave up the attempt to draw them into conversation and rode on my way.

At night I stayed at the house of an aged couple, the husband being eighty-two years old and almost childish. He was a poor man, his wife said, who had begun life as a laborer. Then he had risen to be an overseer, and by dint of hard work and close saving had been able to buy himself a small farm and to stock it with five or six Negroes. But now he was poor again, and had been obliged to work as hard this season as he ever worked forty years ago. Emancipation had taken away all his laborers, and, as if that was not enough, Potter's raiding party had camped beside them for a whole week, and had carried off his mules and horses. She didn't know why the Yankees done her so bad, for she never harmed one of 'em. There was a heap of Yankee storekeepers in Charleston, and she had always preferred to trade with 'em and had never spoken bad of their nation. But they took away everything they wanted, and dug up the yard to see if she hadn't buried silver or a watch or some jewelry. She thanked God that Sherman didn't come that way, for they told her if he had she wouldn't have had her house left.

On the following morning I was awakened by the rain pattering on the roof of my chamber, and it continued to pour steadily down all day, so that the last forty miles of my journey to this city I performed without stopping at any house by the way, and without seeing much more of the country than the muddy road just before me.

PORT ROYAL ISLAND, S. C., November 10, 1865

INTENDING soon to revisit Charleston, I made no long stay in that city, but on the morning of yesterday sailed down the harbor past the famous islands and forts, and, keeping the low, wooded coast in sight during the whole day, in the evening reached Hilton Head. The neat, whitewashed town, built there in the sand by the quartermasters and sutlers during the last four years, with its hospitals, and storehouses, and machine-shops, and offices, has lost much of its old importance, and, instead of being the bustling part of the Department of the South, is sinking back into the quiet dullness of its natural condition as a part of the State of South Carolina. A stumbling walk in the dark up the long wooden pier, which extends far into the shallow water of the bay, brought me to the hotel, where I found the few guests gathered around a box-stove, for the night was windy and cold, and the walls of the house —a portable or sectional building—were thin. There were two or three Federal uniforms in the company, some men who seemed to be Northern traders, and a person who had the easily distinguishable appearance and manners of a South Carolinian. This gentleman, a person of some fifty-odd years old, dressed tolerably well in a suit of gray clothes, with a large display of crumpled linen at the collar and cuffs of his coat, sat before the stove smoking, and talking very freely about his present poverty and his plans for the future.

He had left St. Helena, he said, when Dupont forced an entrance, and captured the Sea Islands, in 1861. He and his family

ran, leaving plate and furniture behind them, and went up to
Greenville, where he'd since been living how he could. The Government took his cotton, and somebody, Government or niggers, got
everything else that was left. Then, in the spring of 1863, they sold
his plantation. Some Massachusetts man bought it, and he didn't
know when he'd get it back. Up in Greenville he soon spent all his
money to support his family, but if he'd had money he couldn't
have saved his property. How was he to come back inside the
Yankee lines and pay the tax? The commissioners knew very well
it couldn't be done; the sale was a perfectly unfair thing. He didn't
know whether the place would be restored to him or not, but at
any rate he intended to leave Greenville, and move down to Beaufort. It was just as well to starve in Beaufort as in any strange
place. He hoped to be able to pick up a little medical practice, but
if his profession failed him, he supposed his son and himself could
put up a cabin somewhere in the vicinity, and get fish and oysters
enough to live on. He intended to go up to Greenville the next day,
and bring his family down immediately. He hadn't a dollar in
money; had thought it would be a good plan to circulate a handbill
among his acquaintances up there, asking them to aid him, but the
trouble was, pretty much all of them were as poor as himself—
better off so far as keeping their land went, but without ready
money. Then he went on to relate, in a good-humored way, many
amusing stories of Sherman's army, and the impudence of the bummers.

This gentleman, it is currently reported, has made several visits
to the plantation which he formerly owned, and the Negroes living
there have collected for his use nearly a hundred dollars. In several
instances similar contributions have not only been accepted but
solicited. In July last, a gentleman who once owned a fine plantation, about ten miles distant from Beaufort, rode out to it in a
carriage hired for him by a Negro formerly his slave, and, having
called together such of the people as would go to meet him and
shaken hands with them all, he told them that he was now a poor
man; that he had even been compelled to beg to support his
family; that the very ear-rings from his wife's ears had been ex-

changed for food; that they all knew that their mistress knew nothing about any kind of work, and had never done any; and he concluded his address by a personal application to each one for whatever money he could spare. The response to this appeal was not a very liberal one, my informant said. Prince ga' 'm seventy-fi' cent, she believed, and several of the others gave him something; she herself would give nothing. "Den mawser git into de kerridge an' drive off," she added. "Him tell bro' Prince take good keer o' all tings. Him for come back soon, him say. But ef dem rebel come back, tell ye wha' no' *our* nigger gwine for stay on dis place, no' one nigger. Wid dem she-shesh! Chuh!"

On another plantation I learn that small gifts of money and poultry have been received from the people by their former master, who himself urged his claim upon their kindness, and who was found willing to accept half a dollar from an old, crippled Negress who now for some years has drawn rations and been furnished with medicine and clothing at the expense of the Government.

Most of the Negroes, I should say, are surprisingly free from a vulgar contempt for these men merely because of their sudden poverty and the shifts and straits to which they see them reduced, and some appear to feel a genuine commiseration for them in their distress. But their kindly feeling towards them extends no further than this, and it is, perhaps, remarkable that it should extend so far, for evidently they fear and dislike the slaveholders, both as a class and individually. The probable return of their former owners to the island, the possibility that they may some time be compelled to work for them and be governed by them, seem to excite the liveliest apprehensions and very strong expressions of hostility.

The swift steamer *Rockland,* plying between Savannah and Charleston by the inland route, took me in a little more than an hour up the river to Beaufort. The town stands on the river of the same name, one of the many streams or inlets which, with their network of endless ramifications and intersections, everywhere penetrate the south-eastern Carolina coast, and, dividing it into many parts, form the Sea Islands. Beaufort is a quiet town, with many handsome houses scattered here and there among the sandy streets, and with abundance of orange trees, and oleanders, and pomegranates; and on all hands the live oaks are to be seen with their gray drapery of hanging moss. The scene was a familiar one to me, and as there was no special reason for my remaining there, I rode out across the island in a north-westerly direction, over what had once been an excellent road, until four years of neglect had injured it, and finally the passage of Sherman, corduroying as he went, gave it the finishing blow and made it execrable. In the country through which it led me there was more woodland than clearing, and of the cleared land much more than half, fenceless, bushy, and unkempt, lay uncultivated. In this region of large plantations, however, it is customary for a planter to divide his lands, and to work each acre every alternate year, the one half being left fallow and used as a pasture while the other is planted. The cabins of the people seemed to be in tolerable preservation, and no better or worse than those commonly found in other sections of the State; but at several points on the roadside, at some distance from any Negro quarters, I noticed small unsightly shanties, made of poles and rough clapboards, which appeared to be occupied by vagabonds or squatters —people who proposed staying but a short time in one place, and working for themselves only. Upon this road, more than in any other district of the South in which I have yet travelled, the Negroes seem to form a part of the commercial world. I was constantly overtaking them or meeting them going into the town with produce to sell, or returning with their purchases, the load being sometimes made into a bundle or laid in a flat basket and carried mile after mile on the head, while the shoes very likely were carried in one hand and an umbrella or stick in the other, and sometimes it would be stowed away into the body of a little, creaky, shaky, home-made cart, with a wooden axle so chafed and worn that the wheels, wandering in a headstrong way hither and thither, each making a serpentine track, gave additional labor to some poor creature of a horse, who tugs at his collar of plaited corn-

shucks, and seems hardly to have strength enough to break his
patched and rotten harness. Many of these travellers are dressed
quite well, and many are literally covered with rags.

A two hours' jolt over this road brought me to the plantation
which I desired to visit, a pleasant tract of land, bounded on two
sides by a blue river, and not far from Port Royal Ferry. The
kindness of the gentleman who plants it, Mr. J. H——, has enabled me to gain some exact information in regard to the general
management and working of the place during the past year. I have
selected this plantation as one that may be taken, all things considered, to furnish a fair sample of the present state of cotton
culture in this part of the country, and of the present condition and
disposition of the free laborers in the Sea Islands.

The plantation contains about three hundred acres of ordinarily
good land, of which, perhaps, a hundred acres are well adapted to
cotton, and a reasonable proportion of the remainder is capable of
producing corn. There is also potato ground, and low, wet ground,
on which rice can be raised. Flowing along one side of the plantation is a creek from which can be obtained salt mud and marsh
grass for manure, and to supply the people with wood there is a
large tract of pine barren. The cotton land is rather high, and the
soil is light, so that a dry season affects the crops unfavorably.

The people who form the working force consist in part of Negroes who were born and bred on the plantation, and in greater
part of people who came from the mainland with Sherman's army,
and were hired as laborers in February last. The whole number of
laborers was fifty-six. Forty-five of these were persons who, in
point of physical ability, ranked as full hands, two were
ploughmen, and nine were people too old or too young to perform
a good day's work. In round numbers, it may be said that the
working force consisted of fifty full hands and two ploughmen. The
season now ending is Mr. H——'s first year upon this plantation,
and the fourth year of his experience as a cotton planter. When the
time came for preparing the ground for planting he had upon the
place only the people who had always lived there, and who for
three years had been free laborers. To them he proposed that they

should work for him for wages in money; they proposed that he should give them half the crop as their wages, which he refused to do. An order had been issued from General Saxton's headquarters directing that whenever laborers worked a crop "on shares," their share should be one-half of all the cotton raised, and of all the breadstuffs, including corn, potatoes, rice, and peanuts. The people sent a deputation to the headquarters of the military governor and complained that Mr. H—— was endeavoring to force them to make a contract, the terms of which were contrary to the instructions of the circular No. 8. Mr. H——, therefore, received a letter calling his attention to the fact that any person violating these directions would be at once sent out of the department. He explained that false representations had been made, that he wished to hire his laborers for money, but they were disposed to insist that he should divide the crop with them. It was necessary that all contracts should be examined and approved at headquarters, and his proposals having been pronounced fair, he was permitted to proceed in his endeavors to hire the people. They, however, were still desirous of having their own plan carried into effect, and still refused to accede to his terms; he was even assailed by outcries of various kinds whenever he visited the Negro quarters, and demands for "half the crop." Meantime the empty houses on the plantation he had been filling up with families of refugees, and the time for planting was very near at hand. The people still remained fixed in their determination, and at last it became necessary to send a guard to the place with orders to remove all persons there resident who would neither sign the contract as prepared by the lessee and approved at headquarters, nor make room for others who were willing to do so. The threat alone was sufficient, and the signatures of all the laborers were at once given. By the time this difficulty was removed, the season was somewhat advanced, and the crop was not planted till more than a fortnight after the proper time. It may be thought that an occurrence such as I have just related is of itself enough to remove this plantation into the list of exceptional cases. But misunderstandings similar to this in their causes and effects, if not precisely like it in their details, are a part of the experiences of a majority, or at least of very many, of the Northern planters in the Sea Islands.

Mr. H——'s fifty laborers, assisted by the two ploughmen, planted eighty-seven acres of cotton, or considerably less than two acres apiece. Up to the 1st of November, 6,716 pounds of seed cotton had been picked, and it is not impossible that before the picking season closes the whole amount of seed cotton may be 8,000 pounds. The cost of the 6,716 pounds already gathered has been $1,631 for wages paid the laborers, exclusive of the interest on capital invested in mules and farming implements, the expenses of ginning the cotton, and the value of the manure. The cotton which is to be looked to for the repayment of this $1,631, to say nothing of the other expenses of the crop and the plantation in general, will, when ginned, amount to something like 1,670 pounds. This very unsatisfactory result is partly due to these three causes: On account of the controversy already mentioned the crop was planted late; it suffered severely from a long drought in July and August; the caterpillar made its appearance in August for the third time in three successive years, and though its ravages were not so extensive as in the two preceding years, they were sufficient to seriously diminish the crop. But for these three things Mr. H——'s enterprise would, he thinks, have proved moderately remunerative, and he intends to plant in 1866. Anything like perfect success, however, he fears, is unattainable at present, and he is not yet quite prepared to say whether the fault is in the Negroes, or in the system of labor and payment that has been adopted in this department. Although in these Sea Islands the Negroes are now in the fourth year of their freedom, he is of opinion that they have never yet been fairly tried as free laborers. And now, he would say, to leave untouched the various questions that have agitated this department at one time and another—whether or not it is well to make the Negroes all landholders by a division of land amongst them; whether or not it was a wise policy to allow Negroes to pre-empt land; whether or not a Negro in Port Royal should receive just the same, or more, or less wages than a stevedore in New York—setting all these questions aside, he believes that the system of wages for labor which has prevailed in this department is of itself an insuperable obstacle in the way of successful cultivation of cotton by free labor. That alone would account for the prevalent ill success. For example, a man comes to his place to work for him, and takes up, say, an acre of cotton. He moves into a house on the place, and in February goes out into the field and lays out his acre into the regular four *tasks*. He chops down the weeds with his hoe, lays them in the furrows between the old cotton beds, and pulls the earth of the old bed over the weeds. That's *listing,* and he gets so much a task for listing. Then he goes out again and pulls up the earth on the listing. That's *banking,* and he has so much a task for banking. Then comes planting, and so much a task for that, and so much a task for each hoeing and each hauling. For such and such an operation so many cents. By-and-bye picking comes, and there's so much a pound for all the cotton picked; everything as easy and regular as clock-work. But if he's wanted to do a quarter of an hour's work at any time, he expects pay for that. If he goes to the house for an axe he's to be paid extra for it. It's well enough to pay a man for all he does, but who can carry on a farm in such a way as that? But suppose you want him very much for some piece of work that must be done. You cannot have him. He's working an acre of cotton for you, but his corn, and his rice, and potatoes make a little farm that he's working for himself, and he can't do job-work for you when he's got his provisions to make; he needs to have control of his own time. He had hardly a single worker out of all his fifty-six who hadn't more land under cultivation for himself than for his employer.

The whole affair down here looked rather discouraging, but at the same time he would not say, and no one ought to say, that the application of free Negro labor to cotton raising was a failure, till he had seen the experiment tried more fairly than it had been in this department. If it were possible to make a change merely in the matter of supporting and paying the laborers, greatly improved results might be expected.

PORT ROYAL ISLAND, S. C., November 17, 1865

WHILE staying on the plantation mentioned in my last letter, I visited a school kept by two young ladies resident there, and attended by about a hundred children from the immediate neighborhood. A portable school-house sent out from Philadelphia last winter was partly destroyed by Sherman's men before it could be erected, and for the present the school-room is the large barn-loft of a cotton-house. Its uses in the past are shown by the broken bits of machinery fixed to the posts, and the dusty, worn-out gins pushed away into a far corner to make room for the blackboards and benches of today. The school has been in operation almost six months. The teachers, like those of nearly every school in the Sea Islands not supported by the munificence of some planter, are paid by some of the Northern charitable associations, and instruction is given gratuitously. Usually, after the children are dismissed, a few of the laborers on the plantation receive a lesson in reading, and at the regular school session I saw three or four adults present; but most of the scholars are between six and sixteen years old. Some of them were very neatly dressed and all were tolerably clean. Their behavior, as a rule, was quite orderly, and in all cases it was obedient and respectful. There was more noise in the room than most teachers of a Northern school would allow, but this was because the lessons are learned out of school hours, and because of the lack of proper school furniture. Nothing could be better than the close attention given to the book and the teacher by each class actually engaged in recitation. There is seldom any need of resorting to whipping or other punishment. The grown people, I was told, are slow to learn, even though they apply themselves faithfully and laboriously; but the children do quite as well as white children in Pennsylvania, for they are willing and eager to be taught, and are very constant in their attendance. The morning of my visit was rainy, but there were eighty pupils assembled, and some of them had walked a distance of two or three miles. After looking at the copy-books, which were singularly clean and contained some very fair specimens of running hand, an opportunity was afforded me to judge of the proficiency of the most advanced class. They had begun their studies in March last, at which time some of them knew the alphabet, and have had a long vacation of three months in the hot weather, so that they have only been five or six months under instruction. First they answered general questions on the map of North America. The relative positions of the various countries were given and cities and chief towns were named with commendable correctness. The worst blunder made was that of a boy who was asked "What large city is on the Pacific coast?" "New York," he said, and the teacher rebuked him: "William has been in New York himself, and he says it is on the Pacific Ocean. He doesn't deserve to go there." When the day's lesson was finished, the class gave definitions of terms in physical geography. Then came a reading lesson and the spelling of words which had occurred in it, some of them being of three or four syllables and each pupil defining the word he spelled. This was very well done. In written arithmetic the class were able to perform long sums in addition with great promptness, and came out easily successful from the attempt to enumerate large numbers made up of significant figures at the beginning and end and ciphers only in the middle. In mental arithmetic the performance was in multiplication, and was equally satisfactory. All this time the primary department was in full operation at the other end of the room, and those on the benches divided their attention between the alphabet cards on their left hand and the globe and the long rows of figures on their right. After a short recess, several patriotic songs were sung and the "shout" chant, "Hold your light," which is religious in its character and hortatory, one and another Christian

brother and sister being addressed by name and urged to hold their
light "on Canaan's sho'." In respect to pronunciation, by the way,
it is noticeable that in the singing and other school exercises, the
peculiar Negro dialect is to a considerable extent discarded; in
their ordinary talk, as might be expected, they again lapse into it,
and the transition is sometimes amusingly sudden.

During the week just past I have visited several plantations on
St. Helena Island, and had opportunity to converse with many
gentlemen who for the last three or four years have been engaged
in raising cotton. They are all Northern men, and some of them
are persons who were sent out from Boston by the Freedmen's Aid
Society, in the spring of 1862, as superintendents of plantations.
Afterwards, when lands in the Sea Islands were sold for the non-
payment of direct taxes, they either purchased plantations for themselves or became managers for other purchasers.

The planter with whom I first talked was of this latter class. He
had in his charge several plantations, containing in the aggregate
eleven hundred acres of land, and cultivated by about one hundred
laborers of both sexes. This year he planted two hundred and
thirty-five acres of cotton, and an equal number of acres was
planted in corn and miscellaneous crops by the people for themselves, so that the total quantity of land cultivated by each laborer
was 3.7 acres. For their manual labor on the cotton crop, up to the
time of laying by, the people were paid fifteen dollars an acre, and
for the picking they received two and a half cents a pound. Mr.
R—— finds that these wages are sufficiently high to stimulate the
people to work, and, as a general rule, to work well. The former
owner of one of these plantations paid a visit to it in the course of
the past summer, and gave it as his opinion that the land was as
well and faithfully tilled now as in old times under the old system.
Mr. R—— speaks of one exception to the general rule. The collection of marsh-grass and marsh-mud for manure is a branch of
farm-work comparatively disagreeable, and the Negroes will not
undertake it except at a price which is altogether exorbitant.

This year's crop was injured by the drought, and very much
diminished by the caterpillar, so that the whole amount of ginned

cotton produced will not exceed 11,000 pounds. The same number of acres in 1863, the most favorable and the most successful season since free labor has been employed, would have yielded 21,-150 pounds, and under the system of slave labor, as the average yield per acre was 130 pounds, the product of 235 acres would have been 30,550 pounds. This difference in production is owing to several causes, but mainly to the fact that formerly the land was much more thoroughly manured than at present, and this will account, also, for an admitted deterioration in the length and fineness of the staple.

As to the profits of planting at the present time, Mr. R—— informs me that, exclusive of the value of the land occupied by the laborer, and of the fuel and house-rent which is given him, each pound of cotton that he can raise in an ordinarily favorable year costs him fifty cents. The business may be made remunerative, therefore, while the present high prices are maintained. It is known that for some years previously to emancipation the cultivation of long-staple cotton in South Carolina was not a lucrative occupation, the capital invested seldom returning in the way of profit a higher rate of interest than four or five per cent. The plough, Mr. R—— thinks, may hereafter take the place of the hoe to a very great extent, and by means of it he expects to lessen the expenses the coming season. Mr. R—— says that he has found the Negroes on his plantations neither improvident nor idle; that, except in the matter of getting marsh-grass and mud, their labor is quite as much under his control as he considers desirable. They cultivate less land now than in old times, when each hand was required to work about six acres; but this is because while the soldiers were here in great numbers the people have been able to obtain money more easily by the sale of fish and poultry and vegetables than by plantation work. Doubtless their experience in that respect has injured their character as hired laborers, but now that the army is withdrawn, he looked for an immediate improvement, if one chose to call it improvement; the money was honestly earned in either way. He had never observed that there was any disinclination to work in the cotton-field; some of the men who owned land of their own proposed to plant cotton for him next year. It would not be easy to substitute the system of day-labor for the task system now in use, for the people preferred the latter; yet it could be done, and the Negroes could become efficient and profitable day-laborers. They would need instruction first, and example; the farmer should take off his coat and work with them.

Each of the plantations, he said, which he was superintending had been divided by the owner, and one-half the land he was now selling in small lots to such families as were living on it at the time of the Government sales in 1863. Five dollars an acre was the price demanded, and the Negroes were very glad to purchase. By the general adoption of some such plan he thought the troublesome question of settling upon a labor system would receive an easy solution.

The possession by every head of a family of such a quantity of land would preserve the Negro from being wholly dependent on the employer, and would not diminish the supply of labor while it improved its quality. The men who were buying these small homesteads still wished to be hired by him, and some were unwilling to purchase until they had been assured that they could continue to get employment on his plantation.

Within the last four years the domestic condition of the people had considerably improved. He could now sell many little articles of household furniture, such as knives and forks, plates, tinware of all kinds, and other similar conveniences, of which their cabins were then entirely destitute; and they all dressed themselves much better now than formerly. There were few families of his acquaintance, he thought, that had not a little hoard of money. He knew some great liars and thieves, but had no reason to doubt that more than nine-tenths of his people were reasonably honest and truthful. They were very much like white men.

The Negroes who hold land, he said, are not managing it so well as the white planters. At the present time, perhaps, no land in the Sea Islands is cultivated as it should be. Theirs, as a general rule, for want of capital and skill, is rather worse cultivated than any other.

Stopping on my way from this hospitable plantation to another, some eight or nine miles distant, I passed a pleasant hour in the largest of the St. Helena schools. It is divided into three departments: a primary, an intermediate, and a higher, each of which is in charge of its own teacher, and occupies a separate room. The branches of study pursued in all the rooms are reading and spelling, writing, geography, and arithmetic; the degree of advancement attained by the pupils constituting the only difference between the departments. The oldest scholar that I saw was a young man, and he was in the primary school-room. The children flock in so numerously that the school accommodations have grown too small—the seats designed for a hundred and twenty scholars being filled full and crowded by the hundred and eighty who are admitted, and not a few are altogether shut out. The exercises were, of course, similar to those already described, and were even better performed, for the school has been longer established; and, as it seemed to me, the length of time during which the pupils have been engaged in intellectual pursuits had not only brought about an improvement in their manners and general appearance, but had worked a visible change in the expression of their faces. One of the teachers apologized for the dress of her scholars, saying that at this season of the year most of them were obliged to work in the morning, harvesting the sweet potatoes, and, as tardiness was not permitted, came from the field in their working-clothes. For most of them, however, no apology was necessary. The school building was a gift from friends in Philadelphia, and is a neat little house, standing surrounded by some magnificent green and gray live-oaks, whose shade was grateful even in November.

The second plantation which I visited is quite large, containing 1,500 acres and supporting a colored population of two hundred and forty persons of all ages. One hundred and forty of these, who are over sixteen years of age, may be called workers, and, during the past season, have cultivated one hundred and ninety-four acres of cotton. As on the other plantations of which I have any knowledge, an equal extent of ground has been cultivated by the people for their own use. Upon their corn land they pay a tax of one bushel to the acre, and they are also expected to supply all the sweet potatoes that may be needed by the white family. The cater-pillar and the drought carried off three-eighths of the cotton crop, so that less than 12,000 pounds of clean cotton will be produced. The cost of production has reached $7,776, an amount which does not include the expenses of the shipment and sale of the cotton, the diminution in the value of the stock and implements, the inter-est on the money invested, nor the sum of $587 expended for the support of a free school in which more than a hundred children have received instruction.

The gentleman who carried on this plantation was of opinion that before cotton-raising in the Sea Islands could become either a profitable or pleasant occupation it would be necessary to make a complete change in the system of labor. The fault of the present plan lay in the fact that the employer had no control whatever over his laborers. They worked when they pleased, and at what they pleased, and only so long as they pleased. It was a fault that made the system almost unendurable. He agreed with his friend, Mr. J——, to live in this country and try to carry on a plantation was a constant tax on a man's self-respect. He could not secure the obedi-ence of the men whom he hired; was under the necessity of coax-ing them to do the work they were paid for, and often he coaxed in vain. For example, Mr. H—— said, he had a good blow of cotton in the field once, and was very desirous of getting it picked; so he told the people to go out and pick it. They were busy at the time ginning the cotton already gathered, and at the end of a week he found that not one person had been into the field. He was deter-mined to get the cotton picked, so he locked the gin-house door. That exactly suited them, however; it was just time then to dig the slip potatoes, and till the slips were dug the cotton was not touched.

Such cases, Mr. S—— said, were of weekly occurrence on his plantation. It so happened that he had found no difficulty in get-ting marsh-grass cut, but some planters had found it almost an impossibility, and every planter was subject to the caprice of his people.

Mr. H—— said that under the present system the laborer worked for his employer rather less than three months in the year; he seldom labored more than five hours in the day, and half of that time was spent in cultivating his own crop of corn or potatoes or groundnuts, so that his employer had the use of his services about one-fourth of each working day. But it was not wonderful that they had become bad laborers. The only wonder was how so much good came to be left in them after all the efforts of their enemies and their injudicious friends. He would like to see all the working people of the Sea Islands hiring themselves out to a set of tight-fisted Yankee farmers, who would be just towards them, taking nothing and giving nothing for nothing, and without a spark of sentiment in them. It would be for the best interests of the people that such a thing should come to them, and come as soon as possible. The present system of things was unbusinesslike and ought to end. He had no objection to the Negroes doing as they pleased; but he had a right to live here as well as they, and they ought to do as they pleased on their own ground. Though, for that matter, the plan of allowing them to take up so much of the plantation for their own exclusive use, and the fact that it had been almost impossible in the past to discharge any laborer, no matter how idle he might be and how ill-behaved, had made them about as independent of the land-owner as if the land were owned by themselves.

I asked these gentlemen what opinion they had formed of the general character of the Negroes in Port Royal. The longer he lived with them, Mr. H—— said, the less confidence he had in their truth and honesty. Mr. S—— said that it would be necessary to admit the Negroes to the witness-box, but he was afraid that very little reliance could be placed upon their word. The taking of an oath would make them not a whit more worthy of belief. They seemed to disregard perjury. There were several cases which had been brought before plantation commissions on St. Helena that still remained unsettled, because, in the confusion of lies and perjuries that must have been uttered by the opposing witnesses, the members of the commission were entirely at a loss. Lawyers would untangle such skeins, he supposed. He had serious doubts if the testimony of one respectable white man ought not to outweigh that of ten Negroes. Stealing is very common; cotton is pilfered on all sides, and sold to unprincipled dealers at Beaufort, who buy and ask no questions. But one great reason for that is because stealing can be done with impunity, there being no settled law now in operation. In respect to chastity, there seemed to be some improvement, though the ties of marriage were yet too easily taken on and thrown off. They were improving, too, in their desire for home comforts, though less rapidly than one would expect.

And many of their faults, Mr. S—— thought, had been encouraged and confirmed, rather than discouraged and removed, during the past four years. He felt convinced that a system of labor which should leave the employer and the Negroes perfectly free would show that the latter were careful, industrious, and profitable servants. Only give him the power over his laborers which a Northern farmer has over his hired hands, and he would ensure as large a crop of cotton as was ever produced in old times.

At the house where I passed the night, that of a Quaker from Delaware, who has been in the Sea Islands a little more than three years, but who never planted cotton till this spring, I had an hour's conversation on the same topics. He, too, had carried on cotton raising at a loss, although he had escaped the ravages of the caterpillar. If he gathers all the cotton that he now expects to gather, it will have cost him when ginned a dollar a pound. His condemnation of the present system of labor was unqualified. For every acre that his people planted for him for wages they planted precisely two acres for themselves, and it was hard to induce them to take up more cotton ground than would supply them with spending money. Their living they expected to make off their own land. As a friend of the colored people, he would say that he would not wish a final judgment of them to be deduced from their present condition in the Sea Islands.

These same opinions, which I found to be held by a majority of the gentlemen with whom I conversed, would be expressed, perhaps, in less temperate language by a majority of the Northern planters in Port Royal. On Thursday next they are to meet in the Baptist Church on St. Helena Island, for the purpose of taking into consideration the system of labor now in use and devising means for its improvement. Whether or not any of the Negroes are to be present at this conference I do not know.

XXI

CHARLESTON, S. C., November 27, 1865

THE various new influences and agencies recently brought to bear upon the freed people of South Carolina are all under the direction and control of officers whose headquarters are in this city. The courtesy of these gentlemen has enabled me, during my stay in Charleston, to gather some information, not easily to be obtained elsewhere, on two or three interesting subjects, such as the Negro schools, the Freedmen's Savings Bank, one of the most useful of General Saxton's institutions, the working of the Freedmen's Bureau throughout the State, and the reports made by its subordinate officers to the Assistant Commissioner.

The task of instructing the Negroes was begun at Port Royal, under the auspices of the Northern Freedmen's Aid Commissions, so long ago as the spring of 1862, and the schools then founded have since been constantly giving instruction to many hundred persons, and are still in successful operation. As soon as Charleston was surrendered, these same charitable societies sent out their teachers and a supply of books; and in March last, under the general supervision of Mr. Redpath, of Massachusetts, several large schools were formed, which were kept open till July. In the autumn, by a happy appointment, Mr. Reuben Tomlinson was made State Superintendent of Education. He at once proceeded to grade the schools in the city, to provide them with suitable rooms, and so far as possible to extend the school system over all the State. To a considerable extent this has been effected. The Freedmen's Bureau is poor, and before the school buildings could be fitted for the reception of pupils it became necessary for the superintendent to expend something like a thousand dollars of his private means in making needful repairs. The houses had suffered from Gillmore's bombardment.

By the middle of October about eighteen hundred scholars were collected into three schools, separated into many classes, and put in charge of forty competent teachers. The largest school, held in the old Normal School building, contains nearly eight hundred pupils. The head-master is a colored man, a graduate of the University of Glasgow, and the various classes are taught by about twenty persons, of whom some are Northern women and some Southern, and of the latter some are white and some are colored. In the other large school the principal is a Massachusetts man, and among his sixteen subordinates are included women from New England, women who were once slaves, and women belonging to Charleston families once wealthy, but made poor by the war. Among the pupils there were no white children, or rather, none of unmixed Caucasian blood; there were many whom most people would have taken for white, and more than a fourth of the children were brown or yellow. I visited many of the rooms, finding the scholars studious and very orderly, and at all stages of advancement. In a room of the Normal School building three hundred children together were taking an object lesson; in another room a class of boys, whose parents, I was told, intended them for professional life, were transposing, analyzing, and parsing a passage from Milton's "L'Allegro," and recitations in reading and arithmetic were going on with more or less success before the other teachers.

A majority of the pupils in these schools were ignorant of the alphabet a year ago, but nearly half of them had received some instruction. The first assistant in the Normal School building, a free colored girl, has kept a private school in Charleston during the past four years, and among her present pupils are many of her old ones. Having been herself educated by her father, she began just before the war to teach a class of forty or fifty free colored girls in her own house. Under the law prohibiting the teaching of Negroes she was twice arrested, but by the interposition of her mother's guardian, Major King, a license was granted her by Mayor McBeth to keep a school for free colored persons, on condition that no slaves should be admitted to it, and that a white person should be always in the room during school hours. She complied with these conditions, hiring a white woman to sit in the school-room with her sewing, and kept the school open till the capture of the city.

I am told that the free Negroes, as distinguished from the freed people, still cultivate a feeling of exclusiveness, and, among other modes of displaying it, still send their children to private schools. Whether or not their action in that particular is justified by any superiority of the private over the public schools, I cannot say.

All the teachers in Charleston, as well as in the State at large, are paid by the New York National Relief Association, or by the New England Freedman's Aid Commission. The buildings now occupied by the schools belong to the State, and as these may soon be taken away from the Bureau, the Superintendent of Education proposes soon to solicit contributions from Northern men in order that he may build a house for the exclusive use of the freedmen.

In the whole State there are now forty-eight schools in operation, attended by six thousand pupils, and taught by one hundred and eight teachers, of whom eighty are from the North and twenty-eight are Southerners. In Columbia, Greenville, Orangeburg, Summerville, Georgetown, and on the coast islands schools are already established; they are in process of organization at Camden, Florence, Darlington, Sumter, and Cheraw, and it is confidently hoped that before the spring at least one teacher will be at work in each county town. The superintendent, after an extended tour through the State, reports the white people as not only indifferent but entirely opposed to the educating of the Negroes, and is of opinion that outside of Charleston no colored school could be maintained a month after the Federal troops are withdrawn.

The South Carolina Freedmen's Savings Bank was founded at Beaufort in August, 1864. The colored soldiers then in the Department of the South were receiving large bounties and good pay, and many of them being unused to the possession of money were in the habit of spending it wastefully and improvidently. For example, after a regiment had been paid off it was not unusual to see a soldier wearing two watches and two chains, and some one of the little jewelry shops at Beaufort or Hilton Head would sell as many as seventy, more or less, worthless watches in one day. It was not uncommon for the officers of colored regiments to borrow their men's money and embark it in some land scheme or other profitable business. If the creditors of these officers chanced to die, they very likely left no heirs, for many of them were refugees from hostile States and without families. It was proved that the captain of one company, after the paymaster had made his rounds, sent his orderly sergeant on a borrowing mission to every man in his command. It was in the interest of the soldiers, therefore, that General Saxton established his bank. Two gentlemen of his staff, who served without salary, were designated as managers of the business, with orders to receive deposits of five cents and upwards. Interest at the rate of 5 per cent. was to be paid on all sums exceeding $25, and when dividends should be declared the profits that had accrued were to be divided among persons who had deposited $25 and upwards. All investments were to be made in United States securities. General Saxton issued a circular explaining the objects of the institution, telling the freedmen, "You will thus have a secure place of deposit for your money, where it will yield you a fair rate of interest, and will at the same time indirectly aid in sustaining the Government which is doing so much for you." Deposits at once came in rapidly, and the enterprise seems to have been very successful. A circular issued on the 16th ult., when the bank was a little more than a year old, makes these statements: "On this day the actual deposits in the bank amounted to $250,-734.74, of which there had been paid out to depositors $73,-690.71. After paying all expenses, the total assets, consisting of United States securities and cash on hand, amount to $179,-066.20, showing a profit to the bank of about $2,000 over and above all liabilities and expenditures."

The funds remaining in the bank on the 16th of October have been turned over to the National Freedmen's Savings and Trust

Company, and I believe the sum thus entrusted to that corporation forms by far the larger part of its capital.

The depositors in the bank at Beaufort were nearly all soldiers. The laborers there deposited very little; for, while they had less money than the men serving in the army, their expenses were very much greater, and less pains was taken to inform them of the nature of the institution. Their small savings were usually concealed in their cabins.

The Freedmen's Bureau was organized in this State by the appointment of General Saxton as Assistant Commissioner. General Ely, at Columbia, is an Acting Assistant Commissioner, and is subject to General Saxton's orders. Subordinate to these officers, there are officials of two classes thinly scattered up and down over the State; in several of the districts there are civilians, called agents of the Bureau, who have no other duty than to attend to the government and protection of the Negroes. The limited fund at the disposal of the Commissioner has kept the number of such agents very small. The great bulk of the colored population where it can be reached by the Bureau at all is in the charge of sub-assistant commissioners. These are military officers who, in addition to their strictly military functions as commanders of garrisons and the like, are expected to carry into effect the orders of the Assistant Commissioner. For this additional duty, as may be supposed, they have little liking and little fitness of any sort. At headquarters it is said of them that a majority of the sub-assistants cannot be trusted to do justice between the laborers and the planters; they invariably range themselves on the side of the latter.

It is beyond a doubt that during the past year many of these officials have permitted the planters to tie their laborers up by the thumbs, to throw them into confinement, and to ill-use and oppress them in many ways. I hear of plantations where Negroes have been compelled to work throughout the season under a contract which gave them as wages only one-sixth of the crop. It is to be remembered that all planting this year was done late, and that there has been almost no attempt to raise anything more than a limited quantity of breadstuffs. As a consequence, therefore, of the mistaken policy pursued in many districts, there are large numbers of Negroes, of whom some are newly discharged from their places, who have only four or five bushels of corn for the support of their families through the winter. Many of them have even less than that. An agent of the Bureau in Beaufort district says in his report for the month of November: "The pressure upon this office for assistance for those who have spent the summer far up in the State, laboring for Mr. Inscot, Robert Barnwell, and others, who have now sent them here without any pay for the summer's work or provisions for the winter, is immense."

Doubtless, an officer of the greatest ability and activity, with the best intentions, would find it almost impossible, with the means now in his control, to protect all the Negroes in one of these wide-extending districts.

Every agent of the Bureau is required to make a monthly report of affairs in his district to the Assistant Commissioner, and he, in turn, at the end of each month sends a concise abstract of the reports to the office of the Commissioner at Washington. The brief for October I have been permitted to see, and I made some extracts from it as perhaps showing more fully than it could be done in any other way some features of the present condition of the freedmen in this State. Reports had been received from eleven districts only, and those for the most part situated on the coast and along the Georgia line. "In the interior of the State," says the report, in conclusion, "where military force cannot readily reach the plantations, affairs are in general worse. It is difficult to reach the murderers of colored people, as they hide themselves and are screened by their neighbors."

Of Edgefield district it is said: "Several affidavits have been received of cruelties practised here. One freedman with two males and one female children were stripped naked, tied up, and whipped severely, threats of murder being made if complaint was made to the military. Another man was whipped severely with a stick and cut over the eye with a knife, and, as he ran away to escape from their cruelty, was shot at. A woman was severely whipped and carried off to jail, and, as she has disappeared, fears are entertained that she has been murdered. Two children were severely whipped and their mother driven off the plantation without any pay for work done."

In Georgetown district "it is reported that the planters, with assistance of the military, compel the freedmen to do work not called for under their contracts. On one plantation a freedman was twice beaten over the head with a stick and was refused rations."

In Beaufort district, "the officer at Beach Branch is reported as assisting the planters in acts of injustice and cruelty to the freedmen. In one case, a woman and her children were brutally whipped and driven off the place after the crop was harvested. Two men were tied up four feet from the ground and left in that condition more than two hours."

In Anderson district, "one man was shot and killed in presence of his wife, who begged for his life. Two other men were tied up, cruelly flogged, then shot (and, it is believed, killed, as the men have disappeared), while the wife of one of the men received fifty lashes."

The report, in speaking of the Barnwell district, after detailing six cases of Negro whipping, and several other outrages that took place during October, goes on to say, that "two freedmen were whipped by their master, who took them to the commanding officer at Barnwell, who told him to whip them again, as they had not had half enough. This officer is reported to pay no attention to the complaints of freedmen. With such an officer in power it is hardly possible to protect them from abuse. Lawlessness on the part of the freedmen must be looked for under such circumstances. It is reported that a band of sixty of them are organized for the purpose of robbery. The leader of it and three men had been captured, and one escaping was shot, and afterwards died of the wound."

Of this district it is also stated that "a regular pass and patrol system (such as was in vogue at the time of slavery) is said to exist."

In Darlington, Williamsburg, and Marion districts, "the reports show in general a better state of affairs than elsewhere. The freedmen are self-supporting, and there is little or no conflict between the two races, though there are individual cases of injustice and dissatisfaction. Many of the planters are not making contracts for the ensuing year, as they are waiting to see what legislation may be made in regard to labor."

Most of these statements are based on affidavits made by the injured parties, and by witnesses of the occurrences. When the report of a case calling for the arrest and trial of any man reaches the office of the Assistant Commissioner, it is necessarily referred to the military commander of the department. It has been usual in this State for the general in command to refer it back to the commander of the district named in the report. Then it is referred by him to the subordinate officer stationed nearest to the place where the outrage is alleged to have occurred. Hitherto it has been found that when this stage was reached the matter ended. Without the cooperation of the military the Commissioner is quite powerless to bring any criminal to justice or to carry the orders of the Bureau into effect.

Just at the cessation of hostilities, in May last, several Negroes living on a plantation in Clarendon district refused to work any longer under the old system. They were full of uncertainty as to the future, and they were very much dissatisfied with their overseer, a man by the name of White. Six of them, therefore, left home one morning in a body. White and several of his neighbors pursued them with dogs, and captured them all. One was shot in attempting to escape; the other five were at once hung by the roadside. For a month after this event the people on the plantation remained at home, but some of them at last made their way to Charleston and Kingstree. Affidavits were taken, and complaint was formally made, but the crime has not yet been punished. Perhaps an offense of so great magnitude, and so easily susceptible of complete proof, could nowhere in the State pass unquestioned at the present time; yet this I think by no means quite certain.

It is probable that during the coming winter there will be a good deal of suffering among the freedmen for want of food and clothing. Even more distress is to be apprehended in the Gulf States than in South Carolina. At present, however, less food is given away by the Government than at any time since Johnston's surrender. The money value of the rations delivered to destitute freedmen in Georgia and South Carolina during the month of October was $29,672.09, which is less than half the value of those issued in those two States in the month of September, and in September the value was not so great as in the preceding months. Throughout the four years of war very few masters gave their people the customary supply of clothing, and the destitution in this particular is, therefore, not wholly of recent growth.

But little, I should say, is to be hoped for from State action in these matters. The Negro code has been framed, and if that fails to be applied it seems unlikely that anything else will be attempted. I observe a marked change in the feeling and language of the people; they seem much less confident than they were three or four weeks ago that the management of their affairs is to be at once entrusted to their own legislation. These apprehensions affect their actions as well as their words. Mr. Wm. Whaley, a candidate for Congress in the Second district, was beaten at the polls by Mr. Aiken and by General Stephen Eliot, "the hero of Fort Sumter," as he was styled in the electioneering placards. About one half of the voters took no part in the election. In Barnwell district, a very large county, Mr. Whaley says that the polls were not opened. Since the day of election his friends, he says, have come to him by scores and excused themselves for voting for his opponent: "The delegation was not going to be admitted, and they thought it just as well to let Governor Aiken stand in the lobby as to let him." In Orangeburg and other districts there was the same indifference, and from the newspapers I might quote many expressions of the despondency that has recently stolen over the community.

XXII

COLUMBIA, S. C., December 5, 1865

THE hardships of railway travelling over the swamps and uplands of South Carolina have been often set forth of late, and have not been exaggerated. Rails worn out, shaky, creaking trestle-works, the slow, thumping motion, the frequent transfers from dirty cars to dirtier ferry-boats and stages, the lack of hotels at the stopping places, and the long delays, with a dozen other inconveniences, rob the traveller of rest and peace of body and mind. After a few hours' ride, everybody becomes fatigued and thoroughly ill-humored, and only speaks to grumble. At Florence, in the dusk of the evening, I heard a small, smoke-dried, vicious-looking boy, a poor white of thirteen or fourteen years old, giving expression to his own feelings and those of his fellow-passengers. He stood on the car-platform, leaning over the brake in an attitude of exhaustion, and accosted me as I went up the steps:

"A'n't there no sellers round yer sellin' snacks?"

"No," I told him; "there's a hotel, though."

"Yes, hominy for a dollar. There'd ought to be sellers. I'm starved myself and so's ma'am. Dog-gorn sich roads anyhow. Wear me out. By G——, I could git down an' walk a heap faster'n these cussed kyars. Creepin' along so durned slow! I'd like to know if they think they're goin' to make connections."

Then he pronounced the engineer and conductor "no account," and imprecated curses on his own head if he ever was hired to run trains on that road. Going into the car he joined his mother, a person even more irascible and fierce than himself, to whom he briefly reported his ill success, and then the two slept, curled up in one seat for the sake of warmth, till we reached Sumterville. A seven or eight hours' ride, at the rate of four miles an hour, brought us, at four o'clock in the morning, to Kingsville. The village never contained more than half a dozen buildings, and, as Sherman's men have been there, only two of these remain. A bed could be had at neither, and the passengers made themselves as comfortable as might be in the cars. The air was full of a white mist, obscuring the stars; but the night was not dark, for the moon was shining, and the weather was unseasonably warm. I walked about, therefore, a little while, and went along towards some fires that were burning in the open air at a few rods' distance. Close beside the track lay a confused heap of bundles and boxes and rude furniture, evidently the household property of Negroes. There were small pots and pans, bags of corn, groundnuts tied up in sheets, three-legged stools, and coops in which hens and chickens were cackling and peeping. Behind this barricade were several rude huts, made of poles or boards, with a covering of canvas or rusty sheets of iron from the ruined locomotives. In front of each shelter was a fire, with men and women round it talking and smoking. Other Negroes lay among the luggage guarding it, and the whole camp seemed to contain about a hundred people. I talked first with one of the old women. She rose from her seat on the ground as I approached and made a courtesy, while her companion, still older than herself, remained cowering over the embers. Both were without shoes and very ragged.

"You're sitting up late," I said.

"Who for watch de tings, mawssa, ef we sleep? Who for watch my leel corn and grun-nut? Tell er, mawssa, 'bleeged to sit up late, 'less dey be gone 'fore day, clean."

"You've got a good deal of corn, have you?"

"Got not but tree peck. Dat's my sheer when dey sheered. Dunno ef I has tree peck."

"Is that what you've got to keep you next year?"

"Dat leel bit o' corn keep me! Can't. Not ef I was to eat it by grains. No, can't, can't, sister," said the other old creature.

"All we gang o' nigger," they told me, "is rice nigger." Three years ago, Mr. H. B——, their master, who was a rice planter on the Combahee, had moved more than a hundred of them up into Richland district out of the way of the Yankees, and, having hired land, had kept them employed in raising corn. They had now for three nights and two days been "waitin' upon de train" that was to take them back to their former place of residence, and they seemed very glad at the thought of returning. I asked if any of their people had died since they were moved up the country. "Oh, 'nough dead," the old woman said, " 'nough," and they called a man from the nearest hut to help them in counting. The three together recollected twenty-eight. Why had so many died? I asked. "Look yer, mawssa," said the woman, "shum? shum?" showing first one bare foot and then the other; "dat's what do 'em. No shoe, no cloes, an' den de fros' git up into deir body, tell when de sun come down so hot, dey dies too fas'. Tight livin' what do 'em so; not'in' to eat. S' help me God, some day I trow my head back so, look up into de heaben—dear Christ, mawssa, I most' starve to death."

The last time when blankets and clothing had been given them was the winter before the war broke out. During the season just closed they had been working for one-half the crop, and some of them had received ten bushels of corn and three or four bushels of groundnuts. Others had received only a bushel of corn; but these were very inferior hands, such as old people who could do no field-work, but had been employed in spinning and minding the children. Their employer had also given them a monthly allowance of corn meal and molasses. I asked the man what were his plans for the coming year. He didn't know; he'd prefer to get a piece of ground for his own, and he looked at me enquiringly. It wasn't likely, I told him, that he would be able to do that. Then he'd work for master, he reckoned, on the rice plantation. If he couldn't be by himself, he and his family working land for themselves, he'd prefer to stay with his fellow-servants. Mr. B—— wanted them all to go back to his place, and that was where they were going now. He'd work for money or on shares.

One of the passengers, a mild-faced, mild-spoken little Irish gen-

tleman, had walked down into the camp, having found it vain to
hope for sleep in the uncomfortable car, and we whiled away an
hour in conversation. He had been an instructor in the Catholic
college or seminary at Columbia, and appeared to have taken no
interest in politics or war. He talked of Kingsville as he had known
it during the past four years. His home was in Sumter, and in going
to visit his family he was often compelled to wait a day or two in
Kingsville. The cars would be broken down, or all the cars would
be needed for the transportation of soldiers or of Federal prisoners
going from Andersonville to Florence. It would have melted a
heart of stone to look at them. Wirtz, the jailer at Andersonville,
had been executed, he believed; if he was responsible for the horrible condition of those men, surely he deserved hanging. He never
had gone but once to the place where they had them guarded; a
second sight of them he could not have borne. All of them were
shockingly filthy and hardly looked like human beings; some were
nearly naked as they were born, some were starved down to skin
and bone, some were begging pitifully for a drink of water, and
some were in the very act of dying. He should not forget to the last
moment of his life two or three that were crazed and ran about
with loud cries and laughter. It seemed to him as if mercy and
humanity had fled the land, and the earth had become a pande-
monium. There was no pity or respect for the dead even; they
were buried as you'd bury an old horse. He pointed out the spot
among the trees, on the north side of the railroad, where he had
seen these things, and declared that he desired never to put his
eyes on it again.

At seven o'clock a train of empty freight cars arrived, with the
engine laboring in the rear, and in the course of the next three
hours we were pushed along to Hopkins's Turn-out, where the
road at present terminates. Here, too, were Negroes encamped
beside the road, with their corn and bedding piled around them,
waiting till they could be carried down to the coast. I learn from
the officers of the Bureau in this city that during November they
sent down about two hundred and fifty persons each week, and
they give transportation to those only who are too old or too

young to make the journey on foot. Through the summer and early autumn transportation was given to none; but it is estimated that in each month more than a thousand Negroes passed through Columbia on their way to the low country, most of them being Negroes whom their masters had removed into the interior for safekeeping. The opinion that land is to be given them by the Government is, or was, undoubtedly prevalent—how generally prevalent it would be very hard to say, but in any case the people would have made very great exertions to get back to their former homes and the country in which they were born—"their old range," as they express it.

At Hopkins's the traveller chooses some one of the several stages which in four hours and for four dollars carry passengers through the mud to Columbia. Even at this distance from the sea the country, though somewhat rolling and not entirely sandy, is still a dreary pine forest, and in the twelve miles' ride we passed but very few clearings. The road, however, is well travelled, and we met more than a hundred wagons, of which most were getting, as best they could, to the railroad with heavy loads of cotton. Four or five Government wagons also we met. "What's them comin'?" said our driver. "Damned Yankee wagons. I hate to give 'em the road, but I'll have to do it, I suppose"; and he gave as little as he could, honoring each teamster as he passed with a long stare, which was duly returned. He drove carefully, however, and brought us through without an overturn, and without obliging us to alight. My companions were two gentlemen, of whom one had been and one now is a high executive official of the State. Fatigue prevented much conversation, except such as grew out of the present perils of the road, or was suggested by the inconveniences of the night before. Even the Negro and the Reconstruction question were hardly mentioned. "Andy Johnson," one said, and the other assented, "has done a great deal better than we could have expected." One of the party remarked that he had read in the late New York papers that General Grant was decidedly in favor of war against Maximilian. "Well," it was replied, "he certainly talked that way to me. He said if he hadn't felt confident last summer that

war would of course be declared, he would have thrown a corps
across the Rio Grande when Sheridan first went down to Texas.
He said he thought he could have got a corps of Confederate soldiers into that service."

"Well, he's mistaken then; he couldn't."

"I don't know. I think it's more than probable he could. There
seems to be such fascination about the life of a soldier that it's
difficult for a man to settle down to work after he's tried it. You'd
be surprised, I venture to say, going into your own district to find
the numbers of men that would enter the army."

"I can speak for one man from my own district, anyhow. *I*
never want to see another soldier or hear another gun fired."

"I don't; but I don't know that we could do anything better with
these Negroes."

"Oh, if you could confine it to them."

It would have been a good thing, it was thought, if the Lieuten-
ant-General had taken a run up to Columbia, and seen the handi-
work of his friend Sherman. It was agreed that if Grant had commanded the Federal army in its campaign in South Carolina, the
American arms and the nineteenth century would not have been
disgraced by such wholesale devastation.

The city is, indeed, a melancholy sight. In Richmond and
Charleston the great conflagrations spared more than they destroyed, but in Columbia one is everywhere surrounded by ruins
and silent desolation. Of the former great beauty of the city only so
much remains as to cause one to regret the more that the work of
destruction was so complete. The wide streets seem all the emptier
for their width; the trees that shaded the walks were killed by the
intense heat, and are now rows of dead trunks, and the pleasant
slopes and hills light up the lonely chimneys and blackened walls
into plainer view. The hatred of the Northern people, which makes
itself manifest more or less distinctly in nearly every Southern community, the Northern visitor is better able to bear with in Columbia than elsewhere. It needs be so, for in no other city that I have
visited has hostility seemed to me so bitter.

XXIII

COLUMBIA, S. C., December 11, 1865

THE town of Newberry, north-west of Columbia and forty-five miles distant, I have recently visited, rather because it is comparatively easy of access than for any other reason. The journey may be made by way of Hope Station in about twenty-five hours, and in returning, if one chooses to forego sleep, he may go by rail as far as to Alston, and, then taking a hack and riding and walking all night, reach Columbia in fifteen hours after leaving Newberry. The railroads are very slow to recover from Sherman's visitation, and, as yet, none of them enter the city, so that the traveller in whatever direction must at first take passage by one of the many stage-lines to some distant way-station or ruined bridge. Into this service are pressed carriages of every kind—coaches, buggies, carryalls, ambulances—and the teams and equipments are as various as the vehicles. From the price of a ticket at the hour of starting to the delivery of luggage or the price of a lodging at the end of the trip, all the accessories and arrangements of this stage travel are excessively and needlessly bad. But, for the time being, the passenger forgets his discomfort in his danger. The loss of sleep is submitted to, and he is willing to go hungry and thirsty and to creep along in the dark at the rate of two miles an hour when he knows that the driver has no lantern and that only a fortnight before, for lack of a lantern, the coach was upset and three passengers killed in one of the enormous gullies by the roadside.

It was in the middle of a cloudy forenoon that we at last got away from the city and set out for Hope Station. The inside passengers were five in number, and an old Negro sat swinging his legs over the edge of the roof. "That cousin thar's got to be car'd somehow," the driver said, when I asked for a box seat, "and there's too much load on top a'ready." But at last I so far prevailed on him as to be allowed an outside place on condition of getting down when the road began to be dangerous. By the time we were ferried across Broad River and were fairly on our way the privileged ill-humor of a coachman compelled to make a late start had given place to a better frame of mind, and he was not indisposed to conversation.

"Dog me, now, but this is cussed mean coachin'. A kind of a drat, no-account team, anyhow. That hoss Dutch, he's a hoss, but the other three a'n't nothin'. Never did believe in puttin' one good hoss with a lot o' poor ones. Git 'em nigh about one thing and let 'em work together. I've coached in Alabamy and in Massissippi, and I druv a hack in Texas when I've had to git off and spade the mud out o' the wheels. Every few rod, sometimes, we'd have to prize out with rails. But, you understand, we had hosses. Look at them leaders, hey? Git up, durn ye! Thar, ye're like a piny woods pond—all over creation."

"How did you like Texas?"

"First-rate. That's the country for a poor man, sir. A year from now and I'll be back thar, too. What do you think o' greenbacks? Good? I mean, will they keep good?"

"Yes, they'll be good as long as the United States is."

"No; I don't believe it. Won't be worth a copper in two years. You never see any war-scrip that was. The Yankees'll call it all in, you see. This 'corn-fed,' as we used to call it, I never had no confidence in it. Some was very confidential, but I warn't. I'm as big a fool as anybody, but I never had no confidence in that, nor in the Southern government nuther. My old uncle in Greenville told 'em just how 'twould come out, and durned if it ha'n't. They wanted to hang him. The first time ever I see our scrip was in Vicksburg, and I told the boys the very first I see: 'Boys,' says I, 'this yer stuff right now it a'n't worth one copper.' And the greenbacks are jest the same. If I thought they'd come out right I'd know better how to do. I want to go to Texas, and take up some Government land, but I've got to have some money. Three years ago I had nine hundred dollars, and now I ha'n't got nothin'. 'Stead o' keepin' it I loaned it out to a fellow; all in silver. He was rentin' a good place down below, and I considered I was safe. But bein' off in the army, only my wife was here, and he jest up and refugeed. That's the last I see o' him. He got up into Illinois somewhar.' I know whar he is, though, and he's good, I know, for I've heerd of him, and I can exactly put my hand on him. But if I was to sue him now I'd be obleeged to take greenbacks, and I don't want 'em. I'll wait awhile and see."

He should settle in the north-eastern part of Texas, he said, and raise small grains. Cotton he'd have nothing to do with, nor niggers, either. What the darkies would do now he be dogged if he knew. Starve, he reckoned. "Mornin', cousin, whar ye bound?" he called out to a Negro woman, who dropped us a courtesy as she passed us on her way to the ferry. "Goin' down to Columby after your 'free,' be ye? Well, go on." She was a middle-aged woman, and appeared to be accompanied on her pilgrimage by her family. A little boy was following her, a little girl she led by the hand, and on her back was an infant slung in a shawl. A heavy bundle was balanced on her head. They all seemed weary as they trudged along through the mud, and their clothing was too scanty for the winter weather.

Within the space of eight miles, over which we passed while I was outside the coach, I counted thirty-nine of these forlorn-looking people travelling to the city, and the driver said he met many every day.

The way to Hope Station lies through the northern part of Lexington district, and is one of the roads traversed by Sherman in advancing on Columbia. For the whole twenty-nine miles there were never, I think, more than fifteen or sixteen dwellings within sight of the road, and of these eleven still remain. Chimneys and heaps of ashes mark the places of the other four. No Negro cabin seems to have been destroyed. On the Alston road, too, which lies in Fairfield and Richland districts, the devastation was far less complete than I had supposed, the proportion of burned houses being about the same.

The country through which we travelled was broken and hilly. The road, at first heavy with sand, soon became steep and filled with a stiff red mud, for the soil changed its character with the surface. The pines were still the predominant trees, but mingled with them, and contrasted with their tall purple stems and evergreen branches, were the several species of oaks with black limbs and withered foliage. For five years no care has been bestowed upon the highways, and driving over them is a trade to be learned. They are full of deep ruts and holes, and fence-rail bridges more dangerous than the sloughs beneath them. Often the wheels were axle-deep in mud, and if both were buried at once we thought ourselves fortunate, for when one alone goes down it is necessary for the passengers, close packed as they are, to throw themselves in a mass towards the opposite window. Mules plastered with mud and cotton wagons broken down were not unfrequent. After three hours I was obliged to go inside. In the course of the day I discovered that my fellow-travellers were a Charleston merchant, a judge, a rich planter, a doctor of divinity, and a wounded man, addressed as captain, in the uniform of the Confederate service. The order relative to Confederate military insignia is not so well carried out here as in North Carolina and Virginia, and the Palmetto button is a common sight. Since leaving Virginia, in my journey through the South, I have almost always been taken for a Southerner, though usually it is supposed that I am a native of some other State than that in which I happen to be, and conversation when I am present is generally quite unreserved. When I am known to be a Northern man, sometimes I am made to feel that my company is not desired, and sometimes there is amicable talk and argument. When I took my place in the coach the doctor was reading a newspaper. "Judge," he said, "here is an ominous erratum. 'Grand chance for Yankee enterprise and *thift*.' The printer has omitted an *r*, and it looks too much like a grand chance for Yankee enterprise and theft. He was thinking of Butler, I suspect, and made the mistake purposely."

By-and-bye the doctor spoke again: "Judge, I see that the writ of habeas corpus is restored except in those States recently in insurrection. Couldn't Mr. Davis's friends effect his liberation by means of it? What would be the process?"

"Well, they would apply for a habeas corpus, and it would be the duty of the judge to examine the facts and see if he was committed by virtue of a warrant regularly issued. If not, the writ might be granted."

"But he's at Fortress Monroe," said the captain. "Yes, Mr. Davis is at Fortress Monroe, and that's in Virginia."

"Ah, well then——" the doctor said.

"Yes, I think you'll find," said the judge, "that the Yankee Government has taken special good care to put all its prisoners into a place of safety before it issued that proclamation. But he will never be harmed."

"Oh, no," the captain said; "that would rouse up the South more than anything else that could be done."

"Shock the whole world, sir," the judge told him; "not the South alone, but foreign nations; the whole civilized world."

The doctor continued the perusal of his paper, while the rest discussed the policy of the Government and the probability that it might be better now that the President had delivered his message, which, according to the telegraph, was favorable to the South.

"A great many men are trying to dispose of their land," said the doctor. "I wonder if they find purchasers readily?"

"Well, yes, sir," said the merchant, "I believe some of them do. Many of the Yankees want to try if they can raise cotton. They think they can do better with the Negroes than we can. And they will do well, I expect. They're making money at Port Royal. They hire the Negroes and pay them thirty cents a task—what we call a task, you know—and then the Yankee keeps a little store on the plantation and gets the money all back again. They have a great ambition to be cotton planters, sir, and I expect a great deal of our lands will change hands, sir."

"That's true," said the doctor; "I noticed that at Augusta. They have a great ambition to be called South Carolinians. On the hotel books there they registered themselves from 'Port Royal, South Carolina.' Fellows that perhaps hadn't been three weeks in the State."

The conversation throughout the day embraced a great variety of topics. The doctor of divinity had been a professor in some college, and he and the judge talked of literary matters. Hobbes's *Leviathan* was mentioned, and the Mishna and Albertus Magnus. Lord Macaulay he considered a brilliant but inaccurate historian. The judge must be mistaken about Bacon's having written upon English history; it was Hume's work that treated of Henry the Seventh. Charles James Fox, too, had tried historical writing, but his mind was not of the historical order. The planter remarked that Fox was a bit of a blackguard and dissipated; probably made some of his good speeches after stimulating. The judge said Canning used to take a very odd stimulant; never spoke in Parliament without drinking a glass of right hot water. The captain agreed with Dr. Johnson that the best stimulant was two or three cups of right strong coffee. Not coffee, the planter said—tea. While he had Bourbon he had no use for tea or coffee. He suspected Canning put a little French brandy into his hot water. It was two years since he had drank a dish of tea. His supply gave out in '63, and he never cared to renew it, and he bought no coffee either. He did well not to renew it, the doctor thought; he paid over two hundred dollars for his last lot of tea. The judge had now fifty thousand dollars in Confederate money. He heartily wished it had been invested in good green tea. The planter was an old man, who smoked all day and told innumerable stories of his old acquaintances, their marriages, their family plate, their drinking bouts, their horses and hunting, their duels, and other adventures at home and abroad, and his reminiscences called forth similar stories from the judge, so that it was late in the afternoon before the merchant and the captain fell asleep, and the rest of the party gave themselves up to expectation of the end of the journey. It was accomplished just after six o'clock, in safety and not unpleasantly. All the travellers seemed disposed to make themselves mutually agreeable. The judge insisted that the planter should not give up his pipe nor the doctor his cigar, for, as he said, he was a great tobacco-chewer himself. The minister was not disturbed at the planter's swearing, and the merchant and captain furnished a lunch for all who would partake.

The house where we stayed at night was that of a farmer living convenient to the station. To every two guests he gave one bed, in which they got what sleep was possible. The house was full of travellers, and some of them chose to sit up till two o'clock, the hour at which the return coach started for Columbia. For an hour after midnight I listened to a discussion of the question whether or not the sun travelled over the earth faster in high latitudes than in low. This was left unconcluded; but it was decided that a fire burns better in the night than in the day, and that sunshine on a fire tends to put it out. Passengers for Newberry were called downstairs at five o'clock, and one after another we washed our faces in a tin basin which was in the porch, and, having been hastily packed in the dark into a coach, were slowly driven down to the railroad. It was dark and cold, and the train was not due for three-quarters of an hour, so wood was collected and a great fire made on the ground, round which we sat till sunrise. The talk was about stage-horses and staging.

It wasn't all profit, the landlord said. All the Government transportation he had to do for little or nothing—soldiers and parties that the Yankees wanted in these nigger cases.

"I wouldn't do it, Mr. H——," said the doctor; "refuse."

"Yes, but here's the thing, doctor. I had a couple of carriages all ready for some gentlemen that had spoken to me several days before. They were all in the house ready, going to start that night. Last week it was. But just that evening down came a Yankee lieutenant with three soldiers—two Yankee soldiers and one o' ours—all wounded they was, and told me they must go down. I told him how it was; I couldn't take 'em; there was the parties in the house all ready; but he just took possession of the baggage-wagon, and they had to go sho' enough. Now, what can you do under these circumstances?"

"That's it," said the captain. "Oh, we'll never get even with these fellows, Mr. H——, till we get a chance to provo' it over them."

"Tell you what, that'll be a long time, first, though."

The doctor made enquiries about the boats plying on Broad River. He had some freedmen up in Greenville—not his, but some that were moved up during the war; they had belonged to a gentleman in Barnwell, and he had undertaken to get them moved back. The men could walk, but to move the women and children and their things three wagons would be necessary. Five wagons, they esti-mated; but he thought twenty could go in a wagon. But the wag-oners wanted six and eight dollars a day, and the people could hardly afford that. From Columbia the Government would trans-port them; but to get them to Columbia was the point. If the boats were cheaper, that would be the way to do it.

He was asked if they had a prospect of getting work and homes in Barnwell. They could get work, he supposed. They wanted to go back there.

The train arrived a little after its time, and in something more than two hours we accomplished the sixteen miles to Newberry. It is a muddy, shabby little village, built irregularly on very uneven ground, and seemed to be full of business. It is the centre of a productive cotton region, and has besides sent to market within the last five months a great number of bales accumulated there during the war. For wagoning cotton out of the district it is estimated that $300,000 in gold have been paid since Johnston's surrender. Trade, therefore, is active in the village stores, the square is seldom empty of country wagons, and the farmers purchase largely of the supplies from which they were cut off by the war.

The garrison commander is also the agent of the Freedmen's Bureau, but having occupied his position only a few days he could give me little information. During the hour that I was there his office was a very busy place. The most important cases were one in which a Negro complained that he had done some bricklaying for a certain man, and had been paid twenty dollars in worthless money; another, in which a Negro was charged with stealing four bales of cotton from the depot; and one in which a white woman, escorted by one of her neighbors, demanded that the Negroes on a plantation near her house should be deprived of firearms: they didn't care where they shot. An investigation of the circumstances was promised her. The alleged thief was put in charge of a little German soldier and marched away to jail. The bricklayer declined emphatically to carry a letter from the lieutenant to the person who had defrauded him; he valued his life too highly; so the summons was entrusted to a soldier, to be given whenever the man should come to the village.

The lieutenant said he had superintended the division of the crop on several plantations, but as yet knew of no agreements having been made for the coming year. The Newberry newspaper, I noticed, urged the need of a district convention of planters, and offered for the consideration of its readers one of those proposed forms of contract between farmer and freedman that now begin to be printed in most of the South Carolina papers.

Alston, the most easterly point to which trains are running on the Greenville Railroad, is several miles nearer Columbia than Hope Station, and I returned by that route. Leaving Alston, after eating what was pronounced "a right genteel supper," we rode all night, and made the trip to the city in twelve hours. The vehicle was a carryall drawn by two mules, and the company consisted of four passengers and the driver. Whenever we came to a long hill we got out and walked. At one particularly bad stretch of road we halted for half an hour, and at last succeeded in making a sputtering fire with wet rails. Then, each taking a couple of brands to light the way and waving them into a blaze when they went out, we picked our steps for a quarter of a mile along the edge of a miry pool, while the carriage was dragged through the middle of it. All my fellow-travellers were young men and had been Confederate soldiers, and the night was chiefly spent in talking about their campaigns and generals and companions in arms. In the midst of a story about old Jubal, who "certainly could just exactly swear," and who, if he believed there was a Providence, could never have expected to win a fight, the driver suddenly interrupted the narrator by stopping the mules and asking us in a low tone if we were armed. It happened that there was not a weapon in the carriage. "That's bad," he said; "however, gentlemen, never mind; when I begin to talk about my pistols you must all say something similar. We're coming to a pretty bad place here. On the next plantation the niggers are a very unruly set, and some of them have guns. We must look sharp." One of our company had several thousand dollars about his person, and, having a very bad opinion of free Negroes, he evinced a good deal of anxiety and trepidation. It was to him, therefore, that we left the duty of responding to the driver. Soon the conversation between them began, the driver directing his voice towards the right-hand side of the road and the passenger towards the left.

"Yes, it's the prettiest rifle powder you ever saw. I wouldn't take any money for it if I couldn't get any more."

"I prefer the cartridges; they're so much handier. A cartridge is always sitting up."

"Oh, well, I always can have twelve shots, you know, and there are always pistols in the coach."

"A man would be a fool to travel these times without his pistols."

"Shouldn't think of it."

"I say, driver, I would like very much to see any six men attack this coach tonight."

"Well, now, they would have a very sorry time of it, sir. But there's no trouble of that kind on this road."

By-and-bye we were informed that the danger was past, and then for a while the Negro was the theme of discourse. My three companions and the driver represented four districts, and each reported it as an undoubted fact that the freedmen were forming themselves into companies and holding meetings at night for the purpose of drill. I enquired if many of them had arms, and was told that every nigger had a gun. The niggers round the driver's house couldn't get ahead of him, for he had two that told him everything. Of General Ely, Acting Assistant Commissioner of the Freedmen's Bureau, who has charge of fifteen districts in Northern South Carolina, I made enquiries in reference to this matter. His attention, he says, has frequently been called to it. In one instance the assertions were so positive and seemed so well supported that he rode out himself to the plantation in order to make an investigation on the spot. Having been posted where he could see and not be seen, he was an eye-witness of the whole parade. Negroes to the number of thirty or forty men, women, and children had gathered themselves together near their cabins and were drawn up in line. Some shouldered sticks, some had gun-stocks, some gun-barrels, some guns, and some were empty-handed. They marched and counter-marched and halted, and marched again in straight lines and curves for nearly half an hour, their evolutions being interspersed with dancing and rough play, and accompanied by much laughter and noise. When he had witnessed these manœuvres for some time, the general went out and had an interview with the people. They said they were only having a frolic imitating the soldiers. None of the firearms were serviceable. In several other instances he had made an examination of the facts and had found them similar to these. Stories about Negroes drilling are not worthy of serious consideration.

As we drove along, the driver pointed out a little hill which he said was the prettiest situation for a house in all Fairfield. In 1861 he had intended to build there, and had engaged the carpenter. "But the war came and broke me up, and then the Yankees done me so bad that when I came back from the army I hadn't a bushel of corn nor a dime in the world. Yes, sir, the woods were just blue with them devils, my wife told me. One regiment from Pennsylvania, Colonel J——'s regiment, camped on my place, and the old colonel made my house the headquarters. My wife thought the house would be burnt before he came. They took everything, even down to my little girl's doll-clothes; and they didn't leave the child a rag but what she had on her back. They took eleven mules and horses, and killed all the poultry and hogs. Just took everything. My wife begged they'd leave her some fodder, but they told her she wouldn't have no use for it; and sure enough they carried off the animals. She told 'em that little corn wouldn't keep her and her family. 'Yes, I reckon——' no, 'Yes, I rayther guess it will,' the

Yankee colonel told her. That G—d-d—d trifling old, cowardly— excuse such language, gentlemen; but it makes my blood boil to think of him. Oh, if I can ever come across that ——, if I don't shoot him! Yes, sir, I'm going to seek a personal difficulty with that man. And, if you'll believe me, he wanted to take my little girl to raise. He'd educate her and bring her up, he said. Why, I'd send her among the heathens first."

"No," said one of the passengers, "we don't wish to affiliate with them. I suppose it would be more Christian to forgive them, and to let all vindictiveness die out, but we never can forget how they have treated us."

"Well," said another gentleman, "I'd like to make a New Year's call on old Sherman, and blow his brains out."

Not long after this conversation occurred, we turned from the main road and pursued our way through a large plantation. It was necessary for someone to take an outside place with the driver, for there were four field-gates to be opened, and I undertook the performance of that duty. Talking with him, as we sat together, he by-and-bye enquired where I lived, and so discovered that I was a Northerner. "Well, now," he said, "a great many of your people are perfect gentlemen. It wasn't the real Yankees that did so much mischief in this country; it was them low-down foreigners and Irish. You know there's mean men in all armies."

XXIV

COLUMBIA, S. C., December 15, 1865

GENERAL ELY, the chief officer of the Freedmen's Bureau in Northern South Carolina, is accustomed to make frequent short excursions into the various districts of which he has charge, for the purpose of conferring with the planters and addressing the freedmen. Last week his duties led him out to Edgefield, and I was invited to accompany him. He was also accompanied by an armed orderly, for it is his opinion, based upon personal experience, that an agent of the Bureau is not so safe in the remote and lonely roads as an ordinary traveller. Edgefield Court-House is about sixty miles from Columbia, and, as there is no public conveyance, we were to travel on horseback and be absent four days. The morning of departure was close and warm, and we set out with our overcoats strapped to the saddle, but soon after crossing the Congaree, a small rain began to drizzle down, making the road a little sloppier than before and lending the landscape an aspect still more cheerless. Not much was to be seen but trees, for the part of Lexington district through which we were riding is a desolate region, sandy and thinly settled. In the first five miles we passed several houses undestroyed and the remains of two or three that had been burnt, and then for twenty miles there was slight evidence of human habitation. Such dwellings as we saw were nearly all of the poorest kind, and more properly to be called huts than houses. At one of them we were accosted by a ragged, unwholesome-looking lad, who begged sturdily for money or bread. It was the first case of the kind that had fallen under my observation, but both of my

243

companions spoke of having met with similar instances, the beggar
being sometimes a child and sometimes an adult. We rode slowly
all day through the wet weather and at evening slower still, for,
just as the night set in, very dark and with heavy rain, we turned
from the main thoroughfare and travelled through the woods along
a less frequented road. After an hour and more a light appeared
among the trees, and soon, emerging from the forest, we came into
a small clearing whose sandy fields could just be distinguished by
their white glimmer amid the surrounding blackness. The light we
had seen shone through the open door of a log cabin, and the
orderly was sent to find out if there was a stable on the premises
and to claim a night's lodging. The name of the general procured
us a grudging admission, for the woman's husband was away from
home and her accommodations for visitors were of the scantiest
sort. She came out with a light-wood torch above her head and
scrutinized us: "Gentlemen," she said, "if I let ye put up, and give
yer critters some corn, ye'll pay me, won't ye? We're poor folks,
and we don't take in strangers, and my husband a'n't yer." She
was assured that our stay should make her no poorer, and, taking
courage, she first lighted us out to the stable and then proceeded to
prepare supper. Her house contained one room, with an immense
fire-place at one end and two beds at the other. It was without a
window, but the two doors stood wide open. An uneven floor of
bending boards was underfoot, and overhead we could see the
shingles, for there was no loft. Besides the beds, the furniture consisted of a table, a clock, four chairs, and a spinning-wheel. The
loom stood under a shed at the back door.

At supper we had cakes of flour and water, fried in lard, and a
panful of fresh pork, for it is now the time of "saving meat," and
pork in some form is a standing dish at all tables. While we ate,
the woman stood near making apologies for the poor fare. She
reckoned we couldn't hardly see, but a piece o' light-wood was all
the candle she had; our women folks made better roll-cakes than
them—they had stoves to cook with; Yankee coffee she couldn't
offer us, for she'd seen none since the war; and, for a wonder, this
remark was not followed by any expression of regret at the depriva-

tion. She'd had to drink cold water in the war, and now she thought she'd stick to it, for she hadn't had the sick headache since she left to drink coffee. After supper she talked about her circumstances.

"She didn't know how much land they had; there was forty acres cleared. It was all mighty poor, through that country, for farmin'. She didn't reckon they got three bushels of wheat to the acre, and it was worse yet for corn. Corn was scarce this year, and when they went up on to the ridge to buy, they axed two dollars a bushel and the greenback money they wouldn't have nohow, but wanted the silver; they said the greenback money wouldn't be good in no time at all; *she* thought it was good, but they thought it warn't. They didn't raise cotton, only a little patch, enough for her factory. She spun and wove all the cloth they needed." Then she went and got out three pieces of cotton goods and brought them for our inspection. "That's some o' my factory," she said. "The black dye was got from the oak bark, and there was a bank of dirt right close that would color red and yellow; roast it and it colored a clever red, and take it right natural and it colored yellow. They hadn't no great use for store goods—a little salt and tobacco sometimes was about the furdest. They lived within themselves altogether. As for the war, *she* niver knowed what they brought it on for. Her old man was out o' age for goin', but two of her boys went, and one got killed the 13th day of July was a year, at Petersburg. And what was the rich folks any better? They'd lost all their niggers, and she was mighty glad of it. She wished them and the niggers had been at the bottom o' the sea." The general enquired how the Negroes were getting along; if the planters abused them?

"They was mighty few in that settlement," she replied; "and where she lived it wasn't any great of a place for news, so she didn't know much about it." She didn't know anything, then, about that preacher up in Edgefield? A Negro preacher, it appears, was killed in that district some three weeks since, and the murderer still remains undiscovered. "She had been told about it only the day before," she said. "Now that man—that Wade—shot up in Newbury, she'd heard about him sooner." This was a case of which the general had heard nothing, and he put many questions in reference to it, without, however, eliciting much information, for she had forgotten the circumstances. A report of it was probably made at the time directly to General Saxton's headquarters in Charleston, and will yet be forwarded to General Ely for his information and action.

At bed-time both beds were given up to us, while the woman and a young girl who was living with her slept on the floor before the fire. Contrary to expectation, we passed a comfortable night, and, after partaking of a breakfast like the supper, willingly paid our hospitable hostess the six dollars which she hesitatingly demanded. She was quite unlearned, and could not read the figures on the Treasury notes.

The day was cold and overcast, and we had a comfortless, muddy ride to Edgefield village. The first few miles of it lay along the Tarbucket Road as the old woman called it, and the country seemed to be worse, if possible—a thirstier sand and more deserted—than what we had seen on the previous day; but after crossing the district boundary, and getting into Edgefield, its appearance became very much better. The houses were handsome and commodious, seeming to be the residences of wealthy men, and the one before us could be seen while the one behind was yet in sight. There was very little wild land. The farm buildings and Negro quarters were in good order, and sometimes very numerous. The fences were still standing, and on several plantations the hands were engaged in the winter work of repairing them; and, altogether, this portion of Edgefield appeared to be better improved and thriftier than any district of equal extent that I have yet seen. The surface is level, and the soil is a light loam, which looks well adapted to cotton. This year but little planting has been done, though I saw a few fields in cotton, and passed some houses in which ginning was going on; also a good deal of old cotton was under the screw in process of repacking. On every plantation where short-staple cotton is raised, the screw is a prominent object. Looked at from a little distance, it may be roughly described as presenting the form of a gigantic letter A. The point is at the top of the screw, and some fifteen feet from the ground. A mule is harnessed to the lower end of one of the limbs, and walks in a circle about the central post. The cotton-bag is placed on a raised platform between the limbs, and, the screw descending, a great quantity of the lint is pressed into a small compass. At one place which we passed, relays of women were substituted for the mules; one would run round once or twice, then another would take her place, and the old planter stood by to superintend.

As we rode along, the general was repeatedly stopped to answer questions: sometimes it would be a planter enquiring if he should divide the crop among the people, or if a soldier would be sent out for that purpose; but oftener it would be a Negro enquiring if he was obliged to work another year on the plantation where he now lives, or was at liberty to seek work anywhere, or complaining that his master would make no new contract with him, but said that after January Negroes would be willing to take lower wages, and he should hire nobody till then. Some expressed themselves satisfied with the treatment they had been receiving, but many charged their employers with having violated the contracts made last summer. Several of the men, after it seemed that all their questions had been answered, would still walk along eagerly asking more, and evidently anxious to ascertain their position and prospects. The enquiries and statements often revealed a total misconception of rights and duties, sometimes on the part of the laborer and sometimes on the part of the employer. From what he heard, the general seemed to conclude that free labor has less chance of a fair trial in Edgefield, and that the Negro may look for more injustice there, than in most other parts of the State. The district is extensive and less remote from the main lines of travel. It was never occupied by the Federal army, and its many large and fertile plantations, owned by men still rich, stand ready for cultivation unchanged and uninjured by the war. As it seems to the people, therefore, more easily possible to preserve the old order of things, and as the material inducements are greater, it may be reasonably suspected that the desire to do so is stronger there than elsewhere. To me, however, it seems not different from other parts of South Carolina.

We reached Edgefield village a little after dark, and were received by the captain of the garrison, who made us welcome at his quarters in the county jail. Notice had been previously given that the general would address the freedmen on the following day, and already they had begun to come in from the neighboring country. A score or two were waiting in the court-house square as we rode through it. I slept in the rambling old tavern at a corner where two roads entered the square, and, being kept awake by the curs beneath the window, who challenged each passer-by, I could hear the people still arriving, one by one, up to a late hour in the night and in crowds after three o'clock. Before eight o'clock more than a thousand had come in, and the number increased afterwards to two thousand. Most were on foot, but some had ridden in; and several whom I asked said their masters wanted all the boys to hear what the general thought, and had loaned them the animals. All were in their best clothes, and, despite the depressing influence of the weather, the crowd was in very good spirits, filling the square with the noise of laughter and salutations, though on some faces there was an expression of expectation and some of the hand-shaking was done with solemnity. The landlord, an irascible old man, was much displeased at the sight.

"Aha!" said he. "Oh, they've come now. Look at 'em. Now they're to get their half o' the land and the stock."

"You don't think they expect that?" I said.

"Don't?" he answered. "Well, now, I'll tell you. If the general don't tell them cuffees they're to have their share o' our land and hosses and everything else, you'll see a hell of a row today. They'll turn their backs on him right here in this square, and there'll be a hell of a row, as sure's you're born. They don't expect nothin' else but they're to have a half."

Before the address was delivered, the general sat in the midst of a throng of people listening to the recital of their grievances and giving them advice. One good-looking yellow man, about thirty years old, waited some time for his turn to speak, and then told this story: He lived on a plantation ten miles from the court-house, and was a stiller by trade. The white people round about had been saying that the Negroes there had guns—Government muskets, of which there are said to be many through the country. On Saturday last, J. R—— and fourteen others of the home guard, with a Yankee soldier, came down to the place and said they were searching for United States arms. He knew this Federal soldier, for the man had once come to him and begged a drink of brandy, "which I gave it to the gentleman freely, and was proud to do it." This soldier told him the guard had a right to search, and were acting in obedience to orders, and then rode away and left him with them. They demanded his gun. He had none, he told them, and for some time they persisted in the demand and he in the denial. At last one said, "I'll get it out of him," and, going away for a few minutes, returned with a chain. With this they hung him "till I lost my sense, and when I come to a good understandin', they asked me 'would I give up the gun, now?' and I told them, 'Gentlemen, I *got* no gun.' " Hung up again, and again restored to consciousness, he made the same reply as before, and was hung for the third time. Then they stripped off his clothes and gave him a severe beating, of which the marks were still to be seen upon his body, as well as those of the chain upon his throat and neck. "I told them the truth," he said, "for I hadn't got any arms. These here is all the arms I has got. And yet they put me to death three times. Which, if I had ha' knowed how easy death was, I wouldn't ha' feared it so. And I don't expect they're agoin' to let me live now I made this complain' to you, gineral; but they may kill me for good as soon as they chooses." Here he began to cry. "Which I hasn't got anything in the world but myself, for I hasn't got any family, nor any parents, nor any land, nor any money, and I know I is not to be any worse off in the grave than I is now."

Two other cases of hanging were reported, names were taken, and an investigation ordered. The home guard, or militia, is now organized in most of the districts. It has its own officers, but is in the control of the Federal commander, and can perform such duties only as are confided to it by him.

The general's speech was, of course, listened to with the utmost attention. He told them, and they heard it with expressions of satisfaction, that it was their right to establish schools for the education of their children; that they were free to meet together for religious worship; that they might seek work wherever they chose; but that a contract once made must be strictly observed. If the employer broke it, he must be sued and made to do justice; and if the laborer broke it, he must expect to be sued and to lose his wages. A Negro's oath would be good as a white man's in all the courts, and in all respects he was now a free man. Honesty, industry, and chastity would give them a good name; and though they could not expect to become rich or well educated in one year nor in two, yet their condition would be all the time improving, and many of them would live to see their race happy and prosperous. The Negro owned the labor, and the planter owned the land; each needed the other, and each must be just to the other. If any freedman wanted land, he must earn money enough to purchase it; the Government had none to give away. It was plainly evident that this part of the address caused disappointment. The faces of the audience showed it; but nothing was said, and they listened with the same patient attention and anxious endeavor to understand every word that they had evinced from the beginning. It was explained to them that one of the Union generals had made a promise of land to the freedmen, but that nobody knew at that time of war what the Government might see fit to do when peace came. It had since been decided that the former owners of land should retain it, and now the United States had no land to give away. Then advice was given them in reference to making contracts for next year, and they were cautioned to sign nothing that they did not understand. It would be best to make the agreement in presence of a Federal officer.

The rain had been falling throughout the time of speaking, and at the conclusion of it the square was immediately emptied, for some of the people had twenty miles to travel. There was no disturbance, except that a drunken man, who cursed the Yankees at the top of his voice, and could not be kept quiet by admonitions, was lodged in jail till the meeting broke up. The weather was such as to prevent a large concourse of the planters; but a few were present, who sat in their carriages on the outskirts of the crowd.

In the afternoon, taking to our horses again, we rode back some twenty-five miles on our way to Columbia, being accompanied by the garrison commander, who was to sit on a court-martial, and at night, dripping wet, reached the house of a wealthy planter, at whose hands we received a most hospitable welcome. He was an elderly man, living alone in a great house full of bare, dismantled rooms—Liberty Hall it might have been styled from the manner of its housekeeping—and waited upon by a crowd of male and female servants. Fires were lighted at which to dry our clothes, a plentiful supper of pork and corn bread was prepared, and we were bidden to make ourselves completely at home. On going to bed a bare-footed mulatto woman carried a whiskey bottle and glasses from chamber to chamber, and in the morning it was brought to us again as soon as we had risen. "Dem boys do jest what they please," the servant said, in apologizing for the absence of light-wood, and master himself had to follow them all the time if he wanted anything. Besides our party there were four or five other chance guests in one part of the house or another. All were bountifully provided for, and I saw, not without surprise, none were allowed to pay for their lodging. I suppose the Negroes on this plantation can hardly be taken as a fair sample of those living about them, for they seemed to live perfectly at ease and uncontrolled. One of them, whom his master laughingly introduced as "the old Adam, the preacher on the place," walked into the parlor after supper, and informed the general that some of the boys had been up to the village that day to hear the speaking. They were dissatisfied with it. The advice he had been giving them all along was precisely the same as what they had now heard from the general, but they could not be content. He would like to hear better what the general had to say, and then he could use his influence over his fellow-servants.

"I offer them a third of the crop," said Mr. N——, "as Adam can tell you, and I believe that's what you advise, general; but they

say that won't do at all. I believe they think they own the plantation. You're their best friend, they all know, and I'm very glad
you've come down this way."

So, for some minutes, the general conversed with the old
preacher, who seemed very sensible of the honor conferred upon
him, and felt confident that now he could keep the people in good
order. They were good boys, but they didn't know.

After getting into bed, I was called on by a gentleman, like
myself a guest in the house, whose visits to the sideboard had been
too frequent, and who now walked into my room and took a seat
before the fire. "Some men," he said, "is dreadful ornery. Beats the
Dutch what ornery men'll run for the legislature. Now I've got
thirty-five workin' niggers; nor they ha'n't been corrected much,
nuther; but they do jest as well today as they ever done. I'll go
home, and I'll skin one o' them cusses, and he'll say it's all right;
for, you see, he knows I'll treat him like a man. You see I never let
myself down to 'em. They a'n't in and out o' my house, and just as
good as I am, and doin' what they please. The worst niggers now
is two kinds o' niggers—them that was cut and lashed and knocked
about befo', and them that never was under rule. Them's the mean
niggers now." I was too sleepy for conversation, and he soon left
me to myself.

On the following day, an uneventful ride of thirty-five miles
brought us to the banks of the Congaree, which was swollen and
red from the heavy rains. The rope-ferry, however, was able to take
us across, and in a few minutes we were riding among the ruins of
Columbia.

XXV

AUGUSTA, GA., December 23, 1865

THE first stage of the journey from Columbia towards Augusta is seven miles long, occupies three hours and more, and is made in the dark. We were called from bed at three o'clock in the morning, several coaches were filled up with sleepy, shivering travellers, and then till after six o'clock the time was consumed in slowly moving through the wind and rain to Hampton's Turn-out. As we passed the College campus the chapel windows were still lighted, for it was the last day of the legislative session, and that body was sitting late. Some of the members already on their way home were in our coach, and spoke together about the character of the two houses, and the work that had been accomplished. The critics seemed dissatisfied upon the whole, though many of their remarks were not quite intelligible. The best part of the Negro Code had been cut out, they said, before its final passage. It was a very good thing, however, that so many copies of it had been printed, for every white man would need one, and probably no law ever enacted in the State had been so generally and thoroughly studied as that would be. The session had been very busy, but more work would have been done if the senate had been less factious and impracticable. Strange to say, that branch of the legislature had been far more radical than the house. It had proved false to all its traditions. The course of "that fellow T——" was then severely reprehended.

"Oh, he had a great deal to say about the poor, patriotic soldiers, you know, and their widows and orphans. They say that

in the conference committee in reference to the usual appropria-
tions, he said before he would consent to pay the judges their
undrawn salaries in good money he would cut off his right hand.
He just as much as said that they left their pay in the treasury
because of the depreciation of our money. Yes, he was exceedingly
enthusiastic. And he is so vociferous! A perfect demagogue, sir. In
point of fact, those gentlemen probably had no use for their
money, and allowed it to remain with the State for the good of the
cause. I am sure a great many of our people down to the very last
retained a great deal of confidence in our currency, and no man of
honor, nobody but some such a fellow as T——, would have
charged them with such motives."

"No. What a curse it is to a country when these low, demagogical fellows of no character are able to rise to the surface! Several of
the upcountry members, gentlemen who were very strong in the
convention for remodelling representation, are said to be quite willing now to undo their work. One of them—you would know him
were I to give you his name—told me himself, that after this
winter's experience of the new system, the people in his section
would be very willing to return to the old. In three years, he
thought, we would be back again."

"Ah," said another gentleman, "it was very ungenerous in them
to force that measure upon the low country at that particular time.
They knew that we had lost everything by the war, and, at least,
they should have given us time. For I think, sir, that the rice country is ruined. Cotton planting may possibly become profitable
again, but no one, so far as my information extends, entertains any
hopes of the rice culture. The Negroes never liked it, you know. It
is very hard work, and it is unhealthy necessarily. I don't know
what we'll do. I am not going to attempt it. This year's experience
in Georgetown district has satisfied us that nothing can be done.
Take one example out of many. Mr. A——, you know A——,
has worked four hundred of the freedmen this year—his own Negroes—with the understanding that they should return to him all
the seed-rice, and that the surplus should be divided between themselves and him. The other day the division took place, and how

many bushels do you think there were to be given to four hundred Negroes? Just nine and a half. There were nineteen bushels over and above the seed. That is one case out of a hundred that I might give you. I am convinced that we shall never be able to do anything till we get white labor. Oh, I have made up my mind fully to do nothing at all with my places this year. Mine came to me, and asked me if I would think hard of it if they tried to find employment off the places. I was very glad to tell them 'No; that they might go as soon as they pleased, and they couldn't go too soon.' I never could stand their impudence, I'm sure."

"Let me see; you have the black troops down there? Though Orr told me they were to be relieved at once. I suppose they demoralize the freedmen?"

"Oh, yes! Yes, sir; their officers have no control over them. I wish you could have seen what I saw the other day in Georgetown. In the middle of the street there was a crowd. I should think there might have been a hundred of these black soldiers surrounding about half a dozen of the white Yankees and quarrelling with them, calling them the vilest names—'D——n their white-livered souls, they could whip any white man ever walked,' etc. Their faces looked absolutely fiendish. They really appeared like demons. The whole street was full of them, and the citizens were in a fright. They would just as soon elbow one of our first citizens as not. And all this was within a few rods of the nigger colonel's quarters. At last one of the Yankees picked up a little courage and offered to fight any one Negro in the crowd. A big fellow jumped out at once and said he was his man; so the two stripped off their coats—"

"Going to fight this nigger?"

"Yes, sir, he was going to do it; but just then the colonel, who must have heard it all—the whole town was in an uproar—walked out of his quarters and spoke a few words to them, and stopped it. Never made any arrests or anything of that kind; seemed to be afraid of them; just walked between them once or twice, and went away."

"One of the captains in Barnwell told me candidly that, in the event of an insurrection, the officers would not be able to restrain the black troops, and they would certainly side with the Negroes."

"Yet some people say they prefer them to white soldiers. A friend of mine told me that in the summer he had some difficulty with his people, and sent up to the Yankees for an officer to come down and talk to them. Well, they had the impudence to send down a black sergeant. My friend thought, however, that he'd let him try what he could do. He was a pompous fellow, he said, and very proud of his stripes; but it was really marvellous to see the influence he had with the people. They obeyed him implicitly. He considered it a proof that the freedmen were disposed to be a law-abiding people. I told him I considered it a proof that the black soldiers have entire control of the whole colored population, and it should be a warning to us to have them removed as soon as possible."

"Well, doesn't it seem as if the United States Government was desirous of bringing on a collision between the races? Its policy can hardly be accounted for on any other supposition; yet that is almost too barbarous."

"We don't know whether anything is too barbarous. However, I believe they will soon be removed."

The conversation, carried on in the dark, was accompanied by snoring from two travellers asleep, and the thread of it was often broken by a jolt, or by the cries of the coachmen giving each other instructions and encouraging the teams to extraordinary exertions. In this, as in other companies of South Carolinians, I noticed that almost always when any man's name is mentioned, someone enquires whom he married. Then the lady's name is given, and it is told whether she was of good family or not, how wealthy she was, and how many children she has brought him. Young men and old seem to take an equal interest in this sort of information, and to possess a great deal of it.

At Hampton's we found the train, and, as usual, quite an assemblage of Negroes clustering around some wood fires and waiting for a passage to the low country. Travelling slowly all the forenoon, we reached Branchville without accident, and there, from twelve o'clock till eight in the evening were detained while the engine was repairing. The little village at the junction, with its half-dozen gaily painted railroad buildings, contained nothing to interest a stranger, and our passengers, after they had wandered for a while about the platform and read the notices of sales by auction posted there and the order prohibiting the sale of intoxicating liquors to Negroes during the holidays, sat and lay on the pine straw in the sunniest spots, impatiently expecting our departure. Some of them derived amusement from the spectacle of a man suffering from an attack of *delirium tremens*. He went from one person to another, falling on his knees and begging for his life. If the gentlemen wished to kill him, of course that was their privilege, and he supposed he deserved it, for it must be acknowledged that he had been in the Yankee army, though he was a Southern man by birth. But he had a wife and two little children. He didn't want to oversize the pile, but he would give fifty dollars, at least, to any gentleman who would save him. If he could have a fair trial, he would be able to show that he had fired on the Massachusetts regiment that came through Baltimore in April, and had made one of them sick, anyhow, and he didn't know but more. Besides, he was an ignorant man, unable to read and write, and never would have gone into the army if he could have got employment. They drafted him after he had travelled about for seven months from place to place to avoid being taken, and he had never shot anywhere but in the air. These, he thought, were mitigating circumstances. He was condemned to death, however, and took the position of the soldier in order to die with dignity. He was repeatedly tried and sentenced and reprieved, and dosed heavily with whiskey and morphine, but nothing could remove from his mind the impression that his fellow-travellers, being Southerners, sought his life, and he continued to weep and supplicate until we arrived at our journey's end.

At Bamberg, thirteen miles from Branchville, there is a break in the South Carolina Railroad, and travellers must take a coach for forty-two miles to Johnson's Turn-out, whence they go by rail to Augusta. It was not possible to get a bed in Bamberg, which was filled to overflowing, but our driver lived upon the road five miles from the village, and to his house accordingly we were carried. His fare consisted of myself, a young lady from Georgia returning from boarding-school, and her brother, who escorted her. The driver was loud in praise of his horses and of a "through cut" which he had made through the woods, and which saved all the danger and mud of the big road. We were mighty lucky to get him, he allowed, if he did say it himself. But we met other drivers in his through cut, each of his horses was thrown down once, the carriage was nearly capsized over a bank, and at last he was effectually silenced by a tall stump which broke one of the single-trees and delayed us fifteen minutes. A little before midnight we reached the log-house he had spoken of, and were very glad of a roaring light-wood fire and beds upon the floor. In the morning the farmer, a paralytic old man, came into our room and talked while breakfast was getting ready.

Sherman had been through that country and made him a poor man. He never was wealthy, but now he hadn't anything. The soldiers came into his lot one morning early, and they just overrun everything. They didn't burn any of the buildings but the cotton-house. It had a matter of thirty bales in it, though. He would have run it out into the woods, and dropped it about, but it was all in the seed. All the poultry went, and all the bacon except some jowl pieces. When he begged for some of the good meat, they turned round and asked him if he hadn't three sons in the rebel army and two sons-in-law, and called him a d——d old rebel. He told them he wasn't much of a rebel at the jump, but when the war got a-going it sort o' inspired him. They seemed to know as much about his business as he did. They got all his honey, too, and his knife. He saw a parcel of the Yankees round a bench in the yard, and some mighty fine pieces of the comb there, so he said to them, "Gentlemen, I reckon I can have a piece of the comb." "All right, old fellow," says one, a little Irishman or Scotchman or German he was: "Dad, lend me your knife and I'll cut it for you." So he handed him the knife, and sure enough he did cut off a big piece, but he put the knife into his pocket, and that was the last of it.

"He had more use for it than I had," he said. Then they took away every horse he had and every saddle. He was not abused himself or any of his family, though he didn't stand back for them, either. They made a fire in the yard, one parcel of them, and began to dance round it, but he went out and told them he could bear to see his property burnt and stolen, but to make him look on and see them dancing over it was a little too much and he wouldn't bear it; so they stopped it. One thing the war had taught him anyhow. He would never try to hoard up money again. What he could make he intended to eat and put on his back. He hadn't eaten cheese for four years, and hardly any meat, but for the future he should live well.

Breakfast, when it was served, hardly kept the implied promise thus made us, but it is seldom in these Southern farm-houses that one finds food at once good in itself and well prepared. The old man surveyed the rye coffee and hominy and corn bread and sausages with audible satisfaction. I asked about the freedmen on the farm. At one time he said he had owned thirty-four. The able-bodied young men, seven or eight in number, had been carried off by the Yankees, but the rest remained and had been at work this year, doing tolerably well. At the division of the crop they claimed a third part, and he wanted to give them only a sixth. Nothing was said about terms at the beginning. Finally he had to get a Yankee from the court-house, and he told him he was poor and pretended to be very obstinate about the one-sixth; so the Yankee gave the Negroes a right hard talk, and made them take one-fifth, and call themselves lucky to get that. Next year he was going to have an understanding. His Negroes said they would work for one-third; he had four white men hired to run the ploughs, at twelve dollars a month and board and washing, and he intended to plant pretty much all his land in cotton. He thought more cotton would be planted in Barnwell in 1866 than in any previous year. Now, if the Negroes would only work, he didn't know but it might be a good thing that they were free, and he asked the Georgian and myself what we thought about it; we were city raised, weren't we? and knew more about things than he did. He also enquired of the Georgian if old Joe Brown was not the governor of that State, and if it was true that England had declared war against the United States.

As we were leaving, I asked what we should pay him for our entertainment. "Nothing," he said, "he never took a dollar from a man for lodging in all his life." In a minute he added, "You must talk to the old woman about that." She entered just then, so we asked her the same question, and paid a dollar and a half apiece. On the way the driver, of course, talked about Sherman's army, pointing out this house as the place where so many hundred bushels of corn were destroyed, that as the place where two splendid pianos were smashed to pieces with axes, that other as having been occupied by Sherman as his headquarters for two or three days. "It wouldn't do for him to travel through this country now. Too many of the boys would want him." As in other parts of the State the devastation was not nearly so great as my preconceived notions of it. But few of the houses near the road had been destroyed, and near the road, I was told, the destruction had been more complete than elsewhere.

"They burnt my house smack clean, sir," said the driver, "and every bit of furniture that I had except some that the niggers saved for me. I was worth fifteen thousand dollars the day the war broke out, and the day it ended I just had my horse that I rode home on. But I'm a young fellow. My father lost everything, too, and he's an old man. They put fire to the corners of the house, and then two of 'em held him and made him look at it burning. The women folks would try to save some of the things out of the fire, and when they came running out with books or anything the Yankees would snatch 'em and throw 'em back on to the fire. The old man had to go down to my sister's—she's married and lives near where you stayed at last night—and she gave him a bed, or he'd had to sleep out in the open air; and when he went down the next morning to look round, sir, one of the niggers told him he might leave; Sherman gave her the place, she said. Called him a grand old rascal and all sorts of names."

"What did he do with her?" the Georgian asked.

"Why, he couldn't do anything. He's an old man, seventy-two years old, and she was a big strapping nigger; could ha' killed him with one hand."

"Does he keep her there now?"

"No, by G——, he don't. You may bet she didn't stay there long after I came home. They told me the story."

"And she's left the plantation?"

"Yes; and when she comes back she'll come back in the spirit. Nobody is exactly certain where she is, you know. Some think she's gone to Charleston or somewhere on the coast, and some think she's got lost in the big swamp."

"A heap of 'em out in my country get into the swamps and get lost. I don't know as it's true, but I've heard that there's men out there that haven't got anything else to do, and if you mention any nigger to 'em, and give 'em twelve dollars, the nigger's sure to be lost in a very few days."

"I know four right here in Barnwell that have been drowned some way within the last two months. Niggers never were so careless before. They go into the swamps and nobody can find out anything about 'em till by-and-bye they're seen floating down the river. Going to the coast, I reckon; that's where they're fond of going."

"Well, now," said the Georgian, "it's queer that the niggers that were the best before the war, the ones that we trusted the most, and thought the most of, and gave every privilege, are the same ones that turn out the meanest."

The driver admitted that this was the fact, and the Georgian continued:

"And the niggers that we thought were the grandest rascals, stealing and lying and everything else, are the ones that do the best now. A nigger has got to know you're his master, and then when he understands that he's content. There was one of our niggers, I'll bet my father has given him more than two thousand lashes since I can remember; he just lived in the woods in old times, but he's the best nigger we've got now. When we hired the hands this year, he was hired with the rest. I was at home myself, and after they'd been working a day or two days, I went out into the field, and they weren't doing anything hardly. So I went up to the house and told my father that the Negroes were not doing anything, and this particular nigger I told him I thought was doing all he could to prevent the rest from working; and I'm going to discharge him, says I. Very well, my father told me. He gave me full power to discharge any of them I wished; but, says he, let's give them a talk first. I was away that evening, but father called them up and told them that I was dissatisfied with the way they worked, and he mentioned this nigger in particular. Well, he stepped out right at once and said, says he: 'Whoever would say that I prevented the rest from working or didn't work well myself, is capable of telling anything.' As much as to call me a liar, you see. Well, the old gentleman told 'em all at home to say nothing to me about it when I came back. He knew there would be a row sure if I heard it, and they all meant to keep it secret from me. But at the supper-table I heard my little brother telling my mother the circumstances, and very soon I got it all out of him. I got up from the table right away and took my walking-cane and a big navy pistol that I've got, and I walked right out of the house. In the yard I met my brother-in-law, and he saw by my looks there was some trouble, and asked me what it was. 'I'd got a nigger to frail,' I told him, 'that had been calling me a liar.' 'All right,' he said, 'he'd go out with me.' So we went on down to the quarters together, he and I. When we got to this nigger's house I called for him and out he came. As soon as I saw him, I jumped for him, and I laid the cane unto him—it was a kind of a riding-cane—just as hard as I could lay it, over the head or anywhere. He didn't like it much, and blamed if he didn't run in on me and get hold of the whip. Then I took the pistol and I didn't stop to cock it, but I hit him two or three times with it as quick as ever I could strike. The pistol went off and the nigger thought I'd killed him. 'Oh! Master Henry,' he says, 'I never thought you'd do one of your own niggers so that you raised yourself.' 'I'll learn you,' says I, 'to call me a liar'; and we took him and tied him up and I gave him one of the best frailings he ever got in his life. My father came out, though, and took him down. He can hardly hobble about, but he was so afraid I'd kill the nigger that he walked away out to the quarters and took him into the house, and washed his head himself and bandaged it up for him. But he's been the very best hand we've had since that time. Frail a nigger and he knows you."

There was much talk of a similar character between the two young men, and they had an inexhaustible topic of conversation in their varied adventures as soldiers and scouts and spies during the late war. All day we were riding steadily at a very good rate of speed, and early in the evening, without accident, we arrived at the Turn-out, where we were provided with beds, or, rather, with certain fractional parts of beds, and with breakfast on the following morning. In that desolate little hamlet I saw nothing and heard nothing which would merit reporting, and the railway ride across the Savannah River into the State of Georgia was equally destitute of incident.

ATLANTA, GA., December 31, 1865

AUGUSTA, the second city in Georgia, and said to be advancing rapidly towards the first rank, is a well-built town, well situated on the Savannah River. My stay there was only long enough for a walk through the principal streets, which are regularly laid out, level, and so exceedingly wide as almost to dwarf the rows of buildings on either side. They were cheerful with a busy press of pedestrians of various colors, and streams of vehicles; there was a vast display of goods in the warehouses and shops, and the newspapers were filled with advertisements of every kind. By its position Augusta is the seat of a large jobbing business, the river and the railroad connect it with the ports of Charleston and Savannah, and it is enabled to avail itself of these advantages, for it has received its full measure of the Northern capital which, since the surrender, has been poured into every Southern town. Concerning this investment of capital, I listened the other day to the opinions of a young gentleman from New York, a man of business, quite young, but with the appearance of a person perfectly well informed: "I'm posted about this thing," he said; "I'm acquainted in Wall Street— very well acquainted for a man of my age—and I know their opinions there, and I've studied the working of it down here. A Northerner needn't come into this country to go into business unless he can put his money into something he can monopolize, or can buy into some Southern firm. You see if these people can trade with one of their own men, they're not going to trade with you and me. It's all natural enough—I don't blame them; but it puts you and me under an immense disadvantage there. Then New York is bound to favor the old houses in every kind of way, and we're under another disadvantage there. You know how it is with these countrymen and country dealers; they're used to coming in and hitching their horses to the same post year after year, and you can't change 'em to a new place; you couldn't if there hadn't been any trouble, and of course you can't now when they're down on us. I don't believe they'd speak to a man if they knew he'd ever passed through Boston. They know in New York that one of us can't compete with these fellows; can't begin to do it. Then, again, nine in ten of the Southern business men owe any quantity of money up there, lots of it, and New York is willing to take them and set them up again, and do a great deal better by them than it would by you or me, in order to get its old debts. Of course, it's all right; I'd do the same thing myself; but that's the way it is. I've got this far looking for a chance to invest $25,000 cash, and I'm going through to New Orleans; but I've made up my mind not to go into business unless I can get in with some old house. It would just amount to this—with their advantages they'd break a new man right down, and he'd just lose his time and money."

Of mercantile and professional pursuits this may be true. But the inducements to Northern men to come here and engage in agriculture, lumbering, and similar branches of business which, being carried on mainly by the services of the freedmen and for a foreign market, are not subject to the drawbacks above-mentioned, seem to be very great. There is apparent a willingness, often an anxiety even, to secure Northern men as lessees of plantations, and large tracts of land, well improved and productive, are everywhere offered for sale at low prices, sometimes at prices that may be called ruinously low. "These freedmen will work a heap better for a Yankee than they will for one of us," it is frequently said. Other causes of this sacrifice of lands and rents are to be found in the belief that the free labor of the Negroes cannot be made profitable, and in the fact that many men who have much land have no money with which to cultivate it. But although much land may still be bought cheap, there are some signs that these causes will not continue to operate so extensively as heretofore. Often I hear it predicted that cotton is going to command a very high price for some years to come; that therefore its culture may be profitable, though the laborers should work a smaller number of acres than in old times; and occasionally some local newspaper announces that the gloomy prospects of the planters are brightening, that the Negroes who, after all, showed so commendable a spirit of devotion, faithfulness, and obedience during the war, are beginning, in certain districts, to make contracts and profess a willingness to receive a share of the crop as wages.

But, however the case may be as regards the business relations of Northern men in the South, I should consider it advisable for the newcomer, if he desires agreeable social intercourse with his neighbors, in almost any part of the South that I have yet seen, to restrain the free expression of any social or political opinions distinctively Northern. Frequently this hostility is avowed, frequently men make a merit of disclaiming it, but no one denies its existence.

The Georgia Railroad, 171 miles long, between Augusta and Atlanta, is the best which I have ridden on since leaving the North, the cars being comfortable and commodious, the officials civil, and the rate of speed more than fourteen miles an hour. It was on a Sunday that I made the journey, and all day the rain was pouring steadily, so that we could see the country turning to mud as we passed and every stream growing yellower. We were able to ride all the way, however, for the bridges stood until the following morning, and our train went on without delay. Among the passengers were Jews, drummers from New York, a few women, and men from nearly every Southern State. Everybody seemed resolved to lighten as much as possible the fatigues of travelling. Some slept, there were many whiskey-flasks in circulation, fowls were eaten, the newspapers of Chicago, Louisville, and Nashville could be bought, a one-armed man in the rebel uniform sold cigars, and it was assumed that the ladies would make no objection if they were smoked. In the course of the afternoon two or three of my neighbors, who had told each other all the stories they knew, began comparing their pistols and disputing about the comparative merits of the various patterns. "Good for your side, gentlemen," said a man, drawing near, "if you've got pistols; but I don't ask a pistol while I've got this fellow," and he displayed a heavy knife with a broad blade some eight or nine inches long. He praised it as a faithful companion during the war and as being a fine imitation of the real old Arkansas toothpick. It might be called a toothpick anyhow, for it was a dentist made it, a right clever, ingenious fellow that could make anything. That silver mounting on the handle was four Mexican dollars melted down. In a difficulty it was the prettiest thing in the world; wouldn't miss and made no noise. All the company handled it and admired it. Then, addressing me, he explained how he could kill me with it in one minute—yes, under a minute, if I didn't understand its use. A man should know the weapon or take something else. Then he showed how a man unaccustomed to it would probably attack with it, and how, in that manner o' fightin', he'd be killed right away. It should be held in the right hand with the point forward, not downward, and in making a pass with it one must thrust over or under the left arm, which is always to be held as a guard across the heart, protecting the body from the blows of one's antagonist. Of course he always expected to get his left arm pretty much cut up when he fought with a knife.

As we approached Atlanta, of course we saw burned buildings at the way stations, rails fantastically twisted and bent, and ruined locomotives—remembrances of Sherman and Johnston. It was too dark when we arrived in the city to see anything but the lights and an occasional rocket shooting through the rain. It was Christmas Eve, and it appears to be usual in the South to celebrate the coming of this festival with Chinese crackers and other fireworks.

Atlanta, as I saw it on Christmas morning, was a most cheerless and mean-looking place. The sky was dropping rain, and underfoot the mud was almost ankle-deep. It had rained for three weeks. People walked slowly, treading with careful steps in the footprints —slowly getting narrower in the soft mud—of those who had ventured before them. The middle of the city is a great open space of irregular shape, a wilderness of mud, with a confused jumble of railway sheds, and traversed by numberless rails, rusted and splashed, where strings of dirty cars are standing, and engines constantly puff and whistle. In one place I saw beside the track a heap of bones and skulls of animals, collected from battle-fields and the line of march for some factory, moulding and blackening in the wet weather. Bricks and blocks of stone and other rubbish were everywhere. Around this central square the city was formerly built, and is now again building. Unfinished houses are to be seen on every hand; scaffolding, mortar-beds, and lime-barrels, piles of lumber and bricks and mounds of sand, choke every street, and the whole place on working days resounds with the noise of carpenters and masons. The city is hardly less pleasing to the eye than the people. A great many rough-looking fellows hang about the numerous shops and the shanties among the ruins where liquor is sold, and a knot of them cluster at each street corner. The gray coats are almost as numerous as the blue uniforms, often very dirty, of the white and Negro soldiers, some of whom are always on guard in the streets. White women are but seldom seen, perhaps because the sidewalks are nearly impassable; the men are obliged to wear the bottoms of their trowsers tucked in their boots. Negroes of all colors abound.

But though Atlanta, in spite of its newness, has a cheap and squalid look, which is depressing, it evinces much energy and life. Trade of all kinds is extremely active; the city is full of goods; and though the number of traders seems inordinately great, new ones are pushing into business. To a stranger it appears as if the feverish activity of the mercantile community must eventually bring on a crash, but the citizens indulge in glowing anticipations of the future prosperity and growth of their town. They point to the railroads centering here, and say that if the country around to be supplied with goods was poorer than it is and less productive, the mere storage and trans-shipment of freight would suffice to make Atlanta a great city.

In walking about the town on Christmas morning my attention was attracted by a crowd of two hundred colored people and a few whites gathered about the door of the City Hall. They were listening to an address from Colonel Curkendall, of the Freedmen's

Bureau. He had made many a horseshoe nail, he said, but he had never before made a speech. All his life he had been a working-man, and he supposed that they too would be working-men as long as they lived. He had the meanest kind of a camp close by, with about 650 colored people in it receiving rations from the Government, and if any one of his audience was not able-bodied and could get no work to do and was starving, he would put him into that camp and let him have a little hard-tack and a poor place to sleep till he could find some work to do. There was no comfort for them anywhere without hard work for honest wages. No land would be given them. They knew that, it was responded from the crowd. Very well, then, they probably knew that some persons were expecting a Negro insurrection about this time. Yes, they said; yes, colonel, they knew that, too, and they agreed with him that, though he was not a very big man, he would be able to put down all the insurrectionary movements that would be made by the Negroes of Northern Georgia. He believed they would behave like men. Every right that he had, except one, was already theirs by law. The right of suffrage they would probably get if they showed themselves qualified to exercise it. In the exercise of every other right he would certainly protect them. Exact justice should be administered, whether it took a black man or a white man to jail. Then the colonel spoke of education, and gave good advice in reference to a great many points of conduct and character, and at the end was loudly applauded. When he told them that there were many good men in Georgia who would be their friends if they were industrious and well-behaved, who would deal justly with them and take care that the bad men of the community did not impose upon them, the Negroes cordially assented. "That's what we want," they said, when he told them that hard work and the education of their children would soon put the ballot into the hands of every Negro in the South.

I noticed in the crowd several men with badges of colored ribbons. They were members of two associations, I was informed—the Union League and the Sons of Liberty—which have been formed for mutual aid and counsel. Neither of them is a secret society, and both have invited the inspection of the Freedmen's Bureau. As the meeting broke up I walked toward my hotel, and was soon overtaken by a soldier who walked along beside me and wished me a merry Christmas. "It's Christmas Day," he said; "that's what's the matter." Then in a minute, as we met two Negroes, he added, "And I'm goin' to punch every d——d nigger I see." With that he struck first one and then the other Negro a violent blow in the face. The men seemed too much astonished to retaliate. Afterwards quite an affray occurred between some white soldiers and Negroes, which resulted in some slight injuries to the latter, two being wounded by bullets, and in the arrest of the soldiers by the provost-marshal's guard, which patrolled the streets for the rest of the day. In the course of the afternoon a colored man was shot and killed by a citizen in an altercation about the right to the sidewalk. I also met a Negro who had been severely wounded above the eyes with a knife, and was then on his way to Colonel Curkendall to make complaint. Besides these, I heard of no disturbances on Christmas. I had believed that the reputation of Atlanta in respect to these things was never very good, but I am told (it would be hard to say how truly, for the police is inefficient) that no more than five assaults ending fatally had occurred in the city in the preceeding months of 1865. In December two were added to this list.

At the office of the Freedmen's Bureau in Atlanta it was said, in answer to my questions, that a minority of the planters are disposed to treat their laborers kindly and justly. A majority are indisposed to give adequate wages and to recognize in practice that the Negroes are free; that the Negroes evinced an unwillingness to make contracts unless in cases where the person wishing to employ them was a Northern man. The names of three men were given me, all of whom had been officers in the Federal army, who proposed planting cotton next year, and who were offering as wages twelve dollars a month, together with board, clothing, and medical attendance; that no courts had as yet been established for the trial of causes in which Negroes are parties, but every case is tried, and all sentences are passed, by the colonel himself; that the operations of the Bureau are to a great extent crippled by the want of cavalry; cases of fraud and cruelty occurring at a distance from the town and from railroads necessarily go unpunished; that the military officers throughout the district of which Colonel Curkendall has charge could probably be depended upon to do justice between the whites and the Negroes; that very few complaints of any kind had ever been reported by the garrison officers in the country. In the Atlanta office I found recorded, as having occurred during the fortnight ending December 13, four cases of abuse and cruelty which had been punished by the imposition of fines varying in amount from twenty to one hundred and fifty dollars. Two complaints, one of assault with intent to kill, and one of assault and robbery, were made while I was in the office. The average number of applications for redress is twelve each day.

XXVII

WHILE staying in Atlanta I heard a strange story, which, perhaps, should not be related in a correspondence professing to give only undoubted facts, for in repeating it I give currency to a report which, indeed, seemed to me probable, but which I am not in a position to prove. If, however, the business to which the report refers is not actually in existence, it would be so easy to establish it, and at the same time secrecy would be so necessary for its establishment, that I may be excused if I give publicity to what I heard.

Since August last, my informant stated, a traffic in Negroes has been carried on between several points on the Southern coast and the island of Cuba. The Negroes are hired as if to work at lumbering in Florida and Georgia, or, in fact, for work of any kind in any place so distant as to furnish a pretext for taking them on board a vessel, and then they are at once run over to Cuba, where purchasers are readily found. The Negroes cost little or nothing, and the business is exceedingly remunerative.

A steamer is spoken of which was partly freighted in Augusta, and made the trip only three weeks ago, and it is said that more than one party in Charleston have made very profitable ventures. Their secret having become known, certain other persons were desirous of embarking in the same enterprise, and it was from some of the efforts of these latter to obtain the requisite capital for their purpose that the facts which I give transpired and became known to me.

In my last letter I spoke of the charge which is brought against the Southern people of being hostile to the settlement of Northern business men among them, and gave it as my own conclusion, from what I had seen and heard, that this hostility did exist to such a degree as that the immigrant, unless he was willing to be cut off from all agreeable intercourse with the people among whom he lived, would be compelled to restrict his accustomed freedom of speech and action and defer to the social and political theories and opinions of his neighbors. Since arriving at Macon, I have heard the particulars of two or three cases which appear to show that in some communities even the acceptance of such conditions as these is not enough to disarm the ill-will of the native population.

Major R——, of the 187th Ohio Volunteers, and Captain C——, of the same regiment, not long ago secured a three years' lease of two plantations situated in Stewart County, and owned by a Mr. W——. They intended to cultivate cotton, and, having purchased all the requisite implements and a sufficient number of mules to stock both places, they sent down forty Negroes to live on one of them, while they themselves remained in Macon and awaited the mustering out of their regiment. This event, however, not taking place so soon as was expected, Captain C—— went down into the country to perfect his arrangements for planting, and, very much to his surprise, was met by his landlord with a proposal that he and his partner should withdraw from the further prosecution of their enterprise, inasmuch as persisting would bring trouble upon all concerned in it. The neighbors, he was told, had given Mr. W—— to understand that no Yankee should be suffered to live in that country; that if he rented land to those two Yankees his tenants shouldn't live to harvest their crops, and his own house should be burned over his head. Out of consideration, therefore, for him and his property, if not for their own safety, he begged them not to disregard these threats, which were made by men who would carry them out, but to abandon their project. If they came down he would be exposed to constant losses and danger, and if they did not lose their lives, their operations would be interfered with in every conceivable way. He would take all the tools and animals off their hands and buy back the lease, or, at any rate, one year of it. Perhaps at the end of a year the feeling against Northern men would not be so strong. These proposals were agreed to, and the captain and his friend have given up all intention of planting in Georgia, and propose to invest their money in some Northern State. Another gentleman who, during the past summer, administered a military office which brought him into contact with very many people and gave him opportunities for conferring obligations upon all of them, said that when a few months since he left the service and went North, he flattered himself with the idea that he had a great many warm friends in Georgia, and was exceedingly popular throughout the district in which he had been on duty. He decided to return, therefore, and establish himself in business in one of the most flourishing towns in the State. He had an intelligent partner, and both members of the new firm worked hard and paid close attention to business, without, however, reaping any adequate reward for their exertions. By-and-bye he learned, through the detectives employed by the district commander, that there were several persons who entertained the intention of killing him as soon as an opportunity presented itself. He became aware, also, that it was commonly said in the town that he should not sell goods there or grow rich on Southern money. He could see nothing better to do than to sell out his share in the business to his partner, who was a Southerner, and the store is now, he tells me, quite liberally patronized. To the recital of these facts he adds the remark: "This country won't be any place for Yankees or niggers when the troops are mustered out. When the military goes, I'm going too."

The knowledge that such a state of feeling exists, coupled with the belief that there is no good reason for its existence, gives rise to a corresponding hostility on the part of those who are its objects. The other day I heard several officers talking upon this subject, and one who spoke as follows was applauded by the company: "My heart never was in this war all the time that I was fighting. I never hated a Johnny, you know, and I guess all our fellows felt the same way. But, by Jupiter, I wish now that they'd leave off singing the 'Bonnie Blue Flag' and damning us poor devils that have to stay down here in their God-forsaken country, and try pitching in again. I want 'em to get up another war, you know, and then I want a cavalry command. Won't I raid through Georgia! There sha'n't be anything left behind me. I'll destroy every house and barn and plantation. The voice of song shall cease; there won't be anything left to feed the little birds, you know, and they'll all die, except the buzzards. Every buzzard shall be filled. No; but, confound 'em, I mean if they have another war I'm going to go for 'em with a will."

The condition of the freedmen in the country around Macon, so far as I could learn from the Sub-Assistant Commissioner of the Bureau, is exceedingly satisfactory. This officer has his headquarters in Macon, and the district over which he presides embraces thirty-four counties. In each county he has three subordinates, who were appointed from among the citizens on the recommendation of the delegates to the Constitutional Convention, and many of the delegates having been willing themselves to accept the government of the freedmen in their own neighborhood, the office was, in many instances, conferred upon them. They receive no salary, but in all cases which are tried before them they are allowed to retain such fees as are customary in justices' courts. The Bureau, I was informed, contrary to the character which it generally bears, is quite a popular institution in the Military District of Columbus.

The Negroes are quiet and well-behaved, and conducted themselves admirably during the holidays, not a single complaint having been made against them. The white people were very apprehensive of a rising of the freedmen, and in some places the militia picketed the roads and patrolled the country in all directions. During the last week of 1865 three Negroes were killed, and, of course, a great many outrages of less consequence were committed. The murderers of one Negro had not been arrested, but those of the other two were caught, and were now awaiting trial before a military commission. The power of the Sub-Assistant Commissioner extends no further than to impose a fine of $150 or a term of three months' imprisonment.

From General Dawson, who is in command of the sub-district, I learned further particulars of the picketing above mentioned. The United States officers in Georgia refuse, I believe, to supply the State militia with arms, call on them for no assistance, and hardly recognize that they exist. In Monroe County, contrary to the proclamation of the provisional governor, the citizens formed not one but two or three companies of volunteers. Then they requested the withdrawal of the Federal troops, and the request was complied with, the garrison being withdrawn a fortnight before Christmas. During Christmas week the difficulties between the militiamen and the freedmen began. Negroes were stopped on the roads, which were all patrolled or picketed; some of them were beaten, all were searched and compelled to give an account of themselves, and one was killed. The general has seven men who are charged with the murder under bonds of two thousand dollars each, and the evidence against two of them is so strong that he expects to secure their conviction before the civil court of the county, and, at any rate, intends that they shall be tried there rather than before a military commission. He wishes to establish a precedent for the conviction of a white man for murder by the testimony of Negro witnesses. The battalion of militia in Monroe County has been disbanded, and the citizens have been threatened with the establishment among them of a garrison of colored troops.

General Dawson, as well as some of the gentlemen mentioned above as having suffered from the hatred of the Southern men towards their Northern countrymen, unite in saying that the persons who disgrace themselves and the community to which they belong by outrageous acts and words are but a minority of the Southern people, and that the men of wealth and social standing, and, in general, the elderly men, as distinguished from the young men and the women, are well disposed towards the United States Government. He deprecated the complete removal of the United States troops from the country, and thought the process of mustering out had already gone too far.

The Negroes, I was told, are very generally entering into contracts with the planters, and it is thought that almost all will have found employers before the 1st of February. All Negroes who at that time shall be unemployed and not willing to make contracts, it is the intention of the Commissioner to arrest and treat as vagrants. The demand for labor is greater than the supply, and the Commissioner has frequent calls made upon him for able-bodied men to go to other States and to other parts of Georgia. With these calls, however, he does not comply, being unwilling to drain off all the young and strong men, and leave in his district a disproportionate number of women, children, and aged persons. By a recent order of General Tillson, the compensation for the labor of a full hand is fixed at $12 a month, food, and proper medical attendance. This order creates much dissatisfaction among the planters, as they had previously been hiring laborers for food, medicine, and $10 a month. I believe the soil in this part of Georgia is not very productive, and that a planter thinks he does well if he gets a bale of cotton of five hundred pounds weight from three acres of land.

An Alabama planter with whom I conversed upon the prospective profits of cotton planting, informed me that in his neighborhood a Negro on a plantation, properly supplied with mules, was in old times expected to cultivate fifteen acres of cotton land, and would now be expected to take care of ten acres. The planter in this part of Georgia may, therefore, calculate on something like 1,600 pounds of cotton from each full hand, the money value of which will probably be not less than $400. As corn is worth $1.50 per bushel and bacon is worth $35 per hundredweight, the food of each laborer who receives his full allowance of 13 bushels of corn and 200 pounds of meat would cost $89.50. His wages being added to this amount makes the total year's cost of the laborer $233.50, and the employer's profit on his labor in an ordinary year may be set at $166.

COLUMBUS, GA., January 17, 1866

In the journey by rail from Macon to Columbus there is little to interest one who has previously travelled for any considerable distance in the South. All along the road is the familiar scene of their desolate-looking forest, with now and then a way-station with its dozen or so of loungers and its Negro women selling cakes; and now and then a watering tank and a wood-pile, where usually the passengers walk about a little, examine the engine, look back at the long, undulating line of the track, and wonder, perhaps, that such rails have been able to bear the train safely thus far. Inside the cars also the scene is familiar—here and there a uniform, gray or blue; one or two families, man, wife, and children, who seem to be seeking a new home, or, more likely, returning to an old one which is safe now that the war is done and the husband is out of the army; a few Northerners and many men unmistakably Southern in manner and language.

The conversation, which may be heard by snatches, is on various topics, the two chief being the war and its experiences and the Negro. I very seldom hear anything said now about colonization, and the race is less frequently pronounced worthless; but the prospects of making cotton by free labor are often discussed, and one man gives another details of his farming plans for the coming season, and tells of the operations of the Freedmen's Bureau, an institution which commonly is severely denounced, though once in a while a man commends its action in his particular case. I hear President Johnson praised at the expense of the radicals in Congress, and not unfrequently Maximilian is mentioned. I judge it to be the prevailing opinion in this part of the country that the United States should let him alone. "When Kirby Smith broke up, you know," I heard a young man say yesterday, "we met one o' them Juarez colonels and he offered captains' commissions to Tom and me if we'd go into his regiment. 'Not much,' I told him; 'I'd been whipped once, and I didn't want to be again.' No, sir; if I was going into that fight I'd go in on the other side. Didn't tell him that, you know, but that's what I'd do."

While riding on this train I noticed, also, one or two illustrations of the fact that the women of the South are outspoken in their dislike of the Federal soldiers. Just in front of me were two young ladies, and, as the cars stopped at a little village, we saw two men on crutches. On the platform were also some of the garrison. "It makes my heart ache," murmured one of the ladies, "to see our poor wounded Confederates. And look at those creatures in blue mixing with them!" Not long afterwards these ladies left the cars and their places were occupied by three others of less pleasing appearance, whose voices could be heard even above the noise of the wheels. Two soldiers sat in a seat across the aisle, and were compelled to hear much loud talk about "the miserable Yanks" who had stolen the corn and meat of such a person, or who were the probable destroyers of this or that building by the roadside "when they made one of their brave raids." Officers on duty in this city tell me that some of the women still carefully gather up the folds of their dresses when they approach a man in the Federal uniform, and prefer crossing the street to walking under the national flag. Manifestations of the same feeling have fallen under my observation at Liberty, Lynchburg, and Danville, in Virginia; at Raleigh and Salisbury, North Carolina; at Charleston, South Carolina, and at three cities in Georgia. The most amusing instance occurred in Lynchburg. A lady called from an upper window to a little girl on the sidewalk: "Julia, come in this minute, child. That Yankee will rub against you if you stay there." The Yankee referred to was a soldier, a dull-looking fellow, who appeared confounded at this attack upon him. He quickly recovered himself, however, and, turning his face towards the chamber window, addressed the little girl, who was obeying her mother with alacrity: "Yaas, go 'long in, you skinny little thing! Don't rub against the Yankee. I guess your father tried it on down at Petersburg, and *he* didn't like it, you know."

Columbus is about a hundred miles from Macon, and the journey was made in nine tedious hours. The town is built on flat land, and is a pretty place, with many trees, and like Augusta in the great width of its thoroughfares. These are not in the best order; but that is a matter of small consequence, for each driver has a broad expanse of roadway from which he may choose a path. Cows and pigs wander up and down in them without molestation. One of the pigs I praised as I was standing in a shop on Broad Street.

"Yes," said the shopman, who was a small dealer in groceries, and an Irishman, " 'tis a fine hog, and ye may be sure it's a nigger's. One o' them would ha' knocked it on the head if 'twas a white man's was runnin' the street like that." Then he went on to lament the changed times and customs. The niggers was above work now and was all for living like gentlemen and ladies. Every one o' them in Columbus had seven or eight other ones living about him and stealing for him. When they was slaves they all had plenty o' money, and eating and drinking to their hearts' content, and now they had nothing, and wouldn't work to earn. It would be a fine day when the Yankees should be off about their business, and the people left to manage their own niggers themselves. Then they'd be brought to their senses. When one o' them runs away from his lawful work, then a man'll just take his pistol in his hand, and get on his horse, and, faith, if the nigger won't come back with that, he'll be welcome to stay where he's left. It was nothing but the Yankees made them so much above themselves.

Like the other large towns of Georgia, Columbus wears an appearance of more prosperity than is seen in other Southern cities, and seems to be a busy place, its show of activity being perhaps partly due to the large number of idle people in the streets. The Chattahoochee, a reddish stream of considerable size, whose further shore is in Alabama, runs close by the town, and adds much to its beauty. The weather during my stay has been charmingly mild and soft; many of the trees are green, the flowers are in blossom in the gardens, it is so warm, and under my open windows the children are playing barefooted.

I find that the freedmen and the farmers in this part of Georgia are now busily preparing for the work of the coming season. Since the 1st of January the officers of the Freedmen's Bureau have recorded in their books ninety-nine contracts, the great majority of which were entered into by the plantation Negroes with their employers, and each day several new ones are brought in for approval. In the month of December six contracts were put on record. The branch of the Bureau here established has charge of three counties, Chattahoochee, Muscogee, and Talbot, and it is by citizens of this district that nearly all these contracts have been made, although a few of them made in other counties, and a few made by parties living across the river, in Alabama, have, for convenience sake, been recorded at the office in Columbus.

The amount of compensation given the laborer is very variable. I was told that the order issued by General Tillson, fixing the minimum rate of wages at $12 a month for a full hand, had never been enforced here, and indeed, that it had never been heard of. Most of the Negroes, therefore, have been hired for less than that, though I am informed that now $14 per month is offered. By permission I copied from the books some of the contracts which have received approval:

This contract, entered into on this 26th day of December, between David J. Shipp of the one part, and the freedmen hereinafter named of the other part, witnesseth that the said freedmen contract to remain on the plantation of the said Shipp during the year 1866, and perform such reasonable labor of any kind as he or his agent may require of them; their whole time to be employed by said Shipp, and they to accept for their services such compensation as is hereinafter annexed to their names, in addition to the usual allowance of shelter, food, clothing, and medicine given to field-hands, except that Silas, Maria, and Billy Shipp and Joseph Jones are to pay for their clothing and food furnished by said Shipp out of their hereinafter named compensation.

Said freedmen are to be obedient, honest, and faithful, and shall remain in the employment of the said Shipp until the expiration of the contract, when they are to receive the full amount of wages due them. But should they prove disobedient, faithless, and dishonest, or leave their employment, they shall be dismissed from service and forfeit whatever wages may be deducted by the proper authority.

In case of illness requiring the attendance of a physician, the employer will hold himself responsible for the bills, and deduct the amount from the wages of those for whose benefit they may have been made, also making a deduction for the time lost in sickness. The said Shipp binds himself to comply faithfully with his portion of the contract, and to treat his employees with humanity and justice, and protect them in all their rights of person and property so far as is in his power.

George Bernell, $60; Georgianna, $40; Little Rick Shipp, $50;

Dock Shipp, $60; Rick Shipp, $60; Amy Totman, $40; Sally Tot-
man, $40; Tilda Shipp, food and clothing; Silas Shipp, one-third of
the produce of twenty acres of land; Maria Shipp, do.; Billy Shipp,
do.; Joseph Jones, do. and $40.

Another contract, which I copied, was the following:

COLUMBUS, GA., Jan. 2, 1866.

Contract and agreement entered into between R. A. Martin, of
the first part, and Kendle Souther, freedman, for himself and family,
of the second part. The second part agrees to labor faithfully for
the first part, and to obey all orders given by the same, and to be
responsible for all property entrusted to his care; the first part
promises to furnish him with a house to live in so long as he may
be in his employment, and to pay him $135 and board for them
that labors, and sell him provisions at the market price for them that
don't work, and nothing more. In witness whereof we have set our
hands and signatures.

R. A. MARTIN,
his

Approved.   KENDLE ✕ SOUTHER.
mark

In the majority of the contracts which I examined, the planter
binds himself to pay the laborer for one year's work $120 and his
board. In the printed forms for contracts which are now used in
this office at Columbus, it is provided that "for neglect of duty—or
other misdemeanor—or any question of doubt arising, the same to
be referred to the nearest officer or agent of the Bureau or justice
of the peace."

I found five instances in which Negroes had leased land. In one
case a third of all the produce was to be given to the owner as
rent; in another, one-fifth; in another, where forty acres of land
were rented, the lessees were to pay $250 and 48 bushels of meal;
in another, one-half of the crops was to be paid, and in this case
the Negro seems to have been considered a farmer of some skill
and character. The agreement reads as follows:

STATE OF GEORGIA, Muscogee Co.

An agreement entered into the 7th day of December between
D. W. Urquhart, proprietor, on one part, and a freedman, Thornton

Allen, on the other part, witnesseth that the said Urquhart covenants and agrees to furnish the said Thornton Allen a house and lands, to wit: The Joe Diamond place, with 140 acres, more or less, of land for cultivation; and, furthermore, to furnish the said Thornton Allen $500 worth of provisions and two mules to assist in cultivating said land. And the said Thornton agrees on his part to well and faithfully cultivate said land, and put not less than 60 acres in cotton, and all the balance in corn and other grain and suitable crops of sweet-potatoes and melons, to put the orchard and vineyard in proper trim and cultivation, and that he, the said Thornton, will faithfully market the products of said orchard, vineyard, melons, and potatoes, and freely and honestly pay over to said Urquhart the one-half of the products of lands so cultivated and the products so marketed, and pay the one-half of the corn and cotton on lands so cultivated into the store of the said Urquhart.

There was one record of an indenture of apprenticeship. A boy of seven years old had been bound out by his mother for fourteen years, the master agreeing "to provide for all his temporal wants and learn him to read and write if he will take it, and at twenty-one give him a suit of clothes."

The officer of the Bureau in Columbus, who is very soon to be mustered out of the service, is decidedly of opinion that a large majority of the planters will be kind and just towards their laborers, and that his successor will have but little difficulty in his dealings with those two classes of persons. He congratulates himself, however, that he is relieved from duty before the militia is allowed to take the place of the United States troops. The withdrawal of the Federal troops he considers equivalent to the withdrawal of the Bureau.

XXVIII

MONTGOMERY, ALA., January 24, 1866

IT was four o'clock of a very dark morning when an omnibus came for me at my boarding-house in Columbus, and it was two hours later, after a slow circuitous drive about the city from one house to another, the driver and his companions kicking and shouting and thumping at many doors, that a load of passengers was picked up and carried across the Chattahoochie into Alabama to the Montgomery train. The rain was falling when we reached the station, there was no depot or ticket office, nobody had eaten breakfast or was wholly awake, and General Wilson became the subject of very acrimonious remarks. A great destruction of railroad bridges and buildings at Columbus was caused by his raid. We waited awhile, and when the fires beside the track and the car lanterns began to burn pale as the day was breaking, we got under way towards Opelika. Meantime I paid attention to the voice of a lady sitting some four or five seats behind me, whom I could not see in the doubtful light, but who apparently had found an old acquaintance among her fellow-travellers, and was giving him an account of her life for the last few years.

It seemed like it was a century since she had seen him, she said, so many changes had taken place. It was befo' the war long enough. And what trials and distress had come upon their country since their last meeting! She was one of those who had shared in the downfall of their cause, for she was now, she reckoned, just as poor a woman as he ever did see. She had very little left but her health and strength, and she didn't feel any older than when he

knew her before, but property—law! No, he had not been misinformed; she had married again, married a Mr. W——. She lived
with him eight years seven months and nineteen days. His death
took place in 1864, and was a great loss to her, for he always acted
the perfect gentleman, in every sense of the word. "He loved our
country," she said, "and was as good a rebel as any man could be."
His health never permitted of his going with the army, but the Confederates had his prayers, and he never was the man to speculate or
make one dollar out of the war. That wasn't his religion, and he
was a true Christian if any man could be such. The curse of God,
he always used to say—the curse of God would follow money that
was made at the expense of the country. All he raised he let the
Government have at the regular prices. Oh, it would certainly have
broken his heart if he had lived to see what she had seen, he had
such faith in the cause. Indeed that was true, that there was too
few like him. He treated her like a perfect gentleman. He gave her
a deed of gift of thirty-five nigrahs, and told her them was to be
hers and she should have land to put them on. She told him she
wished no more than a child's share, but he said he would fix it
this way; he would give her $38,000, and she should buy the
homestead place. She always wanted the homestead place, so she
consented, and it was arranged that way. After his death the South
was defeated, the nigrahs was free of cou'se, and the $38,000 was
worth nothing at all. Then the administrators fixed up a sale, and
pretended to knock down the land to the highest bidder, but in
reality they had an understanding with the company that bought it
in, and it was sold for $3 an acre! One of the best tracts in the
whole State. She said all she could, but that didn't matter to them,
and she and the children were cheated out of their property. All
her little fortune was already gone, for she had been compelled to
make two or three journeys to see the administrators, and each
time she had to live at a hotel for a fortnight, till they could be got
together to do business, and travelling was so disgracefully expen-
sive, and board four dollars a day—at them licks a person must be
made of money to stand it.

At about this stage of the conversation her friend begged leave

to drink from a small flask which he had with him. Her consent
was readily given, although, she said, she was in general very much
opposed to drinking. She had always been used to seeing a great
deal of it round at her own pa's house, and her first husband's, as
well as at Mr. W——'s. It was very seldom indeed, however, that
Mr. W—— ever took anything, except when he was fatigued or
unwell, or perhaps before going to church of a very cold day,
particularly if he wasn't feeling just right. Then he would allow
himself. She hardly knew when she herself had tasted anything of
the kind. The smell was extremely disagreeable to her. She could
remember as well as if it was yesterday the time when she was
intoxicated. They had visitors at home, and she was sent to the
store-room to fill a decanter with peach brandy. As soon as the
spirits began to run from the barrel she inhaled the smell, and it
got up into her head directly. She became so giddy! She fell down,
and when she got up she fell down again, and couldn't walk
straight at all. They thought she was in a faint, but her pa said no;
she had inhaled the smell of the brandy, and it had been too much
for her, and she was really intoxicated by inhaling it. He made her
drink half a glassful.

By-and-bye she admitted that perhaps it might be well enough,
when one was travelling, and had had no breakfast, to take a very
little spirits as a stimulant; and soon afterwards the gentleman procured a tin mug, and we heard the lady say: "Would my friends
believe it now if any one was to tell them that they saw Mrs.
W—— taking a dram of whiskey in a public kyar?"

At half-past nine we had ridden twenty-eight miles, and arrived
at Opelika, which the inhabitants call Oppalacca. It is a wretched
little village, which owes its consequence, and I should think its
existence, to the crossing of the railroads there, and by its appearance recalls forcibly the typical South-western American city which
is to be found in the books of English tourists. I saw it first in a
cold drenching rain. There was a big pine hotel among the thirty or
forty other buildings, a newspaper office, and half a dozen scattered bar-rooms, with mud between them and the wilderness close
around. The bad breakfast, hastily devoured, was there too; the

rough, lazy-looking men; and the long detention round the fire in the hotel, for the train going West was not due till three o'clock in the afternoon. Soon we learned that an accident had occurred near Montgomery, and that there was little chance of our reaching that city until the next day. A discussion of this probability kept us in intermittent conversation for almost an hour, and provoked much dissatisfaction. It was generally conceded that if a man'd got to lie over, he couldn't find a meaner place to lie over at than this yer Oppalacca.

"This lyin' over," one man said with a laugh, "by gosh, gentle-men, we can't affo'd it now. Old Jeff paid yo' way befo', but now you must pull out yo' own greenbacks. Mighty hard on us po' Confeds."

"You're right there," another said. "This is the first time I've been able to leave Atlanta since we went up, and I couldn't do it now but there's somebody pays my expenses." Saying this he slapped his next neighbor on the knee, and asked him: "Did I ever tell you, Mr. L——, what old W—— says about us? I was in company with him in the hotel, and I was a-takin' on powerful about the sorry fix we was in. 'W——,' says I, 'we're nothin' but old, whipped-out rebels,' says I. 'Oh, but a'n't we down?' says I. 'We done lost our niggers; we done lost our money; and the Yanks has whipped us pretty nigh *to* death,' says I. 'I'll be squeezed to death,' says I, 'if I'd ever fight again for any flag that ever was no more than I'd fight for an old dish-rag. I'm subjugated,' says I. You know old W——, what a train of eloquence he can git on to when you git him stirred up. He got up, and says he: 'T——, you lie! I know you, and you can't tell that tale to me. Do you mean to say,' says he, 'that if France and England, or some o' them foreign powers, was to declare war agin the United States, and was to offer us our liberty and all our rights and our independence; was to land a million o' men right yer, and call on us to come out and help 'em lick the Yankees, do you mean to say that you wouldn't fight?' Well, he pictured it all out so fine, and the old fellow looked so earnest, you know how he can talk, and he spread himself out till he looked as big as a skinned hoss, that it worked on me, and I jumped right out of my chair I was sittin' in. I don't never swear hardly, but I did that time. I just flung my hands up like this: 'Fight!' says I, 'may I may be d—d if I wouldn't fight while I had one drap o' blood left in my veins. I'd fight till the last Yankee was the other side the Potomac.' I let out, and the thing of it was there was a Yankee there all the time. I didn't know it, you know, but there was a captain. He jumped up when I got done, and says he: 'My God! what sentiments,' and walked right out. I was caught. And it was the first time I'd said anything wrong since the smash. But that warn't all. When the Yankee went out, W—— says: 'Come up to my room, I've got something pretty funny up there.' We went up supposin' he had some whiskey, and when we got into the room W—— never looked round, he didn't know he'd got anybody else there, and says he: 'Didn't I give that blue-bellied Yankee hell?' and squeeze me to death if there warn't another Yankee in bed right in the room! We had it on old W——. The Yankee seemed to be a good kind of a fellow too; I met him afterwards, and he seemed a right clever fellow."

When the laughter which followed this story had ceased, a gentleman remarked: "The Yankees would be great fools to go into a foreign war, that's certain."

"Why, sir," said another, "you don't think they have any fears of us? They know that we're whipped. They despise us more than we ever despised them. They consider us the most ignorant, low-down people on the face of this earth. They allow that a nigger is on the same equality with the most of us, and some of 'em will just about tell you so to your face."

"Yes, I have seen some that appeared to think so, but I think they very soon give up that idea. In my part of the country I believe they have less use for a nigger than we have."

This assertion called forth from different members of the company many corroborative stories, which were mostly related of Negroes who had been beaten for impudence or knocked down by drunken soldiers merely on account of their color. One man even professed to know of six Negroes that had been shot by soldiers during Christmas week.

"Well," said an old gentleman, "I am like you, sir; I feel that we have no flag and no country. How can we love the United States? We all know it to be an impossibility. When they ask me to be loyal, I ask, 'What for?' We live in troubled times, gentlemen, and I never expect to see peace again. It seems, sir, as if our times were the latter days which we are taught to expect, when there shall be wars and rumors of wars. I believe that we shall see the Jewish people led up to Jerusalem and gathered in from all the corners of the earth, according to the promise, and all the other promises made to the chosen people will be fulfilled. But there will be no more peace for the rest of the nations. That's the way it looks to me. I may be mistaken."

No one seemed prepared for this view of affairs, and a reply was not attempted. When the old man rose soon afterwards and went out, it was remarked that "he felt the thing powerful: broke him up, like."

Cotton-planting was of course discussed—two of the men around the fire asserting that without slavery there can be no cotton: on a well-regulated plantation, in old times, of course the niggers was made to work a heap harder than any man ought to work; well, a heap closer, anyhow; as for workin' harder, a nigger won't be drove to work more'n so much, like a mule in that respect. Now a free nigger a'n't goin' to work from before daylight, from the time he can see a cotton-stalk, till nine o'clock at night, and a white man can't stand it, and of course it stands to reason that cotton-raisin's gone up.

Four or five other men maintained the other side of the question: Take a plantation where the hands get out just before sun-up and work till sun-down, and you make a better crop than another plantation where you kill up your niggers with long hours and cuttin' and lashin'. Do with the freedmen as you did with 'em when we had slavery, and they'll work just the same; you always had to have somebody with 'em before all the time they was in the field.

Yes, it was answered, no doubt a man could make a livin' that way; and the niggers used to be better off, so far as that went, on

one o' them plantations spoken of, and lasted longer. But, dog-
gone it, that warn't farmin'; that warn't makin' what you call a crop,
not what's called a crop in Alabama.

This provoked a Georgian to say that on a plantation where
nobody worked before nor after daylight he could raise more bales
of cotton than on a plantation where the other plan was followed.
And as to white men not being able to work in the field, that was
all a mistake. They could work; he'd seen white men working cotton in Texas, and was mighty nigh being run out of his own town
for saying so, and for telling 'em that the doom of slavery was
written by them Germans. It wouldn't be long before you'd see
white men raisin' cotton in every State in the Confederacy.

Not our white men a'n't goin' to work, said the former speaker.
But if you mean that there won't be any niggers very soon to do it, I
believe you. Why, it's estimated that in the last year or two more'n
a million has perished; and you'll see in twenty years there won't
be five hundred thousand, all told. They're a-goin' faster'n the
Injins.

Upon this ground the disputants came together again, but I
doubted if more than one of the party really had faith in the theory
to which all, as a matter of course, publicly assented. One of them,
a young planter from Western Alabama, shared my room, and
freely communicated his agricultural plans and expectations.

He had been a soldier in the Confederate army, and when the
war closed found himself in Georgia, wounded and without money.
He had a horse, however, which he sold at a good price, and the
money thus obtained enabled him to go to his relations in
Alabama. His uncle knew he had been in the service, and was
therefore disposed to help him as much as possible, and, though
there was really nothing to do, gave him sixty dollars a month till
Christmas for overseeing the place. He got into a little cotton transaction, too, and cleared about four hundred dollars by that. Then
his uncle let him set up a store in the yard. It seemed mighty
curious, but every nigger round there had some silver, and it didn't
take long to clean out all the goods, and at a profit of about a
hundred per cent., too. Then the niggers didn't know the difference

between gold and greenbacks; in fact, they liked the "Yankee money" the best, and he made a pretty good pile selling the silver. Come Christmas, his uncle made him a first-class offer. He went to bed, and laughed; couldn't help it, as soon as he'd closed the bargain. He agreed to oversee the niggers and manage the place for one-half the crop. His uncle was to find corn and mules, and pay all the expenses. He intended to plant 800 acres in cotton, for there was corn enough there now to keep all the hands and stock at least two years. He had fifty-four niggers that belonged to his uncle, and was going to hire about twenty-one more. Three hundred acres were all ready for seed now, and he had more than thirty ploughs running, and plenty of seed on the place, so that he should get a very fair start. The niggers had promised to take up twenty acres apiece, and he reckoned they would, for they were working as well now as they ever did, and they always used to work that much. The Alabama niggers were not like the Georgia niggers; they're just as ready to wait on you now as they ever were, and there's none of this impudence and independence. Then the planters in Georgia were letting niggers have land and giving them their own way, and perfectly spoiling them. There was none of that in this country.

I asked what wages he paid.

At first he had had some trouble, for they wouldn't contract; but an old nigger fellow, a driver, came to him and told him to leave it all in his hands; only let him promise each worker half a dollar a day, and he'd agree to bring them all round before New Year's. The driver was to have six bits a day if he could do it. By Christmas they found that they were not going to get any land, and sure enough every nigger signed a contract on New Year's morning for half a dollar a day and rations. Every morning he gave the old driver about three gallons of whiskey, and he served out a drink all round before they went into the field.

I said I supposed he had to take his contract to the Freedmen's Bureau for approval.

Oh, yes; but they approved it very willingly. The Bureau in his part of the country let you do pretty much as you liked. They had a mighty good man there—let you whip a nigger if you liked. He would give me an instance. One of his uncle's niggers was in the loom-house, a nigger woman it was, weaving, and she kept breaking the thread. His aunt reproved her for it several times, but she kept on breaking, so careless, you know, and wouldn't take pains, and his aunt went up to her to strike her; but the woman made as if she'd strike his aunt, who was obliged to find his uncle and report the facts to him. His uncle went to the loom-house, but the woman had left. He was in the store when he first heard of it, but he knew very well which way she would be likely to head, so he got his horse and followed after her. Sure enough, there she was going to town to complain to the Yankees. She didn't hide nor anything, and when he asked where she was off to, she spoke up as bold as brass, and said she was going to tell the Yankees how she was used. He showed her his pistol, and told her to march back, which she did, of course, and when his uncle got her he gave her the worst whipping she ever got. But she left in the night—she might as well have gone in the day-time, for nobody wanted her on the place; she wasn't good for anything—and told what he and his uncle had done to her, and back she came with a note from the colonel. He supposed she thought something dreadful would be done to them, but when he read the note it just said: "I send back this woman, and advise you not to turn her away from the plantation. Make her behave herself and do her work, and if she needs correcting, correct her." That was all it said. The nigger left the place, for she said she wouldn't stay unless his uncle would agree not to whip her again. He didn't intend to whip her, for she got enough at first, but he told her "he'd see about it," and she got scared and left, for she thought he'd kill her sure.

The young man told me, furthermore, that he should still keep his store open, and expected to find it very profitable. Neither his uncle nor any of the neighbors intended to pay out much money to the hands till the crop was gathered, but he could arrange a system of certificates, he thought, and would be able to sell goods to the Negroes upon credit and not lose anything by it. I congratulated him on the probability of his making quite a fortune from his store and the sale of his cotton, and enquired if he knew anything about another speculation which I had recently heard mentioned—the shipment of Negroes to Cuba and selling them to Spanish planters? Yes, he said, he had been told about that, and if he had good luck he intended to get into it, for it was the biggest thing yet.

Half an hour after midnight our train was ready to start. In the darkness I missed the passenger carriage, and rode in a freight car, fitted up with benches for the conveyance of colored people. The weather had changed to cold and windy, and the box-stove full of pine wood failed to keep us warm. I could only see my fellow-passengers when at rare intervals the stovepipe became red-hot. Then an old Negro in front of it, nodding over a staff, would rouse himself, and poke the door till it opened and threw a flickering glare over the huddled figures, lying in every attitude of sleep and weariness. They looked like field-hands, and seemed to be all from one plantation, to which they were then returning. They seldom spoke, except now and then some impatient youngster sat to "min' chil' " when he wished to sleep, or a woman hushing her baby. When the conductor appeared, however, he was assailed with complaints because colored folks were compelled to pay full fare now, though the accommodations were poorer than when only half price was charged. To this he replied: "You're free now, ain't you? You're as good as white folks, ain't you?" At half-past four I reached my journey's end, having consumed twenty-four hours in travelling about eighty-five miles.

The city of Montgomery is the most beautiful that I have yet seen. The country around is undulating, and the city itself is built on several gentle hills, whose tops are now green with new grass. Standing behind the city and looking south and west to the horizon, a vast basin of wooded land can be seen, green near at hand and bluish in the distance, with the Alabama flowing through it towards the Gulf. Its many trees and broad streets are beauties common to Montgomery and other Southern towns, but here the streets are clean and hard, and the elegance of the private residences is equalled by the handsome and substantial appearance of the business quarter.

XXIX

MOBILE, ALA., January 31, 1866

ON the journey from Montgomery to Mobile I formed a slight acquaintance with two men who seemed to me, as I heard them talking, very fair specimens of two large classes of people that I not infrequently meet with in the South, and, therefore, I describe them.

One, who walked heavily into the car just as the train was starting, was a tall man in the Federal uniform, a staff officer, apparently, and perhaps thirty years old. He carried in his hand, rather ostentatiously, a bundle of official documents. Taking off a military cape, he laid it down, remarking in a loud voice that he had one objection to living in the South—the climate was too fine. Then the documents received each a brief, rustling examination and were placed one by one in his pocket; but, meantime, having discovered that one of two gentlemen sitting near was known to him, he leaned forward, and, shaking hands with him, was introduced to the other, whom I understood to have been a despatch-bearer or envoy of the Confederacy who had never got nearer Europe than Fort Warren. By-and-bye I heard this officer making known his opinions upon the war and the state of the country.

"Oh, sir, the fact that your Government selected you for that position is a guarantee. We shall not differ, sir, I'm sure. When I meet with a Southern gentleman, like yourself, sir, I never find that we can't agree. Some of the warmest and most intimate friends that I've got I've made in the South; some of the people that I have the very highest respect for. It's far from being a recom-

mendation for a man, in my eyes, to disown his cause. You Southern men believed you were right; in some things I sympathized
with you myself; why shouldn't you fight for your opinions?
Pleased to meet you, sir."

Cigars were then offered and accepted, and the major went on:

"I speak out myself, and I like to meet a man who expresses his
sentiments just as he feels them. Though mine are at variance with
yours, I can understand how you should feel as you do. Of course
you are proud of your record in the war. You fought us honorably,
nobly; no people ever fought better in all history, and I hope I can
honor a brave man whenever I find him. I fought you, I confess, as
hard as I knew how, and I know I'm proud of my record. And I
consider that the glory of this war, the glory of each side, belongs
to both. Look at the valor, the endurance, the way our people
fought in this struggle, the military resources we have developed,
the skill and generalship and strategy of Generals Lee, and Johnston, and Grant! They have never been equalled in the history of
ancient or modern times. Where will you find such a long, bloody
war recorded in history? We are invincible. Yes, sir; I consider the
United States more than a match for France and England and all
the foreign nations of Europe combined. What's Mexico?"

Ah, his hearers didn't know about that; they doubted it.

"Oh, certainly. Of course, I mean in defensive warfare. With
the South and the North united, if the powers of Europe were to
attack us they would be whipped. That's what I mean. Of course,
both sections are too much exhausted for us to think of bringing
on an unnecessary war. I've seen enough of fighting. I have been in
the army more than four years, and I've been at the front all the
time. I wouldn't part with my experience for any money. A
wonderful experience for a man. There is only one thing I missed:
I never was a prisoner. I should like very much to look back now
on two or three months spent in Libby. During the war I didn't
think so, for it would have taken me away from the front. That
was my only objection, however. I never was afraid you'd starve
me if you got hold of me. Too many of my friends, ha! ha! received your hospitality for me to think that."

Both the gentlemen joined in the laugh. No, he needn't have been afraid of that.

"Oh, no. You told such stories about us and we told the same about you. Some suffering, of course."

"Of course; the life of a prisoner couldn't be made very pleasant. But," said one of the gentlemen, "from my experience of prison-life I congratulate you, major, that you got through without being captured; at any rate, that they didn't get you into Fort Warren."

"Yes, that was a hard place, undoubtedly. But now it's all over, a'n't you glad that you have that experience to look back on?"

No; the gentleman couldn't say that he was. Of course he had the satisfaction of knowing that he had suffered for his country. But it had been his wish to serve her in some more active way.

"Yes; but you did serve her. I consider it a great misfortune to any man, especially to any young man, North or South, if he hasn't done something on one side or the other. The leading men of the country in the future will all be taken from among the soldiers. You of the South are not going to trust your pretended Union men, those who didn't prove true to your cause; we don't expect it of you; and we are not going to give office to our cowards and stay-at-homes. If a young man has any aspirations, it is a great misfortune to him if he didn't serve on one side or the other."

He himself had no aspirations, he explained. It was not for rank or promotion that he entered the army, and he did not look forward now to civil rewards. He simply wished to discharge gallantly his duties as a soldier. Not that he was gallant either—his duties as a soldier and citizen. He fought because he thought the Constitution should be maintained. He honestly differed in opinion from the Southern leaders in regard to secession, though he had acted with them politically. If he had been born in the South he would, probably, have fought as hard for secession as he had fought for the Union. As for the abolitionists, they were his detestation. Indeed, it was the abolitionists who brought on the war.

And Thad. Stevens and that gang, one of the gentlemen said, were just as bad today as they were ten years ago.

The major assented. Thaddeus Stevens he knew personally. He was deficient in the first qualities of a statesman. Able, very smart indeed; but no statesman. He and Sumner, however, were only fanatics; they could not lead the people. In his own opinion, the people of the South since the surrender had furnished an example of good sense and sincere loyalty unparalleled in ancient or modern history. Sumner and Stevens and the Abolition party were now the only disloyalists left. But the men who had fought who knew the Southerners because they had met them on the field of battle, were willing to trust the South and let the war end, and, if it should be necessary, to put down the fanatics.

There was much conversation of this sort, and all the major's remarks were well received by the two gentlemen. It was gratifying, one said, to hear such sentiments expressed; and the other said that they reflected honor upon the man who felt them. But among two or three young men across the aisle looks and smiles were now and then exchanged which the speaker would not have considered flattering. Just before going to sleep, for we left Montgomery in the night, I heard him replying to an enquiry about some buildings in Mobile which were seized by the Government some months ago and have since been used for the public service. Certainly they ought to be restored, he said, or else the rents ought to be paid. If he had his way the back rents should be paid at once and the buildings turned over to the owners. But, unfortunately, if he had been correctly informed, very recent orders from Washington forbade it, and of course the United States Quartermaster had no option but to keep the buildings and withhold the rents. It was a great hardship. For his own part, he would like to see the Government magnanimous to the South in every particular; magnanimity was the true policy, and the one that would have to be adopted; but still they would admit that it was the duty of a good soldier to obey his orders, although they might be such as he could not help considering wrong, and such as it was painful to his feelings as a gentleman to carry into effect.

This personage belongs to the South of today; the other figure that I attempt to describe belongs to the South which has just passed away. It is that of a man who throughout the rebellion was a loyalist in Georgia. He is a small, pale man, of very unobtrusive manners, and with the look of an artizan, so that I was not surprised when he said he was a cotton-carder and spinner from Rochdale. He came to America when he was twenty years old and had since then lived in the Southern States, following his trade in one factory and another and earning good wages. When the war broke out he was in Columbus, but he determined to get himself out of the city, where everybody was in a tumult, and they were all "through other" with their secessionism, and this and that, and therefore with his savings he bought a small farm two or three miles out in the country, where he could be quiet like. He avoided all public gatherings, gave a civil word to everyone, and never spoke about politics or Abe Lincoln except in secret and to those that he knew were of his way of thinking. The Union men in those days knew each other a deal better than the secessionists, and had a good understanding together. For a time this quiet, inoffensive life kept him out of trouble, though once in a while he'd know that there was talk of making him come out with his opinions; but still he never was visited till they began to enlarge the State militia and to drag in the old men as well as the young. His name he knew would be put down, for his age was within the limit; but he had decided in his own mind that he never would lift a hand for the rebellion, and he set about finding a plan for escaping the draft. He began to wear the oldest clothes he could get, and a pair of shoes that the blacks themselves wouldn't have demeaned themselves to pick up in the streets. He put such a stoop into his shoulders, too, that he was bent almost two double; he didn't shave either, and altogether he looked dreadful decrepit. Often the neighbors passing him at dusk, or riding by quick in the day-time even, would call to him, "Hello, Mr. N——" or "How d'ye do, Squire N——," mistaking him for Squire N—— that lived near him, a man eighty year o' age. But they put down his name and served him with a notice to be at the mustering place on such a day. He just stayed at home and looked after the ploughing, stooped over a little more very like, but paid no attention to the summons otherways. So in the evening a whole committee of them waited on him and wanted to know if he did not know he was enrolled, and why he had not made his appearance. He put them off with some indifferent answer; they wouldn't be wanting men of his age for the militia. His name was on the roll, they said, and he was to appear at the next meeting or take the consequences. Well, he didn't know how ever he'd be able to get there. He couldn't take the mule out of the field. But he told them, shuffling his old shoes and clapping one leg over the other so they could see them, he'd see if he could get something to wear that he could walk in. They said he'd best mind and be on hand, and with that they rode off. He had been careful not to say that he would go, but only to say that he would look up a pair of shoes to walk in, for it never was in his mind to go at all. And he never did. On the morning of the muster the captain of his company, a man that he had known pretty well for some years, rode past his place and said, "Come, Mr. F——, are you going to town?" "Well, no, captain," he told him. "It's younger men than me you want for your company." Then the captain asked how old he was; his name was down, and there had been some talk before because he was absent. "Captain," he asked, "you're a man that has known me for years; what would you set me at?" Well, the captain considered, and looked at him, and all this time the old clothes were on him and the old shoes, and at last he said, "Well, sure enough, Mr. F——, I reckon you're rising sixty. How near have I come to it?" But he wouldn't tell him; he only said, "Captain, you're near about the thing; I'm not that old as I look, but you're near about the thing." So, after a bit, the captain rode along; and he was informed afterwards that when the roll was called and they came to T—— F——, and some of the men cried out that he was not there and never had been there, the captain said that man was too old for duty, and they might just strike out his name. That was the last of his troubles except hat he lived under a miserable tyranny, without daring to open his mouth, until the United States Government conquered them and put them down. It sickened him of the South, and he intended to leave it for good and all. He was only waiting for the winter to pass and then he would seek work in Louisville or St. Louis.

I asked if he thought it would be unsafe for him and other men of his political opinions to live in Georgia and Alabama now.

No; he wouldn't say that. He could get along with them. He had lived with them through all the war; and they were far humbler now than then. The wild young men would bluster, but the most of the people would let a man alone if he went about his business.

The other day I put the same question to a gentleman living in Mobile, Mr. A—— G——, who is perhaps better qualified to give an opinion on this matter, showing him at the same time the anonymous letter of which I give a copy below. It is one of those that are known to have been sent to many different persons within the last fortnight.

MOBILE, ALA., January 25, 1866

Sir: We, the undersigned citizens of Mobile, Ala., give you one week from date to leave the place, and if found within the limits of the city or State after the time specified as above, you and your traitorous offspring will be wiped into eternity as sure as there is a God above you.

"By order of   SPECIAL COMMITTEE.

To the traitor, Francis Lyons, late Commandant of Florida Renegades.

In answering my question, Mr. G—— related an illustrative passage in his own history. Before the war his father, a Northern man, published a newspaper in Macon, Ga., in which town Mr. G—— lived from the time when he was three years old till the autumn of 1855. In that year he was waited upon one day by a number of his fellow-citizens, who charged him with being an anti-slavery man and with having made anti-slavery speeches in New York. He admitted that he was opposed to the continuance of slavery, if any safe method for getting rid of it could be devised, but denied that he had made speeches of any kind during his visit to the North. He was ordered to leave the town within twenty-four hours. At first he thought of disobeying this command. He went about to the shops to purchase a knife or a pistol and ammunition, but no one would sell anything of the kind to him or any member of his family; his friends being called on to aid him, durst not, and pronounced the idea of resistance utter folly; the power and authority of the mayor were invoked for the protection of a peaceable citizen, and the mayor replied that he should be protected up to the expiration of the twenty-four hours. Nothing remained, therefore, but submission, and he left Macon on the next train. None of the usual accessories of such a departure were omitted. He was accompanied to the depot by a tumultuous escort, who cursed, gibed, and flung rotten eggs; one of the newspapers noticed the occurrence in a short local article, headed "Served him right," setting forth that a young man, whose youth and weak head alone preserved him from a severer punishment, had been summarily sent out of Macon for using offensive language in reference to the peculiar institution, and was on his way to the North and the society of more congenial spirits; a telegram was sent to Savannah informing the citizens that an abolitionist might be expected in their city by the next train, and bespeaking a warm reception for him. Going North by way of Augusta, he escaped the tar and feathers prepared for him in Savannah.

One man, Mr. G—— said, caused all this. He felt confident that if the question of his expulsion had been voted upon by the people of Macon, more than three-fourths of them, even then, in 1855, would have voted in his favor. The manner of his banishment was the same with that of nine-tenths of all the men who in those days were driven out of the South. Some one man, a personal enemy perhaps, would take advantage of the soreness of public feeling in reference to slavery to use the ruffianism of the community in furtherance of his private ends. Free speech was not punished in every instance, though it was in his case; he had known many men whose dislike of slavery was as well known as his who were never molested. But let it once become worth anyone's while to attack such a man, and he could not consider himself safe; for though, as he believed, the majority of the people in no Southern community would have borne a part in such outrages, yet as they knew that slavery could not bear free handling in the light, they willingly permitted others to commit them. Now, however, there is no peculiar institution to be conserved, the great reason for hating Northerners has disappeared, and the prominent and influential men whose countenance of these lawless conservators alone made them dangerous, recognize the changed state of affairs. It was not at all his opinion that the memories of the war could furnish a reason for hating Northerners strong enough to take the place of the old reason of slave-holding times. He would be willing to work at his trade in any Southern community and vote the Union ticket. Yes, and read the New York *Tribune* openly. No; perhaps he would not like to avow himself in favor of Negro suffrage. And he readily admitted further that he would by no means consent to continue his connection with *The Nationalist* (a newspaper published in the interest of the colored people of Alabama) a day after the Federal troops should be withdrawn from Mobile. The same people who might concede to a white man the liberty of holding such opinions as seemed good to him, were very far from willing to allow that right to Negroes or to see anything done for their instruction.

I may say that the Assistant Commissioner for Alabama, General Swayne, is of opinion that Northern men may now settle in Alabama without fear of being molested by their neighbors. He inclines to think that such settlers are apt to exaggerate the bluster of a comparatively small number of men into the threatening voice of the whole people. At the same time he would not wish to be understood as denying that quite possibly their view is the correct one. They see in detail, while he gets but a general view, and there may be good ground for the apprehensions which they do undeniably entertain, for it is certain that the Northerners in the vicinity of Montgomery, his headquarters, are unanimous in believing the presence of the Federal troops essential to their comfort and safety.

I am informed by the officers of the Bureau that the freedmen in this part of Alabama have almost all found work for the year, and already entered upon the performance of it. In the immediate neighborhood of Mobile the turpentine business forms the chief employment of the people; and for working in the orchards the men receive some ten, some fifteen, and some even twenty-five dollars a month. Women, engaged in the same occupation, get from six to eight dollars a month; and food, shelter, and medical attendance are furnished at the expense of the employer. This statement is to be understood of the wages of able-bodied hands. The demand for labor both in the turpentine region and in the cotton country, further from the coast, exceeds the supply.

The newspaper which I mentioned above, *The Nationalist,* is conducted by white men, but is owned by an association of colored people, and of course relies mainly for support upon that class of the population. I may remark, in passing, that the publisher announces that he finds it difficult, "owing to some cause connected with the post-office department," to supply the paper to his more distant subscribers. From its columns I quote a report of the number of rations issued to destitute citizens of Mobile, and of the number of cases tried in the Freedmen's Court, during the week ending January 27, 1866:

Total number of applicants for justice from among colored citizens, 335, viz.:

For collection of wages from white employers	301
For whipping and other brutal treatment from the hands of white citizens	18
From the hands of colored citizens	4
For protection from white mobs in the streets while employed in their daily labor	3
Total	335

Number of rations issued to destitute citizens for the past week, 5,194, as follows:

Number of white persons drawing rations	624
Number of colored persons drawing rations	51
Number of persons in hospital at Dog River, of both classes, drawing rations	67
Total	742
Number of days	7
Total number of rations	5,194

Besides their attempt to establish a newspaper, the colored people here, in their desire to elevate themselves, are making efforts in other directions that merit a favor and encouragement little likely to be given them by the white citizens of Mobile. The books of a branch bank of the National Freedman's Savings and Trust Company have within a month been opened, and the deposits made already exceed $4,000. By means of a fair recently held in the Medical College building they succeeded in raising $1,200, to be devoted to the founding of an asylum for orphan children. Six hundred children are under instruction in the schools, which are to a considerable extent self-supporting, the scholars buying their own books and paying the salaries of two teachers out of eight. In these schools the scholars were well behaved, and the lessons were recited very well. The teachers, who have been engaged in the schools since they were first opened in May last, speak in high terms of the docility of their pupils, and say that it is seldom necessary to resort to punishment. Here I saw, for the first time in the Southern States, colored boys reciting in the same class with white. The latter, however, were children of the teachers, and not natives of Alabama. I saw, too, among the children one old white-headed man, who, when I asked him why he was there, told me with great earnestness that he wouldn't trouble the lady much; but he must learn to read the Bible and the Testament. He and his grandchild attend the same school, and the old man supports them both by what work he can do in the morning and evening.

As everywhere else, except in Port Royal, the teachers of these Negroes are bitterly disliked by the white people around them, and complain of many insults.

X X X

At Mobile I took passage by steamboat for New Orleans, gladly bidding good-bye to that disagreeable city, to the mud-banks of its harbor, with the flocks of carrion crows—turkey buzzards—always streaming and hovering over them, to the narrow and dirty streets, infested as they are by hundreds of ill-looking men, whose profession, said to be gambling, seems to be hanging about the innumerable bar-rooms. Nor was I at all sorry to go away from the boarding-house where I had heard so much about the irreclaimable worthlessness of the niggers, about the gallantry of various Confederate regiments, about the vast preponderance of foreigners among the dead men in Federal uniforms on several battle-fields, and where the lady sitting next me at table used to quiet her child whenever it made a disturbance by threatening to leave it and let the Yankees catch it. As we moved down the bay and past Fort Morgan the water became quite rough, and the weather, windy and piercing cold, was thoroughly unlike what one is accustomed to fancy of February on the Gulf coast. There were many little indications, however, that we were not travelling on Northern waters. On board that boat a placard notified us that gambling on Sundays was strictly prohibited. The bar was open, and a handsome young mulatto behind it, extravagantly dressed and fluent in French and English, was kept pretty busy throughout the afternoon and evening. There was ice in all the water jars, flowers adorned the tables at dinner, and there was a plentiful supply of fresh vegetables and fruits. Gentlemen were introduced to others as having been in Mexico, or intending to go there, or being well informed on Mexican affairs. It is noticeable, as one approaches New Orleans, that the dress of the men and women is better than that of the Southern people further north—homespun coats, Confederate uniforms, and clothes of the fashion of twenty years ago being an exception.

At the end of eighteen or nineteen hours we reached New Orleans, and I was walking through the French quarter and towards the river, eager to see the Mississippi, and intent on comparing the real city with that New Orleans which for many years, from the time when I first read pictorial geographies, had existed in my mind as the most interesting of American cities, seeming further off and more foreign than Europe or Egypt. But the Department of the Gulf has recently been too much written about for a description of the city to be now of any value. It will be of more general interest to give the substance of a series of conversations which I have had since my arrival with several men, some of them natives of Louisiana, some of them citizens of Northern States, but residing here, who may be supposed capable of giving a correct opinion in regard to the tone of public feeling in this community. The disposition of the people toward the Government and toward the Northern men living here were the points to which my enquiries were chiefly directed.

I talked first with a young gentleman from Massachusetts, an educated man, a lawyer, who, having come out here as a lieutenant in the Federal army, served till the end of the war, and is now practising his profession in New Orleans, and also has some money invested in carrying on a plantation in a neighboring parish.

"These people," he said, "are in this frame of mind: they are as firmly convinced as ever that they were right in this war, but they see and admit that secession from the Union is an impossibility; that the attempt to secede was a great mistake, and one that they have no desire or intention to commit again. Every one of their soldiers will tell you—I hear it said almost every day—that he is tired of fighting, that he has taken the oath of allegiance, and that he means to keep it, and to be a good citizen; and when they tell

me this I believe them. Talk with the business men, and you hear
the same thing. The war is over, slavery is gone. They have no
wish to see it restored; they want to see business reviving—that's
what they say. These classes of people will treat a Northern man
well enough. I don't wish to be better treated than I have been
treated by them, both here and in the country. My profession has
brought me into contact with a good many of them. I have acquaintances with lawyers in almost every parish in the State, and I know
I am always treated with courtesy, and I think they show me their
honestly felt sentiments and opinions. As for Northern capital,
they welcome it. Men come to me in this office; they have come
recently, anxious to get help from Northern men. I am endeavoring now to induce some Northern men to send their money out
here, and I am authorized by the parties here to guarantee them
fifteen per cent. interest on their money, and give them the control
of the crop. If they direct it to be consigned to Boston, why, my
client will agree to do so. His case is not an isolated one. The
whole planting community here is wishing for Northerners; they
want them as partners or as capitalists; and whatever money is
loaned the planters are ready to secure by a mortgage of their
lands—not their crop, mind, as they used to in old times, but their
land—or they will sell land to the Northerner. And if he buys he
will be kindly received. I go down once in a while to the plantation
that I am interested in, and I never was better treated than I am
there. They bring out their wine, I am taken to ride, I am introduced to the neighbors, and yet they know perfectly well that I am
a radical, that I believe in emancipation, and that I fought them
for four years in the Federal army. Yes, I believe that all the men
of wealth and influence and integrity, the solid men, are disposed
to be loyal, and to behave like good citizens. It is a few brawlers in
bar-rooms and billiard saloons—fellows who do not represent public opinion, who are not responsible men, and whom the sensible
people despise—these are the fellows who are always damning the
Yankees, who haven't had enough of fighting yet, who declare that
they owe no allegiance to the United States, and all that kind of

talk. They make a great noise, but I know that the respectable people are not with them. I believe I have as good opportunities for getting information as anybody."

I remarked that these men whom he described as bar-room brawlers, who had never owned Negroes, and whose opinions were not worth regarding, were commonly said to be in a majority here.

"No; I don't believe they are so numerous, and I don't believe they wield any influence. I don't deny that of the better classes some cherish the recollections of rebellion, are proud of Lee's army and Stonewall Jackson and so on. That I look upon as natural, and so it would be natural if some of them did hate the Yankees. Suppose the North had tried to secede, and the South had whipped it back into the Union, and there was a Southern garrison in every Massachusetts town, wouldn't we take it out in hating the South, though we might conclude that we ought to be loyal to the Government?"

Another Massachusetts man, an ex-captain in the Federal army, had entered the room while the foregoing conversation went on, and at about this point he said:

"Why, hang it, L——, a'n't you getting a little touched with secession? You've been here a little too long. You don't believe any Northern men would have any sort of a chance down here if the military was removed? You wouldn't dare to stay here yourself, now, would you?"

"Stay here? Certainly I would. And I believe I should never be troubled, no matter how long I stayed."

"Well, now, I can tell you that you would be troubled. I can tell you that you'd stop here a mighty short time after the military went away. I can tell you that there's a secret society in this city— and I know it's so—where your name and mine have been brought up before the whole crowd, and canvassed, and our antecedents discussed, and a mark put against us both. Not us alone, you understand, but every other Northern man in the city, too. They intend to drive us all out. And it a'n't your rapscallions either; some of the first merchants in town belong to it," and the captain mentioned some names.

"I don't believe a word of it. We've heard of this conspiracy before. I don't believe there is any such society."

"Well, tell me what made Governor Wells, in his message to the legislature, talk to them about secret societies, with grips and passwords and mysterious meetings, that he wanted to have put down? Didn't he say they were political?"

"Yes; and didn't he afterwards admit that he was mistaken, and had been humbugged?"

"I don't know whether he did or not. If he did, he needn't, for there is such a society, I know."

"All right; you can have it stopped then. But you'll find there's nothing in it. We've heard too much about it. It's an old story, you know. I've been all through it. Why, I was very sure myself that I'd got on their track, and I even was enough of a fool to write to the State Department and beg to have it investigated. And very soon I had to send another letter apologizing for the first one. For two of the best detectives in the United States came down here to investigate. I felt sure then. They got in with the suspected men, dined with them, drank with them, damned the Freedmen's Bureau for two months, and then they went away laughing between themselves at the idea of a secret anti-Northern society in New Orleans."

"Very well. But you find out, if you can, what they think of it at General Canby's headquarters. There they believe it."

This was a matter of which I could learn but little further, and that little was chiefly corroborative of the captain's assertion that, at headquarters, a secret society, which the governor refers to in his recent message to the legislature, is really believed to exist. It was vaguely hinted to me that I might believe the objects of the society to be more nefarious than an attempt to injure the trade of Northern men in business here, and to discourage immigration from the North. On the other hand, a Southern gentleman, a member of the State senate, said that he thought the governor was entirely mistaken, for he himself, in endeavoring to hunt out the conspiracy, which he denounced as odious, had exhausted all the resources that freemasonry placed at his command, and had been unable to find the slightest trace of it. But whatever the fact may be, the suspicion certainly exists, and in quarters generally considered very well informed.

Mr. L—— thought that as a rule the freedmen in Louisiana would receive kind treatment from their former masters, and inclined to think that eventually they would find their former masters their best friends. So far as his observation extended, most of the planters had tried hard to conform themselves to the new order of things.

A gentleman with whom I conversed shortly afterwards was a planter and the owner of three plantations. All the people on his home place had stayed with him, he said; but on his lower places they had been burnt out of their homes by General Smith, and he had been obliged to cut that up into small lots and put on white people. Nineteen families of poor devils were there doing what they could, and they were to give him half of what they made— they to find themselves in provisions and to furnish their own stock. His niggers on the home place were doing pretty well. He knew how to manage them. In old times almost every boy of his had a little horse, each family had a patch of ground for its own use, the men had one Saturday in every month as a holiday, and the women had half of every Saturday, no matter how much the plantation work might be pressing him. They never went to the field till broad daylight, and when it was cold they never went out at all. The result was that all his neighbors called him a nigger-spoiler; but he beat them all on crops, and a sick nigger was a rarity on his plantations. It was always his rule when engaging an overseer to tell him that his niggers were not to be whipped unless their owner was present; that in the absence of the owner he might give eighteen lashes over the nigger's clothes, and that if he ever violated those instructions he should leave and leave his wages. By this management he always had civil, industrious niggers. He knew how to manage them. They ought to be treated kindly, of course. Probably they would be, for the planters of Louisiana as a class were good masters. But Northern men did not and could not understand the Negro character. Therefore, the old harmony and confidence once existing between the black and white races in the South would never be restored; the golden age, if he might call it so, would never return until the Freedmen's Bureau should be removed. He would give me a sample of the working of the institution if I didn't know much about it: A friend of his went to Natchitoches the other day and engaged fourteen hands to work for him, and got the agreement countersigned by the Bureau officer. Thought he was all right. Coming into town the next day for his niggers, he found that another man had hired them, and that the officer had approved that contract too; so he went to the Bureau and said to the lieutenant: "Lieutenant, you've let those boys that I hired only yesterday, and brought before you to make the contract, go and make a contract with another man." But the officer would give him no other satisfaction than telling him that "the niggers were as free as he was." The Bureau certainly made trouble everywhere, and he asked me what I thought of the prospect for its discontinuance. I replied that its powers would probably be enlarged, and that I believed an agent was to be appointed in each county of the Border and Southern States. If that was so, he said, and if Andy Johnson didn't veto the bill, he thought he'd try to be appointed agent in his own parish. Of course it was reasonable to suppose that a native Southerner, who knew all about planting and all about the Negro, would make a better agent than a Northern man.

This gentleman described the people of his State as being loyal to the United States. Some few men were still rebellious, but even those few were gradually getting more sensible, and there was not nearly so much bitterness now as three months ago. This he could see in his own circle of acquaintance. And what was the use, he wished to know, of talking about the Southern hostility to Northern men when anybody could see it was for the interest of the South, that it was absolutely a necessity for her, to invite capital and enterprise from all quarters? And Northern men, in thinking of the subject, ought to remember that the State of Louisiana was in reality opposed to secession from the outset. It was nothing but that cursed Democratic party which took the State out, and the honest men, the men of character and standing, did all they could to resist it, but unfortunately failed.

Another man who gave me his opinion of affairs in Louisiana was a Northern man by birth who had lived in Arkansas and Louisiana thirty years and more. When the war began he was a steamboat captain and pilot in New Orleans, and being, as he says, an outspoken man, was soon thrown into the parish jail for being a Unionist and a Lincoln spy. When the city was taken he joined the Federal army and served during the war as a soldier and as a pilot. His property was destroyed by the Confederate army, and since the war he has been endeavoring to earn his living by following his profession. This he finds impossible, and the reason, as he gives it, is the hostility towards Unionists which is felt by a large portion of this community. When Butler's order compelled the people of New Orleans to divide themselves into two classes, registered friends and enemies of the United States, three-fourths of the members of the Pilots' Association were enrolled in the list of enemies and were sent outside the lines. Now, after four years, they have returned, and the Pilots' Association is revived again. A list of pilots has been prepared by the association and is used by the inspector of steamboats for the Board of Underwriters. It is charged by my informant, and, whether mistaken or not, he attests his sincerity by preparing to bring the matter before the courts, that this list ranks the pilots not according to their ability, but according to their political opinions; that an unqualified pilot, if he was a registered enemy of the United States, is classed as a No. 1 pilot, but that a Unionist, no matter how well qualified he may be, is omitted from the list; that he has been informed by steamboat captains that they would willingly employ him, but that they are told that no boat in charge of a man whose name is not enrolled will be able to effect an insurance. Feeling sure, therefore, that there is a combination to keep honest men out of employment for no good reason whatever, he proposes to bring a suit for damages in one of the courts here, and has sent a petition to Washington setting forth the facts and praying for justice.

This person thinks that the men who fought in the Confederate army are honest in their professions of loyalty and wish for an enduring peace; but the great body of the people are, in his opinion, as rebellious as they were two years since. The men who are reasonable and desire to give up contention are kept in awe by the opinion of their neighbors. He mentioned what he considered the strongest of many instances of this kind which he had observed. On one occasion during the war he had befriended a young Confederate prisoner whose family he had known in former times. Recently, while travelling in the Washita country, he met the boy's father on a steamboat, and the old man, after some time, came over to him and returned thanks for his kindness. This he did in a hasty whisper, showing every sign that he desired those about him to remain ignorant that he had received or acknowledged favors from a Yankee. He would like to talk to Andy Johnson for one half hour, and he would prove to him that he ought to raise the number of regular troops to one hundred thousand men, and keep these States garrisoned for the next three years. If the troops were removed now no Union man could stay here a week.

I find the greatest diversity of opinion prevailing among the men with whom I have talked as to whether or not public opinion is growing more hostile to the North. I judge that the Northern men now here would, for the most part, think it not dangerous to remain after the troops are gone; and I think most of them would not expect their stay to be so profitable to them as it is at present. I speak of professional men and merchants. I believe there was but one of my many questions that received always the same answer. When I asked if there is any town in the State where they thought a man might, with safety to his life, publicly advocate, or be generally known to advocate, the propriety of allowing intelligent, educated Negroes to vote, the reply was uniformly in the negative.

XXXI

NEW ORLEANS, LA., February 20, 1866

ONE day this week I made a visit to the house once owned by
Mr. Pierre Soulé, and now in the hands of the Government. For
nearly a year it has been used as an asylum for colored orphans. A
young lady from Boston, Mrs. De Mortié, has been its manager
from the time when it was founded, and, indeed, may be regarded
as its founder and preserver, having successfully overcome the
many obstacles which stood in its way at the beginning, and the
perils which have threatened its existence since. It was only after
wearisome delays that the Federal officers quartered in the house
could be got out of it in order to make room for Negro children.
The citizens resident in that quarter were, of course, violently opposed to the establishment of a Negro school and house of refuge
in their neighborhood; and others, not aggrieved by its vicinity to
their residences, were very angry at seeing so elegant a mansion
given up to such uses. A guard had to be stationed round the
building to protect it from destruction and its occupants from insult. This was furnished by General Banks, who warmly befriended
the enterprise from the outset. On the part of some people who
had been expected to render aid there was a good deal of back-
wardness at the first, and it is only recently that a society, called
the Louisiana Association, and made up for the most part of
wealthy people of color in New Orleans, has been formed, and has
pledged itself to give the institution pecuniary assistance. At one
time it was in great danger from an order issued by the Assistant
Commissioner of the Bureau, which seemed to contemplate the

apprenticing of all the inmates of the asylum. There were at once a great many visits from Southern men demanding apprentices in the most confident manner, one even threatening the matron that she would do well to be careful of her language or she might find herself apprenticed. Prompt recourse to General Canby averted that danger. Courage and patience constantly exerted have kept the asylum in existence and successful till the present time. And now a French gentleman, who has recently visited this country, and while here gave a careful examination to the institution, offers to bestow upon it $10,000 on condition that $20,000 additional is raised, and Mrs. De Mortié entertains the confident hope of soon seeing her enterprise carried to a prosperous conclusion.

That there is need of such an asylum is evident from the fact that it is now giving support and an education to fifty-six children. The number of inmates was at one time as high as one hundred, but that was while many of the Negroes of this city and the neighboring country were yet in the Federal army and the Confederate camps. In many of these cases the mother died during the father's absence, and the child found refuge in the asylum. Then upon his return it was removed and cared for by him.

I found children of all ages, from those of four months old up to fourteen and fifteen years, and some whom I did not see, and who are more than fifteen years old, were away at work, and are only to be found in the asylum at night. The school is held in what was once the dining-room, and contains about fifty pupils, two of them being day-scholars, who pay for their tuition. An increase in the numbers of this latter class may be expected, I was told, and their tuition fees will be applied to the expenses of the establishment. The list of studies embraces the common branches of an English education, history and physiology among the rest, and there is a class of ten who study French. Plain needlework is also taught. One of the teachers is paid by the National Freedmen's Relief Association, and the others by the Freedmen's Bureau. One of them informed me that her scholars behaved very well in school and gave her no trouble, so far as discipline was concerned, but she thought them indolent and averse to study. I only heard them singing, an exercise which they performed with a great deal of spirit. The dormitories, dining-rooms, playrooms, and the grounds were all very neatly kept, and evidently pains had been taken to preserve the house from injury.

The general work of educating the freedmen of the State seems to be carried on with considerable vigor and probably with more success than in any of the other Southern States. I learn that on the 1st of February, 1866, the whole number of schools for freedmen was 140, with 267 teachers and 14,500 scholars. These schools are nearly all in the eastern part of the State, near the Mississippi River, although efforts are now being made to extend them over the other parishes. The cost of supporting the 140 schools now in operation is not far from $20,000 per month. It is defrayed by the United States Government, but the Bureau is charged with the expenses, and they in turn charge them to the State of Louisiana, which, it is probable, will eventually be compelled to pay them; for in 1864 a tax was imposed on the real estate in Louisiana by General Banks, who intended thus to support the schools which he had been mainly instrumental in establishing. For some reason this tax was not collected in 1864, and it was not until 1865 that a small portion of it, about $40,000, was paid into the treasury. Just then, if my information is correct, General Fullerton, the successor of Mr. Conway in the office of Assistant Commissioner, ordered that the collection should cease. Meantime the Bureau had been allowed to borrow from the Quartermaster's Department about $300,000. General Canby has recently declared that the tax was imposed by proper authority and must be paid, so that it seems likely that the instruction hitherto given to the colored people of Louisiana will be paid for by the State. For their future instruction General Baird, the present Assistant Commissioner, adopts a new plan. To the people in each district he gives their choice whether or not they will have a school. If they decide to have one they are obliged to pay its expenses. The agent of the Bureau is instructed in the case of such Negroes to direct the employer to withhold from them and pay over to him five per cent. of the laborer's wages. This cannot be done where Negroes enter into contracts that are not submitted to the Bureau for approval, and it cannot well be done in the cities, where few laborers work under a written contract. In the cities, therefore, each child is expected to pay a tuition fee of $1.50 per month. The Superintendent of Education is now sending his agents into all parts of the State to urge upon the Negroes the importance of supporting schools, and hopes for good results from the new policy, which, except as to its principles, it is of course too early yet to judge. The hostility of the white people to the Bureau, so far as his official information enables him to reach a conclusion, is decreasing, the good influence being exerted by the best class of planters. But there is still much of it in exist-ence, and it is only this week that one of his subordinates comes to him severely beaten, with the complaint that he has just been driven out of the parish of Point Coupee.

In the plantation department of the Bureau I was told that there are not laborers enough to supply the demand of the planters, and that in consequence some of the contracts made very recently give the Negroes $18 a month. But the greater number of contracts filed in the office set forth $10 and $12 a month as the rate of wages; and I am told that not only shelter, food, fuel, and medical attendance are given by the employers, but clothing also. Five-sixths of all the contracts made agree that the laborer shall be paid in money; the rest give him a share of the crop.

Outrages upon Negroes are said to be of infrequent occurrence, for very few complaints reach the Bureau; and cases of fraud, though by no means so rare, are not remarkably numerous. The gentleman at the head of this department of the Bureau is often in receipt of letters from Northern men who are cultivating cotton here. He believes that the danger of injury and insult to North-erners from their neighbors is very much less than it was a few months ago. He mentioned as one instance—and was able, he said, to give many—the case of a Mr. R——, a Massachusetts man, who, three months ago, found his neighbors so hostile that few of them would speak to him, and he had even received threatening letters. Now, he reports, there is very little trouble of that kind. Some of them come to him for advice as to the proper management of free labor, for he is a more successful planter than they. That circumstance, by the way, was an illustration, he thought, of the great difficulty which every officer of the Bureau found constantly coming up in his own experience. The planters as a class required more teaching, before they could adapt themselves to the new system, than even the Negroes. At any rate, they required as much teaching, and they were less willing to be taught.

On this same question of Southern hostility to the North and the Government I talked not long since with a staff officer, who gave me as an example of it this account of an affair in which he had borne a part: He happened to go with some friends not very long ago into a hotel that has recently been opened here, and in the office he saw hanging up a printed announcement that on such an evening a concert or lecture, or some entertainment or other, would be given, and then came the big letters, "for the benefit of the Hon. Jefferson Davis and family." A portrait of Davis was fastened to the lower corner. The sight of the thing stuck up there made him angry, and he at once jumped up and snatched down handbill and picture. Going then to the clerk he demanded his reason for insulting a part of the guests of the house. The clerk said "no offence was intended, they had to please everybody," and made other lame excuses, and referred him to the proprietor. The proprietor was away at the time and could not be found. Well, on the next night there was quite a company of Southerners assembled in the hotel office, and the handbill and Jeff's picture were hung up again. Of course he did right in pulling it down the first time, but what should he do the second time? Consulting with his friends he decided that he would not be justified in going there without business of any kind just to make a quarrel, kill somebody, or get killed. He could not go there and let it hang; so he decided to stay away altogether. But he believed that was the way they all hated the Union.

XXXII

I WISHED after leaving New Orleans to visit Baton Rouge, and, for the sake of seeing the country and the people between these two cities, I decided to make the journey on foot. My valise and overcoat, therefore, were sent forward by express, and I carried with me only a very light equipment of such things as would be indispensably necessary during a week's walk. I reached the little suburb of Carrollton before twelve o'clock, and there enquired for the road to Baton Rouge. "The river," everybody answered with a stare; "a boat; nobody went by land," and at last they told me to take to the levee. Accordingly I climbed the bank and was fairly on my way. At the end of the first five hundred yards a colored soldier ordered me to halt, and referred me to his officer for the reason. The lieutenant said that he had orders to keep all Jews and peddlers out of the camps; the men were being paid off. Satisfying him that I was not a peddler, he suffered me to pass on, and for a little way I walked in company with two Negro women who were going into the country to make a Sunday visit to their relatives. They talked about the capture of New Orleans, the cannonade at the forts, the first appearance of the fleet, and the fright among the citizens. That was the day, one said, when them rebels run all about. Yes, said the other, that was the time when the stripes come off'n their pantaloons! They told her the d——n Yankees had come, and the very first thing they'd blow up the city and kill all the people. They wouldn't kill her, she told 'em. She knowed she'd never done nothin' but work hard; not her, not since they done sell her out o' old Virginny. They told her a heap more'n she believed. Same as they said that Confederate flag never should come down off'n the Custom House; the man that laid a hand on it should die sure. But she noticed the Yankee flag went up very quick. As for herself, her mind was all made up to run for them same cannon that talk' down the river, if the Yankees didn't come up.

These recollections the women dwelt on with much apparent enjoyment, as is usual with the Negroes whenever they talk of Federal successes. By-and-bye we came upon another guard, and I went on alone, leaving the soldiers examining the baskets of the women to see if they contained whiskey, and soon I fell into the company of a young man who, after finding out my business, informed me that he was a teacher employed by the Freedmen's Bureau, and urged me to spend the night with him. He would show me a *lusus naturæ,* he said. He would introduce me to Mr. B——, a man born in the South, once the owner of several slaves, afterwards for a long time an overseer, who was not only a Unionist, but actually believed that the Negro was the equal, and in many respects the superior, of the white man, and should be allowed to vote. Mr. B—— was manager of the plantation he was living on, which was only twenty-five or thirty acres further up, and I would find him very hospitable.

I consented to go with him, and as we walked along he bade me remark that the surface of the river was eight or ten feet higher than the land, and that the field-ditches all ran not towards it but away from it. The country along the Mississippi for many miles above and below New Orleans and Baton Rouge was a narrow strip of good land, with the river on one side of it and a swamp on the other. Then each plantation was a strip of land, the most of it worthless, extending back, sometimes many miles, into the swamp water; and in estimating the size and value of the farm the important element entering into the calculation was always the number of acres fronting on the levee. The country is exclusively agricultural. It is customary, therefore, in measuring length to use the measure applied to the farms, and to speak of points upon the road as being so many acres or so many arpents distant from each other.

It was not long before we came to the dwelling place of my new acquaintance. The house was a low building, shaded by magnolia trees, in the middle of a flat yard, which looked like a goose-pasture with its slippery mud, its short green grass, and shallow pools. His school-house was on the next plantation. On first coming into the service of the Bureau he had been compelled for several months to live in a part of one of the Negro cabins; but Mr. B—— had taken him out of those disagreeable quarters, and established him more comfortably where he was then. His pay was eighty dollars a month, the same with that given other teachers of his rank. Those of lower grades received sixty-five and sixty dollars a month, and no one was employed without first passing a thorough and severe examination. In no other State, he thought, had the rate of wages for teachers in freedmen's schools been so very high, and from all I hear of the examination to which teachers in Louisiana have been subjected, I should say that the standard of qualification also has been exceedingly high. General Baird's recent order, directing that the Negroes shall hereafter pay the expenses of their schools, goes into operation in March, and during February all schools are suspended. Meantime agents go about explaining its provisions to the people. Its effect, this teacher thought, would be to diminish considerably the number of persons under instruction. Anticipating its promulgation, he had offered to keep his school open during the intermission if each pupil would pay one dollar. Formerly, he had eighty-three pupils; now he has only thirty-five. But, if I am not mistaken, a compulsory support of schools is intended.

At night we walked out half a mile to the Negro quarters of a neighboring plantation, and visited the cabin of one of the laborers. Several of his friends dropped in, and the schoolmaster directed the conversation to the subject of education. Two men were spokesmen for the others, and presented the different aspects of the question. Here they were, one said, working for only twenty-five dollars a month. Out of that amount they had to buy food and clothes and everything else they wanted, and were also taxed half a dollar a month to pay for the regular visits of the doctor. If he

ordered medicine, that had to be paid for. Mr. M——, their employer, didn't want women in the field—not now, at any rate—and
the man's wages were all that was coming in. It was pretty tight
living, and come to put on a school tax on top, nobody could stand
it. The wages all went for victuals. How could they save a dollar a
month for schools?

The other man, a carpenter and engineer, said that the school
tax wouldn't be a dollar; it would be only seventy-five cents a
month. Mr. M—— had explained that all out to them; and by-
and-bye the women would have work as well as the men, and
would be getting half a dollar and a dime a day for it. Education
was the greatest of all things. What made the difference between a
white man and a black man? Knowledge and wisdom. Look at
this: Mr. M—— hired him and paid him thirty dollars a month,
and he had to find himself out of it; but he hired Baptiste and paid
him a hundred dollars a month and found him everything he
wanted. Now he could do the work Baptiste did, just as well, and
perhaps a little better; but when it came to taking a pencil and
paper and calculating and figuring, he couldn't do it. Baptiste could
tell the feet in a load of boards; he couldn't. Education was the
thing. "For we old gineration," he thought, it was too late to go to
school; but the children ought to be educated. Leaving learning to
your children was better than leaving them a fortune; because if
you left them even five hundred dollars, some man having more
education than they had would come along and cheat them out
of it all; but learning they could keep. He ended by begging the
teacher if his boys would learn their lessons in no other way to
whip them night and morning. The little girl was more easily managed; she sometimes sat up half the night over her geography
book. The other men fully agreed with him as to the importance of
education; it was the tax that frightened them, and they so poor;
but of course they meant to keep their children in school as long as
they could.

Going back in the dark, we could hear the steamboats panting
down the distant river, but could only see them as moving clusters
of lights, floating as it seemed in the air, the river was so high

above us. Mr. B—— had returned in our absence, but had immediately gone away again, for a squad of soldiers, searching for a stolen mule, had forcibly taken away one of his, and he had ridden to the camp to recover his property. He had not come back when I rose in the morning, and I lost the opportunity of talking with him.

February 18, 1866

The morning was close and warm when I set out again, and it was a constant pleasure to walk through the unfamiliar scenery in the delicious weather, the air full of the earthy smell of the new herbage and ringing with the songs of birds. For miles together the appearance of the country is the same. On the levee one is in the middle of a great oblong space, almost flat. The bank he walks on is about six feet high and a yard wide at the top. Its sides are covered with sods, and a trodden footpath, edged with grass and small-leaved clover, and slightly elastic beneath the step, winds away before him and seems like a green ribbon with a wood-colored stripe running through it. On the left hand is the yellow stream of the river, more than a mile wide. The trees along the further bank are not thick together, and the white houses, never far apart, shine through them. For the most part they are leafless and indistinct, and as one looks away up the river the low shores of the distant loops and bends range themselves irregularly behind each other, and at last would almost fade into the hazy sky, but that one sees the globe-like deep green mass of some live-oak standing out against the dim background of blue-gray. There is little on that side to break the monotony: the shadow of a buzzard skims along the bank; a skiff runs out and, making fast to the roots of some floating pine, tows it in; a Negro silently fishes, swinging a long-handled scoop-net; a steamboat is seen now and then, and perhaps she suddenly turns her bow to the shore, the current carries her stern down the stream, she swings to the bank broadside on, picks up a passenger, and is off again.

On the right hand, at the foot of the levee, is the dirty road. Behind this road the brown fields, with spots of green, and marked

by fences and long ditches and canals, stretch back for a mile or
two, sloping with an almost imperceptible inclination to the
swamp. This appears as a line of bleached and leafless forest,
hung with heavy masses of what one knows to be gray moss. Dot-
ting the great muddy plain are the various farm buildings, the
dwelling houses near the road, further in the rear the village of
Negro houses, then, sometimes a mile away, the sugar house with
its massive red chimneys, and furthest of all, on the edge of the
swamp water and close to an unseen levee, the roof that covers the
cumbrous draining machines.

These lowlands of Louisiana are in appearance by far the richest
country and the best populated that I have seen in the South.
Sometimes for a mile or more the houses stand so close together as
to form a continuous line, and one is never out of sight of some
dwelling place. In walking twenty miles one usually passes two or
three of these villages, with their foreign-looking inhabitants, the
shop signs in the French language, the chapel where a bell is ringing for service, and the little houses sometimes plastered with mud,
but usually seeming neat and clean. The planters' houses are often
handsome buildings, and it is common to see them standing in a
fine grove of evergreens, orange trees, perhaps, with loaded
branches, while the ground beneath is golden with the fallen fruit.
At two o'clock it began to rain, and I took refuge in a wayside
grocery, where a young man talked with me about political questions. It was strange, he said, to see what fools the Southern people
had been since the surrender. They wouldn't wait till their Con-
gressmen were admitted, but showed their hand plainly. He had
told a good many men that all this legislation about the niggers
ought to be put off; there was no hurry; but they thought things
ought to be fixed right off, so that they could make a crop this
year, and they went on doing what he called playing the radicals'
game. Of course the North would stand by the nigger. A couple of
months ago he had been in Alabama, and two niggers came into
that country from the North; one was a well-educated fellow, too,
and had something to do with a newspaper in his own State. The
young men run 'em both out of the country. He told them they had

no business to do it; of course that nigger told his story when he got home, and made it ten times worse than it was. The result of that kind of thing would be that Negro suffrage would be forced on the South. He had prophesied it for months; but they laughed at him, and said that anyhow they could control the Negro vote. Well, when a man was d——d fool enough to talk like that he'd better be left alone. The niggers would vote for the men that gave them their freedom.

While I sat there several Negro men and women stopped on their way home from church and bought whiskey and tobacco. The store was a miserable little room in the yard of a large house, and the storekeeper was the planter's son, a young man and apparently a person of some education. The rain ceased for a little while, but before I had walked far recommenced, and I began to look for a place to stay in for the night. I found it at what is called Rost's Colony, a plantation twenty-five miles distant from New Orleans. It was for some time held by the Bureau as confiscated property, but the owner, having been pardoned, now receives rent for it. It is not only worked as a plantation, but is also an asylum for Negroes disabled by age and sickness. There are now 745 people living there, of whom 100 are able-bodied persons receiving pay for their labor. Fifteen dollars per month is the amount given to each full hand, in addition to shelter, food, and two suits of clothing yearly. They are said to work very well, although a man formerly employed as overseer went away in disgust at free labor. The expense of carrying on the farm during 1866 will be about $40,000. Should the season not be a bad one, it is estimated that the value of the molasses, sugar, and cotton produced will be $90,000. The cost of maintaining the colony will be $25,000, including the expenses of supporting an hospital and keeping a physician at a salary of $100 a month. Six per cent. on the net profits is paid to an experienced sugar planter who acts as overseer. This is the only institution of the kind in Louisiana, I am told.

Here I met the agent of the Freedmen's Bureau for the parish of St. Charles. He reports the condition of the freedmen as being satisfactory. They are all at work, except upon some few plantations which are not under cultivation, the lessees having abandoned them for one reason or another. Ten dollars and fifteen dollars a month are the wages commonly paid, and where more than this is given the laborer buys his own food and clothing. The women are not paid so much as the men, and are not always hired by the year, but often by the day. No planter gives his laborers the whole amount of wages due them when the monthly pay-rolls are made out, but one-half of the money remains in the planter's hands until the end of the year. Outrages or frauds upon Negroes were very infrequent.

There was only one opinion among the gentlemen at this house about the political sentiments of their Southern neighbors—that they were hostile to the Government and to Northern men. None of them, however, complained of having been himself injured or insulted.

February 19, 1866

In the morning I was invited to ride out and see the plantation, which is considered a model, and has evidently been carefully managed for some years. The powerful and complicated machinery for sugar-making is said to have cost nearly a hundred thousand dollars. There was also the gin-house with its separate engine, the grist-mill and the engine, and the heavy water-wheel of the draining-machine in the swamp. The Negro houses formed a long street, and, like most that I see in Louisiana, were superior to the laborers' quarters in other Southern States. The house, now used as an hospital, had been built for that purpose by the owner of the place; there are now twenty-one inmates, some of them men more than a hundred years old. After looking at these things I bade good-bye to my kind entertainer, who insisted on my taking one of his horses and riding two or three miles. A little Negro boy, mounted on a creole pony hardly bigger than a yearling calf, accompanied me, and was full of chat. When he grew up he intended to be a hand on one of the steamboats; that was better than working on a plantation, only they turned a man away too quick.

Freedom was better than slavery, he thought; for one thing, in free times, you could go to school. His horse could run mine down; it was God's truth, and, if I didn't believe it, I could try it. Then he rode straight up the steep bank of the levee, showing off the powers of the animal, and brought her down again safely, and made her jump a ditch. He was sometimes whipped in school, he said. Leaving him to go back with the horses, I walked on in the face of a strong wind which ruffled the river into waves, and made me glad when the levee now and then forsook the bank and interposed between me and it a screen of willows growing up out of olive-colored pools of water. Soon a young man on horseback overtook me, and we travelled together. He was a Bostonian, who came into this State in 1864. Last year he cultivated a plantation on "the coast," as everybody calls the river-shore, and this year he rented one place on the coast and two in the Red River country. The Negroes worked as well as could be expected of people who had been brought up as they had, and fed on such food as the slaveholders gave their hands; of course, they were not so efficient and profitable laborers as whites were. He intended to make his home in Louisiana, and desired no better country to live in. He weighed ninety pounds when he left Massachusetts, and now he weighed a hundred and forty, and was afraid of no kind of weather or work. The people always treated him like a perfect gentleman, and there was no greater mistake than to suppose that they didn't like the Northern men. When the war first broke up a Yankee was not very favorably received; it was much the same in the South as it was then in the North when a Southerner was seen; people looked at him and said: "Perhaps that's the scoundrel that killed my son or killed my brother." But that feeling had worn away. He had lived among the people of this State, he had recently made a long journey on horseback into Texas, and everywhere he had been treated as well as he could ask. And he never denied that he was from Massachusetts nor concealed his hatred of slavery. So far as danger was concerned, there were many mean fellows in the country, who cared nothing for law, who always had been in the habit of using the pistol in any little dispute; but it was easy to take the necessary precautions against such men, and he felt just as safe here as in New England. As to Negro suffrage, universal Negro suffrage, the men that advocated such a measure as that must be lunatics or fools. At any rate, they had a very poor idea of what made the glory and strength of true republican governments. The niggers were destitute of honesty; they didn't know the meaning of principles; they were ignorant and debased; and to put the ballot in the hands of such a set as the common plantation Negroes would be ruinous. Couldn't any man of common sense see that the country would be filled with a tribe of miserable demagogues, worse, if possible, than the John Slidell democracy, the moment that the Negroes got political power? Of course, if a man could honestly believe in the right of these ignorant men to vote, he had a right to uphold his belief by speech and writing. It would partly depend on how he talked about it whether he could talk with safety in this country. Let him be as civil to his neighbors here as he had to be in New York or Massachusetts, and there was no doubt he could express any opinions that he might hold. Intelligence and good character, in his opinion, should be made the conditions of exercising the electoral privilege; but Congress had no right whatever to interfere in the matter; it should be left to the States.

The gentleman's plantation on this road, a small farm devoted to the culture of rice, was not far from the place where I first met him, and he invited me to dinner. The house was a small cottage, with about two hundred acres of land behind it, and was occupied by his overseer, who has entire control of affairs here, his employer being absent most of the time on the Red River plantations. As we entered the gate a bell was ringing calling the laborers to their afternoon work. They go out at six o'clock in the morning and work till sunset, an hour and a half being allowed for breakfast and three-quarters of an hour for dinner. The food of each laborer consists of a peck of meal every week and five pounds of bacon, or three pounds of mackerel, the cost of a week's rations being $1.40. Two suits of clothing—one worth $25 and one worth $15—are furnished each laborer yearly, and he is paid $15 a month. The quality of the food and clothing is better on this plantation, I am told, than on any other in the neighborhood; and the general management of the place is so well liked by the colored people that when, on commencing work, the overseer wished to hire seven hands, he had more than fifty applications. Seven men receive permanent employment, and there are six women who work occasionally, and are paid fifty cents a day.

At night I stayed at the Gray Eagle Coffee House, the tavern of the creole village of Bonnet Carré, where there was no one able to speak English but the old Negro cook. They made me a bed on two benches in the billiard room, and I went to sleep to the sound of my landlord's voice, who read aloud to his wife from a copy of *Les Trois Mousquetaires.*

February 20, 1866

In the morning I found him again at his book, from which he was once in a while called away by men, some of them barefooted, who came in with their hands in their pockets and drank absinthe at the bar or played billiards. I received a dozen *bon jours* when I left the party and walked briskly on till noon. Then I stopped at a little shop to buy bread and cheese. Half a dozen creoles were lounging there, and my appearance excited a good deal of curiosity. They gathered round me while I ate, and one who could speak English asked many questions, interpreting my answers to his friends. From New Orleans, eh? When did I leave? I was out of my work and was seeking for place? Perhaps I was a schoolmaster? At last I gave him a full account of myself, but he seemed unable to believe it; a newspaper correspondent was an unknown personage to him. It must be there was something wrong with me. Oh no, not that I was not all right; but there was some trouble, it was plain, or why should I be travelling on foot. Was there no trouble, no sweetheart? But it was very strange. I knew my own business, but I did not tell to strangers. He liked my look in the face, however, and, though he was a poor man, if I would come dine with him I should be very welcome. He had been a traveller himself.

I should say that nearly three-fourths of the white people along the road from New Orleans to Donaldsonville are creoles, and a great proportion of them are ignorant of English. They are neither large nor handsome, and have the name of being an indolent, careless race. Most of them cultivate no cotton or cane, but raise crops of corn and vegetables on their little farms, which border the road, while the larger property of their neighbors extends behind theirs, cutting them off from the swamp. They live for the most part, one of them told me, on chickens and eggs, and their wood and water comes from the river. A ball on Saturday night and billiards on the other six evenings of the week, it is said, are their pleasures. But some of them are both wealthy and well educated. I stayed at night in the neighborhood of a great white convent, with a family of these creoles, who readily received me. None of them, except the oldest son, spoke English, and he seemed little inclined for conversation, but showed me silently to my room. I learned afterwards that the father had died only the day before.

DONALDSONVILLE, LA., February 21, 1866

Today I was for the first time afloat on the Mississippi, having been ferried across at a point seven miles below Donaldsonville. The ferryboat was a light skiff, manned by a creole and a colored man. Their little pine oars were rudely shaped, but they handled them well and took the boat over in a straight line in less than ten minutes. The row-locks were iron pins driven into the gunwale, to which the oars were tied with cowhide thongs. Landing on the western shore, I was told that the distance to Donaldsonville was six miles and seven or eight arpents by the levee, but by the "cut-off" it was only five miles and two arpents. I therefore chose the cut-off, and was soon exceedingly tired of it, the sun being oppressively hot in the fields and the road now painfully rough and now muddy. I was glad of half an hour's rest under the roof of a lonely draining-machine, and a drink from the ditch, for a walk of seventy or eighty miles enables one to relish very simple pleasures. A little after noon I reached the town.

XXXIII

BATON ROUGE, LA., February 27, 1866

I STAYED in Donaldsonville three days, weather-bound, and, though it was reasonable to expect very bad walking, I escaped from that dirty, squalid little town as soon as blue sky showed itself, late on Saturday afternoon.

I found no opportunity of talking with any citizens of the place except my landlord, a German Unionist, who considered himself a bad representative of the community; but I met two Northern men, one a lawyer settled there and the other a cotton planter, and the agent of the Bureau gave me some information about the freedmen in his district. He said he had no paupers on his hands, and the Negroes were all at work at wages varying from ten to fifteen dollars a month for the best hands. The women on almost every plantation were hired by the year as the men were, and not by the day, and yet the demand for labor was not fully supplied. Cases of violence to Negroes were of rare occurrence, and the feelings of the planters and laborers towards each other were better than in 1865. While we were conversing a Negro came into the office and asked that a letter should be written to his old employer, Mr. La-C——. As the lieutenant knew, Mr. LaC—— had promised the boys a part of the crop if they would stay and work with him, but at the end of the year he made it out that the hands owed him over $300, and refused to give them their portion. They had worked hard, till they puffed same as a bellows, but Mr. LaC——'s hand was locked, and it was no good trying to get so much as a copper out of it. Not if he was offered four thousand dol-

lars he wouldn't work for him again. While he lived there he
had built himself a dwelling-house, a corn-house, and a hen-house,
and there was a patch of ground that he had cultivated as a
garden. He intended to move his forge to Donaldsonville and work
at his trade, whenever he could get a job in the town or on the
small plantations, and he wanted authority to move the buildings,
and also still to use the garden ground. But the garden belonged to
Mr. LaC——, he was told, and it would be impossible to grant
that part of his request; two of the houses he built, on his own
showing, seven years ago when a slave; he might take away the
corn-house, which was but three months old and built of wood
saved from the river, but he must touch nothing for a fortnight. A
letter was given him ordering Mr. LaC—— to permit the removal
of a certain corn-house now on his plantation, or to appear within
ten days and show cause why it should not be removed, and armed
with this the man went away. As a general rule, the officer said,
the Negroes were willing to listen to reason and justice, and in
words, at any rate, paid respect to equitable decisions. The case I
had just listened to was one of a great many. In 1865 about one-
fifth of all the plantations under cultivation in his district were
worked on shares, and he believed that without a single exception,
in every case where persons worked under such a contract, they
found at the year's end that they were in debt to the employer, or
that the amount which he owed them was the merest trifle. The
accounts kept by the planter always showed that the expenses of
the plantation had eaten up the value of the crops, or that the
laborer had violated the contract, or was heavily in debt at the
planter's store. But even when he was well satisfied that the accounts were fraudulent it was difficult for him to put his finger on
the exact spot where cheating had begun. He thought he should
have less trouble from this and other causes during the coming
season, and that the condition of the freedmen was improving.
This he attributed to the operations of the Bureau, declaring that if
the South today has anything like food enough to keep her people
from starving before a new crop comes in, it is due to the good

influence which the Bureau has exerted upon the Negroes through its officers and upon the planters through the military.

Northern men in Louisiana might get into difficulties, especially if the military should be withdrawn, for a good many of the people that he heard talk were just as loud-mouthed secessionists as they ever were. In such a little hole as Donaldson you could hear it especially frequent; the young fellows and roughs from all around came in there to drink and play billiards; and, if I had ever noticed it, they were very fond of playing the bluff game in their talk when they knew a Yankee was listening. But he himself intended to stay in Louisiana. It was the place for a young man, more money could be made than you could make in the North. That gentleman that I saw come in a few minutes before had been a captain in the United States army, and was running a plantation not far from the town. Some time in January he was riding out to his place and he was shot at from the side of the road. He saw the fellow that did it sneaking off. The ball went just across the back of his neck, grazing his coat-collar. He was going to stay, though, for all that. It was only a certain class that did that kind of thing, and sometimes the other side shot too. There had been a fellow living in Donaldsonville, by the name of Le B——, a notorious bully, that everybody hated, but everybody was afraid of. He had killed two men in fights, and had never been put through for it, and nobody dared say a word to him. It was well understood, so the sheriff had informed him, that there was a reward ready for any one who would kill Le B——, and get him out of the way. But nobody killed him, and during the war he was a rebel, of course, and after the war he was bitter. There was a man by the name of F—— keeping a drinking saloon in town, who had been in one of the Louisiana Union regiments. So, one day Le B—— went into F——'s place, drunk, and began to abuse all Yankees and traitors, and finally he drew a pistol. F—— drew his pistol at once, and shot him dead. They arrested F——, of course; but they only put him under two hundred and fifty dollars bond to appear for trial in May, and nothing would be done to him. It would be different if it had been any other Confederate but Le B—— that was killed, but everybody was too glad to get rid of him.

On the second morning of my stay in his house, the landlord called me aside, and said he knew what my business was, and he was desirous of some conversation with me. He wished to explain to me the political situation in Louisiana, so that I might expose the treachery of Governor Wells. The Union men of the State had taken that man up and made him. They put him on their ticket as lieutenant-governor when a nomination was equivalent to an election. Then, when Governor Hahn was sent to Congress, Wells got into power, and in order to perpetuate it he sold out the party that elected him—sold it out to the rebels. Union men were put out of office all over the State, and red-hot rebels were put into their places, and had everything just as they wanted it. He himself was the Union sheriff of his parish, and of course the rebels wanted to put him out; but a sheriff can only be removed by the Senate, and they could find nothing against him. Resign he wouldn't; but when he saw how everything was going, how Andy Johnson was doing on a large scale what Governor Wells was doing on a small one, he gave up, and did resign. He was getting more and more discouraged every day. While General Canby was at New Orleans, the loyal men knew they had somebody to look to; but when the military were taken away, and he supposed that would be the next thing done, a loyal man might as well go away from Donaldson, for the rebels already had their heels on the necks of everybody not of their way of thinking; and if they were so bold now, what would they do when the soldiers were gone?

I asked him for some facts in support of his assertions.

Why, were there not men, he said, who openly threatened that, before long, no Yankee would be suffered to live in the town? Were there not men who would never come into his house because he was loyal, and other men who always looked in at the billiard-room windows before they entered, and would not enter at all if a Yankee officer was there? There was a person living on the bayou, a few miles from Donaldson, who had been fined five dollars, in 1861, for not being present at a Confederate muster. He was prosecuted, and judgment was obtained against him, but the fine and the costs were never paid. Here, last week, a rebel justice had endorsed the old writ of seizure, and a constable had actually gone to the man's house and levied on his goods for the amount. The facts had all been made known to General Canby, and he would straighten out these fellows; but what would be the condition of things when there was no General Canby in New Orleans? A neighbor of his, a shopkeeper, was notified, not a month since, to pay his tax. All right, he intended to pay it, he was an honest man; but it is customary to allow ten days after such notifications, and the man, relying on the custom, did not immediately carry in the money. In a day or two he was arrested and carried before the mayor, as big a rebel as could be, who fined him thirty dollars and confined him in jail forty-eight hours as a punishment for refusing to pay his tax. If I thought that was improbable, here was another case that he would prove by two or three good witnesses. When his own tax bill was brought in, he was surprised at the largeness of the amount, and resolved to make some enquiries at the collector's office. But the fate of his neighbor had been a warning to him, and he therefore took two or three military men down with him to hear what he said. He did not come down to refuse to pay his taxes, he told the collector, but they were so much larger than he had been expecting to find them, that he wished to talk the matter over with the collector. He could get no satisfaction from him, and soon came away. By-and-bye an officer came from the mayor, and made him go up to the mayor's office, where he was at once charged with refusing to pay his tax. But he was too strong in his witnesses, and they could not effect their purpose. It was such things as these—there were plenty of them—that made him say the rebels had their feet on the loyal men's necks. It would soon be time for the loyal men to leave, before things got to be worse. There was Mr. N——, the lawyer, he had been stopped in the street and threatened with death because he wrote letters to a radical paper.

The facts in this last-mentioned case seem to be these: The newspaper referred to is the *Tribune*, published at New Orleans, and, if I am not misinformed, owned by a number of colored citizens of that city. It maintains the right of the Negroes to complete political equality with other men. It has published recently several letters dated at Donaldsonville, for the most part devoted to setting forth the injustice and inexpediency of shutting out the Negroes from the polls; but some of the series have touched on matters of local interest, and in one of them reference was made to a citizen of Donaldsonville as trembling at the ghost of a certain man who was described as having been murdered, and whose name was mentioned. The letter-writer might almost as well have mentioned the name of the citizen, too, for it is well known that he killed the other in a quarrel. The citizen, a doctor by profession, accosted Mr. N—— in the street, and demanded of him if he was not the author of the letter in question. In one hand he held a copy of the *Tribune* and a pistol in the other. Mr. N—— said he was not the author. He was commonly said to be the author, he was told, and if it was only certain that he was he should be shot there and then.

The landlord's story about the writ of seizure was confirmed by the lawyer who drew up the papers to be submitted to General Canby and by the officer who forwarded them; and these gentlemen confirmed also, in all its essential particulars, his account of the mayor's action in reference to the taxes, and drew from it the inference which he had drawn. I asked him how he accounted for the fact that two Northern men, both of whom had served in Negro regiments, and who were well acquainted with the community which he described as so hostile to loyalty, were intending to live in it even after the Federal troops are taken away? Neither of these men had done that yet, he replied, and their intentions would be changed. At present they were making money, and the troops were not gone. And though one of them had been shot at, they did not yet know so well as he did the community they were trying to live in.

The rain had hardly ceased when I resumed my journey and was ferried over the river. The levee was wet and slippery, and the afternoon was raw with a north-west wind. I have been told by a Northern man, who expressed some contempt of the natives for never discovering what he pronounced a fact not to be doubted, that an acre of land on the western shore is more valuable by several dollars than equally good land on the eastern, because the season there is warmer and nearly a fortnight longer. The prevailing winds along the coast, he said, are northerly and westerly, and they blow cold from the river, shortening the summer on the eastern bank and retarding the spring. I found the plantations above Donaldsonville larger than those below and the houses more widely separate, so that the road at first was lonesome. The river serves for company, however, with its bends and turns and the plash of its motion, and with its color changing, as one sees it from different points, from silver, through many shades of stone color and dull yellow, to russet and even to red, with patches of blue as the sun shines on the surface and the wind ruffles it. Till half an hour after sunset I walked fast, and then, stopping at the one house in sight, asked leave to stay all night. But the head of the house was away from home. Soon a mule-cart overtook me driven by a Negro, who said if I would ride with him as far as he was going he would find me a lodging. I mounted the cart, therefore, and we went on together, he relating his history as we went, for he soon found out that I was from the North, and announced himself as "a whole, thorough-breded Yankee." He was fifty-two years old, and was born and raised in Tennessee. He had never had but two masters. The first was a fine man, Major W——; I must have heard of him? No? well, he was a fine man. He used to be always lending somebody money; 'peard he'd lent out pecks of silver, and he used to say to him: "Now, master, you'll lend out all your money till you won't have not a dollar, and some day I'll see the sheriff come and sell us all up." "Oh no, William." But it was so. The sheriff came and took all the people, and his master had to run off to New Orleans very quiet with him and sell him so as to get a little money. That was the way he came to Louisiana. His wife was left behind, and he took a new one down here. For some years they worked him on the sugar plantation, and then he was made a cooper, and that was his regular trade till the Yankees came. He had done something for his freedom, for whenever the rebels came down in the woods towards the Federal camp, he always left his work, no matter what he was at, and took word to the colonel. And when they began to raise Negro soldiers, he started right off for Thibodeauxville, he and another complected fellow, and offered to join the ranks. But the walk swelled up his knees and feet so bad—working in the wet and cold, you see— that they said he was no good for a soldier and wouldn't take him. That was in 1864. In 1865 he left his master and got work on a place up the road, where the planter promised him one-twelfth of the crop. He worked all the year, found himself a good deal of the time, and how much did I think he got?—and Mr. D—— didn't pay him till the day before yesterday either—how much did I think Mr. D—— gave him for all his share of the crop? And there was nine bales of cotton made too. Just excisely eleven dollars and ten cents!

But he owed Mr. D—— for rations or for goods?

Not a copper. He could prove that Mr. D—— owed him. He let him have a half-barrel of pork, although it was the agreement that Mr. D—— was to feed him. No, there was no bill presented. Old Mr. D—— had his two witnesses there, and called him in as he was going past and offered him the money. He refused to take it; there ought to be over a hundred dollars coming to him, he said, for the pork and all. Then Mr. D—— said the expenses were so great that he himself hadn't hardly got five dollars left from his own share; and just think of the old rascal! while he was a-talking he took out his pistol and changed it out of one pocket to another to skeer him, you see. But that didn't skeer him. He had a pistol of his own, and he told Mr. D—— that the pistol was a thing he didn't care about. At last he took the eleven dollars and ten cents and signed his name.

Why did't he go to the Freedmen's Bureau if he could prove that he was cheated in the settlement?

Well, he'd been there too much. And he couldn't prove how he made the contract. But old Mr. D—— couldn't get a colored man to work for him now. One of his friends told him that he was going past the house the other day, and the old man was walking up and down with his hands under his coat behind, and called out to him, "Boy, you want to make hire? You want to make hire?" No, Antone told him. He couldn't get anybody to go work for him. Antone knew him, and so did all the colored folks.

He had never been whipped but once in old times, and that was for swimming across the river in trying to save a raft that came floating down. "S'pose you'd got drowned in that river, you d——d rascal!" his master said—his master owned him, you see—and then he give him, oh, a *fair* whipping. But, gracious goodness, there was licking along that coast! Whoo! They used a hand-saw sometimes; struck with the flat of it; but mostly a whip, or a cat-o'-nine tails, or a strap. The strap was the worst, because it raise a great welt on your skin, and the blood was drawed right through the little holes in the straps. If it was only light he'd show me a house up above with a big iron ring in the side of it, and the marks of the blood where they whipped the people were on the boards of the house, to be seen to this day. It was a devil owned that place then, but he couldn't lick now. He was working this year for a very good man, he said, who gave him his rations and clothes and sixteen dollars a month, and paid the hands their money whenever they asked for it.

It would be long past supper time, he told me, before we reached the house where I could stay, and I therefore stopped at a grocery store to buy some eatables and talked with the storekeeper. He asked for news, but I had none to tell. He never got a paper except by chance, he said. He had heard that the Legislature had passed some bills over the governor's veto, but he didn't know what they were. On this point I was able to give him some information, and he approved the action of the Legislature. Our governor was shaky, must have been shaky, or he never would have vetoed them. Vetoing was the order of the day, though; he reckoned I knew about Johnson's vetoing the Freedmen's Bureau bill. Wasn't that a noble piece? I had not seen it, and he proceeded to tell me what it was. He was sorry he hadn't the paper with the message in it; every Southern man ought to study it. It took the right ground. It proved that the Bureau concern was a complete tyranny; that it cost more to feed and teach niggers than it cost to support the whole of John Quincy Adams's government. He set it all out, and showed that the radicals were an unconstitutional set, and were keeping the South out of the Union. But they were no-where. Johnson was doing fine; no doubt about that. He thought we had a right to take our places; so the message said. It was the grandest thing he'd seen.

We rode five miles, the mule going slowly, and then my guide went to procure me admission to a farm-house a little way from the road, but came back with the statement that no one was at home, and his promise was broken. At the next house I applied in person, but unsuccessfully, and, as it was cold in the night air, I decided to travel no further in the dark, but to sleep in the same house with the driver. It was a Negro cabin on a plantation which is in litigation and occupied by but one family. There was only one room for us all, and that a small one, and the family were embar-rassed by the presence of a white man as a lodger; but we were received with apparent willingness, and the old couple stripped their own bed to make a pallet for me. A fire of drift-wood smoul-dered on the hearth, and we sat before it for an hour talking. The husband was younger than his wife, a little black woman with white hair visible under her turban and a troubled expression of countenance. She spoke French better than American, as she called it, for she had been bred in a creole family. The creoles were better masters to live with than the Americans, she said, and the men agreed with her, for though they did not feed or clothe their hands so well as the Americans, they granted more liberty. On the big plantations in old times the hands were never allowed to go anywhere except on the levee in front of the overseer's house, and that made that now they didn't know nothing but just crop. This may account for their ignorance of distances along the road, for I seldom get a correct answer to my enquiries. But, for that matter, a creole family with whom I breakfasted on the follow-ing morning, who lived about sixteen miles from Baton Rouge and about the same distance from Donaldsonville, could tell me the distance to neither place.

The old Negro, Lewis, told me that the plantation was in court, and that consequently he could make no crop on it this year. Three men claimed it, and none of them would let either of the others give him leave to go to work. My guide explained to Lewis that the reason of their unwillingness was this: when men claimed a farm and another man was living on it, the one of the two men who gave the first order on the place would get it into his hands when the trial came on. That was a rule in law. But it would be much better for Lewis to move away from there, and get work down where he himself was. His boss would pay him good wages and feed him five pounds a week, and, best of all, would give his money whenever he wanted it—even once a week. Lewis had been thinking he ought to go; he was spending his last dollar there and making nothing, and he had told Mr. L—— so. Mr. L—— wouldn't make objections to his going either, he thought, but the old woman was too timorous.

"Yes, William," the woman said, "I tell him not to go. Stop where you is, Lewis. Behavior will carry a man. Money thinks it will go furder, but behavior carry you." And she seemed obstinate enough as she shut her eyes and smoked in silence. Lewis changed the conversation, and for some time we talked of the fish of the river, and of the bayous, and of the various reptiles with which Louisiana abounds. I heard such stories of alligators, of scorpions, of moccasin snakes, of rattlesnakes as big as a man's thigh, of the rattlesnake spider, whose bite is more deadly than his namesake's, of the thunder-snake, who can kill a hog, even, and who looks, till you tread on him, like a bit of rotten wood, that I walked more warily all the next day, though as yet I had seen none of these creatures but the scorpion.

Rising at daylight on the next morning, the old woman brought me a tiny cup of very strong coffee, unsweetened, and I went away without breakfast. Lewis, with a readiness to serve me which I have found almost universal among the Negroes as soon as they learned me to be a Northern man, walked with me half a mile or more to put me into a road that would shorten the journey. He was anxious to know if it was probable that the Negroes would get land of their own, by gift or by purchase. While he had to labor for what the planters would give him, he wasn't hardly free from them, he thought. "I's thankful," he said, "for what I is got. I never 'spected I'd see it, me"; but still land was a great thing for a man, and made him free and his own man.

"What," I said, "without religion and education?"

Well, he was a member, sinful, he knew that; but he'd been a member this many year. He was too old to go to his book; but them two little chaps I saw at his house, he wanted them to learn. They knew some reading now, for he sent them to school awhile, as long as there was a school. But the people broke it up, took all the doors and windows out, and the teacher went away. That was one of his reasons for wanting to move away, so he could put the children to school. They were not his sons; but if he was earning he would be willing to pay for their schooling.

The children were two light yellow boys, grandsons of his wife. He enquired also about the death of Mr. Lincoln, of which he had heard something, but he didn't know if he was really dead. He expressed wonder that any Yankee should have been the assassin. Though he did know one or two Yankees that were like the rebels in everything; they turned the point of the sword at a colored man's back, though they were good to his face.

I walked then two miles through the fields, which were, in some places, covered with water, and the ditches were brimming full. Getting out upon the levee again, I met the people going to church, some in heavy coaches and some on foot, but most on horseback. The young men wore plated spurs and the tails of their horses were braided and the ends of the braids tied in a knot. They rode in little companies, talking gaily and bowing to the ladies in the carriages. The church was one of the queer little structures common along the levee road, weather-beaten and picturesque, and, I suppose, like nothing between here and Lower Canada. People were waiting at the door as I went by; but the horses of the young men I passed further up were tied before the door of the St. Gabriel grocery. The stores by the roadside were all open and so were many stores in Baton Rouge. At a point nine miles from

Baton Rouge I turned my back upon the river and travelled over a direct road to the city. Soon I came to a gently rising ground and good walking, the narrow way for miles together lying in the shade of tall hedges of rose-bushes, which grow in continuous clumps and form a beautiful green wall impervious to anything larger than the small birds. Baton Rouge came into sight long before I reached it, the city being situated on a considerable hill, and the glaring white of two large buildings, the asylum and the capitol, being visible far off. The latter building is ruined, and I am told that the finest part of the city was also destroyed during the war. Certainly what remains is not fine. But I see it without its green trees.

From the reports made to his superiors by the agent of the Bureau stationed here, I take some information about the Negroes in the parish of East Baton Rouge:

> Jan. 20, 1866. The majority of the planters in the parish are offering from $12 to $15 per month without clothing.

> Jan. 31. Many of the planters are giving the freedmen a share in the crop. Those who are paying wages generally offer from $12 to $18 per month without clothing. . . . The conduct of the freedmen seems to be very good. I have heard but few complaints of them, and I think nearly all the planters are dealing very fairly with them.

At present the common rate of wages for hands of the first class is $18 a month and rations. Clothing is offered by a few men, but not by all.

> Jan. 2. I have conversed with several of the planters in the parish, and they all agree in saying that they prefer to keep the old colored people on their plantations and support them, as they find they are but little expense, and can often pay their way by doing light work. The mayor of the city informs me that there is not one colored pauper fed by the city. I would state that during the months of September, October, and November, 1865, while the poor of the city were fed by the military authorities, out of 180 paupers there was not one colored.

I called the captain's attention to an editorial article in the Baton Rouge *Advocate* of Feb. 21, with the caption, "The Pauper Question," which, among other things, says:

Baton Rouge is the great centre of attraction. Before the war there were but six hundred Negroes in this place. Now there are as many thousand. . . . We have to support them, nurse them, and bury them, and this at an expense of $6,000.

The article does not expressly say that the paupers crowding in from the adjacent parishes are Negroes, but no other impression could be produced by it. The captain said that laborers were scarce, and that for some days he had kept a person employed searching the town for vagrants. He had been able to find three Negroes without employment. He had no knowledge of any colored paupers except the sick and aged, and the number of those was extremely small.

I hear of but one opinion held by Northern men living here as to the loyalty of the people. Much that is told me is told on condition that I do not repeat it. The letter, of which I give a copy below, is pronounced by the colonel commanding at this post a concise expression of the feelings entertained by a majority of the citizens. It was sent on the 19th of January to a Mr. Rider, an Englishman, who for the last thirty-five years has resided in East Feliciana:

We have been informed that you are 'lowing niggers to squat about on your land; or, in other words, you are renting niggers land. One of our committee told you that you would be burnt out, but you would not pay any attention to him. Now, sir, your gin-house is burnt for renting niggers land. If this is not sufficient warning we will burn everything on your place. If that don't break it up, we will break your neck. If that don't break it up, we will shoot the niggers. Beware, sir, before it is too late, or you will be waited on by   A COMMITTEE.
The niggers are not to be blamed. You are the villain.   C.
[In pencil:] Since writing the above we have decided to burn more than your gin-house, and will kill you if you don't break up your infamous nigger camps.   COMMITTEE.

Mr. Rider is a gentleman of wealth and respectability, who, it is believed, has never given his neighbors other grounds of complaint than they find in this endeavor to introduce upon his estate a system of labor resembling the English tenant system. It was not his gin-house that was burned, but a corn-house with four hundred

bushels of corn. The fire at the gin-house was put out by the Negroes. Colonel Edgerton sent an officer into East Feliciana to investigate this matter, who succeeded in getting the testimony on oath
of one of seven men, planters in that parish, who, having met
together, had taken Mr. Rider's affairs into consideration, and had
decided on intimidating him. The evidence being sufficient, the
colonel proposes to General Canby that these gentlemen be compelled to pay for the property destroyed, and he is confident that
the general will adopt the course which he recommends. It is sure
of the cordial approval of General W. T. Sherman. General Canby
has not yet spoken, but great confidence appears to be placed in
him by all Union men whom I meet.

XXXIV

VICKSBURG, MISS., March 8, 1866

I SET out from Baton Rouge for Vicksburg and the North on the steamboat *Columbian*. At the place where I went aboard, as at most other points, she followed the fashion of Mississippi steamboats, and made the landing with more haste than ceremony. It was pleasant to look on one Southern scene full of business-like activity and bustle—the bow scraped the bank, gangway planks were instantly pushed out, freight was rolled ashore in a hurry, people crowded aboard, jostling each other to beg a late newspaper from the clerk; the steam, all the time roaring and hissing, made the boat itself seem impatient to be off, and at the end of five minutes we were making for the middle stream.

The few passengers were mostly Northerners bound for St. Louis. One reads of the strange characters, of the gambling and hard drinking on these river boats, and I looked for something of the kind, but saw nothing of it; everything was orderly and commonplace. We were going up "against a rise," I was told, so that the water was thicker than usual with mud, and great quantities of driftwood were carried past us on the strong current, but our rate of speed was nearly eight miles an hour. Let the traveller forget that not unlikely he may be scalded to death or blown to pieces, and a voyage up the river is pleasant travelling, if only because one is constantly astonished at the grandeur and immensity of the stream, recognizes the river as a wonder of nature, and because, as he sails for days after days on into the heart of a continent, he is forced to see the vastness of the country and to think of its wealth and strength in the future.

346

I became acquainted with but one of my fellow-passengers. He was a man from Maine, and was then on his way home again from Texas, whither he had gone at the end of the war. He had been a photographer, he said, in Austin, and away down there that was a very profitable occupation; pictures commanded big prices. He'd have liked to stay there if the people had been a little more reasonable; but they were so down on Yankees that he was a little afraid to risk it, and, as he had been offered a good price for his gallery, he decided to sell out and get away. The soldiers were there now, but nobody knew how long they'd remain; as soon as they should go, all the Yankees that didn't want to turn rebels would have to go too. A regular Yankee soon finds out how he's looked down on, and he do'n't trust them. He himself had learned to carry a pistol all the time; everybody had to do it, and a Yankee in particular ought to go armed. Here was an example of the way in which they felt: One day he was in his back room, finishing a picture, and a couple of ladies walked into the reception room and began to examine the specimens. It so happened that he had photographed a good many of the officers, and he heard one lady say, "Why it's a regular Yankee concern. 'Most every picture is some beast of a Yank." That was a kind of talk that always made him mad; he'd heard about enough of it, so he stepped out and said, "Madam, if those officers are Yankees, they are all gentlemen." The women walked off disgusted, and wouldn't have anything done. It was that style of thing that disgusted him with the Southerners. At one time they were decent, comparatively. "We're whipped," you'd hear 'em say—"fightin' 's played." But after the women folks got hold of them the men gave up all that, and now men and women were about alike—more disloyal than they were in '60. The niggers were going to have a good time.

This person's view of these matters was the same with that of an intelligent Northerner, whom I met in Baton Rouge. He had been travelling from Ohio to Louisiana, to seek for the remains of some unfortunate friends of his who had perished miserably in a steamboat explosion, and whose bodies, it was possible, might be found at some point between Vicksburg and the Gulf. His search had brought him into contact with all sorts of persons in several States, and he had endeavored to find out as much as possible about the opinions and feelings of the Southern people. I asked him to let me know his conclusions.

"You must understand," said he, "that in 1860 I was a strong Douglas man. I didn't like Lincoln, and the abolitionists I hated; but, of course, I was Union. As the war went on I began to believe in Lincoln, and, by the time the Emancipation Proclamation was issued, I had been educated up to it and endorsed it. As a war measure, I mean; that was how Mr. Lincoln regarded it, and so did I. Well, since the war ended I've been a conservative; I've considered Stevens and Sumner dangerous men, who didn't understand the South, wanted to humble it and so on, and were standing in the way of peace. I believed what we used to hear, that the North didn't understand the South. I believe it yet, but in a very different sense. This journey has been the greatest that I ever experienced. I came out with the kindest feelings for these people down here; I wanted to see it made easy; we had whipped them, and I wanted it to rest there. I thought the South wanted it to end there. But I was tremendously mistaken. They hate us and despise us and all belonging to us. They call us cut-throats, liars, thieves, vandals, cowards, and the very scum of the earth. They actually believe it. They won't even allow that we won our own battles. 'We were overpowered by numbers,' they say; 'of course we couldn't fight all Europe.' They've said that to me more than fifty times within the last few weeks. And they say that they are the gentlemen; we are amalgamationists, mudsills, vandals, and so forth. And I've heard and seen more brag, and lying, and profanity, and cruelty, down here, than I ever saw or heard before in all my life. The only people I find that a Northern man can make a friend of, the only ones that like the Government and believe in it, are the Negroes. I'm convinced they can vote just as intelligently as the poor whites. A Southerner would knock me down if I said that to him; but it's true. I tell you I'm going home to be a radical. Fight the devil with fire. I've learned to hate Southerners as I find them, and they can hate me if they want to. I'm a Sumner man after I get back, and I shall write out my experience for some of our papers. Every man that's seen what I've seen ought to let it be known. 'The North don't understand the South,' you know, and I'm going to help our people to see two or three things: that the chivalry hate us and despise us; that a 'nigger' they don't consider human; that whatever harm they can do us without getting another whipping, they've got the will to do, and mean to do, too. I wish every county in the North would send out two men, who have the confidence of their fellow-citizens, and make them travel through the South and report the true condition of things. They couldn't make a true report without changing every honest administration man into a radical. I know what I was when I came out, but I couldn't resist the evidence of my own senses."

It was eight o'clock in the morning when we reached Vicksburg, and it was not till the following morning that we could fully perceive the repulsiveness of the place. On that night, however, the landlord of the principal hotel assisted us to form a correct notion of it. He walked into the hall or office where most of his guests were assembled, and cried out in a loud voice as he walked up and down through the crowd, "Gentlemen, I warn you to take care of your money. Hardly a night passes that some gentleman in the house is not robbed. Let me beg you to look out for your money." Upon this my next neighbor said to me, "These d——d niggers, you see"—a reference to the waiters. But in fact the rooms contained two or three beds, and no one knew whether his room-mate was not a Vicksburg gambler or one of the people who make the city streets unsafe after nightfall.

On the next morning I walked about the place, observing with curiosity the singular bluff on which the town stands and overlooks many miles of the surrounding lowlands; and saw the semi-circular sweep of the Federal earthworks. In the streets there are still vestiges of the innermost lines of the besieged, and also of the caves or burrows in which people hid themselves from Grant's shot and shell. Not much, I suppose, has been done to remove the traces of the siege, and, if so, it is evident that the city suffered little by it.

The day was chilly, and in the afternoon I sat before the red-hot stove in one of the hotels and listened to one of those conversations which so displease most Northern travellers in the South. Perhaps a dozen people sat within hearing of the three speakers. Of the latter two were elderly men of good appearance, and the third was a young man of twenty-five or twenty-six, with a dyed moustache and insolent manners, who chewed tobacco and nursed one of his small feet, while, without modesty or hesitation, he engrossed the principal part in the conversation.

"Well," said one of the old men, "you were luckier than I was. They broke me up. I lost about fourteen thousand dollars' worth of niggers, and they've taken that lot of mine, and I've got to go to work and make it up."

"They didn't make much out of me," the young man said. "Put a bullet through me at Baton Rouge; but I reckon they owed me that much, some of 'em. I hadn't anything to lose. I was raised to work myself since I was that high."

"Ah, you were? At the North?"

"No, *sir*. Never was north of the Potomac till John Morgan went into Ohio, and if I live a hundred years I'm never going again. Got no use for wooden hams."

"And these yer shoe-peg oats."

"What's that?" said the other old man.

The young man explained to him: "Why, these Massachusetts and Connecticut Yankees make shoe-pegs by machinery, and they make 'em cheap, so whenever they can they shove 'em off for oats on some trader at a distance. Put a few sacks of pegs among the piles of oats, you know. You go to New Orleans, and any of the grain-dealers will tell you all about it. Wooden nutmegs, wooden clocks, wooden hams—every d——n thing. I was talking to one of these fellows not long ago, and he beat round and wouldn't talk out openly. Trying to make me think he was a Southerner. Says I, 'How long have you been out from Boston?' 'Haow long have I been eout from Boston?' says he. 'Yes,' says I; 'I know a Yankee from Massachusetts whenever I see him. You're no Southern man'; and then he owned he wasn't."

"Ha! How did you know him?"

"His talk. And then they've all got short fingers—picking up pegs, I tell 'em—and think more of half a dime than you would of a dollar. I can't stand 'em."

"But, by George! though, I don't see but what we've got to stand 'em."

"Yes, if you stay here you have. What's more, you've got to stand nigger suffrage. You'll have your niggers voting within a year."

"Oh, no; no, sir. That wouldn't be constitutional."

"Constitutional! How much constitution have you got left? Look at the nigger soldiers in the streets. You'll have nigger suffrage in a year. Didn't you see that the niggers in Texas have sent up a petition for it? They have; and they'll get it. Well, I expect to be in Mexico three months from now."

"You going to that new town some of our folks have got there? But a'n't the United States going to drive Maximilian out?"

"It's none of the United States's business."

"Oh, but there's the Monroe doctrine. We've told Europe that our people a'n't going to have kings and monarchs on our soil, and you'll see Maximilian'll have to quit."

"Well, I a'n't in for monarchy myself. But the Mexicans are better than the Yankees and the niggers."

"Well, Johnson's doing very well now. He don't believe much in the niggers, neither, and when we're admitted into Congress we're all right. The men that tyrannize over us now won't be in a majority then."

"All the men, North and South, that are conservatives, must unite together. There are some men at the North that behaved very well all through the war, and we must unite with them."

"All right; you gentlemen can try it."

"Well, if we can't get in we can stay out, anyhow, and we'll see how they can get along without us."

"If it wasn't for these niggers. There's the difficulty."

"They a'n't going to be in the way long. There a'n't half the niggers that there was. A heap of em's dead. You may know that by its being so hard to hire 'em; there actually a'n't the niggers;

and now they're retaking 'em to Cuba, and selling 'em. Did you see that Toombs met his coachman in the street in Cuba, and found he'd been sold there?"

"Yes," the other old man said; and Mr. ——, of Hinds County, "had told him that he knew it for a fact that one cargo had gone over certain."

Then the talk went on about the injustice and folly of emancipation; how miserable the lot of the freedman must necessarily be; how cotton and sugar and rice never could be cultivated except by slave labor, and how the United States undoubtedly ought to pay the value of every emancipated slave. The young man for his part told of his battles, and, as I have repeatedly noticed on similar occasions, his audience received quite readily more than one story of cold-blooded cruelty, which, at the North, would not have been listened to by any circle of persons of equal intelligence and apparent respectability, if any one could be found to tell them there. For example, he and half a dozen of his companions being at some little distance from their command, came upon a straggling party of four Federal soldiers. Immediately after capturing the squad they stripped them of their shoes and hats. "We wanted them, you know; and if they had a fine watch or a roll of greenbacks, we wanted them too. Being on foot, they couldn't keep up with us, and, of course, we were in a hurry about that time; so when we got into a piece of pine the Yanks didn't come out when we did. Don't know whether any stray Yanks were seen round there after that. Maybe."

The headquarters of the Freedmen's Bureau for Mississippi is at Vicksburg. It is chiefly busied with a general supervision of the affairs of the colored people, and occupies itself with details only when its interference is necessary. The examination and approval of contracts is not a part of its work, and the relations between employer and employed are controlled, in the first instance at least, by the civil authorities. Through its subordinate officials, its influence is extended to every part of the State, and, as might be expected, it is not a popular institution. Every sub-assistant commissioner, the Assistant Commissioner informs me, needs military force within call to sustain him. The freedmen are working very well, and are receiving good treatment; their labor being in great demand, it commands very good prices, and the planter finds it to his interest to use his laborers well. It is not from the oppressive acts of individuals, therefore, that the Negroes suffer most injustice, but from the spirit in which the civil authorities enforce the laws. Under the provisions of the vagrant law, for example, a white man as well as a Negro might be arrested; but in practice it is found that while honest and industrious Negroes are often arrested and punished, there is no arrest of notoriously idle and worthless white men. For this state of things the spirit of public opinion is responsible; and because this state of things exists the Bureau is a necessity. The hostility to schools for the Negroes is very general, and often very bitter and dangerous. In the middle of February a Dr. Lacy, an old man who had started a school in Okolona, was four times shot at as he walked in the street for no other reason than that he was a teacher of Negroes.

Such cases, whenever they occur, are reported by the officers of the Bureau to the military commander, General T. J. Woods. The case of Dr. Lacy has been reported. As yet nothing has been done in reference to it. In the town of Fayette the people will not permit schools to be maintained, and in Grenada they will not permit them to be opened.

In the face of such opposition, 5,240 children have been gathered into schools, and are receiving instruction from about 70 teachers, who are paid in small part by their pupils, but mainly by the Northern charitable associations. In the monthly reports returned by these teachers they are required, I notice, to give the number of pupils in their charge whose blood is mixed, and the number of those whose blood is purely African. Taking the returns of twelve schools which happened to be first set down in the consolidated report, I find it stated that, in the opinion of the teachers, the children of African blood number 287, and those of mixed blood number 777. A majority of the scholars live in the towns and cities.

In the office of the Assistant Commissioner, Colonel Thomas, I met several gentlemen attached to the Bureau, and resident in different parts of the State. They spoke of the condition of the Negroes as being generally prosperous, but there is much hostility, they say, on the part of the native white population to Northern men. The large landowners are anxious for immigration, but it is not so with the mass of the people. It is for their property rather than for their lives that the new-comers fear; but in respect to their lives they are by no means at ease. It would be easy to multiply instances, one gentleman told me; he would give me two. Not long since Colonel S——, of Hinds County, a Southerner, and a gentleman from the North were in treaty about going into cotton-planting together, and probably would have done so. But Colonel S——, after a little while, saw with regret that it would be necessary to break off the arrangements. He informed his prospective partner that he had reliable intelligence that more than a hundred men in the neighboring county of Holmes had bound themselves to prevent the settlement of Northern men among them, and had also determined that no discharged Negro soldier should be suffered to find employment in that section of country. My informant said it was beyond a doubt that Colonel S—— acted in perfect good faith.

Another case was that of Mr. A——, of Boston. He moved into Mississippi after the war, with the intention of becoming a planter, and at first was very much pleased with his prospects—so much pleased that when a little while ago he made a visit to Massachusetts, he wrote a letter to the Boston *Post* and praised his new neighbors highly. Soon he came back, and it was not long before he began to think himself mistaken. By-and-bye he became convinced that the people were too much opposed to Northern men for him to stay among them with safety. So he paid a considerable sum of money to the owner of the lands which he had intended to cultivate, was released from his bargain, and has left Mississippi.

On the last night of my stay in a Southern city I attended a political meeting, which had been called to endorse the President's recent veto message. It was held in the court-house, and was composed of about two hundred persons, who were by no means enthusiastic. Resolutions were passed, and many speeches were made, in all of which the President was lavishly praised, and the Senate and House of Representatives spoken of with great disrespect. "The war being over," said one speaker, "we were looking for peace, but it seems that the rebellion has only changed hands; that treason has reached the halls of the Congress of the United States. But there is a man at the head who is able to cope with it. President Johnson has put down the rebellion at the South, and he is now prepared to put down the rebellion at the North."

Another speaker warned the Southern people to remember that there was a party at the North, the Radical party, who would never be content till the last silver spoon was taken from them and their lands divided; but there was also in the North a Democratic party which needed the active cooperation of the Southern people, and only needed that to hurl the Radicals from power.

The evening was not very far advanced when Colonel Joseph E. Davis, a brother of Jefferson Davis, was seen upon the floor and a committee was appointed to lead him to the platform. A speech from him was demanded, and he complied, speaking three or four minutes, when, as I think, at the suggestion of the chairman of the meeting he brought his remarks to an abrupt conclusion. The Vicksburg *Journal* says:

> He fully endorsed the action of President Johnson in vetoing that accursed measure to enlarge the powers of the Freedmen's Bureau. The bill, if passed, would have caused a revolution equal to, if not more dreadful than, the one through which we have just passed. We have a branch of the Freedmen's Bureau in our midst headed by officers of the most infamous character; who hold the offices for a given purpose; who gladly record the abuses and murders of Negroes, and forward such information, rather than assist our people without homes and means in obtaining the necessaries of life. You have these officers among you. I charge you to look out for them. Mr. Davis's feeble health would not admit of any extended remarks.

I might give many passages from the various speakers, but they would be wearisome. I give but one.

Mr. McKee, formerly a general in the Federal army, stepped forward and said that he approved of the veto message of the

President and endorsed it fully. "But in that hall on that night he had heard language used by some of the speakers that made his blood run cold."

Though it seemed to me not very successful as a political gathering, the meeting revealed very plainly the feeling which prevails in all the Southern country. The speakers represented the South as being cruelly injured, insulted, and oppressed, and the North as her wanton oppressor.

XXXV

In coming home from my long journey in the South, I travelled by rail through Connecticut, and it happened that for several hours my seat was shared with a merchant from Rhode Island. I expressed to him my pleasure at sight of a country so different from that with which the last eight months had made me familiar, and contrasted the pretty villages and busy, prosperous towns which we were passing, the trim fences, the neat dwellings, the frequent school-houses and churches, the carefully cultivated farms, and all the other evidences of intelligence and industrious thrift, with the dreary region I had just left, thinly peopled, full of uncleared forests and undrained swamps and sandy levels, the wretched railways and worse roads, the slovenly plantations with their mean houses, the hovels of the laborers with their degraded population, and the disorderly towns. Even in my seat-mate I found a striking contrast with a person whom he recalled to my mind, and whom I look upon as being in many respects a typical Southern man. I found that the merchant had cut from a newspaper, and had preserved with great care, a copy of the official telegram which announced the death of Mr. Lincoln—"the President," as he still called him— "Abraham Lincoln died this morning at twenty-two minutes past seven o'clock." The South Carolina planter, I recollected, had his memento also. In a fight with a marauding party of Negro troops or camp-followers he and his neighbors had been easily victorious. He was willing to keep on his piazza floor, and I saw them there, the bleached skulls of the two men whom he had killed with his hands.

My companion questioned me about the Southern country and people. I had been for some time endeavouring to generalize from the mass of facts which I had collected. On some points my mind was made up, and on others I was still in doubt. Many of my conclusions, whether correct or incorrect, answered questions which I was aware were not of general interest. Therefore, when I fell into this gentleman's company, I took note of those questions which he seemed to think most important, and resolved to let them guide me in the preparation of this paper.

In his first question he asked for my opinion of the loyalty of the South.

I left New York at the end of June last, and before the steamer had reached Virginia began conversing with Southern men; and I remained in the late Confederacy until the beginning of March. During July and August I was in Virginia, and often talked with people of all classes, and heard them talking among themselves. It is commonly said that the Virginians were then more loyal than they are now; but this, in my opinion, is a mistake. By loyalty I understand fidelity to the Union and love for it. The vast majority of the people were as disloyal at that time as we may suppose them to have been in 1862. I very seldom found a man who thought that his State had done wrong in seceding, or that he had done anything but right in following her fortunes. Many men were ready enough to call secession a great mistake, and I heard more than one wish that Roger A. Pryor had been hung. Lincoln, it was said, would probably never have harmed the South if she had not seceded, and, of course, that policy must have been a bad one which needlessly provoked so disastrous a war. But it was not a wrong thing that had been done; only an inexpedient thing. To be sure, the South had been dreadfully defeated by the overwhelming hosts of their enemies—mercenaries from Europe and Yankees and Negroes outnumbering General Lee's army in the proportion of five to one. But the South had been in the right. The first Southerner with whom I talked said that "anyhow, the war was all a d——d foolish piece of business, he supposed. Still, his State went out, and if she was to go again he'd go with her." He was travelling on the steamer with me, and of him and his companions I said: "Rebels, I suppose, they may fairly be called, for those with whom I have talked, while ready enough to admit themselves conquered, still declare that it is only because their country is subjugated that they now pay obedience to the United States." A few days afterwards, another gentleman whom I met upheld strenuously the doctrine of State sovereignty and the right of States to secede. Coercion was tyranny, he said, and "he believed all Southerners felt so. From the meanest private in the army up to the highest men in the land, up to General Lee, all felt that the South had been most deeply injured." This same gentleman, in speaking of the likelihood that the freed people would be oppressed by State legislation, said that "the remedy for the evil would be found in requiring the States to take such action as should be satisfactory to the general Government. The general Government seemed to be doing what it liked." And this remark of his brings me to another statement which I would make in reference to the feelings of the Virginians at that time. They had never in all their lives been loyal as we understand loyalty, and they hated the Federal Government with a hate that had been growing for four years amid the passions of war and the humiliation of defeat; but the power of the Government they feared, and they respected its authority. Pardoning had hardly begun; the country was full of soldiers. President Johnson, it was generally said among these people, was a bloodthirsty, narrow-minded, demagogical "poor white," who would wreak vengeance on the Southern aristocracy, which he had once envied and which was now in his power. So I used to hear Mr. Lincoln mentioned with respect and his death was regretted. The Virginians seemed ready to accept whatever conditions it might please the North to impose, and to look on all favors conferred upon them as concessions of the conqueror and not as rights to be demanded. This was the feeling among the mass of the people. It seemed to me that they recognized the fact that whatever the war may have been at the beginning, however technical may have been the questions then involved in it, it had grown to be before its end a struggle for mastery between contradictory social and political principles. Perhaps most Northern men had accustomed themselves to look upon the rebellion as a work of destruction merely, a movement designed to effect only negative results. As a nation the Confederacy, we thought, even if it conquered its independence, could live but a short life; its great work would be the disruption of the American Union. But the Southern people believed their success would mean not that alone, much as that was to be desired. It would mean, also, the maintenance of a peculiar social system, the establishment of a government with certain very positive and admirable characteristics. Naturally enough, then, and logically, they saw in the defeat of Lee the defeat of the principles he represented. Their army and all their cause was lost. Then, too, so very many Southern men knew almost nothing and were not given to close thinking. They had been beaten, they knew, and they expected to take the law from their conqueror. This was far from being the view of the politicians, though, as they were for the most part unpardoned, they were saying less then than afterwards, and it may have been a very incorrect view, but I think it was the one generally prevalent. Then, better than at any other time, the North might have reaped the fruits of the war. Even universal suffrage the Southern people would have accepted. Not willingly, more unwillingly, probably, than they accepted the Constitutional Amendment abolishing slavery, but with far less resistance than would be opposed to it now.

The Union men at that time were rejoicing, but they rejoiced in secret, for they had served a long and hard apprenticeship to humility and every species of prudential dissimulation, and they knew that they still lived among rebels, though rebels without arms in their hands. I knew several men of this class, and before the middle of August they were beginning to doubt if they had not been too hasty in rejoicing at all, and to wonder and fear if the secessionists were not more powerful at Washington and more in favor than the Unionists. Without any exceptions, they disbelieved utterly in the loyalty and good faith of their secessionist neighbors.

As the fall passed away and the winter began I travelled southward. In North Carolina, and only in that State, I found native Southerners in whose eyes it was a recommendation of a man that he was from the North. For it was true that the Northerners had beaten their secessionist neighbors and set free their slaves, and might perhaps confiscate their property and punish them for driving poor men into the woods; and they, if they did not love the Union much, hated their secessionist neighbors perfectly. But even there such people were not in a majority. On the edge of that district I even found one man who was in favor of equal suffrage for whites and blacks. As he told me so he lowered his voice and looked carefully to the fastening of the door. If the fact was known, his village would be no place for him, he said; he intended to leave it. In North Carolina there is more of the soil in which true loyalty may yet grow than in any other Southern State that I have visited. But even in that State Jonathan Worth was elected governor over William Holden, because Holden was opposed to the payment of the debt incurred to support the rebellion.

As I went on from North Carolina to the Mississippi, seeing much of the people everywhere, I concluded that they were but little inclined to accept what may be called the natural results of the war. And by that phrase I mean that the war seems to have settled that the political and social condition of the South is eventually to be the same with that of the North. The Southerners saw that slavery was destroyed, and in their conventions they were forced to say so and to ratify the Constitutional Amendment. Their conventions were also willing to rescind the ordinances of secession, and in the case of North Carolina, after a long debate, the secession ordinance was even declared to have always been null and void. It is my belief that when the States are left to untrammeled action it will be found that these enforced and reluctant admissions, and the further admission that in one civil war the South has been overpowered by the North, and in another civil war probably would be overpowered, are all that the South of today will concede. I am convinced that in all those cases in which the consent of the South to the demands of the country has not been so expressed as to be irrevocable, there is great danger that its consent will be revoked. For I could not see that, as regards loyalty, the South was different in any important respects from what it was during the war. The people were sorry for nothing but their ill-success, and they had more curses for the men who led them badly during the war than for the men who led them into the war. If their feelings and opinions in 1863 were such as the country then condemned, it seemed to me that the country could not help condemning them today. In 1863, to be sure, they backed their opinions by bayonets, and there is little danger that they would again choose to make war upon the North. They seem to be thoroughly convinced that the North is an overmatch for them. But what was worth fighting for through so many years must have been dear to them, and what remains of it is worth voting for. What harm they can do the Union by political action I do not know; but whatever harm they can do will, I think, be done.

For some time to come the South will be a unit on all questions of Federal politics. If the few Union men in each State had been supported by all the might and influence of the general Government, if treason had been made odious, the Union party might, perhaps, have gathered to itself all that class of doubtful and wavering men that exists in every community, and so have made some head against its opponents. But that opportunity has been lost.

I was constantly hearing abuse of the North and of Northerners. Yankees were stigmatized as cowards, robbers of women and children, vandals, braggarts, low fellows, avaricious, cruel, and mean. Not that every Southern man and woman talks in this way, and that every Southern child is brought up to despise Northerners; but a Northern man travelling in the South is continually made uncomfortable by such insulting language, and is never safe from it for two days together. If he hears nothing of it in the railroad car today, tomorrow he may be shut in a stage with people who entertain him with nothing else. It is perhaps excusable in the mouths of a defeated people, but it does nothing to convince those who hear it that the victorious people are well liked.

XXXVI

I was not able, in the space afforded my last letter, to complete the résumé of my observations in the South. I undertook then to describe the feelings of the white population there; today I wish to speak of the blacks.

The present condition of the Negroes in the States which I have been visiting, if it be compared with their condition during the summer and fall of last year, will be pronounced prosperous. Though it is often denied, there must have been a great deal of anger and dislike in the feeling with which the Southern people regarded the newly emancipated slaves. The newspapers did now and then print an editorial article recommending a kind and generous treatment of the freedmen, and praising them for a faithful adherence to their masters through all the war. This I learned to look upon as being very often only an indirect expression of the Southern theory that the system of slavery was not hated by the race subject to it. For constantly, in almost every issue of almost all the newspapers, sometimes even in the columns of advertisements, were many contemptuous and injurious flings at the Negroes, and the talk of the people among themselves showed that their opinions were better reflected in the correspondence and local paragraphs than in these occasional editorials. They were very ready to hear and repeat any story that made against the freedmen. The ignorance, the viciousness, the insolence of Negroes, were insisted on. It was always assumed that the unknown perpetrator of any crime must be a Negro; and in every way the observer was made to feel that in

the South, however great in old times may have been the love for
the slave, there was not much love for the freedman. He was led
also to reflect that if the saying is a true one that man cannot be
just to his neighbor unless he loves him, the future of the colored
population, so far as the Southern whites should have power over
it, would be anything but bright.

The Negroes themselves were at that time furnishing people
who were inconsiderate or prejudiced with an excuse for declaring
that emancipation had ruined them as laborers. Impelled by various motives, many were wandering about without regular occupation or fixed abode. I met men plodding along Virginia and North
Carolina roads who had come from distant parts of those States, or
from distant States, seeking work or looking for relatives. One man
I remember who had walked from Georgia in the hope of finding
at Salisbury a wife from whom he had been separated years before
by sale. In Louisiana, I met men and women who since the war
had made long journeys in order to see their parents or children. I
dare say there must have been thousands of such cases. Traversing
the South Carolina roads in December, it was common to see parties of hungry, ill-clad Negroes moving towards the coast country,
whence, during the war, thousands had been removed for safety's
sake, when it was feared that the lower districts would be invaded.
They wanted to get back to the region with which they were familiar, or they thought to find employment in labor which they understood better than that which they were leaving, or they were set
adrift by their employers, or it might easily be that no place could
well be worse than the region in which they found themselves
when the war closed. These were sights that seemed to fill every
white Southerner with anger. A public officer of the State said to
me, as we rode together in a stage, "See those d——d niggers! They
think of nothing but crowding into Columbia. What do they want
there?" Next day, in the office of the Freedmen's Bureau, I found
an answer to his question. I saw there one of the men whom we
had passed upon the road, and whose laziness had been bitterly
condemned. He was old, half naked, foot-sore, and hungry. They
had given him some army biscuits and promised him trans-

portation by rail towards Georgetown district. "He could get work on a rice plantation there," he said, "and rice was his work; he didn't know cotton very well. He had been discharged by the man who hired him that year and had received no wages for all his work, except some bushels of corn, which he and his family had brought away on their backs. He had lived in the up-country three years, ever since his master moved him, but had been born and raised in the Pedee rice country." Of such cases as this too there must have been many thousands. I saw them occurring in all the months between August and January.

Undeniably the Negroes were at that time somewhat ignorant of the right use to be made of their freedom, though the extent of this ignorance has, in my opinion, been much exaggerated. At no time, I think, has anything like a majority of the Negroes thought that freedom meant exemption from labor. I have never met one who seemed to think so, and certainly at no time has the behavior of a majority of them shown that they entertained such a notion. Yet many of them were idle for weeks together, and were too apt to be lazy and refractory, to violate the contracts which they had made, and to set too high a value on their services as laborers. I remember talking with an old Negress in Louisiana, who spoke contemptuously of the stupidity of the Negroes living on the great plantations; they knew "nothing but just crop," she said; they stared at every little thing; it made her laugh. She accounted for their ignorance by saying that they were never allowed to go anywhere except on to the levee in front of the overseer's house, and so never saw anything. That such a people, and almost all were such to some degree, should have taken advantage of their new liberty to go away from the plantation and see what the world outside was like, is not strange. Moreover, on many plantations their freedom was only a name, a rumor. In many cases to leave the plantation of their birth was to leave a tyrannical master. In the towns they could see the Northern troops, and talk with the agents of the Freedmen's Bureau. So for months the Negroes were restless, and got the ill word of every one incapable of making allowances for their peculiar position.

It is to be remembered, too, that most of the farmers and planters were cultivating but little land in 1865, and confined their
attention to the raising of breadstuffs, so that many laborers were
necessarily idle. In the summer and early autumn of that year,
then, the popular Southern opinion of the Negro was, very probably, lower than it had ever been before, and the Negroes, without
the aid of the Freedmen's Bureau, would have been more nearly
defenceless before their enemies than at any previous time. The
almost universal judgment was that laziness and improvidence
were inherent in the Negro nature, and that in much less than a
century the Negroes as a people would be extinct. The more hopeful saw in emancipation a great blessing to the South; white laborers would come in, and the black race would perish. The de-
spondent thought that their country was utterly ruined by emancipation, the long heats of the Southern climate precluded the
employment of white laborers, and the black race in a state of
freedom was sure to perish. I may remark, in passing, that most
Southerners who were much interested in the question seemed
rather to look upon the expected immigration of white men as a
means of supplying Southern landholders with a laborious and
obedient peasantry than as the incoming of a class of men who
soon would cease to be hireling laborers and become landholders
themselves.

Before January was gone the condition of the Negroes began to
improve. The operations of the Freedmen's Bureau, of which the
influence was felt in almost every country, had at least familiarized
the minds of the Negroes and their former masters with the fact,
not learned at once, that the slaves had been really emancipated.
Numberless instances of wrongs redressed, of misconceptions
cleared away by reiterated instructions, had taught both classes of
persons much that both needed to learn, for it is true that the
master has been found as much in need of enlightenment and advice as the freedman and more in need of close watching. Not
infrequently, too, the master has needed assistance and protection,
and I have never, I believe, known assistance to be withheld. I
think the Bureau to have been of the greatest value to the South.

Not that I have not met with officers belonging to it who were unfit for their positions. Some that I have seen were unfit to hold any office which would require judgment or character in him who administered it. But most of these officials whom I saw were laborious and tolerably competent public servants, and even in the rare instances where I found them disgracefully unqualified to discharge the duties of the post, it was impossible for me to deny that, on the whole, it was better that even they should be there than that no one should be there. Both the white and black population of the South are, in my opinion, incalculably better off than if the Bureau had not assisted in the passage from the old system to the new. Even some Southern men admit this to be true; but, of course, to the mass of the white people the Bureau is odious.

As the public mind became accustomed to the new order of things and was able to look forward instead of around, the planting community found itself in better courage than the planters themselves six months before would have thought possible. The change came over them about New Year. It often encouraged me, after the hopeless and truculent talk that I had been hearing about the worthlessness of the niggers, and the speedy extermination of the niggers, to observe that the actions of the speakers belied their words. For example, a man would say in the hotel parlor that no free nigger could be made to work, that the country was ruined, that the extinction of the whole race of niggers was a certainty and very desirable, and an hour afterwards I would perhaps learn from him that he was getting a vast farm under cultivation, that he was expecting to earn his living and probably make a fortune from the paid labor of some sixty or seventy freedmen, and that his intentions, so far as I could judge, were to treat his laborers with reasonable kindness.

This practical and humaner view of the matter was much more the general view in those States where I was travelling after January than it had been during the summer in the more northerly States. I ascribed it mainly to the fact that the Negroes held in their hands, if no other power, the one power of freely selling their labor in open market. No doubt the existence of the Bureau and the consequent absence of State legislation in reference to this question had much to do with keeping the market an open one. Judging from what I saw in Georgia, Alabama, Mississippi, and Louisiana, I should say that a great majority of the freedmen are now receiving tolerably good treatment and tolerably good wages. To pronounce whether or not their wages are good enough I am not competent, and when I say that they are well treated, I speak of them merely in their character of men hired to labor. That there is any general desire or even any general willingness on the part of the Southern people to aid the Negro in becoming as valuable a member of society as he might become, in educating and otherwise elevating himself, I do not believe. Whether or not the ability which just at the present moment he possesses, to secure for himself fair wages and exemption from bodily hurt, is to be taken as proof of the further ability to extort from his employers a fair chance in life for himself and his children, may well be doubted. It has not always been found the fact in other countries that a laboring class, because its labor is honestly bought and paid for, necessarily obtains all its social and political rights. And no such class in other countries, at least in modern days, has been opposed by prejudices so strong as those against which the Negro will have to contend. Indeed, in my opinion, what he has gained already cannot yet be regarded as his permanent and secure possession.

I did not find the freedmen taking much interest in topics of this nature. They are, of course, very deficient in all knowledge of the life outside of their own painfully narrow experience. I speak now of the mass and not of a considerable class of Negroes who seemed to me as well informed and as clever as most other men of my acquaintance. The majority are densely ignorant, and comprehend nothing of the meaning of politics. I suppose it may be called a deficiency of knowledge merely. Certainly I did not come away from the South believing that there was any body of men there unfitted by nature for exercising any rights that are exercised by American citizens. During the war the Negroes, of course, sided with the North. They believed that if the North should be successful they would be freed. And today, so far as they can understand the questions which agitate the people, they are of the Union party. But I hesitate to apply the name of loyalty to their feeling towards the Government. They have never had a country.

Leaving out of view the present fitness of the freedmen to exercise the elective franchise, one who sees the condition of the South and perceives the general feeling of hostility to the Government is forced to consider the expediency of proclaiming universal suffrage. There is little doubt in my mind as to the side on which the Negro vote would be cast. Years from now, it is possible to conceive, every planter may control the votes of all his Negro laborers. But so far as this is a question of expediency at all, it is a question of today, and the pressing problems of American politics at the present time are such as touch the Negro so nearly that they may be said to be his own personal concerns. As regards these matters he would not remain in ignorance as to what men were his friends, and what men were not. The class-leader and preacher, the intelligent house-servant, the black men who are able to read, would save the voter from the deceptions of his employer. In the minds of the Negroes there is always a secret distrust of the white man, and especially of the Southern white man. The coercive power of the employer, the coercive power of bitter prejudice among the great mass of Southern white men, would be obstacles more formidable. I think that the Negroes unprotected by the military authority of the general Government would hardly be able to cast votes enough to alter the elections of any one Southern county. Yet I found some men, Northerners mostly, and Negroes, who seemed to believe that the competition of parties would soon produce a favorable change in this regard, and they took a more hopeful view of the matter than I was able to take. I found the Union men nearly or quite as unwilling to see Negroes voting as the secessionists are. All parties, I think, would agree that the first step must be taken by the general Government, or the desired end is many years distant.

I say nothing of the more general aspect of the grant of the franchise as a means of gradually elevating the freedman by giving him a power which might be as efficient to elevate him in other respects as the new power of selling his labor has been efficient in improving his condition as a laborer. As a means of aiding the loyal people to retain what has been won by war, it would, in my opinion, be powerful at the present time only when joined with the other means of doing the same thing—the military occupation of the South until she gives guaranties which cannot be revoked.

The work of teaching the freedmen, which is now going on, will not greatly affect the adult Negroes. No great number of them, I should say, are under instruction. I found that the children, wherever it was possible for them to reach a school, were docile pupils, regular in their attendance, more laborious in application and more rapid in their progress than white children accustomed to the regular routine of school life. I think the parents are anxious to have their children taught, and may be expected to make sacrifices for the sake of educating them. It is not in their power to do much. It will be interesting to watch the course of affairs in Louisiana during the current year, where, since February, the colored people have been required to support their own schools. They believe that learning is to raise them to an equality with the white race, and are, therefore, eager for schools. I do not know why this feeling should not be of permanent operation.

I see that encouraging accounts of the industry of the freedmen are coming in from all parts of the South. My experience in the South, both as a traveller and as a resident and an employer of Negroes, was such that I needed no reports of this sort to convince me that a Negro fairly paid and otherwise justly dealt with, living under the same restraints of law which are found necessary for white men, is a satisfactory laborer.